OXFORD CULTURAL BIOGRAPHIES

Series Editor
Gary Giddins

A Generous Vision: The Creative Life of Elaine de Kooning
Cathy Curtis

Straighten Up and Fly Right: The Life and Music of Nat King Cole
Will Friedwald

Music by Max Steiner: The Epic Life of Hollywood's Most Influential Composer
Steven C. Smith

Music by Max Steiner

Music By Max Steiner

The Epic Life of Hollywood's
Most Influential Composer

STEVEN C. SMITH

OXFORD
UNIVERSITY PRESS

OXFORD
UNIVERSITY PRESS

Oxford University Press is a department of the University of Oxford. It furthers
the University's objective of excellence in research, scholarship, and education
by publishing worldwide. Oxford is a registered trade mark of Oxford University
Press in the UK and certain other countries.

Published in the United States of America by Oxford University Press
198 Madison Avenue, New York, NY 10016, United States of America.

Library of Congress Cataloging-in-Publication Data
Names: Smith, Steven C., author.
Title: Music by Max Steiner : the epic life of Hollywood's
most influential composer / Steven C Smith.
Description: New York City : Oxford University Press, 2020. |
Series: Cultural biographies | Includes bibliographical references and index. |
Identifiers: LCCN 2019058681 (print) | LCCN 2019058682 (ebook) |
ISBN 9780190623272 (hardback) | ISBN 9780190623289 (pdf) |
ISBN 9780190623296 (epub) | ISBN 9780190623302
Subjects: LCSH: Steiner, Max, 1888–1971. | Film composers—United States—Biography.
Classification: LCC ML410.S8163 S65 2020 (print) | LCC ML410.S8163 (ebook) |
DDC 781.5/42092 [B]—dc23
LC record available at https://lccn.loc.gov/2019058681
LC ebook record available at https://lccn.loc.gov/2019058682

9 8 7 6 5 4 3 2 1

Printed by Sheridan Books, Inc., United States of America

For James V. D'Arc and John W. Morgan,
who preserved the scores, the letters, and the stories,
and made this book possible

Contents

Foreword

BIOGRAPHY IS A KIND OF ONE-SIDED MARRIAGE in which a writer lives with a subject for years, trying to bring him or her to life, while the subject, usually long deceased, is by turns inspiring, infuriating, frustrating, helpful, honest, mendacious, indifferent, and, perhaps most often, maddeningly elusive. The marriage may be self-imposed—an undertaking of devotion, abhorrence, even of commercial practicality—or arranged by a third party. But a crucial consideration is invariably the suitability of the match. *Music by Max Steiner* is an ideal biographical marriage.

In 1991, Steven C. Smith published his first book, the prizewinning *A Heart at Fire's Center: The Life and Music of Bernard Herrmann*. It was not only the finest biography ever written about a film composer, admittedly not a high bar to clear, but also a dramatic exposition of the way film scoring really works. Smith showed how film composers, once regarded as musical hacks, could achieve enduring greatness in a profession that consists largely of composing fastidiously timed "cues," frequently no longer than seconds in duration. When I approached him with the idea of embarking, after twenty-five years, on another biography, I figured it might be a long shot. Smith has written extensively about film and film music but is best known as the producer, writer, and director of two hundred or so documentary films for network and cable television stations, as well as "bonus" short subjects for every kind of home video media.

Happily, he leaped at the challenge of writing a life of Steiner, the man who, more than anyone else, advanced the paradoxical art of movie music—music that must not call attention to itself at the expense of the story, even as it rivets the filmgoer's mind and heart. As an essential collaborator on some of the most durable pictures ever made, Steiner lives on in *King Kong, The Gay Divorcee, The Informer, Dark Victory, The Charge of the Light Brigade, Jezebel, Gone with the Wind, The Letter, Casablanca, Now, Voyager, The Big*

Sleep, Key Largo, The Treasure of the Sierra Madre, White Heat, and *The Caine Mutiny*, among hundreds of other films and television shows. Few composers are more widely heard and less recognized by the general public. Twenty-four of Steiner's scores have been nominated for Academy Awards, and his "Tara's Theme" remains among the most familiar of melodies. He never created a Broadway hit or a concert hall staple, and not for want of trying, but in 1960, he had the number one song in the country (charting 21 weeks), when Percy Faith recorded his "Theme from *A Summer Place*."

In Smith's telling, Max Steiner, about whom little is generally known, comes alive as a splendid character in his own right, the wizard behind the curtain who turns out to be a genuine wizard. Unlike most great cultural figures, his career threatens to be a long apprenticeship without a payoff. The bright child of a farsighted but often hapless Viennese showman, Max enjoys a few triumphs as a prodigy, before making his way through European capitals and New York, exhibiting undeniable gifts, experiencing champagne coups and utter insolvency, rising and falling with flukes of luck, indulging in serial marriages and other impulses, working closely with artists already destined for immortality. Yet as he commences his 41st year, he is little more than a footnote, a mention-in-passing.

Then, after an uproarious Broadway disaster called *Rainbow*, Max conducts a couple of Broadway hits that lead to an invitation from RKO in Hollywood to work in the new business of talking pictures. It is December 1929. Music had been vital to silent pictures, producing several hit songs, but audiences could see that it was performed nonstop by a pianist or ensemble in the theater to enhance the mood of the story. Talkies were different: it was one thing to show characters singing and dancing, but would audiences accept "invisible" offscreen music popping up out of nowhere? Mel Brooks satirized that conundrum in *Blazing Saddles*, as his two western heroes ride across the plain, accompanied by radiant orchestral riffs played, as we eventually see, by the orchestra of Count Basie, who waves them on as they pass.

Steiner soon overcame objections as he revealed himself to be a visionary composer, arranger, and conductor who wrote memorable themes to play behind the credits, and increasingly nuanced musical cues that intensified the onscreen drama and comedy, suspense and horror, romance and sex. Smith takes us deeper into the process, demonstrating how Steiner's music made audible the psychology of characters, portended bombshells, and heightened climaxes. He shows how Steiner developed his art from broad accompaniments to the kind of subtleties derived from studying speech cadences and vocal ranges of actors in order to find just the right musical timbre and resonance to complement them. His music managed to be at once unobtrusive and indispensable and has thus survived the decades. Beyond establishing him as one of the undisputed titans of film composing, it has found an independent life on recordings and in concert halls, where excerpts from his scores are performed internationally to much acclaim. Steven C. Smith tells a remarkable story that will change forever the way you watch and hear movies.

Gary Giddins, Series Editor

Prologue

THE SOUND OF A RINGING TELEPHONE in the dead of night was not unusual in Beverly Hills—especially on Saturdays, when the movie industry's finest celebrated the end of their six-day work week. Home screenings of a new release, late-hour story meetings, romantic assignations—all were common in the west side neighborhood whose occupants were known by surnames alone. Chaplin. Colman. Dietrich. Astaire.

But on the night of Saturday, November 11, 1939, the call that came for the owner of 1012 Cove Way could not have brought more unwelcome tidings. Exhausted by months of little sleep, working at a frenzied speed fueled by daily injections of Benzedrine, Maximilian Raoul Steiner, age 51, listened with mounting rage to his caller's news.

David O. Selznick had asked Metro-Goldwyn-Mayer's top composer, Herbert Stothart, to write music for *Gone with the Wind*.

As Steiner listened, his tipster—a fellow musician—described the party he just left, at which Stothart, lips loosened by drink, blurted out that Selznick had hired him to "fix up Max's work."[1] That "work" was a three-and-a-half hour score-in-progress that was pushing Steiner to the verge of a breakdown. A score he had begged to be assigned, for a film so anticipated that even Adolf Hitler, two months after his invasion of Poland and the start of World War II, expressed eagerness to see it.[2]

Steiner did not doubt that the story about Stothart was true. Seven months earlier, independent producer David O. Selznick had agreed to pay top dollar to Max's tight-fisted employers, Jack and Harry Warner, to borrow their busiest composer. But the scoring of Selznick's four-hour epic had been largely delayed until October. Now, just 34 days remained before *Gone with the Wind*'s world premiere.

And much of its score had yet to be written.

Max himself had set the crisis in motion, telling Selznick days earlier that he needed more time. The producer immediately strategized. "Tomorrow, Friday, he is recording the first several reels," Selznick wrote business partner John Hay Whitney. "If quality is disappointing, this, together with his pessimistic statements, would warrant pulling him off, particularly in view of the fact that Herbert Stothart is dying to do the job and guarantees he would get it through on time.... Very secretly we ran the picture for him today, and he is simply frantic with eagerness to do it."[3]

Selznick's willingness to change composers so close to the film's release date reflected a temperament as mercurial as it was meticulous. But ultimately, he realized that the ideal pick remained Steiner—the man who, in the course of his 35-year career in Hollywood, would win three Academy Awards and receive 24 Oscar nominations.[4] During that time, he would do more than any other composer to invent and codify film scoring as we know it today. At a time when talkies were new and dramatic underscoring almost nonexistent, Steiner's psychologically astute, tailor-made approach to a project convinced skeptical producers to finally stop asking "Where is the music coming from?"

From 1929 to 1932, that question had led to arid, crackling movie soundtracks and sluggishly paced action. But with such titles as *Bird of Paradise, King Kong, The Lost Patrol,* and *The Informer,* Steiner not only proved that "background" music was a crucial element in motion pictures; he established its basic vocabulary.

His innovations also set the table for what has since become an international revenue source generating millions of dollars each year. Albums of the scores for 1977's *Star Wars* and 1997's *Titanic* outsold most contemporaneous pop offerings.[5] It was an industry Steiner helped launch, as one of the first screen composers to have his work released on commercial recordings. In the 1950s and '60s, his music bolstered another new revenue stream: television, as stations across the United States used Steiner themes to introduce prime-time programs, like New York's *Million Dollar Movie.* By the late twentieth century, film music had created its own cadre of superstars, led by John Williams, whose net worth reportedly exceeded $100 million.[6] That number was partly thanks to Steiner, who spearheaded a multi-decade fight for film composers to receive royalty payments.

The commercial value of movie soundtracks today is also reflected in the thousands of screenings of motion pictures with their music performed live by symphony orchestras—titles that include Steiner's *Casablanca.* And in the age of digital downloads, entire scores or single cues are offered for sale with a single click on a smartphone.

NONE OF THIS EXISTED at the time Max Steiner came to Hollywood in 1929, initially as a lowly orchestrator, before his swift ascent to become the industry's highest-paid, most honored composer. He was also its hardest working. During Max's crisis month of November 1939, Angelinos seeking escape from war news might hear as many as ten Steiner scores in local theaters. They ranged from romances (*Intermezzo*) to Cagney crime thrillers (*Each Dawn I Die*) to Bette Davis tearjerkers (*The Old Maid, Jezebel*) to edgy propaganda (*Confessions of a Nazi Spy*). Weeks earlier, those options also included westerns (*Dodge City*) and revivals of films already considered classics (*Of Human Bondage*).

The dramatic language Steiner helped create was quickly adapted by others: recurring leitmotis linked to specific characters, climbing key modulations to intensify emotion, precise orchestral colors to evoke place and psychology. But Steiner's own musical genius was sui generis. No other film composer possessed such a seemingly inexhaustible gift for melody. His choice of musical key signatures carefully considered the pitch of an actor's voice, as well as sound effects (Steiner would compose above or below them).

Just as important, he imbued his music with his own philosophy of life. It was one highly sensitive to romantic desire and longing—for what else is the music of *Now, Voyager, Casablanca,* or *King Kong*? When required, his depiction of violence or psychopathy, in such scores as *The Searchers, The Treasure of the Sierra Madre,* and *White Heat,* could be as unnerving as Bernard Herrmann's. But closer to Steiner's nature were dramas that reflected his own innate optimism and generosity of spirit.

Whatever the genre, and however brutal the schedule, Steiner's employers knew he would deliver the goods. His reputation as a workhorse was well-earned: few others could have written and/or supervised music for some three hundred movies, starting at the advanced age of 41.

The answer to how he achieved such a high level of quality and quantity is the subject of many of these pages. His methods included a unique system of studio support, and assistants who could translate his detailed shorthand into full scores within days or hours.

Geography and genealogy were also on his side. He was born in Vienna, in an era of exceptional musical diversity: the symphonic neo-Romanticism of Brahms and Mahler, the dissonance, and proto-cinematic opulence, of Richard Strauss, the light-as-air operettas of Johann Strauss Jr. Steiner knew or met many of these composers, thanks to another gift from the gods: his father, uncle, and grandfather managed several of Vienna's most important musical theaters.

His own journey from the Austro-Hungarian Empire to Hollywood is a narrative as eventful as the Warner Bros. movies enlivened by his music. His long life began just two decades after America's Civil War, and ended on the eve of Watergate. And it is likely that no other human being knew both Gustav Mahler and Frank Sinatra, Johann Strauss and Nat King Cole, Richard Strauss and W. C. Fields. His scores were critiqued and approved not only by the usual studio bosses, but also by political powerbrokers from J. Edgar Hoover to Joseph Stalin.

Steiner's exploits, set against a backdrop of imperial Austria, pre-WWI London, Gershwin-era Broadway, and mid-century Hollywood, provide a biographer with enviable color. In an unpublished memoir written late in life, Steiner tried to tell his story as a series of whimsical adventures, most of them ending with a comic punch line. The tone reflected his reputation as a joke-loving, affable Austrian, for whom life was not as serious as good cigars, alcohol, or beautiful women.

But there is a darker side to Steiner's story, one that is less Viennese operetta than classical tragedy. In it, the relationships of fathers and sons begin with grand dreams and end in tragedy. Fortunes are made and lost, by a man driven by the desire to redeem a lost family dynasty.

It should not be a surprise that for Max Steiner, *Gone with the Wind* was not only the most prestigious project of his six-decade career. It was a Technicolor mirror of his own extraordinary life.

PART ONE

The Little Prince

1

Elegant Revolutions

The frightful times are over,
We are cheerful again!
The Viennese merrily row their boats
To "Venice in Vienna."
There is now a Ferris wheel
That merrily turns . . .
How moral principles come into doubt
When one glides along in a gondola.
There is only a "Venice"
In Prater Park in Vienna.
     Der Floh (The Flea), Vienna newspaper, 1897[1]

FOR A CULTURE ENRAPTURED by the waltz, merry-go-rounds, and all things rotational, the circular shape of the great machine could not have been more pleasing.

At 210 feet tall, 430 tons strong, Vienna's Riesenrad—or, as its English admirers called it, the Ferris Wheel—proved as impressive on the day of its unveiling as eight months of publicity had promised.[2] But on the afternoon of June 21, 1897, as the eyes of invited guests traveled from the wheel to the figure below it, some visitors standing in the northwest corner of the Prater must have noted an amusing contrast. The Riesenrad's scale was as epic as the man who willed it into existence was diminutive.

He was handsome and thin. Dangling down across the buttons of his coat was a long cord attached to eyeglasses, which he was never without. Like most Austrian men, he sported a moustache, and a dark beard that neatly rounded a strong chin. Most striking were his eyes: when photographed, he invariably gazed to the right, with an expression that suggested his ambition and restless imagination.

What 39-year-old Gabor Steiner lacked in height—he was under 5-1/2 feet tall—he made up for in daring.

Gabor Steiner, ca. 1880.

In the 1850s, Emperor Franz Joseph had commissioned another great circle: the "Ringstrasse" of civic buildings and concert halls that formed an architectural crown around Vienna's center. The wheel instated by Gabor would prove just as iconic.

That day in June 1897, its red passenger gondolas were "festooned with giant garlands," *Illustrated Vienna* reported.[3] Lady Horace Rumbold, wife of the British ambassador, "solemnly" installed its final screw. Her presence was a tribute to the builder, London engineer Walter B. Bassett. After three sharp hammer strikes, a boys' choir sang "God Save the Queen." They were followed by operatic arias . . . a dramatic recital . . . a ballet . . . and a symphony concert.

The program reflected an impresario who spent his peripatetic career blending "high" and "low" entertainment. Gabor Steiner had noted the popularity of the Ferris Wheel's predecessors in Britain and America. Within a year of its unveiling in Vienna, the Riesenrad was as much a symbol of the city as ancient St. Stephen's Cathedral.

But it was just one attraction within an entire mini-city of Gabor's creation. Two years earlier—and sixty years before the gates of Disneyland opened—Steiner had masterminded "Venice in Vienna," a 12-1/2-acre complex nearly a third as large as the grounds of Buckingham Palace. Open from May to September, it was built in the elite Kaisergarten section of the three-mile-long Prater, Vienna's most popular park.

Gabor based his dream city on smaller Venice exhibitions he had visited in London and Germany. With architect Oskar Marmorek, a student of Otto Wagner, Steiner designed scaled-down replicas of Venice's most enchanting sites, from St. Mark's Square to the Grand Canal.[4]

Gondoliers rowed patrons along interconnecting canals, under neo-Gothic arches and bridges of actual marble. Guests rambled past mosaics and frescos from square to square. Each was filled with palazzos, whose seeming authenticity disguised what was inside them: jewelry stores, drama theaters, pastry shops, restaurants, beer halls, and much, much more.[5]

A cultural hodgepodge? Absolutely. Yet so was Vienna. The Ringstrasse was a cacophonous riot of neo-Baroque, neo-Gothic, neo-Renaissance building, "all quite new, barely weathered, and not yet, if ever, real," historian Frederic Morton observed.[6]

Austrians embraced cultural synthesis. And within weeks of the opening of "Venice in Vienna" on May 22, 1895, twenty thousand visitors had strolled under its arched entrance.[7]

Many of its attractions reflected Gabor's obsession with new technology: the twinkling electric lights lining the trees of the English Garden . . . the Concert Edison Hall featuring the gramophone, a device introduced just eighteen years earlier. "'Venice' is a city in and of itself," one reporter enthused. "It has its own post office, its own fire department, its own medical services. . . . In the evening, the glow created by colorful electrical lights and arc lamps is magical."[8]

Gabor installed a 230-foot roller coaster climaxing in a water slide. Cuisine from across the continent could be sampled in the Restaurant Français and the large café at Campo #1, which became a favorite meeting spot for restless bachelors and single women. Indeed, ads for the park often featured

A canal within "Venice in Vienna," ca. 1895.

curvaceous fräuleins and male admirers, leaving little doubt that the charms of "Venice" were not only for families.

The slow-turning wheel was a favorite spot for dalliances. Wrote one historian, "Many couples behaved so that the ride often had an unpleasant ending for them at the police station."[9] Despite, or because, of these illicit acts, Vienna's police chief was among the earliest supporters of "Venice." "I have nothing against a great establishment," Franz von Stejskal told Gabor. "Until now, the police have had to look for crooks in all districts. Hopefully, we now will find all the criminals in 'Venice in Vienna.'"

Casablanca's Captain Louis Renault could not have said it better.

Symphony concerts in the park drew crowds, but not all could afford a ticket. One music student, Arnold Schoenberg, was said to haunt the Prater's entrance, too poor to afford admission.[10] On a June afternoon, sculptor Auguste Rodin and painter Gustav Klimt "seated themselves beside two remarkably beautiful young women," a patron recalled. "Rodin leaned over to Klimt and said, 'I have never before experienced such an atmosphere . . . this garden, these women, this music . . . and round it all this gay, child-like happiness. . . . What is the reason for it all?' Klimt slowly nodded his head and answered only one word—'Austria.'"[11]

Park advertisement, ca. 1897.

"Venice" even captured the imagination of Emperor Franz Joseph. A year after its opening, Gabor Steiner was summoned to Hofburg Palace. There, "my name was called and I entered the emperor's parlor. He took several steps to stand before me and launched into a long conversation, asking me many questions. He wanted to know where I got the water for the canals . . . how many people visited 'Venice in Vienna' during its first year . . . and many other things. [Finally] with a warm smile, he nodded his head and the audience was over. The unusually long duration of this audience granted to a mere mortal had caused astonishment."[12]

No one loved Gabor's new park more than its most frequent visitor: his own son. Maximilian Raoul Walter* Steiner, age seven in 1895, enjoyed the unique privilege of unlimited access to the world of his father's creation.

Gabor encouraged Max's enthusiasm. Just as Franz Joseph was grooming his son, Crown Prince Rudolf, to rule the empire, Gabor hoped that Max would guide his franchise of entertainments into the next century . . . just as Gabor had inherited the Steiner dynasty from his own father, after whom Max was named.

---

* The middle name of "Walter" does not appear on Steiner's birth certificate but was used by the composer when listing his full name as an adult. Whether it was simply omitted on the original form or added later is unknown.

The entrance of "Venice in Vienna" (at left) beckons below the Riesenrad, ca. 1897.

IN HIS BRIEF 49 YEARS on earth, Maximilian Steiner the First had led a life of achievement that any grandson would have difficulty surpassing. Born in Ofen, Hungary (now Budapest) in 1830, Maximilian traveled to Temesvár to become an actor.[13] There, he found a champion in stage director Friedrich Strampfer. In 1862, Maximilian traveled with his mentor to Austria, hoping to become a theatrical producer.

Strampfer had leased Vienna's legendary Theater an der Wien, whose stage had seen the premiere of Mozart's *The Magic Flute* and Beethoven's *Fidelio*. Perched by the river Wien, it boasted a seating capacity of 2,000.[14] Strampfer made Maximilian his secretary. Soon, servant had eclipsed the master; he was dubbed by the press "der kleine Diplomat" ("The Little Diplomat"),[15] gaining fame for his canny musical programming. In 1869, as the end of Strampfer's theater lease approached, Maximilian was named its new codirector.

Steiner and his business partner, former soprano Marie Geistinger, shifted the theater's focus to a genre exploding in popularity: operetta. Its acknowledged master in Vienna, Franz von Suppé, wrote mostly for the rival Carlstheater. Maximilian set out to find a composer to eclipse him—and his choice was inspired.

For most people, 44-year-old Johann Strauss Jr. *was* Viennese music. The world's "Waltz King," a celebrity ranked only behind Queen Victoria in international popularity, Strauss wrote pieces that were the musical accompaniment of Austrian life, whether emanating from elegant ballrooms or the whistling of a window washer. "Tales from the Vienna Woods," "The Emperor

Waltz," "On the Beautiful Blue Danube"—these and dozens more gave proof to Strauss's comment that for him, "melodies gush out like water."[16]

Rich and sedentary, he composed only instrumental music, and rejected suggestions to write for the stage. But Maximilian was determined to change his mind. In 1869, Steiner convinced Strauss's wife Jenny to join him in a scheme: at Maximilian's request, she took from her husband's desk sketches of Strauss works in progress. Steiner commissioned lyrics for their melodies, and days later, Strauss arrived home to find inside a group of singers flanked by Jenny and Maximilian. The Waltz King listened, stunned, as vocalists trilled arias based on his unpublished melodies.

According to one biographer, "Strauss's eyes lit up. He listened, smiled. 'Not half bad.'"[17]

Maximilian quickly signed Strauss to a contract. Their first two productions at the Theater an der Wien, *Indigo and the Forty Thieves* and *Carnival in Rome*, confirmed that the Waltz King was as adept writing for singers as he was for orchestras. But it was the composer's third-produced stage work that changed musical history.

Today, *Die Fledermaus* (*The Bat*) stands unrivaled as the world's most popular operetta. It was Maximilian who alerted Strauss to its story, based on the hit comic play *Le Réveillon*; and although the operetta's 1874 premiere was marred by mixed reviews and poor box office—probably due to a concurrent financial crisis in Vienna—*Die Fledermaus* became an international sensation.

Maximilian Steiner had ushered in the Golden Age of the Viennese operetta. He was decorated with France's Legion of Honour, made Knight of the Italian Crown, and given Russia's Order of Saint Stanislaus.[18] And for the next four decades, the Theater an der Wien was the most democratic hall in imperial Austria. Royalty and shopkeepers alike succumbed to musical fantasies that mixed gentle social commentary with lush romance, until true love finally prevailed in three-quarter time.

By 1877, Maximilian was not the only Steiner employed at the Theater.

Before coming to Vienna, he had married Rosa Kollinsky, who became the mother of his five children: Franz (1855), Gabor (1858), Eugenie (1860), Alexander (1867), and Bruno (1870).[19] During Maximilian's first year as director, 11-year-old Gabor began performing at the Theater an der Wien in small roles. He became a skilled pianist, and in 1876, the 18-year-old convinced his father to hire him at the theater. "One of my favorite activities was communication with Johann Strauss," Gabor later wrote. "Almost every

Maximilian Steiner, the master juggler of talent. Caricatured in the Viennese press, 1873.

day I came to [his home] and Strauss played for me what he had just created. Often I summoned [assistants] to help preserve what he had written."[20]

The Great Man's cantankerous temperament often made him difficult company. "Grandfather Maximilian, who was supposed to be the boss, was deathly afraid of him," our Max recalled. "Therefore, when Maximilian wanted Strauss to make any changes in his scores, he would always use my father as a go-between, because the maestro was extremely fond of my father, and respected him for his musical knowledge."[21]

By the late 1870s, Gabor would become even more invaluable when Maximilian, now the theater's sole manager, received devastating news: a medical diagnosis of rectal cancer. In January 1880, Gabor and brother Franz took over management. Four months later, on May 29, Vienna's theatrical community shed genuine tears at the news that Maximilian Steiner was dead.

At first, his dynasty seemed to have passed into capable hands. Franz Steiner, senior to Gabor, assumed sole management of the Theater an der Wien; and that October, a new Strauss operetta, *The Queen's Lace Handkerchief*, became the composer's biggest hit since *Fledermaus*.[22] But within weeks, a scandal threatened to destroy everything Maximilian had built.

In an act of career suicide, Franz Steiner had embarked on an affair with Angelika "Lili" Strauss—the second wife of Johann Strauss, who had remarried in haste after Jenny's death.

In 1882, Lili fled her husband's estate and moved in with Franz. Real-life and theatrical melodrama collided in 1883, with news that Johann Strauss's next operetta, *A Night in Venice*, would premiere not in Vienna but in Berlin. The message was clear. And although Franz eventually snapped out of his romantic trance and left Lili, the Theater an der Wien had amassed a debt of 250,000 florins.

By 1884, Franz was out.

The scandal has a fittingly Viennese coda. After divorcing his wayward wife, Johann Strauss fell deeply in love and married again. Adele Strauss proved the ideal partner for her demanding husband, and as Strauss resumed composing with new vigor, he renewed his friendship with Gabor. The Waltz King may have realized that in ridding him of Lili, Franz Steiner had done him an inestimable favor.

AS THE FRANZ AND LILI SCANDAL exploded, Gabor left Vienna to manage a theater in Hanover, Germany. But soon he was eager to return to Austria's capital, to forge a fresh career.

Fortunately, Vienna moved on from *le scandale Strauss*. In 1887, Gabor applied for and received the post of artistic director at Vienna's Carlstheater, second only to the Theater an der Wien in presenting popular musicals.[23]

All around him, momentous events were taking place. But most were hiding in plain sight. At the new Court Theater, Gustav Klimt, not yet renowned, hung high on a scaffold completing his two-year ceiling panel *The Chariot of Thespis*. In the Jewish Innere Stadt district, 32-year-old Sigmund Freud had begun testing the use of hypnosis on patients—a step that led to *The Interpretation of Dreams*. Inside Vienna's General Hospital, medical graduate Arthur Schnitzler was soon to quit his job, to pursue playwriting. His depictions of sexual compulsion, like the revolutionary work of Klimt and Freud, anticipated a new century of radical ideas and artistic explosions.

Vienna also offered much opportunity to its burgeoning middle class. It was an audience to which Gabor catered for the rest of his career—with help from a hard-working partner.

A former dancer at the Theater an der Wien, Mirjam Maria Josefine Hasiba Hollman was known to friends as "Mitzi." Six years Gabor's junior, she came from the Austrian town of Graz, Styria,[24] and possessed a pragmatic intelligence that set her apart from other chorus girls. On March 29, 1883, she and Gabor married, and the pair moved into the Hotel Nordbahn at 72 Praterstrasse.[25]

It was there that their son Max was born, on May 10, 1888.[26] "As far as I have ever been able to find out," Max Steiner would dryly note, "I was the only child of my parents."[27]

HE WAS BORN INTO A TIME of warring emotional extremes. Amid the almost desperate gaiety of Vienna, some sensed an encroaching darkness. Suicides had risen to an alarming level. "Nervousness is the modern sickness," observed one paper. "Outside, everything is gleam and gorgeousness . . . one no longer expects anything from the inner life, from thinking or believing."[28]

That ominous mood literally echoed outside the Steiner home on February 5, 1889. At 4 p.m., the tolling of bells rang across the city; they mourned the mysterious death of a young man who had seemed destined to continue his father's greatness.

On January 30, the corpse of Crown Prince Rudolf had been found at the prince's shooting lodge at Mayerling. Rudolf had shot his mistress and himself in a suicide pact. It was a tragedy set in motion by the prince's manic depression and the growing divide between Rudolf, eager to enact social reforms, and his conservative father, Franz Joseph.

For the next five days, all music in the world's most melodious city stopped.[29]

There was another shadow over Austria's future: anti-Semitism was on the rise. Two months before Max's birth, politician Georg von Schönerer led a cadre of thugs into the offices of the *Neues Wiener Tagblatt*, where they brutally beat the mostly Jewish staff.

These and similar events led Gabor toward a step of reinvention. On July 14, 1894, Gabor, Mitzi, and six-year-old Max were baptized in Gustav-Adolf-Kirche, Vienna's first Protestant church.[30] To readers who have

RESTAURANT-HOTEL NORDBAHN
Praterstrasse 72 ✴ WIEN II ✴ Praterstrasse 72.

Hotel Nordbahn, the Steiners' residence, ca. 1890.

assumed that the hero of our narrative was Jewish: he was—until legally at least, he was not.

Gabor's Hungarian ancestors were Jewish, and father Maximilian was buried in Vienna's Jewish Cemetery. Mitzi converted from Catholicism to Judaism by the time of her marriage. But in 1894, the Steiners left the faith—Gabor for Protestantism, Mitzi for Catholicism.

Gabor's conversion had a likely explanation. Not long after his baptism, and after two years of fruitless civic meetings, his plan for "Venice in Vienna" was finally approved.[31]

Within a year of the amusement park's opening, the phrase "We're going to Venice!" was familiar across all strata of society. Gabor became a favorite of newspaper caricaturists; typical was a drawing of him rowing a gondola through the city streets, after Vienna was flooded by a storm. "Is this a case of Gabor's refined advertising campaign?" the cartoonist asked.[32]

OVERSEEING A PARK with constantly changing attractions and 1,500 employees, Gabor's energy seldom flagged. It was a quality his son would inherit, along with his father's diminutive height. A reporter later described young Max as "spindly-legged, large-headed."[33] Nevertheless, his status as the son of Gabor Steiner instilled in him a sense of privilege and curiosity.

Seventy years later, he could vividly recall the forty-foot tower inside a man-made lake in "Venice,"

> with a springboard on which were performed all kinds of water acts. Annette Kellerman [international swimming star] was one of the performers, but the most daring act was performed by a man with one leg. He rode a bicycle off the tower into the water. This act not only thrilled me but was a challenge. One morning when the park was closed, I crawled up the forty-foot tower, mounted his bicycle and away we went.
>
> I woke up in a hospital with my irate parents by my side.
>
> The Park and its restaurants and theaters were only open during the summer months. My father always tried to stage the season's Grand Opening to coincide with my birthday in May.
>
> What a wonderful, colorful world for a boy to grow up in![34]

The palazzos of "Venice" housed attractions that, in retrospect, seem to preview the life that lay ahead for Max. The aforementioned Concert Edison House trumpeted the sounds of early music recordings. On an outdoor stage, African tribal performers danced and chanted native songs, decades before Max scored similar rituals filmed on an RKO soundstage.

Even more relevant to his future was a device Gabor read about and imported, sight unseen, for 18,000 francs (more than $19,200 dollars). Brothers Auguste and Louis Lumiére had introduced their "Cinématographe" in Paris in 1895; soon thereafter, Gabor made room in Campo #3 for Vienna's first "Kinotheater"—moving picture theater.[35]

IT IS IRRESISTIBLE TO IMAGINE seven-year-old Max transfixed by its flickering images. Irresistible, but unlikely. Young Steiner probably saw the Kinotheater in action, but its "operation had to be stopped before the season's end,"

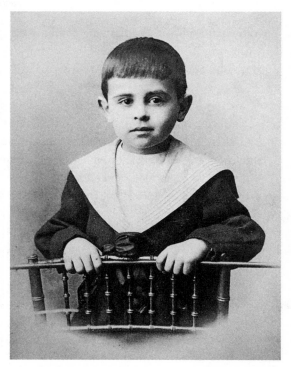

Already showing confidence, ca. 1895. (Louise Steiner
Elian Papers; L. Tom Perry Special Collections, Brigham
Young University)

Gabor's Kinematograph Theater, "Venice in Vienna," ca. 1896.

Prater historians recorded.[36] "The images of the light shimmered so much that spectators complained of eyestrain and headache. The apparatus often failed, and it was even necessary to return the entrance fee to the disillusioned visitors."

But Gabor was undeterred. For the rest of his career, the entrepreneur would offer improved versions of his early cinematic experiment.

In time, Vienna—and Max—took notice.

2

Heir Apparent

FOR MITZI STEINER, "Venice in Vienna" was far less enticing than it was for her son. The former dancer was the Prater's hardest-working employee, overseeing two of the restaurants of "Venice." They included the two-thousand-seat Roman Hall, advertised as "a true El Dorado for the public on languorous Viennese summer evenings."[1]

Languorous hardly described Mitzi. Behind her son's soft-filter affection ("She was widely hailed as the most beautiful woman in Vienna"[2]) one catches glimpses of an earthy laborer who channeled her frustrations—including those toward the spendthrift Gabor—into making her restaurants a success. "My mother became wealthy, but not without hard work. She attended to all her own marketing, leaving the house at six in the morning and choosing her own vegetables and her own meat right out of the stockyards. She was a wonderful cook."[3]

One day, shortly before the park's annual re-opening, Max visited his mother in the main office, where she was

preparing foods and attending to other details. An insurance man came in and advised her that her renewal premium was due for the fire insurance in the restaurants. Mother was so busy that she asked if he could come back the next day.

The park opened according to schedule, but during the night [of May 8, 1902], the Roman Hall was almost completely destroyed by fire—and no insurance. When I came upon the scene, my mother was screaming and three men were trying to keep her from leaping into the flame, attempting to retrieve just anything at all. The greatest loss suffered was not the building alone, but the supply of fine linens, silver, crystal, and furnishings. But my mother didn't give up. The repairs took eight weeks, and then she opened again for what was left of the season.[4]

When Steiner scored the film *Mildred Pierce* half a century later, a real-life role model for its heroine—an unstoppable restaurant operator—lived in his memory.

WITH NO SIBLINGS, Max grew close to his extended family—especially Mitzi's father, Rudolf. A watchmaker in Salzburg, he was "a man whom I adored. I spent my school vacations with him and Grandma in that beautiful little village.

But Grandpa was a gay blade. Every Sunday, he and I would go fishing for trout in the Salzach River. After having caught a few fish, we would go to visit Grandpa's little girlfriend in the town. I would sit in the drawing room and look at all the pretty books while Grandpappy made love to his lady friend. We would then return home to Grandma, and present her with our catch of trout for the day.

On one Sunday, we failed to catch any trout. Grandpa came up with a wonderful idea. We would go to the fish market and purchase our trout.

At home, Grandma accepted our trout, unwrapped them, and then to our surprise became outraged and started beating Grandpa with her shoe and anything else she could get her hands on. I came in for my share, too. Alas, we had forgotten to remove the price tag from our purchase.[5]

One day, while sitting at home, a large picture of Grandfather—hung over Max's bed—came crashing down. "It was 3:15 in the afternoon, the hour and minute, we learned later, when my grandfather passed away in Salzburg. It seemed to me that my beloved Grandpa wanted to let me know he had gone."[6] Although Steiner would grow up to be an atheist, Grandfather Hollman's passing at age 63 would give him a flicker of hope in an afterlife.

During boyhood, Max seemed to find little pleasure among children his own age, preferring the company of adults. Few acquaintances made a stronger impression than the man still key to the family's success: Johann Strauss, whose music was played daily at "Venice in Vienna." "One time during a rehearsal, Papa walked down to the orchestra pit and stopped Strauss, saying, 'Maestro,

Max and his favorite childhood pet, Waldie. (MS Papers; L. Tom Perry Special Collections, Brigham Young University)

we are going to have to do something about this march. It is too close to "Light Cavalry" by Suppé.' Strauss looked down at him and said irritably, 'So what? He doesn't need it anymore, he's dead!' Ah, shades of Hollywood!"[7]

The irascible maestro seemed to have genuine fondness for Gabor—a frequent card partner—and young Max. "Papa told me at the age of four I used to sit on the piano bench next to him while he played. On my eighth birthday, Strauss gave me a most interesting piano. It was made in 1840 and had been in his family. It is a small grand, but up-ended flat against the wall like a harp. It is called a giraffe piano, a sort of harpsichord. Drums and cymbals are built in.

Strauss had a wonderful fruit garden in his summer villa where he grew about every kind of fruit. His favorite was ribisl, or red currants. I was the only one permitted to pick Herr Strauss's ribisl."[8]

STEINER'S COMPOSING STYLE would have much in common with Strauss's. Max's gift for comic music mirrored a core quality of Strauss's writing: a "contagious bonhomie," to quote historian Richard Traubner, "the impulse to relate one's good feelings to the other members of the audience."[9] Steiner's love of Strauss waltzes led him to a mastery of that most romantic of forms.

But despite apparent encouragement from Johann Strauss himself, Max did not take music seriously as a child. "When I was six, I took three or four piano lessons a week. I hated it. My father had to give me a kronen for every lesson I took. But when my teacher left, I would go on playing for two or three hours, just so long as I didn't have to practice the lessons he gave me."[10]

Around 1897, an astute teacher named Edmund Eisler found a better way than bribery to focus Max. "Eisler let me play whatever I wanted, but he played it first. Then he would say, 'Now you play.' Because I couldn't, it made me mad. I really started to practice to show him that I could do it, too." Seemingly overnight, "I didn't want to do anything but play piano." Max began improvising and creating his own compositions. It was the breakthrough Gabor had waited for. "Papa would always encourage me by saying, 'Write it down! Write it down!' "[11]

Gabor's influence lay behind another milestone: the publication of Max's first song, at age nine. Like later Steiner works, it aimed straight for the heart. "Lasse einmal noch dich küssen" ("Let Me Kiss You One More Time") is a simple, attractive melody, with lyrics by Gabor associate Carl Lindau that are surprisingly romantic for a child's tune. The song was dedicated to Gabor and Mitzi, whose side-by-side photos adorn its sheet music.[12]

Short compositions began to flow from Max's pen. Their international titles reflected the eclecticism found in "Venice in Vienna," and their composer's curiosity about the world. Sheet music for "Alvaneda: Indianisches Intermezzo" boasts an illustration of an American Indian girl. "Russian Patrol: A Descriptive Piece for Piano" shows an early talent for imitation, with martial rhythms a la Tchaikovsky (Russian music would be a lifelong passion for Max).

By his early teens, the boy who once yawned over Bach and Beethoven had fallen madly in love with the classics. Two hundred years of concert music became his daily study.

Max's first published song, 1897.

Ironically, the composer to whom he would be most often compared—Richard Wagner—was among his least favorite. "Wagner was undoubtedly a great composer. I just don't particularly care for his music," he said in the 1960s. "It's too Nazi; he was one of the first Nazis. [Steiner meant this philosophically.] He used to hate the Jews. . . . He was a son of a bitch."[13]

But Max could separate man and artist. He memorized the German composer's operas, each a textbook in orchestration and psychological drama. "Listen to the incidental scoring behind the recitatives," Steiner told an interviewer. "If Wagner had lived in our times, he would have been our top film composer."[14] (Wolfgang Wagner shared that opinion: "If my grandfather were alive today, he would undoubtedly be working in Hollywood," he said in the 1970s.)[15]

Max also sought out the avant garde. That quest led him to the luxuriant harmonies of two Frenchmen who would rank among his favorite composers: Maurice Ravel and Claude Debussy. Steiner later claimed to have seen Debussy perform in concert twice: during the first, in Vienna, there was "dead silence from the audience. Some people even started hissing."[16] For Steiner, the lesson was probably twofold. Music was evolving into new, exciting forms. But if one planned on making a living, it was best not to be *too* far ahead of the public.

A CHANCE FOR MAX to conduct may have come as early as age eleven, when Gabor handed his boy the baton for a "Venice in Vienna" performance of *The Geisha*, a popular *Mikado* imitation.[17] When Gustave Kerker's Broadway smash *The Belle of New York* came to the Prater, Max—according to his own recollection—was again permitted to conduct.[18]

Surviving programs for *Geisha* and *Belle* do not list Max in any capacity; but if his oft-repeated accounts are to be believed, his conducting may have been done unofficially, and perhaps for only part of a performance. Less plausible is Steiner's claim that Gustave Kerker heard Max's conducting of *Belle* and offered to take him to New York, to study as a prodigy. Mitzi is said to have killed the plan with a terse remark: "All musicians and waiters are stinkers."[19]

Only the final sentence rings true.

IN OCTOBER 1900, Gabor expanded his empire by taking on management of another theater: Danzers Orpheum.[20] For the next seven years, it hosted vaudeville-style entertainment during the months that "Venice in Vienna" was closed. Gabor not only booked his performers, he often discovered them, in travels that took him across Europe and even to Africa. (Egypt was a mere three days' boat trip from Italy.) Max sometimes joined his father, as Gabor groomed his heir apparent.

During their travels, Steiner Jr. reportedly was allowed to conduct at London's People's Palace.[21] And as he took note of folk melodies from Germany and exotic modal scales from Cairo,[22] Max expanded his musical vocabulary in ways he would use to the end of his career.

Danzers Orpheum showcased half a dozen acts a night. In October 1902, a program of Offenbach operetta and ventriloquism was upstaged by

a deadpan comic juggler from America. "W. C. Fields has developed an in-
credibly dry sense of humor," wrote the *Vienna Morning Paper*. "He evoked
storms of laughter with quick, succinct gestures and grimaces."[23] Max was
an instant fan, and during Fields's month-long engagement, the 22-year-old
comedian and 14-year-old music student struck up a friendship that would
last for decades.

IN AND OUTSIDE Gabor's emporiums, military bands were everywhere. Max
was drawn to marches—not only their sharply accented rhythms, but their
cultural symbolism: "I had always wanted to be in the army, and have a military band and perhaps be another Sousa."[24]

Around age 15, he saw his idol in person. John Philip Sousa ranked high
among the world's most admired figures; tours by his 63-member band carried
the brash, optimistic ethos of the United States around the globe. In Sousa,
Max found a model for his future career: a commercial composer and conductor whose concerts blended the highbrow with the latest hits.

Max never forgot watching Sousa conduct during a visit to Vienna. Initially
audience response was tepid. It was only when the conductor gently brought
down his baton, and the hushed open of *On the Beautiful Blue Danube* wafted
over the crowd, that "the audience went out of their minds. I think he played
it four times."[25]

Performing the best-loved piece by Vienna's favorite composer—one
who had passed into immortality in 1899, age 73—was a bold choice for an
American. It also was a triumphant example of what Sousa called his "mes-
meric process"[26] of sensing what his listeners wanted, then adjusting and
accommodating.

BAND CONCERTS WERE far more thrilling than the lessons Max endured at
Franz Joseph Gymnasium, Austria's version of high school. Mitzi hoped
her son would abandon music for the new field of electrical engineering.[27]
But Max dreamed "only of becoming a great composer," he later said.
"Thanks to my father's position . . . I was already a fairly good one at the
age of fifteen."[28]

In 1902, Steiner made the friendship of another world-famous composer
who would become a role model. That June, 38-year-old Richard Strauss made
headlines by conducting at "Venice in Vienna," leading performances of his
tone poems *Till Eulenspiegel's Merry Pranks*, *Death and Transfiguration*, and
Ein Heldenleben. Some 150 musicians joined forces for his three "Venice"

concerts; they included 25 members of Vienna's Court Opera Orchestra, supplied by its conductor, Gustav Mahler.[29]

This cameo appearance by one of the twentieth century's greatest composers leads us to the most puzzling part of Max's education. To the end of his life, Steiner cited Mahler as one of his teachers, mentioning him in dozens of interviews and printed biographies from the early 1930s to 1971.[30] Facts suggest otherwise. At the time of Max's studies, Mahler worked in Vienna not as a teacher but as a conductor.

But Max seldom invented important autobiographical details, however much he embellished them. The cultural standing of Gabor, an impresario decorated by the emperor, would likely have given Max entry to Mahler's rehearsals of the Vienna Philharmonic. There, the gregarious student could have engaged in conversations with Mahler, who had come to Gabor's musical aid in 1902, and whose own Jewish heritage kept him in need of supporters in Vienna. Mahler also may have welcomed a friend of the late Johann Strauss; for although Mahler's own music was dark and unconventional, he adored Strauss waltzes and operettas.

THREE YEARS AFTER CONDUCTING at "Venice," Richard Strauss tested the social mores of his time with the revolutionary opera *Salomé*. And if the Dance of the Seven Veils and Salomé's erotic caress of John the Baptist's head weren't shocking enough, Strauss's fortissimo dissonances made the work incendiary.

In 1905, the composer whom Max "always called Uncle Richard"[31] invited Steiner to *Salomé*'s world premiere in Dresden. Many first-nighters were repulsed by the opera, but Max was transported. *Salomé* would provide him with a template of future tools: character leitmotivs, modulations of keys to heighten intensity, polytonality (two musical keys played against each other), and more. Little wonder that Max "was so excited that after my return to Vienna, I could neither sleep nor eat for days."[32]

AROUND THE SAME TIME, "Venice in Vienna" received a visitor even more prestigious than Richard Strauss. The park was to be patronized by the emperor of Austria, Franz Joseph.

The occasion was 1904's First International Exhibition of Spirits and Alcohol, held in the Prater. Gabor created a special "Spirits Theater" for the emperor; it featured a musical revue titled *The Spirits Fairy* depicting the "history of alcoholic spirits," and offered a *mise en scene* worthy of DeMille, as Gabor recalled:

I had the walls decorated with luxurious hangings and covered the floor with a red carpet. Onstage, I arranged a living tableau around the emperor's bust. Flower garlands encircled the orchestra pit, and hundreds of tiny lights created a bright glow.

As the emperor entered, everyone in the theater began to sing the national anthem. The emperor said to me, "You're doing this in addition to running your businesses, which is beautiful and remarkable." It was clear that he remembered me, even though eight years had passed since my last audience. His parting words were: "It was truly delightful. I thank you very much." He left with a smile on his face.

That November, I received the Knight's Cross of the Order of Franz Joseph.[33]

Max also benefited from Franz Joseph's largesse. Soon after Gabor's honor, Steiner Jr. donned the blue-plumed fedora hat and gray uniform of the Emperor's Imperial Shooting Club, whose members included Franz Joseph's bodyguards. Steiner reportedly became a crack shot.[34]

BY 1904, GABOR RECOGNIZED that if his son were to succeed as a musician, he needed more formal training. That year, he enrolled Max in Vienna's most prestigious musical school: the Imperial Academy.

For decades, Steiner would proudly recall completing the school's rigorous exams in a single year, instead of the usual four. That boast was an exaggeration: Max studied at the Academy for two years, from 1904 to 1906.[35] The record of his departure is ambiguous. Did he complete his studies in half the normal time, or did financial illiquidity require Gabor to remove him?

Whatever the case, Steiner learned much. He studied under two esteemed professors: Hermann Graedener, course leader, and Robert Fuchs, teacher of counterpoint and harmony. He mastered piano, and showed talent on organ, trumpet, and trombone. And in his greatest coup—if Max is to be believed— he won the school's coveted gold medal:

At the end of the year there was always an examination on counterpoint, harmonies, etc. Professor [Josef] Brenner wrote on a blackboard an example of a melody which we students were to work out as a fugue. The boys were given three hours. I stood up and said, "Why do I have to stay here for three hours? Couldn't I just write my fugue on the blackboard and then leave?" The Professor said, "You couldn't possibly do a thing like that." Herr Brenner smiled tolerantly and said,

"This I've got to see. But the rest of the boys will have to leave the room or the example will be ruined."

I worked out my fugue and wrote it on the blackboard in about twenty minutes. My fugue was correct, and I was awarded the Emperor's Medal.

The same night, at dinner with my family at one of my mother's restaurants, the evening paper was brought to the table. There was the story about my winning the medal. Father was so proud he started to cry, but Mother said: "What are you crying about? I'll bet you paid for this."

It was not too long after this episode that my professor of harmony, Hermann Graedener, called my father and said, "You might as well stop Maxie coming to me because I can't teach him anymore. He knows as much as I do now about harmony and orchestration."[36]

After leaving the Academy, Max found work from a predictable source: Gabor. At "Venice in Vienna," Steiner "made out the payroll for his employees, ran errands, but somehow I found time to watch all the rehearsals

for the different shows. It was here that I learned my trade. I loved every part of this period. I would haunt the music publishers for the newest music. At home with a bowl of fresh fruit by my side, I would study scores until five or six o'clock in the morning. I attended every symphony concert and opera that came to Vienna, especially anything that was considered new or radical."[37]

Over time, Max's study endowed him with an instinctive sense of the rhythm of drama: the need for an arresting opening; the power of a strong melody; and the methods of developing musical ideas. As early as 1904, Gabor began featuring his son's compositions at Danzers and at "Venice." But Max's interests were not solely compositional. Thanks to Gabor's largesse, he pursued "a number of hobbies, such as painting and drawing and illustrating the covers of the sheet music for my songs. I loved sailing, swimming, motorcycle racing, and 'das Frauleins.' "[38]

Young Steiner bought guns, jewelry, a horse, and a boat. Fascinated by the automobiles now sharing roads with horse-drawn carriages, he asked his parents for a motorcycle. The answer was a rare "no"—but Max got his way. "Its upkeep was expensive. But never have I known such ecstasy as I did while dashing over Austria's countryside." One summer, "I took part in a motorcycle race called 'the serpentine.' The track was a winding road up into the mountains, about an hour and a half from Vienna. Whenever I entered a race, my mother, who was a devout Catholic, sat in the window praying with her rosary until my return." Max's daredevilry ended abruptly after a race: "a cylinder cracked, and in a state of unconsciousness, I was pulled out from under a pile-up of men and motorcycles. I was in a coma for days."[39]

Max suffered eye damage in the crash. Initially the injury seemed minor; but it would have serious consequences in the future.

STORIES OF STEINER'S RISK-TAKING suggest a rebelliousness that he acknowledged when an adult. "My father often told me that the worst time he had with me was when I was between the ages of fifteen and eighteen," he wrote in a private letter. Commenting on his own son's temperament in 1956, Max wrote, "There is very little anybody can tell him. He knows everything. But then so did I when I was 16."[40]

Despite a height that would never exceed 5 feet, 4 inches, and looks that might be called unprepossessing, Max displayed confidence, a quick wit, and charm. He seldom lacked female company.

He soon replaced his motorcycle with a car; and in 1906, at age eighteen, he wrote another one-act operetta: *Der Kristallpokal* (*The Crystal Cup*). A company in Russia agreed to perform it, and according to Max, its composer traveled to Moscow to conduct its premiere. "It played in an enormous variety house," he recalled, "and was quite a success. The royalty and other aristocrats had their own boxes in the theater. Behind these boxes, after the performance, late suppers of pheasant, caviar, wine, and other delicacies were served. Every night I was invited to one of these gay parties. The Russians were intrigued by so youthful a conductor and composer, and I received many a proposition! My stay there was a very happy time."[41]

With his father's theaters serving as creative workshops, Steiner saw his future as a writer of operetta—and in 1907, he made his most ambitious move to date. It would provide his most frequently told anecdote in interviews, including this version: "When I was about fifteen [thirteen in some tellings], I wrote my first complete operetta, *The Beautiful Greek Girl*. Julius Wilhelm, who wrote the book for me, took the manuscript to my father. Papa turned it down. He thought it was no good at all. We then went to my father's competitor, Karl Tuschl. Mr. Tuschl accepted it. It ran in Vienna for a full year."[42]

Truth parts company from the above. Max was nineteen when he wrote *Die schöne Griechin* (*The Beautiful Greek Girl*), based on a comedy by August Neidhart and billed as a "Vaudeville in Two Acts." It premiered on December 20, 1907—at Danzers Orpheum, home of many Steiner first performances. As for its "full year" run—it is true that *Griechin* opened in 1907 and ran into 1908; but it played for *two months*, from December to January.[43]

Nevertheless, the operetta's success was real and its importance for Max considerable. After its premiere, *Griechin* was selected to headline on Christmas Eve, Christmas Day, and New Year's Eve—proof that it was more than a piece of nepotistic programming.

Max would date his true beginnings as a composer to the work.

FOUR MONTHS AFTER *Griechin*'s last performance, Max Steiner turned twenty. With multiple theaters featuring his music, often under the imprimatur of his celebrated father, a future following in the steps of Strauss and Franz Lehar (*The Merry Widow*) seemed possible and probable.

But as Max should have known from studying countless operas, scenes of triumph were invariably followed by sudden, precipitous disaster.

PART TWO

The Wanderer

3

Come Over Here

IF *THE BEAUTIFUL GREEK GIRL* showed Max Steiner's career on the ascent, the opposite was true of the man who made it possible.

Gabor had spent twelve years juggling multiple ventures, as money flowed from his pockets as freely as water in the Danube. One "Venice" production, recreating the 1683 Turkish siege of Vienna, employed a thousand cast members, plus elephants and camels from a Hamburg circus.[1] But by summer 1907, pleasure-seekers had tired of the palazzos of "Venice." Its popularity was also hurt by growing fears of infectious disease from its lagoons and canals.[2]

The inevitable crisis came that November: after amassing debts of some 800,000 krone (about $10 million today),[3] Gabor declared bankruptcy. "Considering the environment of success in which I had grown up," Max recalled, "You may imagine my shock when I awoke one morning and saw the headlines in the paper: 'GABOR STEINER BANKRUPT.' I did everything I could to help. I sold my horses, my automobile, motorcycle, sailing boat, gun collection and jewelry. Papa had around 200 antique clocks in his collection. Mother sold most of these and, together with part of her own money, finally succeeded in settling the matter."[4]

Gabor supervised one last season at "Venice." But by September 1908, with debts again climbing, he was forced to surrender directorship of his beloved park, months after giving up management of Danzers Orpheum.[5]

MAX'S PROSPECTS HAD GONE the way of his family's possessions. It was time to chart a new course, away from the city where "Steiner" was a name most often uttered by debt collectors.

Over Mitzi's objections, the 20-year-old decided to emigrate to Britain. "Because of the then-current popularity of Viennese and Hungarian music, I thought I would have no trouble finding a job as a conductor, orchestrator or composer."[6] Max probably spoke at least some English by his teens. He was fascinated by the phonetic similarities of words and their multiple meanings; his addiction to puns would be one of his enduring traits.

"I purchased an English grammar and a German-English/English-German dictionary. Every week I would buy an English newspaper and diligently follow word for word this week-old news, looking each word up in the grammar and then in my dictionary."[7]

His decision to leave Vienna was fortuitous. Musically, the romanticism of Strauss would soon be challenged by the dissonant atonalism of Schoenberg. Politically, the emperor would extend Austria's "sovereign rights" into Bosnia and Herzegovina in October 1908. The annexation lit a fuse that exploded in war six years later.

FOR STEINER, TRAVELING to a new country was an adventure. Years of interaction with entertainers instilled in him a sociability and self-confidence that won him friends quickly.

But Max had another reason for the journey: he had fallen in love.

Mabel Funston was a 21-year-old British singer and dancer he had met in Vienna. Surviving photos show a pretty, round-chinned brunette whose wide smile, sparkling dark eyes, and coquettish poses suggest a gift for seduction. From England, she kept up a correspondence with Steiner. In an early sign of a lifelong weakness, Max impulsively decided to pursue her and propose. More than 50 years later, the details of that pursuit remained vivid in his mind.

> Some years before, my parents had taken me with them to London on one of their talent searches. We had stayed at the Ritz at something like five pounds a day. This time, my "Ritz" was a small, furnished room over a French bakery in the Soho district.
>
> The first thing I did after setting my baggage in my room was to take a bus to Brixton, to the address given me on my letters from Mabel. When I arrived at 16 Rushcroft Road (you see, I still remember it), the door was opened by the landlady. I inquired whether Mabel was at home. She replied, "No, they went out to dinner." I asked weakly, "They?" "Yes, Mabel and her husband."
>
> I stood there, stunned, then turned around and started the long, tedious journey back to Soho.[8]

But heartbreak is seldom wasted on an artist. Years later, Max would put his unrequited passion to good use, in music.

STEINER HAD ARRIVED in a country making swift technological strides into the new century. In 1908, taxicabs sped across town with alarming speed, passing the suffragette rallies that began in force that summer. The months ahead saw the launch of the modern department store (Selfridge's), modern spycraft (the Secret Service) and modern movie exhibition (the Cinematograph Act, regulating the industry).

Amid so much activity, Max was sure he could find work. But whether due to prejudice toward foreigners, or the reason he later gave—"Although [twenty] years old, I looked fifteen"[9]—no one would hire him, and soon he was broke. The pampered composer who two years before had dined on pheasant and caviar in Moscow was now "close to starving."[10]

To fill empty days, he indulged in a favorite pastime: drawing. Steiner was a gifted artist, and his early sketches suggest someone already keenly observant of character, and eager to capture psychology in his art.[11]

After weeks of struggle and anxiety, Max found salvation that, in his account, came with a coincidence worthy of a Danzers Orpheum operetta:

(Louise Steiner Elian Papers; L. Tom Perry Special Collections, Brigham Young University)

One cold, wet and foggy night, I stood shivering outside a delicatessen named Appenrodt's. I had three shillings left and stood wondering whether to spend it on a sandwich or buy cigarettes or a cigar to still my hunger (I was already a heavy smoker).

As I tried to decide, a gentleman emerged from the delicatessen and stood beside me. Finally he said, "I beg your pardon, son, but are you Viennese?" I said yes. "Is your family alive?" I answered, "Yes, they are in the theatrical business." The man shook my hand and said, "You must be the son of my dear friend, Gabor Steiner."

He then took me into the restaurant and bought me perhaps the most appreciated dinner of my life. He told me he recognized me because I looked so much like my father. He himself had been musical director of my father's theater in [Germany]. After giving me twenty pounds to pay my rent, he told me to meet him the next day at George Dance's office in Leicester Square.[12]

Theater promoter George Dance excelled in a facet of show business that still thrives today: sending hit shows on tour after their London runs ended. Steiner was hired as one of Dance's rehearsal pianists. Soon he was promoted to musical director of the touring operetta *The Girls of Gottenberg*.[13]

Success on tour with the operetta *Veronique* led to an offer from the London Hippodrome, reportedly to serve as musical director.[14] This event marks another fork in the road between Steiner's recollections and surviving records. The latter contain few mentions of the man who later claimed to conduct at the London Palladium, the Tivoli, Gaiety, Adelphi, and Empire. But Steiner's accurate memories of obscure musicals suggest a compromise truth: Max probably worked on many of the shows in a more junior capacity than principal music director.

Either way, his stage experiences in Britain were the start of his education in how to work quickly and efficiently under pressure. Upon arriving in Dublin to conduct the musical *Amsterdam*, Max discovered that instrumental parts for his twenty-five players had been lost in transit. In a 20-hour marathon, Steiner is said to have played each part from memory on the piano, as the musicians hastily handwrote new scores for themselves.[15]

AMID THE MANY FORGOTTEN OPERETTAS and revues that Steiner conducted in the UK, one engagement stands out. Actor-impresario Sir Herbert Beerbohm Tree was a lion of the British theater; during the early 20th century, his productions of Shakespeare at Her Majesty's Theatre in London became

Steiner sketches, date unknown. (MS Papers; L. Tom Perry Special Collections, Brigham Young University)

national events. "Sir Herbert had quite a large orchestra playing during his performances" at Her Majesty's, Max recalled.

"The pit was covered over with a netting. On top were beautiful flower arrangements. The orchestra was hidden beneath this netting. Sir Herbert had a musical director named Adolf Schmid. I used to help him now and then, writing little cues and orchestrations. One day Sir Herbert walked in, and Schmid introduced me to him. His Lordship told me, 'You know, Mr. Steiner, the day will come when all these old plays will be underlined with music. I like to have as much music as possible with my plays. Music helps me to be a better actor.' He was certainly farsighted. Sir Herbert made his statement long before talkies had even been thought of."[16]

Steiner never forgot the productions' hidden placement of the orchestra, which created an effect not unlike music on a film soundtrack. And in a time before microphones simplified the blending of human voices with an orchestra, Max was gaining invaluable experience in learning how to orchestrate in support of speech.

STEINER'S BREAKTHROUGH YEAR of 1909 ended with another step forward. That November, he was hired to compose and conduct for John Tiller, founder of the Tiller Girls, a touring troupe synonymous with precision dancing. Their high-kicking routines inspired countless imitators, including New York's Rockettes.

While in London, Max renewed an old friendship, with W. C. Fields. "He was so much fun, and he had a marvelous touring car, built very high. It had a step on hinges which hung down because the seats were about four feet from the ground. After you climbed into the car, you reached down to a handle on the side and pulled up the step. When Bill had to leave for an engagement in America, he wanted me to buy it, but I didn't have any money to speak of. Bill asked, 'How much do you have?' I had 75 pounds, then worth about $375. Bill smiled and said, "Oddly enough, that's the exact price.' So I bought the car and said goodbye to my friend. A month later I received a letter with a check for $375. 'I've decided," he wrote, 'that I cannot accept money from a broken-down musician like you. You stink. Love, Bill.'"[17]

THE FACT THAT DESPITE REGULAR EMPLOYMENT Max "didn't have any money to speak of" suggests that the 22-year-old was returning to the lifestyle of his youth. Expensive meals, cigars, and liquor were lifelong vices for Steiner. In London, they propped up an insecure ego still recovering from his family's fall from grace.

The follower of Strauss dreamed of writing his own hit stage musical; and in 1910, he found a collaborator in Raoul Lurion, a would-be librettist with a wealthy father. Raoul proposed an original story called *Topsy Turvy*, set on an island "where everything was turned around. The women, all Amazons, were the army, the police. The men did all the women's chores."[18] Lurion and Steiner dashed off a first draft. With funds from Raoul's father, they hired popular stage comic Fred Emney to star in a tryout in Manchester.

Topsy Turvy lasted exactly one night. Max blamed its failure on a final gag that didn't come off, but clearly its problems ran deeper: Steiner never revised it, and he would not attempt another stage show for 13 years.

A WARNER BROS. MOVIE would compress Max's next two years with the Tiller company into a montage of maps and marquees—so let us imagine such a sequence, with glimpses of Hamburg, Johannesburg, Cairo, Brussels, Norway, and Sweden.[19] In December 1911, he enjoyed a two-month engagement in Paris. The following July saw the premiere of a Steiner ballet, *Bits of Dresden*.[20]

And by 1912, he had again fallen in love.

Beatrice Tilt was an attractive soubrette from the London suburb of Brixton. Max had met her in Vienna; in Britain they reconnected, and that September, the 24-year-old composer and 28-year-old former actress married.[21] Beatrice was typical of the women to whom Max was drawn: pliant "pretty little things"[22] who were not his intellectual equal, but who could provide sex and creative encouragement.

But their honeymoon was brief. Weeks before their ceremony, Max had received an urgent telegram from his father. Gabor was again in trouble.

FOR A WHILE, STEINER SR. HAD RISEN from the ashes of his 1908 bankruptcy. The following year, he won the lease of another crown jewel among Viennese theaters, the Ronacher.[23]

Since opening in 1872, the Ronacher had survived a devastating fire and rocky attendance, but only barely.[24] Gabor believed he knew how to make it a success: like the shuttered "Venice in Vienna," the Ronacher would be a pleasure palace. He enlarged its stage and auditorium, and turned its modest café into a glittering after-hour nightclub, the "Establissement Parisien," which offered risqué performances of the cancan.

From 1909 to 1912, Gabor filled the Ronacher with an eclectic array of entertainment: classical recitations, acrobats, magicians, operetta, and the cinematic flickering of the "Ronacher-Biograph." Gabor hadn't given up on movies.[25]

Once again, his outsized vision ended in debt. Enter 24-year-old Max, after receiving his father's telegrammed S.O.S. "I had recently come into a small trust fund from my grandfather. I used this to straighten Papa out as well as I could. Then I took over management of the theater."[26] Max's own handling of finances hardly made him an ideal manager—but desperate to aid the father he idolized, he reached out to every star performer he knew, to give the Ronacher a season the public could not ignore.

He delivered at least one superstar: stage and screen comedian Max Linder. A talent revered even by Chaplin, the elegant, mustachioed Frenchman added the Ronacher to his current stage tour, and performed his much-loved "Pedicure par Amour," a one-act comedy routine.[27]

But not even Linder and an uptick in sales could pay off Gabor's debt. A harbinger of the future came late one night when, just as patrons settled into the Parisien Café to cheer its half-clad dancers, the nightclub was plunged into darkness. "We had been unable to pay the electric light bill," Max recalled.[28]

IN DECEMBER, THE RONACHER LOCKED its doors. Gabor fled to Switzerland,[29] and although he was still married to Mitzi, their life together was over.

For Max, worse lay ahead. On December 21, while still in Vienna, the ex-manager of the Ronacher was approached by police—and arrested.

Among the theater's many creditors was Frau Theresia Sinek, who brought charges against Max for failing to honor a contract he signed for future theater programs. Steiner also had failed to return the Ronacher's lease deposit of 22,000 kronen.[30] His imprisonment made the papers in Vienna, Britain, and even America. Max's humiliation deepened with a visit from his mother—who refused to bail him out. "She was still resentful of my becoming a musician and going away to England, so there I remained for several weeks. All of the jailers knew of me and my family. They were very nice to me. My cell was never locked. Christmas Day, they invited me to their quarters, and we had a lovely dinner."[31]

In January 1913, Max was finally cleared of all charges. "I went to live with my mother in her house in Hietzing, a suburb of Vienna. But I had no money and mother wouldn't give me any. I might just as well have stayed in jail."[32] The fact that Steiner preferred a miserable coexistence with his mother to re-union with Beatrice in London suggests two possibilities: either Max's bride could not afford to join her husband, or Steiner was already tiring of the marriage. Their union would also have a tragic element—a baby who lived for "only a couple of weeks," according to a later confidante.[33]

SURPRISINGLY, 1913 BEGAN with a burst of good fortune. A colleague of Uncle Franz, theater manager Clifford Fisher, had leased the London Opera House and needed a musical director. A mammoth edifice, the Opera House occupied an entire city block and accommodated 2,600 patrons. Few productions could attract such a crowd, but Fisher assembled a blockbuster that defied the odds.

Come Over Here offered the kind of spectacle that Gabor Steiner could only dream of: an onstage chase between car and locomotive (the latter projected on film); globe-hopping scenes from France to Arabia; and a rousing musical finale improbably titled "Everybody Loves a Chicken." That tune was "a first-rate ending to a great entertainment,"[34] gushed one reviewer, before praising the "delightful music" under "the direction of Mr. Phil Saxe."

Phil Saxe?

Max had chosen to conceal his identity with a pseudonym. Were Steiner family creditors lurking as far as London? Or was British sentiment toward Germans and Austrians already harming career prospects? Whatever the case,

The new manager of the Ronacher Theatre, 1912.

Come Over Here gave its conductor more than six months of steady work.[35] It also introduced him to the show's co-composer, later a major ally.

New Yorker Louis A. Hirsch was soon to become one of the early 20th century's best-loved songwriters. Two of his tunes remain standards: "Hello, Frisco!" (aka "Hello, Frisco, Hello") and "The Love Nest," which George Burns and Gracie Allen adopted as their theme on radio and television. In the wake of Irving Berlin's smash "Alexander's Ragtime Band," producers were eager to find the next American syncopator. For *Come Over Here*, Hirsch wrote catchy facsimiles of early jazz.

By now, Steiner was a master at conducting shows that switched musical style as quickly as their actors changed costumes. He also enjoyed a memorable liaison during the production, in further evidence of his estrangement from Beatrice:

> The boys and I began to notice the presence of a woman in the first row, every night. We began to call her "the lady in red" because she was always attired in a red costume and had flaming red hair.
>
> The boys began to tease me about her, saying that I was the attraction. So one night at the end of the performance, I addressed her. "Aren't you tired of this show?" I asked. "I'm so tired of it, I'd like to quit." "If you did that, I wouldn't come anymore," she answered with a quiet smile. "I only come to see you." I was flattered and intrigued.
>
> The lady turned out to be a Russian countess-in-exile. She must have made off with some of the Crown Jewels, because she maintained a luxurious suite in one of the best hotels and wanted to lavish gifts on me. The romance lasted until my friend told me one day that she must go to Switzerland on business. She did not know when she would return, but no matter what transpired, she would always love me.
>
> I have never seen or heard of her again from that day.[36]

In July, singing star Anna Held—ex-wife of Florenz Ziegfeld—joined the cast and lived up to her diva reputation.[37] When Held departed the show after one month, she was replaced by another import from America: five foot, six inch comedienne Fanny Brice.[38] Given their similarly mischievous temperaments, Fanny and Max probably had fun together.

In November 1913, *Come Over Here* closed after 271 performances. But sometime before its final car chase raced across the boards, it inspired a small piece of history: Steiner's first recording session. Singers and orchestra crowded into an RCA Victor studio in London to record "*Come Over Here* Selections" that filled two sides of a 78-rpm record.[39]

Its musical director may have sensed a moment of significance. Instead of Phil Saxe, the conductor listed on the label is Max Steiner.

DAYS AFTER *COME OVER HERE* CLOSED, Max was at work on another high-profile project. On November 18, 1913, he was one of four conductors leading a charity show at the London Opera House.[40] After the show, he and the orchestra were introduced to its patron: Hugh Grosvenor, Duke of Westminster.

"The Duke was so pleased with our work that he rewarded each of us with a beautiful silver cigarette case. I liked his impartiality in presenting this gift, because so often the orchestra leader or headliner is given a handsomer gift than the orchestra boys who have worked just as hard."[41] No wonder Max was seen by musicians as a friend and advocate.

Steiner's next job was less glamorous. Carl Hamburg's *Wonder Zoo and Big Circus*, staged at the Olympia, demoted Max to the status of orchestra pit cellist. Its run was short but unforgettable. "One of the animals, a lioness, didn't like me. She kept staring at me during rehearsal. Finally, on opening night, she came right to the front of her cage, which was almost down in the [orchestra] pit, and urinated all over me and the cello. She had taken perfect aim and hit me right in the face with a scalding acidic stream. The stench was so terrific that it cleared the first few rows of the orchestra seats in one minute. Some of the instruments were ruined, but somehow the show went on, as it always does."[42]

STEINER FACED BIGGER PROBLEMS than a discontented lioness. On June 28, 1914, a week before Max began conducting Louis Hirsch's musical *Dora's Doze*, the assassination of Austrian Archduke Franz Ferdinand and his wife, Sophie, triggered a chain reaction of military movement across Europe. Two weeks into *Dora's* run, Steiner was released as conductor;[43] and on August 4, Britain declared war on Austria's ally, Germany.

Max Steiner had climbed his way up in London from penniless accompanist to musical director in one of the world's great cities. Now, he had a new identity: enemy alien.

By September, four hundred Germans and Austrians in Britain had been arrested and interned. In October, Austrians in the UK were banned from jobs in most businesses. Having recently seen the inside of a jail cell, Max grew anxious. "I had neglected to become a naturalized citizen during my years in England, which I now regretted very much."[44]

Steiner knew it was time for another emigration, to a nation that was not part of the Great War. He chose the country that, more than any other, offered growing opportunities for a conductor/orchestrator/composer. And for help, he raced to the office of Frederick Day, whose company Francis, Day & Hunter had published some of Max's compositions.

> I said, "Freddy, maybe I should go to America." Freddy thought for a moment, then said, "We'll finance you." These dear souls collected money from their publishing contacts, all my old friends, and raised my fare, plus $57 pocket money, to go to America.
>
> Next I had to get a passport to leave the United Kingdom and enter America, which was almost impossible at that time for an Austrian. At this point, I remembered the Duke of Westminster. I wrote him a note and asked if he could help me. He wrote back and instructed me to see the Secretary of the Interior, William Haldane Porter, who would arrange a passport.
>
> I went at once to Mr. Porter's office at Whitehall. The Duke had already called and the passport was ready.[45]

And what of Beatrice? Max later claimed that "there was no money available for my wife to go to America with me, so we were forced to separate until such time as I could afford to send for her."[46] Given the support Max found among friends, his excuse for leaving behind his wife of two years sounds more convenient than truthful.

ON OCTOBER 29, 1914, MAX STEINER went to sea aboard the steamer *Lapland* from the port of Liverpool.[47] He would not return to Britain for more than 40 years—and he would never see Vienna again.

In nine days, Steiner would arrive in what would become his new and permanent home: the United States of America.

4

Stairway to Paradise

ON NOVEMBER 7, 1914, 26-year-old Max Steiner arrived at New York's Ellis Island.[1] "I was rather green," he would recall, "for as soon as I came off the boat, a drunk 'borrowed' five dollars from me."[2]

For the second time in seven years, Max was in a strange country starting over. But unlike London, he had family waiting. Gabor's brother Alexander lived in America; there, "Doc" Steiner had become a talent agent for the Keith-Albee theater circuit, one of the United States's largest booking companies.[3] (Years later, the same "Keith" would provide the "K" in RKO.) Max settled into a furnished room on 44th Street. Its cost of $15 a month was more appealing than its interior: "It was an attic room with no windows, only a skylight, but I was happy to get it."[4]

Fortunately, Manhattan was enough like London for Steiner to assimilate quickly. But despite letters of recommendation from UK producers, employment proved impossible. "Nobody thought to warn me that I was ineligible to join the union. I first must have my U.S. citizenship papers. Moreover, you had to be in the country at least six months before you could even apply for your papers. So here I was with six months without work staring me in the face."[5]

But Gabor Steiner's son always found a way. He took on copying work at Harms, one of the world's largest music publishers.[6] An affiliate of his London publisher Frederick Day, Harms was run by Max Dreyfus, who was starting to assemble a stunning roster of songwriting talent: Jerome Kern, George Gershwin, Rodgers and Hart, Cole Porter, and many more.

Steiner also found work at another publishing house, Waterson, Berlin & Snyder. Whether Steiner made the acquaintance of its middle partner, Irving, is unknown; but decades later, Max surely pondered the turns of fate after working with Berlin on three of his greatest successes.

BY 1915, MAX SHARED his second-floor apartment with a pair of equally desperate lodgers. Emanuel Liszt was a handsome bass baritone, later to find success with the Metropolitan Opera. Hungarian Ota Gygi was a violinist whose thick-lidded eyes endowed him with the look of a sad philosopher. "We didn't have money to eat half the time," Max remembered. But

> every night, the occupant of the fifth floor apartment ordered dinner from the delicatessen and had it sent up on the dumbwaiter. We got wise to this and waited for the dumbwaiter to go by. As it passed our dumbwaiter door, two of us grabbed whatever we could.
>
> This went on for about two weeks. Then Ota got a job with the Keith-Orpheum circuit. He sent us money back right away. We decided to go upstairs and confess to the fifth floor tenant what we had been doing. When we told him, he almost collapsed with laughter. He said he had had more fights with the delicatessen about how his orders were not properly filled. He turned out to be a bookie, which was why he was always home in the evening. We told him we wanted to make it up to him and were now going to take him to dinner for two weeks straight.[7]

In April 1915, after five months in America, the 27-year-old was thrilled to get a job as a paid musician, joining the ten-piece band that accompanied the revue *Too Much Mustard*. But playing two shows nightly inside Reisenweber's Restaurant on Coney Island was hardly a source of pride. The revue's chief attraction wasn't musical, as *Variety* made clear: "The costumes worn by the chorus girls [are] chiffon draped over hardly anything at all."[8]

That June, Max finally brought Beatrice from London to join him. Her mother followed. But in what would prove a familiar pattern, Max's workaholic nature, and his addiction to late-night carousing and gambling, strained the marriage to a breaking point. "We also had a conflict concerning her mother. She was a dear soul, but she became a harmless but embarrassing mental case. Beatrice refused to place her in a rest home. We tried hard to work everything out, but we finally came to the decision to part."[9]

Guilty over his long neglect of Beatrice, Max agreed to a generous alimony—one that would continue until the 1950s. Steiner was already sending money to his separated parents; his payments to Beatrice would be the second of several long-term drains on Max's income.

AGAIN, SALVATION ARRIVED from an unexpected source. During the run of *Too Much Mustard*, Max was introduced to "a gentleman by the name of Rothafel."[10] Samuel "Roxy" Rothafel was a theater impresario and future founder of Radio City Music Hall . . . the man whose nickname inspired the moniker for the Rockettes. Impressed by Max's versatility, Rothafel hired him to lead a 43-piece non-union orchestra accompanying silent films at William Fox's Riverside Theater on 96th Street.[11] Thus began Max's professional career in the movies—although 15 years would pass before this flirtation became a love affair.

By 1915, America was home to 21,000 movie theaters. Investment in U.S. film production had reached half a billion dollars;[12] Griffith, Chaplin and others were turning a money-grab industry into an art form; and the first major movie companies were being born. These included Fox Film Corporation, Max's new employer. Steiner's job conducting silent film scores at the Riverside Theater involved choosing stock music and making "an attempt to fit it to the action as best we could. I must have done a fairly good job, because on the retirement of his general music director for the Fox circuit, William Fox made me the music director for all his theaters."[13]

By 1915, William Fox was among the most ruthless moguls in his nascent industry. After fighting his way up from newsboy to nickelodeon owner, he helped create the integrated movie business, one in which Fox-owned theaters showed Fox-produced films. And while many employees found him unpleasant in his avarice, Max—ever-positive, and understandably grateful—remembered him as "one of the finest men the world has ever known."[14]

Fox also allowed Steiner considerable freedom.

[In March 1916] we were showing a picture called *The Bondman*. I had an idea. Until about 1915 there was no special music written for motion pictures. We just used to take the albums publishers put out and would play "Hurry No. 1, Hurry No. 2, Love Scene No. 6." I said to myself, "This is a lot of baloney. I'd like to do something new." I talked to Mr. Fox and told him I wanted to write music for the picture.

"Go ahead and do whatever you want."

. . . And I wrote the music for *The Bondman*. We put together a 110-man orchestra. After that, Mr. Fox always called me Professor.

. . . We used to have theaters in Jamaica, Long Island, and up in the Bronx. I would have to drive from one theater to the other in order to check up on what these different orchestra leaders were doing.[15]

Contrary to Max's memory, a few original film scores were written prior to 1915.[16] Still, his music for *The Bondman* was a milestone: for the first time, Steiner wrote music to fit a motion picture image. Since this score does not survive, we can know little else about the project, except for Max's review of the movie: "A perfectly terrible picture."[17]

STEINER'S ASSOCIATION WITH FOX was a turning point. When the mogul signed a contract with the musicians union, "The union automatically took all the musicians in," Max recalled. "I, at last, was in, too."[18]

For reasons unknown today, Steiner's promising start in the movies was over by mid-1916. The cause may have been an offer from a pair of Broadway powerhouses, producers Lee and J. J. Shubert, who invited him to conduct a new musical. Max still dreamed of fame as a composer-songwriter, and he knew that success with the Shuberts might lead to his own stage project. But during tryouts in Buffalo of the new show, whose name is lost to history, calamity struck: Max slipped on an icy sidewalk and shattered his left kneecap. For weeks, "I had to conduct with a broken kneecap and torn tendons. The doctor came during the two intermissions and gave me an injection to help relieve the pain."[19]

Flash forward to Manhattan, where the Shuberts decided the show was a dog and would go no further. Steiner was again unemployed and broke.

Adding to his stress was a more troubling physical problem. Since his teenage injury in a motorcycle crash, Steiner's vision had slowly worsened. In New York, he began seeing a Dr. Krug, who told him that although his eyes required strong prescription glasses, he would not lose his eyesight.[20]

As the years passed, Max would have reason to doubt that verdict.

AMONG STEINER'S FEW JOBS of the time was orchestration work for Broadway's fastest rising composer, Jerome Kern, on the new show *Have a Heart*.[21] But despite an elegant score, *Heart* failed to spark ticket sales and closed after two months. Max had no choice but to travel once more to parts unknown. In the 1800s, fellow Austrian Franz Schubert wrote of the lonely trek of an artist in his song *The Wanderer*: "I wander silently and am somewhat unhappy / And my sighs always ask—Where?"

For Steiner, the immediate answer was California.

"A WEALTH OF WHIRLING GAIETY, a Lively Lilting Laughing Luxurious Musical Confection," *The Masked Model* offered more adjectives than quality—but the show gave Steiner his first job in America as a conductor of musical comedy. Impressed by Max's orchestrations, producer John Cort asked him to be music director for its low-budget road tour, headed for San Francisco and other cities in northern California.[22]

During its run, Max became friends with an Italian dancer in the company. Steiner recalled his pal Rudy as "very poor, but a wonderful dancer. In Sacramento, where we played three days on our way to San Francisco, Rudy had a falling out with the manager and left the show. Since he was broke and had nowhere to go, Lew Hearn, a funny little comedian, bedded him down in the hotels where we were staying, and took him out to eat with us."[23]

Max's itinerant friend drifted to Los Angeles. Five years later, as Rudolph Valentino, he would become one of the most famous people on the planet.

Steiner's sympathy for a struggling performer demonstrates a quality that would be among his greatest strengths as a film composer: empathy. Despite a life filled with disappointment and occasional exploitation, Max remained at heart a hopeful, generous person, who—perhaps due to the kindnesses he was shown—was predisposed to find the best in others.

The short-lived company of *The Masked Model*, 1917. Max Steiner second from left, Rudolph Valentino at center. (Denver Public Library)

THE MASKED MODEL STUMBLED on to Los Angeles, where it closed after two weeks. Max's first impressions of southern California were colored by the familiar condition of poverty. "We hadn't been paid in a couple of weeks, so we had to get back the best way we could."[24]

Back in New York, Max faced a new source of anxiety. America had entered the war, and propaganda against Austria-Hungary was everywhere. His nationality may help explain why for over six months Steiner had little work. But in spring 1918, an offer finally arrived—one that pointed him toward his ultimate career path.

It came from another unlikely savior. Producer Abraham Erlanger, in the words of historian Ethan Mordden, "was hated by virtually everyone in the business, and he basked in it. . . . Yet in his greed, Erlanger contributed to the amazing expansion of theatergoing in the 1890s and in the three decades after by building more theaters to control."[25] Charles Dickens would have smiled at the name of Abe's producing partner: Klaw.

Erlanger had hired composer Louis Hirsch to write a new Broadway musical, *The Rainbow Girl*. Hirsch recommended his friend Max as conductor, and Steiner eagerly accepted "the first decent salary I had received since my arrival in the United States."[26] It was also his steadiest: he would conduct the hit musical from April to August of 1918.

Its home, the eleven-story New Amsterdam Theater, was another sign that Max was moving up. The theater's cavernous Art Nouveau interior had hosted annual productions of the *Ziegfeld Follies* since 1913. After months of bitterly cold winter, the New Amsterdam's 1,750-seat auditorium, graced with two balconies, twelve boxes, and gorgeous murals in green, pearl, and mauve, must have felt to Max like heaven. He also made a friend in 38-year-old Englishman Sydney Greenstreet, cast as a comic butler three decades before appearing in *Casablanca* and other Steiner-scored films.[27]

FOR THE NEXT DECADE as his Broadway network grew, Max was seldom unemployed. Among his most celebrated collaborators was Victor Herbert, a titan of popular music whom Steiner had met in Vienna; Herbert had been a cellist at the Theater an der Wien during Gabor's management.[28] After contributing orchestrations to Herbert's *Angel Face*, Steiner rejoined the composer in the elevated post of musical director, on 1920's *Oui Madame*.

The show was a flop, but its 21-year-old rehearsal pianist became a close comrade of Max's. Aspiring songwriter Vincent Youmans "was not an educated musician," Steiner remembered, "but he had the most uncanny knack for harmonies. He was a wonderful boy and we became very close."[29] Thirteen years later, their friendship would produce memorable dividends.

1920's *Dere Mabel* is remembered solely for the writers of four of its songs: George and Ira Gershwin. "Swanee" had just brought 21-year-old George national fame; and while Max's work on *Mabel* was brief—Steiner left during tryouts due to illness—his friendship with the Gershwins stuck. "George, Ira, Oscar Levant, and I were the four indestructibles. We were always together. Sometimes we would play music, discuss what I wrote, what the other guy wrote, have a few drinks, get plastered, and go to bed. Those were the good old days."*[30]

Oscar Levant was also a struggling composer, and soon to be the finest interpreter of Gershwin's piano work. Facile, funny, and neurotic, he found a kindred spirit in Max, and for decades they shared a spiky camaraderie that was equal parts affection and competition. Steiner was hurt in 1940 when Levant described Max in print as a "little man who was the kind of a conductor that a producer of musical comedies always thought of third. He would be called in to conduct if the two conductors you thought of first couldn't be had. An overrich orchestrator for the theater, Steiner's abilities in this field were suitable for occasional spots but not for a whole musical comedy."[31] Levant's account may have been colored by envy: by the time of its writing, Oscar was an embittered also-ran in the field of film scoring, and Max its most successful practitioner.

The year 1920 also brought *Good Times*, a Steiner-conducted revue at the Hippodrome—a block-long "spectacle house" with room for 5,200 patrons and 600 performers, "not to mention elephants, waterfalls . . . and a nearly full-scale baseball game," author Martin Rubin itemized.[32] *Good Times* lived up to its title. Packed houses cheered the upbeat show for 456 performances, and Max must have grinned when a reviewer cited Steiner's ballet "Shadowland" as a highlight.[33]

One wonders if he ever chatted backstage with a 17-year-old stilt-walker in the show, newly arrived from Britain, named Archibald Leach. Years later, as Cary Grant, he would star in three Steiner-scored movies.

MAX HAD NOT LOST HIS LOVE of concert music. He kept apprised of the newest composers and closely followed the work of two Russians, Sergei Prokofiev and Igor Stravinsky. Their sharply rhythmic, harmonically daring

---

* Steiner's memory conflates time—Levant and Gershwin did not become friends until the late 1920s—but there is no doubt that Max knew both men during this decade.

works would have a major impact on Steiner's writing. And although Max himself composed little original music during the 1920s, his theater jobs built creative muscles that would prove invaluable in Hollywood: the ability to work quickly under pressure, to balance an orchestra with the spoken voice, to weave a songwriter's melodies into dramatic underscore (Max often wrote the music leading in and out of songs), and to create a specific orchestral color with a limited number of instruments.

HE HAD ALSO LEARNED a valuable lesson from his years in Britain, taking time to become an American citizen. And in December 1921, after nearly a decade of separation from his parents, he convinced both Gabor and Mitzi to join him in New York.

At age 63, Gabor had lost his youthful good looks but little of his ambition. Since fleeing to Switzerland in 1912, Gabor had tried producing, running a music publishing company, and selling inventions. Naturally, he hoped to launch a new venture in New York: a theater exchange bureau, which would allow him to present U.S. musicals in Vienna.

In bringing his parents to America, their sentimental son no doubt hoped Gabor and Mitzi would reunite. But both Steiners soon felt homesick and overwhelmed, and returned to Austria. "Mother couldn't speak one word of English, and father only knew a few words. As much as I regretted it, I had to let them go back."[34]

Max would never see his mother again.

FOR THOSE WONDERING if Steiner's Broadway career included any shows that remain well known, patience is about to be rewarded. In 1922, George Gershwin invited Max to serve as musical director, on the most important project for both to date: *George White's Scandals*.

A former Ziegfeld dancer, producer George White imitated the legendary Flo with his own series of revues that replaced Ziegfeld's polish with speed and irreverence. White's shows were built on bathroom jokes, send-ups of Prohibition, and sex-farce blackout scenes. "White didn't follow Ziegfeld," Ethan Mordden observed. "He passed him at ninety miles an hour."[35]

On August 28, 1922, Max Steiner conducted an Act One finale built around a new Gershwin song, "I'll Build a Stairway to Paradise." Joining Max's pit ensemble was a second orchestra led by Paul Whiteman, a rotund, mustachioed bandleader soon to be world famous as "The King of Jazz." The resulting number became one of Gershwin's favorite theatrical memories.

"Two circular staircases surrounded [Paul's] orchestra on the stage," George recalled. "Mr. White had draped fifty of his most beautiful girls in a black patent-leather material, which brilliantly reflected the spotlights."[36]

Less successful was Gershwin's most daring composition for *Scandals*, which Max also conducted: a one-act "Negro opera" initially titled *135th Street*, later known as *Blue Monday*. Opening night audiences were baffled by Gershwin's attempt to meld operatic tragedy with African American blues, especially in the middle of a glorified girlie show. Only later would the work be seen as the first step toward *Porgy and Bess*.

No American composer would have as great an impact on Steiner as Gershwin. Their teamings were a priceless education for Max in real jazz, as opposed to the synthetic imitations he conducted in Britain. George's influence can be heard in many Steiner film scores, from open emulation in *State's Attorney* and *Crime School*, to jazz-infused tone poems in *Four Wives* and *City for Conquest*. Steiner also would employ a device common in Gershwin songs, repeating and modulating a melodic fragment "with a different and unexpected harmony underneath,"[37] as done in the opening of *Stairway to Paradise*.

Perhaps it was Gershwin's dynamic creativity that led Max to tackle his first original stage musical in twelve years. *Peaches* began with a stronger pedigree than its predecessor, *Topsy Turvy*. Its producer was George W. Lederer, who had known the Steiners since 1900, when his early hit *The Belle of New York* played at Danzers Orpheum.

Peaches' lyrics were by Robert B. Smith, the libretto by his brother, Harry B. Smith. A one-man industry, Harry is believed to have written over three hundred librettos and over *six thousand* song lyrics.[38] But his achievements belong more to the *Guinness Book of World Records* than the Great American Songbook. A competent writer, he was rarely a fresh one. *Peaches'* plot involved Vivien Grey, society girl, who pretends to be a maid to infiltrate the home of her fiancé's family to see what they're like. When a real maid arrives and is mistaken for Vivien, the story takes on enough farcical twists to support a musical hit—at least if that musical's composer was Kern, Berlin, or Gershwin.

Songs from *Peaches* survive; all offer pleasing, polished melodies, but none rises to the status of memorable. A tryout at the Garrick Theater in Philadelphia opened on January 22, 1923. Good reviews were scarce. According to the *Philadelphia Inquirer*, Smith's "trite" book employed "humor which was on its last legs during McKinley's administration ... or even Thomas Jefferson."[39] Max's score was deemed "attractive but routine." Shorn of 30 minutes, it played one week in Baltimore—then closed, never to be seen again.

Peaches' failure discouraged Steiner from ever composing another stage work. Shortly before his death, "Max said that he wished he'd been able to write a big Broadway musical, because there was a gravitas to having a show on Broadway," a friend recalled.[40] In a private letter, he acknowledged his shortcomings in assessing a stage piece: "I disliked *My Fair Lady, Oklahoma,* and *Can-Can* intensely," although "I loved *South Pacific* and *Carousel*. History has proved that I can be wrong."[41]

Fortunately, history had other uses for Steiner, and they were soon in coming.

5

Roaring in the Twenties

MAX STEINER COULD NOT WRITE HIS OWN Broadway hit—but as an orchestrator and conductor, he knew that he could shepherd the work of the top composers in the field. In 1924, Steiner became musical director of Jerome Kern's latest show, *Sitting Pretty*. The collaborations of Kern, librettist Guy Bolton, and lyricist P. G. Wodehouse had yielded success after success; and Kern's melodic style, with its flowing lyricism and ineffable sense of yearning, was another important influence on Max.

Sitting Pretty featured extensive underscoring between songs, giving Steiner and team ample chance for composition. An essential partner on the show was Robert Russell Bennett, a brilliant orchestrator Max knew from Harms. For decades, Bennett's deft instrumental voicings and propulsive countermelodies would enrich such scores as *Show Boat, Oklahoma!, South Pacific,* and *Kiss Me Kate.* Bennett enjoyed a level of trust with Kern that Steiner could never quite achieve, which may explain the low-simmering resentment Max felt toward the senior orchestrator.[1]

Sitting Pretty laid the groundwork for that tension. After Steiner's death, Bennett gave an account of the show's rocky evolution, and the emotions Max bared under pressure:

> Max . . . a good arranger . . . helped me with a few of the orchestrations . . . and I remember him in tears once when the show was on the road during the tryout weeks. The music was not as exciting as had been hoped and [Kern] was inclined to blame his music director. He sent to New York for his old conductor Victor Baravalle to come out and tell us what was wrong. Vic Baravalle was one of the very best at that job, but as a diplomat he was not talented. He was very tough on poor little Max—hence the tears on my shoulder.

[Kern] was a tough man on these jobs, but he could be appealed to and he was smart. He realized what shape Max Steiner was in and he realized he might not have a conductor at all if too much happened to Max. Nobody else knew the show from the conductor's standpoint well enough to give a performance. Kern said to me, "You know Vic Baravalle is not a discreet and delicate personality. I'll make it up to Max somehow."

The next morning, Max showed me a check from Kern amounting to an extra week's salary, but he asked me if I didn't think it would be a good idea to send it back with a polite note of thanks. This he did and he stayed with the show as long as the show stayed with anybody, which was not very long.[2]

Sitting Pretty failed to attract the audience its enchanting score deserved. Kern had banned its songs from being played by dance bands or on the new medium of radio; he hoped the ban would inspire New Yorkers to come to the Fulton Theater to hear for themselves.[3] But the gambit backfired. *Sitting Pretty* ran for just 95 performances, and although Kern and Steiner remained friends, Kern never hired him again as a musical director.

Bennett's description of "poor little Max," breaking under criticism, is echoed by another friend of the time, lyricist Edward Eliscu. "Max was a little darling," he recalled. "He was a very conscientious man who felt the weight of the world on his head. Not on his shoulders, but on his head."[4] Hollywood would help Max grow used to pressure—but his insecurities, and the stresses of work, endured for decades.

The brevity of *Sitting Pretty*'s run had one upside: it allowed the 36-year-old to work on two other shows in 1924 that featured the best of Broadway past and present.

It is a testament to the standards of the *Ziegfeld Follies* that 1924's edition was considered slightly sub-par, despite comedy by Will Rogers and W. C. Fields, dancing by the Tiller Girls, and songs by Victor Herbert. Steiner was enlisted mainly to assist Herbert, in what would be their last collaboration.

Herbert had a heart condition and was not very active after that time. One day in May 1924, he invited me to lunch with him at the Lamb's Club. Ziegfeld had given him another assignment and he wanted to see what I could do to help him. We had a pleasant lunch. I offered him one of his favorite cigars, but he refused, saying his doctor wouldn't let him smoke. Finally I put him in a cab, and we arranged to meet the next day.

I walked the short distance back to my office at Harms. I had settled down to work only a short time when Max Dreyfus came in. He was crying as he said to me, "Maxie, Victor Herbert just died." I was one of the last people to see him alive.[5]

Max's best 1924 project, and his most enduring Broadway work, was saved for last. Weeks after the premiere of *Rhapsody in Blue*, George Gershwin brought his innovations in jazz to a new stage musical, which starred his friends Fred and Adele Astaire, and marked George's first exclusive collaboration with brother Ira.

When *Lady, Be Good!* premiered on December 1, 1924, "the American musical finally found its native idiom," wrote Philip Furia,[6] serving up music whose rhythmic cleverness and syncopated melodies owed nothing to European operetta. Max's main contribution was orchestration of the Act One Finale, a lengthy sequence reprising most of the hit songs amid Steiner-scored dialogue. But he was present from start to finish of the production, and in 1925 he became musical director of *Lady*'s post-Broadway tour, also featuring the Astaires.[7]

It is the one show of Steiner's Broadway years that still sees occasional performance, thanks to a score packed with future standards like *Fascinating Rhythm* and the title tune. For Max, it proved ideal training for his later work on RKO musicals, several of which reunited him with *Lady*'s elegant, tap-dancing star.

LADY, BE GOOD! UNOFFICIALLY LAUNCHED the golden age of Broadway. Old-school operettas like *The Student Prince* and *Rose-Marie* hardly vanished, but they were joined by insouciant offerings like De Sylva, Brown, and Henderson's *Good News!*, Rodgers and Hart's *A Connecticut Yankee*, and Irving Berlin's annual *Music Box Revues*. During the late 1910s, roughly 120 shows opened annually on the Great White Way; by 1927 the number had climbed to over two hundred a year.[8]

Big business meant near-constant employment for Max. It is proof of Steiner's talent and reliability that he was sought out, as orchestrator or musical director, by Gershwin and other Broadway masters for a string of shows from 1925 to 1927. Highlights included the Gershwins' *Tell Me More*, *Castles in the Air*, with Busby Berkeley choreography and "burlesque music" by Max,

Lady, Be Good! newspaper advertisement, 1925.

and *Twinkle, Twinkle*, starring Joe E. Brown and Ona Munson, later *Gone with the Wind*'s Belle Watling.

With no larger game plan in mind, Max seemed content to float on a tide of touring shows, brief but intense friendships, and passing amours. All were lubricated by the best Prohibition-era booze he could buy; and too much of the latter may have led him to embark on another hasty marriage, to another alluring chorine.

Aubry Van Liew, born in Illinois in 1905,[9] was among the cast of *Castles in the Air*, billed as Audree Van Lieu. Her sole other stage credit of note was in *The Desert Song*, in which she doubled as "French Girl" and "Spanish Cabaret Girl." She and Max wed on April 12, 1927[10]—after which Steiner promptly returned to his bachelor lifestyle as if nothing had changed.

His wanton waste of money also continued. Around the time of his marriage, one of *Twinkle Twinkle*'s stage managers, Sam, "was going out to the track.

I had to do an overture for Sigmund Romberg, who had just written a Shubert revue. Sam agreed to place a bet for me if I picked a horse.

I made a selection: French Princess. I gave Sam ten dollars to put on its nose. It turned out to be a rainy day, so I didn't feel too sorry for myself for not being able to go with him.

About five o'clock, the racing results were front-page news. My horse won and paid $245. I was walking on air. I wasn't making much in those days, and my bet amounted to over $1,200. I couldn't wait to spend the money. The following week was my wife's birthday. I knew she was dying for a sealskin coat. I had already priced one—it was over $600. I went out in the pouring rain to the furrier's. I ordered the coat and told the man I would return in the morning with the money.

Our gang used to eat at a kosher delicatessen near the theater. I was so happy I treated everybody. Then I returned to the theater. When Sam finally showed up, he came over and said, "I'm sure sorry you lost, Max." I was flabbergasted. "What do you mean I lost?" I screamed. "My horse won. It paid $245!" "Yes," he said sadly, "but I didn't bet him. It was raining and he's not a mudder!"[11]

This anecdote is Max's only public allusion to Aubry Steiner, who goes unnamed. She is never cited in a single press profile of her husband between 1928 and 1932; and the sole clipping about her in his personal scrapbook is annotated with two handwritten words: *"Poor Steiner!"*[12]

Future events suggest that Aubry was less than a model wife. But Max was hardly an ideal husband, thanks to his constant absences. It was a pattern that continued for decades.

The man who kept Steiner from the racetrack in 1927—composer Sigmund Romberg—was something of a leitmotiv in Max's life. Steiner first met the future king of Broadway operettas (*The Student Prince, The Desert Song*) at the turn of the century, when the Hungarian-born Romberg spent evenings at the Theater an der Wien, and summers enjoying concerts at "Venice in Vienna."[13] Reunited in New York, Max served as musical director of Romberg's *The Love Call*, a 1927 romantic western and a rare "floperetta" for its composer. Audiences were more interested in a different entertainment offered blocks away that October: the world premiere of Warner Bros.' part-silent/part-talkie, *The Jazz Singer*.

IN 1928, AS IF TO COMPLETE his list of work with Broadway legends, Max teamed for the only time with Oscar Hammerstein II. The 33-year-old lyricist was fresh off the triumph of *Show Boat*, a milestone with its integration of song and story, its exploration of serious issues including racism and alcoholism, and tunes by Kern that blended musical comedy with the tragic sweep of opera.

Expectations for Hammerstein's follow-up, *Rainbow*, were sky high.

Max Steiner, New York City, ca. 1927.

With conductor Victor Baravalle committed to *Show Boat*, Steiner won the job of *Rainbow*'s music director. It is likely that he was recommended by the show's 30-year-old composer, Vincent Youmans. Since working with Max on *Oui, Madame!* Youmans had become one of Broadway's most inventive composers, with hit songs like "Tea for Two" and "I Want to Be Happy" from 1925's *No, No, Nanette*, and an equally popular score for 1927's *Hit the Deck*. (Max briefly conducted *Deck* during its Boston run.)[14]

As work on *Rainbow* began, Steiner had just turned 40, and with a perennially empty bank account and a wife with a taste for furs, he welcomed the idea of a long-running hit. But nothing onstage could match the behind-the-scenes drama of *Rainbow*'s unmaking, which can be encapsulated in four real-life scenes:

Act One, Scene One: Leroy Sanitarium, New York. Enter Oscar Hammerstein, voluntarily admitting himself after an emotional breakdown precipitated by divorce proceedings.

Act One, Scene Two: A hotel room in Manhattan. Vincent Youmans, lyricist Gus Kahn, director John Harwood and co-librettist Laurence Stallings (*What Price Glory?*) gather to write a gritty tale of love and betrayal during the 1849 Gold Rush. Absent Hammerstein's steadying influence, tempers flare. Finally, Hammerstein makes a dramatic return, fires Harwood, and announces he will take over direction.

Act Two, Scene One: Philadelphia. During out-of-town rehearsals, as Steiner supervises orchestrations, spirits are buoyed by the hiring of a new performer: Libby Holman. The cabaret torch singer's seductive purr inspires Youmans and Hammerstein to write a sultry ballad, "I Want a Man." Steiner's orchestration complements Holman's husky timbre—something Max will do later when writing underscore for actors with low-octave voices. Maybe they have a hit show after all . . .

Act Two, Scene Two: Broadway, opening night. Audiences eager for a tune-filled romance sit with growing impatience as a dour mining camp drama unfolds. Boredom gives way to laughter, as star Brian Donlevy declaims a love song while a live mule relieves itself "copiously down front center stage."[15] Laughter turns to irritation when a mechanical set refuses to budge at scene's end. A desperate Max conducts his orchestra for a full half hour amid a crescendo of audience heckling. The show's first act finally ends . . . at 10:45 p.m.

Rainbow's end came after just 29 performances, although Steiner would remember it with affection thanks to Vincent Youmans. The songwriter

had a working schedule much like my own. We both liked to work all night until eight in the morning, then have breakfast at Lindy's, sleep all day, then start to work at eight at night and work all night again. [During try-outs] the *Rainbow* troop had gone on ahead, but my orchestrations were not quite ready, so Vince offered to drive me to Philadelphia on Sunday. The night before we worked all night, sent the copyists on by train and then got ready to drive down.

Vince had a two-passenger Mercedes Roadster. There were no windows or top on the car. We started out from Youmans' office on 45th Street. Two huge suitcases were carried out for him. There was no trunk on the car, so we tied them on with rope. There was no room for my little suitcase, so I had to hold it on my lap all the way. The temperature was around 26 degrees. All I had on was a thin overcoat with a little velvet collar and a derby.

By the time we reached Philadelphia, a 2-1/2 hour trip of fast driving, and checked into the Sylvania Hotel where we had a suite, we were half frozen. Vince suggested that we go downstairs to the drugstore for hot coffee. It was one of those drugstores that sold everything. Vince bought shaving cream, a razor, handkerchiefs, shirts, even pajamas.

When we returned to the suite loaded down with his purchases, he said: "I must remember to buy some pants tomorrow." I looked at him and asked, "Didn't you bring anything?" "Nothing," he said. "Well, what's in those two big suitcases?" He answered simply, "Gin." This was, of course, during Prohibition. Vince had brought two cases of gin with him, but no clothes or toilet articles at all![16]

Max's penultimate Broadway show partnered him with another future Hollywood collaborator, Dorothy Fields. *Hello, Daddy!* was a family project befitting its name: Lew Fields starred, while daughter Dorothy wrote lyrics and co-authored the book with brother Herbert. Its racy plot may sound familiar: three men are led to believe that they are the father of an ex-lover's illegitimate daughter. (In 2001, the plot of the ABBA musical *Mamma Mia!* drank from a similar well.) *Hello, Daddy!*'s well-received score yielded one hit song, "Futuristic Rhythm," and the jaunty "In a Great Big Way," staged by Busby Berkeley. It didn't hurt that Max's pit orchestra included Benny Goodman, Glenn Miller, and Jack Teagarden, all on the verge of stardom.[17]

Broadway had enabled Steiner to transition from a world of European operetta to the free and easy syncopations of American jazz. By 1929, he was adept at creating nearly any type of music. But the nightly slog of conducting was becoming a chore. Max grew to loathe the restricting cut of tuxedos, the required dress for any conducting job, and years of late-night orchestrating had worsened his eyesight. The powerful glasses he wore completed the transformation of his once-boyish features into those of an owlish, middle-aged man.

But Max's years in New York City were about to come to an end.

THREE THOUSAND MILES WEST OF BROADWAY, major Hollywood studios were completing their conversion from silent pictures to sound. Musicals dominated the screen; and on October 6, 1929, RKO Pictures released the splashiest entry in that studio's one-year existence.

Rio Rita, with music by Max's friend Harry Tierney, was a faithful screen adaptation of Ziegfeld's long-running Broadway show. Sparing no expense, the movie featured two-strip Technicolor sequences and the stage show's breakout comedy duo, Bert Wheeler and Robert Woolsey. The result was RKO's first blockbuster, with a profit of nearly $1 million.*[18] Not even the Wall Street crash two weeks later could dampen the studio's enthusiasm for big-scale musicals.

RKO had arrived late to the Hollywood party. It owed its existence to communications visionary David Sarnoff, head of Radio Corporation of America (RCA). Sarnoff saw the value of integrating America's two most popular forms of entertainment, radio and motion pictures.[19] By 1928, he and RCA had their own film soundtrack recording system, "Photophone." Although superior to AT&T's Western Electric system, Photophone was less used, and Sarnoff planned to rectify that with his own movie studio.

In 1928, he acquired Film Booking Offices (FBO), a modest movie production and distribution company in California. Its seller was Joseph P. Kennedy, father of future U.S. president John. Kennedy also sold Sarnoff the Keith-Albee-Orpheum chain of theaters that stretched across America. Now, the RCA chief owned "a vertically integrated movie company whose product would demonstrate the quality of RCA sound equipment," historian Richard B. Jewell noted.[20] With its own production unit, its own sound system, and its own movie houses, the newly christened "Radio-Keith-Orpheum Corporation"—RKO—was ready to take on Hollywood's biggest players.

Its production chief was William LeBaron, a holdover from the Joseph Kennedy era and a former Broadway playwright. Unlike most studio heads, LeBaron was generally liked by his staff: he was "a very charming man," one employee recalled, "and he knew his business."[21]

By the time of *Rio Rita*'s release, $2 million had been spent to upgrade a studio that now included ten production stages, an administration building, and a music department.[22] To head the latter, LeBaron hired Victor Baravalle, who had left Broadway for Hollywood. Oscar Levant joined the studio in 1929, writing negligible tunes for quickly forgotten musicals. Disillusioned by such projects as *Tanned Legs*, Levant returned to New York the following year.[23]

---

* Some sources credit Steiner with work on this film. In fact, *Rio Rita* was released by RKO months before he came to Hollywood. The error probably stems from the fact that Max reportedly filled in as conductor during the show's two-year Broadway run. It is also possible that Max assisted when the movie version was dubbed into German in January 1930 ("Rita's German Voices," *Variety*, January 1, 1930, 47).

As RKO's production roster expanded, more music staffing was needed. And in November 1929, *Rio Rita*'s composer, Harry Tierney, suggested a perfect candidate.

AT THE TIME, HARRY'S FRIEND MAX was conducting what would be the third most successful musical of the Broadway season. *Sons O' Guns* was a WWI-set comedy whose cast included Lili Damita (later Mrs. Errol Flynn). "I had an orchestra of 35 men," Steiner recalled, "and every one played about five different instruments. One time we had thirty violins, then we had twenty trumpets."[24] The resulting sound suggested an ensemble much larger than its actual number.

Precisely what happened next is clouded by contradictory accounts from Max himself. In his most colorful telling, William LeBaron was in New York, saw *Sons O' Guns*, and went "out of his mind" with excitement over the big orchestral sound. "When the show was over, he came down to the pit. . . . He says, 'Max, will you come and see me tomorrow at four o'clock?' He says, 'I've never heard such a performance in my life.' "[25]

More prosaic is the version in Steiner's autobiography. "Three or four weeks after the opening, Harry Tierney called me to Hollywood with an offer to orchestrate for RKO."[26]

The more dramatic account may be the truth. According to *Variety*, LeBaron was in New York that December.[27] Whichever story is true, on December 10, 1929, 41-year-old Max Steiner signed his name to his first Hollywood contract. It committed him to six months of work as an orchestrator, with an option for six additional months. RKO would retain all rights to whatever music Steiner created.[28]

The timing was fortuitous: within months, the impact of Wall Street's collapse shuttered nearly half of Broadway's theaters. And after more than two decades of stage work, Max Steiner was ready for a fresh challenge in Hollywood.

Hollywood, however, was not quite ready for him.

PART THREE

The Apprentice

6

Where Does the Music Come From?

ON DECEMBER 24, 1929, Maximilian Raoul Steiner arrived by train in Los Angeles.[1] He was, he later said, "in high spirits" as he devoured his first Hollywood meal inside the hat-shaped Brown Derby.

If Aubry was at Steiner's side, her presence was not recorded. Eventually she did join her husband, sharing with him a furnished home in Hollywood. Its address—2706 Beachwood Drive—was a convenient ten-minute commute from RKO.[2] But like Beatrice, Aubry would play second fiddle to her spouse's chief passion, work.

Max was joining an industry in chaos. The five major studios—Warner Bros., Paramount, MGM, Fox, and RKO, aka "Radio"—had agreed to produce only talkies, and their leaders were struggling to understand the new technology and oversee the costly conversion to it. Although 1929 proved a banner year in terms of profits, it also resulted in unemployment for up to seven thousand musicians, no longer needed to accompany silent films.[3] But talkies were a boon for composers. The westward migration of New Yorkers included not only Steiner, but other future masters of the craft—Alfred Newman, Herbert Stothart, and Dimitri Tiomkin among them.

The studio to which Max reported hardly resembled the sprawling facilities of its rivals. Lyricist Edward Eliscu recalled RKO's street-facing façade as nondescript, "where Paramount had gates like the gates to heaven, and MGM had tall pillars like the richest slave-owner in the South."[4]

Equally underwhelming was RKO's fledgling sound department, which in 1929 occupied a small area on the top floor of a two-story building. Fortunately, its staff included a new hire destined to become one of Hollywood's greatest audio pioneers.

A jazz and classical percussionist, 26-year-old Murray Spivack added sound recording to his resumé while living in New York.[5] Invited in April 1929 to set up RKO's sound department, he discovered "there were no offices for us, so they put me in a tin barn that had housed Tom Mix's horse."[6] Eventually Spivack moved to an office where—lacking any instructions—he recorded the sounds of traffic outside at Sunset and Gower. "If mixers were out on location, and they heard any noises that would be interesting—airplanes, train noises, streetcars—they were authorized to shoot part of that [on film], which became part of my sound effects library."[7]

Spivack and Steiner formed the bond of adventurers traveling to uncharted regions. That spirit was shared by a third Manhattan import, composer Roy Webb. Five months Max's junior, the two had become friends while both conducted on Broadway.[8] None of the trio received a salary rivaling Garbo's; but as financial panic swept America, weekly pay of $250 (for Spivack)[9] and around $450 (for Max)[10] was plenty to live on. And for Steiner, money wasn't the chief draw. "I really came out because I had a hunch that I knew more about the picture business than some of these people out here."[11]

For decades, accounts of early film music have characterized the years of 1929–1931 as almost completely devoid of underscoring. Recent research reveals a more nuanced picture.[12] Cartoons never lost the tuneful accompaniment that had supported them through silent days; and as early as 1929, comedy producers like Hal Roach commissioned original music, which often played from start to finish during the antics of Laurel and Hardy and Our Gang.

The first all-talking picture, Warner Bros.' *Lights of New York*, includes scenes in which the source of music being played—say, a nightclub—is clearly

RKO proclaims its arrival with typical Hollywood understatement.

shown: *diegetic music*, in the terminology of scholars. The movie also has moments in which dramatic scoring is added later, and clearly is not something the characters are hearing: *nondiegetic* music.

In the part-sound *Weary River*, underscoring "occasionally pauses for a particularly pointed line of dialogue and accompanying action," historian Michael Slowik noted. "During [a] line of dialogue, a sustained, tense minor chord is heard. This chord ends with a brief *sforzando* followed by a quick timpani roll. Then, [the heroine's] second sentence is spoken during a rare moment of musical silence."[13] Shades of Wagner, Richard Strauss, and soon, Steiner.

But by 1930, most films followed a simple formula. A musical could have underscoring between songs; but in any "realistic" genre, score was usually restricted to opening and end titles, or "source music" heard by the characters. ("Source music" and "diegetic music" are interchangeable terms.) Instrumental accompaniment of singers was recorded at the same time as the vocalists—a nightmare for sound engineers and film editors. Separate audio tracks could be combined only through "re-recording." Each track was recorded optically on film, like a movie image. The tracks were then played back simultaneously on large speakers. This playback was recorded by another microphone, thus creating a single soundtrack. By around 1930, Spivack recalled, "they finally were able to [combine] three tracks: one for music, one for dialogue and one for sound effects."[14]

When it came to recorded sound, Max proved as quick a study as he'd been in balancing theater orchestras. His bosses were just as quick to promote him. By early 1930, he was composing as well as orchestrating.

His first tasks included writing music for movies being dubbed in Spanish. He acquired "quite a reputation in the trade for this," recalled Oscar Levant. "Actors were employed to speak Spanish dialogue . . . but as they never utilized nearly so many words as the original script specified, there remained many lacunae which Steiner filled with music."[15] Steiner and Webb also were likely tasked with adding music to silent versions of RKO talkies, created for foreign markets and U.S. theaters not yet wired for sound.[16]

Success led to a more prestigious assignment for Max: writing original music, uncredited, for a new sound drama. *The Case of Sergeant Grischa* starred Chester Morris as a Russian soldier in WWI facing execution in a German prison camp. Surviving pencil sketches reveal a process that changed little during Steiner's career.[17] First, Max wrote a simple version of a cue on four-staff music paper—a page containing four separate lines of treble and bass clef combinations. Next, that draft was expanded into a larger orchestration sketch, which contained individual lines for woodwinds, brass, percussion, and string instruments. (On later movies, this task was handled by an orchestrator.)

Finally, a copyist would turn the orchestration score into separate parts for each musician. A "conductor's part" also was made, containing all important orchestral voices grouped together in chords, so that it resembled sheet music of a song.

Grischa required little music—a "Revolutionary Song," some theater source music, and a main title, which ran precisely 1 minute and 24 seconds. Still, it is one of the astonishments of Steiner's career that although he had written only light *divertissements* for some 30 years, upon arriving in Hollywood he could instantly compose music in the idiom of symphonies and opera. That shift was possible thanks to his lifelong study and love of concert music.

Grischa's main title is a compact overture that conveys the movie's themes with power and economy. Written in the dark key of A minor, it opens with a hushed, sustained chord, over which Steiner places a clear melodic idea introduced by solo English horn, representing the hero. Flutes and muted trumpets provide a martial answering figure . . . and so begins a concise encapsulation of the man-versus-military conflict that lies ahead.

Film composing may have come easily for Max, but capturing that music on optical film was more difficult. Microphone limitations meant that string sections were lost behind brass and percussion. Restricted frequency resulted in little bass, and woodwinds barely registered. To capture his intended sound, Max strengthened bass lines, often by adding two tubas. He used two to four saxophones to double woodwinds, since saxes recorded with more clarity. He would keep modifying those choices as technology improved.

NO RKO PROJECT OF 1930 was more important—or more costly—than *Dixiana*, a part-Technicolor musical that hoped to encore the success of *Rio Rita* by reuniting much of its team. That group was joined by a staffer whose name made its first screen appearance, with the credit "Orchestrations by Max Steiner."

With *Rio Rita*, RKO had replicated a well-oiled Broadway hit. *Dixiana* had no road map to follow—and it showed. The tale of a circus performer (Bebe Daniels) in the antebellum South, the film goes clattering off the rails as early as its opening credits. "Mr. and Mrs. Sippi," a tenor sings in faux-minstrel dialect, "I miss you so, I's just dippy!" What follows suggests *The Birth of a Nation* as musical comedy: joyfully singing slaves, who love their master "because [he's] always freeing some one of them," and crass slapstick from Wheeler and Woolsey, who knock a black servant on his face to avoid giving him a dollar.

Harry Tierney's melodies yielded no hits, but Steiner dressed them elegantly. One highlight is "I Am Your Baby Now," a theater number introducing Daniels's circus queen. Max's zesty orchestration evokes Russell Bennett's classic work for similar stage scenes in *Show Boat*. It also features an instrument that would be a Steiner favorite: the harp.

The most succinct review of the film came from pixiesh co-star Dorothy Lee: "*Dixiana*—that was a bomb!"[18] The movie that cost $750,000 to make lost $300,000.[19] But RKO was not alone in seeing black ink turn red in 1930. Hollywood had produced too many musicals, most of them static in their filming and clichéd in their telling. Three years after *The Jazz Singer*, even Al Jolson couldn't draw a crowd.

RKO, new on the block, suffered more than most, and *Dixiana* was a turning point. Gone were the days of wild spending—and that fall, Steiner's worst fears were confirmed in a letter from the front office, "telling me that they would not require our services any longer and to dismiss everyone not under contract."[20]

Max's salary was already proving inadequate to cover alimony for Beatrice, support for Gabor in Vienna, and the needs of his neglected wife Aubry. His pessimism grew after the dismissal of RKO's music director Victor Baravalle, for reasons that remain murky. Naturally, a salacious rumor made the rounds: "I heard he got mixed up with his secretary," Murray Spivack said, "and his wife went chasing him down the lot with a gun."

Not long thereafter, Steiner would remember,

I was called to the front office and told that they had no use for me either. What, they asked, would I take for a settlement of my contract? We agreed on six weeks. Here I was out of work, with a furnished house on my hands in Hollywood and an apartment in New York, which I had rented to a singer who never paid his rent.

I called Jennie Jacobs, an agent in New York, and asked her to look around for a job. She told me [about] an operetta breaking in Atlantic City: *Luana*, with music by Rudolf Friml. Jennie advised me to fly to Atlantic City and take over. I went immediately to Mr. Watson, a business manager for RKO. I told him I had a job and wanted to collect my check and leave. He told me that he'd have to check the matter and I could leave the following day.

The next afternoon I went to Watson's office. His secretary asked me to come back around six o'clock. When I did, Watson said, "Max, I have just talked to Mr. LeBaron and he wants you to stay on a month-to-month basis without a contract. There are some interesting things cooking. How would you like to be the head of the music department?"

I was only too happy to accept.

I have always felt this was a crossroad in my life. If I had gone to Atlantic City, I probably would never have seen Hollywood again.[21]

Max never learned what transpired while he waited for Mr. Watson. According to Murray Spivack, William LeBaron decided to keep Steiner after days of campaigning on Spivack's part. "Max was a very likable guy, quite talented, and we needed a musical director. I said, 'I think that Steiner would make a good music director if you gave him an opportunity.'"[22]

On November 5, 1930, *Screen World* magazine announced the appointment of RKO's new music chief. Steiner moved to an upper-floor office "equipped with a piano, several kinds of phonographs, a stopwatch, a musical library, and other aids," according to one reporter. Within the office was a smaller space—"a funny little cubby hole off his office where he composes his music."[23]

Steiner's new title brought a flood of responsibilities. He was in charge of hiring composers . . . assigning orchestrators . . . supervising on-camera music groups . . . and in a typical Hollywood irony, the composer who couldn't hold onto a dollar was in charge of controlling costs.

"He hated being head of the music department," a friend recalled. "You don't have any time to compose. He told me that he wasn't very good at negotiating, at telling a composer, 'Oh no, we can't pay you that.' He also said, 'Look out for a compliment from an RKO executive, because that meant you're getting your pay cut.'"[24]

Spivack helped Max with the paperwork, and organized RKO's catch-as-catch-can approach to music recording. During a live take of the orchestra, a music mixer would have to select which microphone to raise in volume. "Many times you'd get a mixer that didn't understand one note of music," Spivack recalled. "In desperation I finally went into the booth and would cue the mixer from the music, and say, 'Clarinets coming up . . . violin or harp . . . ' But many of them without knowing it would grab the [mixer] after the solo had started, so they'd miss the first two or three notes. . . . So ultimately I started mixing some of the music."[25]

One more person joined Max's circle at this time, and proved the most essential of all. Marie Teller was a 30-year-old secretary put in charge of Steiner's correspondence and schedule. For the next quarter century she became his most trusted confidante, bringing desperately needed order to his chaotic life. At a salary of $30 a week (later $50), Marie's duties went beyond clerical work. She became Max's protector, as calls and correspondence multiplied from ex-wives, lawyers, job-seekers, and friends in search of handouts.

Her impeccable record-keeping, her friendly but formal style, and her quiet diplomacy make her the unsung hero in Steiner's life.

ON DECEMBER 20, 1930, MAX SIGNED his second contract with RKO. It did little to inspire confidence, guaranteeing work for just six months. Worse, it reportedly stipulated a 30 percent pay cut that studio president B. B. Kahane tried to soften with praise for his overworked music director.[26]

Max didn't stay because of rich opportunities for composition. Most 1931 movies were as bereft of scoring as Depression-era audiences were of funds: music was usually heard only during brief opening and closing credits, or for scenes of on-camera bands or singers. Instead, pauses in dialogue were accentuated by the distracting crackle and hiss that resulted from film emulsion. Even the year's best releases, like Universal's horror hits *Dracula* and *Frankenstein*, suffered from the absence of a score.

Producers "were not merely unfriendly to music," Oscar Levant wrote in 1940. "They were actually suspicious of its potentialities. They made a great fetish, for example, of pointing out the conflict between the so-called 'reality' of the movies and the 'unreality' of music. Always when a situation seemed to demand a heightening by musical effect they would come back at the composer with the question, 'But where would the audience think the orchestra is coming from?' "[27]

With few opportunities to compose, Max experimented in other ways. One milestone came in an otherwise dreadful film: *Beau Ideal*, a histrionic sequel to the silent foreign legion classic *Beau Geste*. With no score, its tedium was worsened by long stretches of audio pops and jarring sound cuts. Fortunately, Max was allowed to write music for a harem dance; its foundation is the same four-note, rising/falling pattern later made famous as the opening of the James Bond theme. More significantly, Steiner would recall the movie as the first on which he used a device still essential to score recording: the click track.

The process was simple. A member of the sound department fixed "an additional track onto the film that was punched with holes," historian Peter Wegele explained.[28] "When playing the film, the hole running through the projector would produce an audible click. The distance between these holes was determined by the tempo desired. If, for example, the tempo was sixty beats per minute, the film had a click every twenty-four frames.... If the composer wanted to hit a cue in the sixth second of the film (the 144th frame of this reel), the cue would be the seventh click."

The conductor of a score wore headphones, through which he heard the clicks while watching the movie projected above the orchestra. The movie had visual "punches" corresponding to key moments needing synchronization, and "streamers"—rolling lines—indicating the imminent appearance of a "punch."

Beau Ideal marked what may be its earliest application in a drama. One sequence showed a foreign legion band. As Max recalled,

> My budget was so low that it only allowed me the use of about twenty musicians. It was not easy to make any musical impression.
>
> Well, I had what I thought was a brilliant idea. I hired twenty men, all of whom played two instruments; the trumpet, flute, trombone, etc. I orchestrated the march for approximately forty men. Then I made one recording with twenty men—maybe all brass against this tempo track, because they had to be in sync with the men marching. Then I had my men double and I did the same thing over again with all the woodwinds. When I got through with that, I used about six drummers, also the same men. In the dubbing we put the three tracks together according to the click track. When we were finished, it sounded like a sixty-piece band.
>
> The producer, who had insisted that we needed only twenty men, said afterward: "You see, Max, these twenty men of yours sound just as good as the sixty. Why did you want any more?"
>
> I recognized immediately the click track's adaptability for scoring, as well as for things other than marching, such as montages, fast-moving scenes, trains, and especially for dances. We could match the movements on the screen with complete accuracy.[29]

Max's discovery coincided with the next major turning point for RKO.

It was story editor Kay Brown who recommended filming *Cimarron*, the latest novel by *Show Boat* author Edna Ferber.[30] RKO spent over $1.4 million on what would be its most expensive production to date.[31] A total of $40,500[32] was lavished on a thrilling recreation of the Oklahoma land rush of 1889, which introduces Yancey Cravat and wife Sabra (Richard Dix and Irene Dunne). The pair struggle over four decades to defeat murderous outlaws, introduce "civilization," and overcome their own prejudices after the marriage of their son to a Native American.

Only one category in the budget—music—was miniscule. Some $1,600 was slated for "one 15-piece Orchestra, 2 days," for main and end titles, and any incidental music. And $800 would cover "one 15-piece Brass Band" appearing onscreen.[33]

Nothing was allotted for the composer or conductor of that music.

What happened next is another case of legend versus fact. Steiner would claim that RKO approached several known composers to write a full score, but all declined. The executives then prevailed on Max to "Knock out a score for us. Just give us enough so we can have a preview." "I scored the picture," he later wrote. "It previewed and was a smash hit. Both *Variety* and *The Hollywood Reporter* wanted to know who wrote the music and why didn't he get credit on the main title. This was my real beginning in Hollywood."[34]

The movie was indeed a critical success—it would win 1931's Academy Award for Best Picture—but Max's remarks are disingenuous. *Cimarron* contains *five minutes* of non-source music: a main title, a cue for its penulti-mate scene, and finale music that leads into the end title. Also, it is doubtful that RKO approached multiple freelancers before Max stepped in, given *Cimarron*'s music budget and the small amount of score planned for it.

But Steiner *was* correct in claiming that his music won attention. Declared *Hollywood Daily Screen World*, "A man named Max Steiner, whose name does not appear on my screen credit sheet, wrote and put in the fine music which introduces and closes this great picture."[35] Other press mentions followed, although the breathless tone of some suggests RKO's guiding hand: "MAX STEINER—CREATOR OF MUSIC FOR 'CIMARRON' / ADMITTED THE MOST PERFECT TO FIT THE CHARACTERS ON THE SCREEN."[36]

Buried amid such praise and banana oil is one important question: how much does Steiner's music actually contribute to *Cimarron*?

Exhibit A is his scoring of the main title. It is twice as long as the norm for the era: two minutes and 45 seconds. Its visuals also are unconventional. An extended cast montage shows in succession footage of twelve of the ac-tors. Each, dressed in character, is given five seconds of screen time, as he or she offers a pantomimic display of their character's behavior (e.g., Edna May Oliver signals her role as comic support with haughty sniffs and a double-take).

Steiner treats the main title as the overture that director Wesley Ruggles clearly intended it to be. Rather than provide one musical theme, he offers three. First comes a fierce, minor-key "Indian" theme for orchestra and tom-toms, establishing the western genre. Next, a lively gallop describing the heroic settlers prepares us for the land rush sequence that will follow. Finally, as Richard Dix is shown, Steiner introduces a stately, Elgarian march. Its second note is a major-fifth above the first—the same interval John Williams would use to begin *Star Wars*, and which countless other composers would employ to signify heroism.

Steiner, who dreamed of being "another Sousa," would use marches in his opening titles more than any other musical form at RKO. As in *Cimarron*, most began quietly before building into a strong emotional statement. These are not marches of militarism; they are portraits of individuals with idealistic dreams.

Jump ahead two hours in the film (as many viewers will wish to do; *Cimarron* may be the most plodding of Best Picture winners). Sabra Cravat is now a congresswoman, abandoned by Yancey. As she reflects on her life at a reception in her honor, Steiner subtly segues from a salon waltz—music heard by the characters—into the quietly heroic march theme from the main title. It tells us that Sabra is thinking of her husband, in possibly the first instance of Steiner using music to reveal a character's thoughts. Minutes later, Yancey reappears for a dying reunion with his wife. Finally, as townspeople unveil a statue in his honor, Steiner brings back the march in a triumphant coda.

So is *Cimarron*, then, a real film score? Consider this: Steiner's cues establish the story's dramatic themes. They musically define its protagonists, and reveal to us a character's thoughts. Verdict: the music *does* enhance the experience of *Cimarron*. But given its brevity and Steiner's newness to the form, it could only be a preview of bigger and better things to come.

DESPITE HEALTHY BOX OFFICE and an Oscar win, *Cimarron* still lost over half a million dollars due to its massive cost.[37] But with Broadway becoming a no-man's-land of closed theaters, Steiner was committed to staying in Hollywood. *Cimarron* had brought him a taste of acclaim. Now, the 43-year-old set out to prove he could help guide the industry to a brighter future.

Movies, he believed, were an ideal medium in which to sell a hit song, via sheet music and/or a 78-rpm recording. With this in mind, Max contributed a fox trot-tempo ballad, "There's a Sob in My Heart," for the drama *Traveling Husbands*. The film depicts a weary group of Depression-era Willy Lomans bouncing among cities in which every hotel band and radio station seems to be playing Max's song. Steiner employed the hot jazz band of Gus Arnheim to play the attractively propulsive tune;[38] but *Traveling Husbands* was a flop, the song ignored.

Far more rewarding was a social drama so grim and violent that it would be banned from re-release.[39] *Are These Our Children?* charted the de-evolution of a likable teen into a cold-blooded killer—the result, the movie suggested, of Depression-era social conditions. In a striking innovation, dialogue scenes were linked by silent, stylized montages showing light beams, fireworks-style explosions, and other metaphors that mirrored the hero's gradual downturn.

Musically, Steiner took full advantage of the expressionistic style. A lightly dramatic theme, introduced in the main title, continues under the first scene, as a young woman leans back in the arms of Eddie (Eric Linden). Gradually, the characters refer to the music as coming from a record: Steiner's score has morphed imperceptibly into source music. As Eddie leaves, he whistles the main title theme, linking it to his character. Later, during the planning of a crime at a social dance, that main theme begins as party music, then takes a minor-key turn on the soundtrack as details of a burglary are planned.

RKO was supportive of Steiner's contribution, to the point of self-parodying hyperbole. "I have to hand a publicity story which cannot be lightly dismissed," deadpanned one columnist. Max Steiner "completed a symphony today for use in *Are These Our Children?*, wrote several original boleros for 'Marcheta' and between inspirations, translated a German play.... A whole day, mind you, and only one symphony! What do they pay these fellows for, anyhow?"[40]

Steiner's efforts were accelerated with help from a dedicated orchestrator. Born in Milwaukee but of German ancestry,[41] Bernhard Kaun, 32, had written several chamber works, and in 1931 composed a memorable main title for Universal's *Frankenstein*. For the rest of Max's RKO tenure, Kaun translated the composer's pencil sketches into full orchestral parts. Steiner was more than capable of doing the job himself; his only enemy was time. In Kaun, Max found a partner who could rapidly turn his ideas into faithful realizations of his intentions.

THE FILM SCORES OF MAX STEINER

The list below and in subsequent chapters includes films to which Steiner contributed significantly as a composer during the period covered in each chapter. Dates in parentheses indicate month(s) of a score's recording; composition in most cases was during the prior weeks and through recording. A listing of multiple months often indicates that Steiner contributed source music during filming, before writing underscore later.

Noteworthy facts or authorial opinion not found in the main text is included for some titles.

AA indicates an Academy Award win. AAN indicates an Academy Award nomination.

All titles in Chapters 6 through 11 were released by RKO. As RKO music director from mid-1930 to early 1936, Steiner had involvement in dozens of additional titles during this time.

1930 Releases

The Case of Sergeant Grischa This film is now considered lost, although Steiner's pencil sketch of the score survives.

Dixiana (3/30–5/30)

Half Shot at Sunrise (7/30–8/30). Steiner's first credit as RKO Musical Director.

Check and Double Check (7/30–9/30). The radio success of black-face comedy duo Amos and Andy (white actors Freeman Gosden and Charles Correll) led to this slapdash movie tie-in, notable only for its stellar musical artists: Duke Ellington and his band, songwriters Bert Kalmar and Harry Ruby ("Three Little Words"), and, uncredited on the soundtrack, the Rhythm Boys: Al Rinker, Harry Barris, and 27-year-old Bing Crosby, on the cusp of stardom.

1931 Releases

The Royal Bed

Beau Ideal (9/30–10/30)

Cimarron (12/30)

Kept Husbands (1/31)

Bachelor Apartment (2/31)

Cracked Nuts (2/31)

Traveling Husbands (2/31–3/31). The Rhythm Boys, including Crosby, made their second uncredited appearance on a Steiner soundtrack, singing Max's "There's a Sob in My Heart."

The Runaround (3/31)

White Shoulders (5/31)

Young Donovan's Kid (4/31)

Everything's Rosie (4/31)

Transgression (4/31–5/31). Steiner's first-known use of a stirring theme best known as the main title of 1932's *The Animal Kingdom*.

The Public Defender (5/31–6/31)

Fanny Foley Herself (5/31–6/31)

Friends and Lovers (6/31)

The Gay Diplomat (6/31–7/31)

Consolation Marriage (6/31–8/31). Includes the Steiner song "Devotion."

Are These Our Children? (7/31–9/31)

Secret Service (8/31–9/31). One of Steiner's first interpolations of Civil War melodies in a score.

Men of Chance (8/31–10/31)

Way Back Home (8/31–10/31)

Girl of the Rio (9/31–11/31)

Peach O'Reno (10/31–11/31)

Dates on RKO titles in this and following chapters come primarily from production and music files held at RKO Radio Pictures Studio Records, Performing Arts Special Collections, University of California, Los Angeles, California. Additional information on RKO titles and most Warner Bros. titles comes from papers held at the Max Steiner Collection, L. Tom Perry Special Collections Library, Harold B. Lee Library, Brigham Young University, Provo, Utah.

STEINER'S GENIAL NATURE and lack of pretension made him a popular figure at RKO. But his habit of hard drinking after a long workday hadn't tapered since his years of "getting plastered" with the Gershwins in New York.

Alcohol could also bring out resentment. In 1931, RKO held a banquet hosted by David Sarnoff, to announce the studio's merger with a smaller RCA unit, Pathé. While serving as the night's orchestra leader, Max reportedly downed several Old Fashioneds with director Victor Schertzinger, who at 6 feet, 220 pounds, towered over 5-foot, 4-inch, 128-pound Max.

By the time of the Pathé announcement, Steiner recalled, "Schertzinger and I were pretty well loaded. Just for the fun of it, we changed coats. He had on my little coat, which he had ripped to pieces, and I wore his big one. I made my way carefully to the dais, arms flapping and coattails hanging below my knees. When I at last stood before David Sarnoff, he addressed me: 'Maxie, because of your wonderful work, you are now also the head of the RKO Pathé Music Department.' I shook my head sadly. 'I'm sorry, I can't accept.' Mr. LeBaron spoke up quickly: 'Why can't you accept?' 'Because I cannot possibly take another cut,' I said."[42]

If true, the story shows how poorly Max could time his jokes—a proclivity destined to endanger his career.

ON NOVEMBER 27, 1931, Steiner signed a new contract with RKO, for the reduced salary of $400 a week.[43] His daily work anxieties were fed by the seemingly endless firing of executives, amid declining faith in the leadership of William LeBaron.

Few heard Steiner's complaints more often than Murray Spivack, who remembered Max as being "as crazy as anybody I'd ever worked with.

> Max would call me up at nine o'clock at night. I was just sitting down to dinner, and he'd say, "I quit. You go in tomorrow morning and tell them I quit. They don't like my music." I said, "Who'd you talk to?" "Well... I know they don't like my music." I said, "You could only have spoken to the gateman. Is he the fellow that told you he doesn't like your music?" I said, "Would you mind waiting until I finish my dinner and then I'll make a note of what you want me to tell them." He did this half a dozen times.
>
> He had a great habit of picking his thumb, and his nail was worn down to about half. He had very poor eyesight, and many times he fell over my piano stool.

He was wrapped up in his own work and worried primarily about Steiner. And this was normal for most people, I don't condemn the man for that, because in that business we have a lot of that.[44]

MAX HAD REASON TO WORRY. By October 1931, the majority of RKO's releases were box office losers.[45] By year's end, the studio was on the verge of shutdown.

But that November, New York executives were quietly making plans to install a production chief they hoped would be their savior.

His name was David O. Selznick.

7

Revolution

THE SIMILARITIES ARE MANY between Maximilian Raoul Steiner and David
O. Selznick, the *enfante terrible* who made possible Steiner's future success.

Like Max, much of Selznick's drive came from the desire to restore a once-
great family name. His father, Lewis, was a Russian Jew who emigrated to
America, where he traded life as a jeweler to make movies. David spent his
youth shadowing his father and learning his business—until 1923, when Lewis
declared bankruptcy after years of unchecked spending. Three years later, 24-
year-old David became a story editor at MGM, then moved to Paramount in
1928. There, he confidently guided the studio into the era of the talkies.[1]

Like Max, Selznick was near-inexhaustible. When an employee arrived
one morning to open windows in David's smoke-filled office, he found the executive asleep on a sofa. "What time did you get here?" a bleary-eyed Selznick
asked. "Eight o'clock," the boy replied. "Fine," said Selznick. "You're my alarm
clock from now on."[2] Recalled producer William Dozier, "He would never sit
down. If you would be in a meeting with him he'd constantly walk back and
forth. He was a human metronome."[3]

The musical metaphor was apt. Selznick loved silent films and their orchestral accompaniment—"a wonderful medium we've lost," he told a reporter.[4]
After becoming RKO's production head in November 1931, the 29-year-old
bespectacled dynamo was eager to experiment with music in movies.

Among his first tasks was finishing *Girl Crazy*, based on the Gershwins'
Broadway smash. Under William LeBaron, RKO had turned the show into
a second-rate Wheeler and Woolsey comedy, its musical numbers mostly an
embarrassment. Selznick ordered reshoots, nearly doubling the budget.[5] (It
didn't help.)

Those changes brought him in contact with Steiner, who ably carried out
the studio chief's directions. Max was even given an onscreen cameo: during

the opening credits, we see him from the back, casually dressed and conducting the RKO players with zeal. Superimposed over the image are the words "THE ORCHESTRA"—a sign of the importance Selznick would place on music in the years to come.

THE FIRST FILM a new studio head greenlights is always revealing. David's choice was autobiographical in its themes, and revolutionary for the future of music in motion pictures.

Symphony of Six Million tells the shamelessly melodramatic story of a Jewish doctor (Ricardo Cortez) who drifts from his beliefs and faith, as he neglects his treatment of the poor to become a Park Avenue physician. The movie offered a depiction of Jewish life more central to the story than most Hollywood releases dared to be. And it was bold in another way: as its title suggests, music would be a *character*.

Page 1 of *Symphony*'s screenplay makes this explicit with a note unprecedented in American sound film: "The entire picture is to be accompanied by a symphonic underscoring."

The script repeatedly reinforces this idea during key scenes.

> Page 157: "OPERATING ROOM / CLOSE UP: Felix ... NOTE: The Symphonic Underscoring hits a higher pitch than ever before."
>
> Page 195: "Felix is in the sunlight . . . as he raises his eyes to the light, the very picture of a man reborn, the underscoring music rises to a climactic finale."[6]

Daily filming reports included a column for "MUSIC," with "Symphonic underscoring" listed as a factor to consider during shooting. The budget reflects this expanded use of score: $13,150 for musicians.[7] One year earlier, a typical RKO movie allotted $390 for 13 players, to record a main and end title.

These documents refute another oft-told Steiner anecdote, in which Max claimed to have delivered a last-minute rescue of a film with no score and no life, over Selznick's reluctance to have music with no apparent motivation. "I said, 'Why don't you let me try it, I have a feeling it might work. He said, 'Go ahead, do one reel. Just one reel' . . . Well, the thing was a sensational success."[8] During the 1930s and '40s, when Selznick was most active in Hollywood, Max accurately gave the producer credit for the idea of featured underscoring.[9]

THE INNOVATION OF STEINER'S SCORE wasn't just its prevalence. Max's break-through was in the way he tailored music carefully around dialogue and screen action, and in his sophisticated use of Wagner's system of leitmotifs—giving characters and settings their own themes. These themes would be modified throughout the score, to comment on character and story development.

Leitmotifs predate Wagner—Cherubini, Berlioz, and others used character-linked mottos—but the German composer developed themes with unprecedented complexity, especially in his opera cycle *Der Ring des Nibelungen*. "These melodic moments," Wagner wrote, "will become emotional guides through the complex construction of the drama."[10] Steiner echoed that thought in describing *Symphony*: "The music . . . matches exactly the mood, the action, and situation of the scene on screen."[11]

Silent film accompanists had often connected screen characters with specific themes. But as the historian Peter Wegele noted, in the 1910s and '20s, "leitmotivs were rarely developed in complex fashion; rather, they were simply restated when the characters linked to them appeared."[12]

For *Symphony*, Steiner sketched out each key theme as its own piece, before writing the scene-specific cue in which those motifs would be developed. After devising these themes, the composer's approach was more instinctual then intellectual, as he allowed characters' emotions and their unspoken desires to dictate his writing.[13]

The resulting score may be simplistic compared with Steiner work to follow; but it proved a milestone in film music, and is worth exploring in detail. At its heart is Steiner's main title, the theme for Dr. Felix Klauber: a slow, dignified march. An ascending seven-note melody is introduced, then played again steps higher. Steiner knew that an upward-modulated repeat of a phrase would create a sense of excitement.

With a startling fortissimo (*ff—very loud*) chord, we're transported into the opening scene and a new recurring motif. "The Ghetto" is a bustling $\frac{2}{4}$ scherzando whose minor-key tune suggests Hebraic folk music, as we see the crowded sidewalks and street vendors of Felix's childhood. It is the first of many themes to root the film in Jewish life. Moments later, Steiner introduces a third motif, for Felix's childhood friend Jessica, who limps because of spinal damage. As street kids mock her with the sing-song chant "Felix loves a *cripple*," the orchestra picks up the chant, but plays it with a tenderness that suggests Jessica's sensitivity and kindness. In seconds, Steiner bonds us to her, the story's conscience.

Inside the Klauber home, Felix's sister plays "Auf'n Pripetchok" on piano for her father. Steiner adopts the theme in his score, linking the Yiddish song with the devout Papa Klauber, just as the main title march will be heard in variations that accompany Felix, the young idealist.

An original "family" motif connotes faith without saccharine. Romance between the adult Felix and Jessica (Irene Dunne) is also given a theme, in Viennese three-quarter time. This meter for Steiner signifies genuine love as opposed to mere seduction; for Max, a waltz never lies.

Scenes depicting Felix's practice on Park Avenue are left unscored. In *Symphony*, music represents family, faith, and love—qualities missing from Felix's lucrative but empty "treatment" of rich hypochondriacs.

Steiner weaves Jewish themes throughout his score to convey subtext. A blind child awaits surgery, but Felix has forgotten the appointment, distracted by a wealthy client. Steiner gives the contrived sequence genuine poignance with a wordless setting for strings of "Eli, Eli" ("My God, my God, why hast thou forsaken me?"). When Felix learns that the boy has died, Steiner incorporates "Hatikvah" (The Hope). Its unsung lyrics mirror Jessica's hope for Felix: "Oh while within a Jewish heart / Yearns true a Jewish soul / O then our Hope, it is not dead."

In the drama's third act, Papa Klauber collapses; a brain tumor is diagnosed, and Felix will operate. As his father is wheeled into the operating room, the "Kol Nidre"—a prayer associated with Yom Kippur, the Day of Atonement—rises to an orchestral crescendo. Felix dons surgical garb with religious solemnity. For minutes, there is no dialogue—only music, as score puts us inside Felix's anxiety.

As he begins the surgery, Steiner's music ends. Silence. Then gradual realization: the operation has failed. Papa's body is covered, as a high-angle shot of Felix is accompanied by "Auf'n Pripetchok," its melody played softly on piano. It is the instrument on which we first heard "Auf'n Pripetchok" in the Klauber home.

Symphony's finale gives Felix his chance at redemption and Steiner his biggest showcase. Jessica's spine requires an operation. As Felix marches down the hospital corridor to prepare, orchestral quarter notes mimic, but do not precisely match, his steps. As Felix enters surgery, the camera surprises us by staying behind him—in a Hitchcockian touch, we wait in the corridor as the operation takes place off-camera. The scene has been conceived with music in mind: it is score that speaks for our anxiety over Jessica. *"Bernard: Please make this very dramatic!"* Max writes in his pencil sketch.

The camera finally moves forward toward the operating room. Violins leap an octave, playing a spiraling allegro pattern whose similarity to a famous concert piece was entirely intentional: *"Bernard: I'd like this to sound like the similar passage in [Tchaikovsky's] 1812."* As this dynamic phrase crescendos and expands across the orchestra, the surgery doors open. Felix's march theme plays triumphant, as the camera pushes into the face of the doctor, eyes raised in supplication and gratitude.

MAX MUST HAVE EMPATHIZED with the story of a gifted man who struggles to rescue the father who made his success possible. As for whether he related to its Jewish themes—or put another way, whether Max himself was Jewish— the answer lies in how one interprets the following:

- Max was born into the Jewish faith, as were his father and grandfather.
- At age six Max was baptized in a Protestant church.
- Max was never known during his adult life to attend any religious cere- mony, except for his son's Christian baptism.
- When asked, Max cited his religion as Christian.[14]

His knowledge of Jewish music is obvious from *Symphony's* score; and throughout his life, his pencil sketches are full of joking references to the faith, in a "member of the tribe" spirit.

Culturally and genealogically, Steiner satisfies the criteria for being a Jew. Spiritually, Max's only true religion was music.

ACCORDING TO THE HISTORIAN RONALD HAVER, Max "began composing while the film was still on the stages, looking at the daily rushes of scenes with [producer Pandro S.] Berman and the editor, getting ideas for the music, then waiting till the scenes were finally edited before finishing the composing."[15] Three weeks after shooting ended, Max began recording the score with a 23- piece orchestra. Eight sessions followed, with the orchestra expanding up to 30 players. Surprisingly for such a trial enterprise, musician and copyist costs came in nearly $2,000 *under* budget.[16]

Steiner was exhilarated by the greatest creative challenge he had faced in his 43 years. "The music for the picture is written in symphonic form," he enthused to a friend. "The themes appear and disappear, sometimes I bring them back for two bars, four bars . . . I've used some original Jewish melodies, but all of these have been rearranged . . . and you can't tell where the originals leave off and my own stuff comes in."[17]

Steiner's front-and-center score was a major stylistic departure, and *Symphony's* press book tried to prepare critics. Heralding a "symphony" written by Steiner, it promised "a distinct novelty in talking pictures. . . . While hundreds of pictures have had musical scores none was developed to the extent heard in *Symphony of Six Million*."[18]

After two years of mostly music-free films, *Symphony* proved a revelation. The *Los Angeles Times, Herald-Express,* and *Time* were among those singling out Max's "soul-stirring"[19] work. *The Hollywood Herald* led its review with praise of "a splendid musical score [that points] the way which may be followed with profit by others."[20]

Commercially, *Symphony* returned a modest profit. More important, it marked the true beginning of dramatic underscoring in sound film. Recalled John Morgan, a Steiner friend in the 1960s,

> When I said, "*King Kong* was the first . . ." Max said, "No, no, it's all wrong. It wasn't *King Kong. Symphony of Six Million* was the most important picture I did as far as trendsetting. But who's heard of it today?"
>
> He was proud that the film wasn't a spectacular fantasy. It was a "normal" drama that used music as underscore, and it proved that music could be played under dialogue and intimate scenes. Alfred Newman was writing film music at the time, but what he did was more like the silent *Don Juan* [1926] with a synchronized score: you have the general "right" music for a sequence.
>
> What Max did was get really specific and start to create a film language that was unique. He took from opera and ballet, and combined it with his own creativity, to come up with what we know now as film music. Today, we go through phases where producers want more music, they want less; but the classical way of scoring movies today is still based on the technique Max Steiner provided.[21]

STEINER'S MUSIC FOR *SYMPHONY* may now seem rudimentary, at times excessive. But in 1932 it served as a starter's pistol. By year's end, Steiner and Selznick collaborated on more than two dozen films, at least ten of which featured substantial passages of score.

None was more extravagant than *Bird of Paradise.* The overripe jungle romance was rooted in a cliché older than its 1912 source play: the taboo passion between a Westerner and an Eastern island beauty. Or as its ads proclaimed, *"White man . . . native girl . . . two hearts in a flowery paradise!"*[22] David had inherited the project, then super-sized it, sensing that Depression-era audiences would embrace its tropical setting, sexy leads, and literally explosive finale. "I haven't read [the play] either," Selznick reportedly told director

At RKO, ca. 1932. (MS Papers; L. Tom Perry Special Collections, Brigham Young University)

King Vidor. "Just give me three wonderful love scenes . . . and del Rio jumps into a volcano at the finish."[23]

The jumper was Dolores del Rio, cast as Luana, a lei-bedecked island girl. Joel McCrea was her lover Johnny, a visiting yachtsman. After filming in Hawaii was abandoned because of storms, choreographer Busby Berkeley led painted Caucasians through "native" dances on the backlot, while Max supervised source music.[24] But Steiner did not plan on writing the score: with a vast slate of films ahead, he hired W. Franke Harling as composer.[25]

Harling was a London-born musician and Broadway songwriter whose first screen credits were mostly musicals, like Ernst Lubitsch's *Monte Carlo*, in which Jeanette MacDonald introduced the Harling hit "Beyond the Blue Horizon." With four years of movie experience and a gift for melody, Harling seemed ideal for *Bird of Paradise*. But after *Symphony of Six Million*, Selznick decided that Steiner was a safer bet, and he asked Max to write the score.

When Steiner asked the boss how much music he wanted, Selznick replied, "For my money, you can start on the first frame and finish on the last."[26] Max took him at his word: only two of the film's 82 minutes are without score. It would be his most lyrical screen work to date—there are at least eleven different themes—as he blended traditional orchestra with ukuleles, steel guitars, marimbas, tom-toms, and other percussion—a musical analogue of the movie's West-meets-East narrative.

Steiner starts his second major score as a seduction. *"Bernard: Make flowing and indefinite. It's supposed to be an imitation of Birds, Water, etc."*[27] The film's first image is a tropical beach with swaying palm trees. Tremolo strings suggest the wind; a dialogue of bird calls is evoked via flute and oboe a la Respighi. Only after half a minute of score does *Bird's* title card appear, as we hear the main love theme, "Out of the Blue," led by languid steel guitar.

Dolores del Rio and Joel McCrea in a publicity still from *Bird of Paradise*.

Bird was the first of many scores in which Steiner proved himself a master of evoking the ocean. Johnny is introduced riding his yacht through a swell. A barcarolle-like triplet rhythm grows urgent; finally, a rushing wave splashes into the screen (and into us) as Turkish cymbals crash, and a *ffff* brass chord triumphantly proclaims *"the climax of the wave."* Three minutes into the movie, image and music have established a world of sensuality and sexual freedom.

Island beauties dive and splash around Johnny's boat, in a scene scored as water ballet. *"Girl overboard . . . Harp, etc. Bernard: If you can improve this, do so, I love it! I am trying to imitate her splash . . . All through this keep the 'water' going."* Native children have a more delicate sound: *"Steel guitar, celesta* [an ethereal-sounding keyboard instrument]—*a sort of Hawaiian music box effect."* Here, another Steiner trademark makes its debut: many of his scores will include a "music box effect" to convey delicacy, nostalgia, or loss.

For a torch-lit dance by native girls, Busby Berkeley's kitsch gyrations are accompanied by expanded percussion: *"I want to use the drums a la Ravel's Bolero—only better?"* Max will use the "only better" joke often in his sketches, when requesting a sound comparable to a famous piece. As he pushed himself and his team to find the best effect, he invariably did so with humor.

The score's highpoint comes 17 minutes into the film, with Johnny and Luana's underwater swim. Luana appears to be nude, Johnny nearly so. Steiner treats the sequence as the movie's true dance number, accompanying the swimmers and the shimmering underwater photography with his love theme, "Out of the Blue." Its Polynesian colors—steel guitars, ukuleles—disguise the fact that it is at heart a *Valse lente* (slow waltz), per Max's score.

One scene lets Steiner experiment with the psychological effect of music by playing against the visuals. As Johnny describes "civilization" to Luana, the score switches from island sounds to 1930s jazz: *"Bernard: I'd like this to sound like a high class Dance band: Tenor Sax (or Baritone), Banjo, Piano . . . But on account of the DIALOGUE, it's got to be soft!"*

Paradise's eroticism inspired Max to fill his sketches with decidedly nonmusical comments. For decades, these private notations to his orchestrators would reveal a striking contrast. Steiner the composer is sophisticated and empathetic to the characters—but Max the man-child fills the same pages with sex jokes and heckling of onscreen action. Reel 3: *"SHE SHOWS HIM THE COVE. NOT 'HER' COVE! YOU RAT."* Reel 5: *"Luana cracks the nuts. 'THE' Not 'HIS.' "* The latter note is supplemented by a fastidious drawing of a penis and testicles—another familiar leitmotif in his sketches.

Some might see this as an invalidation of the music's sincerity. In fact, it was the opposite. Max and his orchestrators—the sole audience for these jibes—often worked all night to meet a deadline. For Steiner, jokes were a vital source of stress relief, and a way of keeping his creative partners—all male—awake, amused, and alert.

Bird's sketches are filled with comments that became favorite shorthands. *"Witch doctor speaks . . . the **KITCHEN STOVE ON IT**" "Johnny, Kiss me, they are coming for us etc. **HEART BREAKER**"* Its final pages reflect another recurring trend: an adrenalin rush as musical demands increase and the end of composition nears. *"EVERYTHING that can read music must play in this masterpiece!" "IST DAS NICHT DIE SECOND PAGE, YAH, DAS IST DIE SECOND PAGE!"* And at its conclusion, a cartoon of Max kneeling: *"Thank God!"*

With a robust music budget of $12,500, plus thousands in overages,[28] Steiner conducted seven days of recording with up to 41 musicians. Sessions ended as late as 4 a.m.[29] What the players lost in sleep they gained in earnings: most had studio deals guaranteeing a minimum number of hours per year, making them among the best-paid musicians during the Depression.

Bird's massive cost doomed the project to commercial failure, but again Steiner was singled out. *Hollywood Herald* praised his "beautiful musical score. . . . Imagine it: Mr. Steiner never once intruded with 'Aloha.' This is recommended to the Academy as cause for a special award for musical courage."[30] (The Academy would not honor music until 1935.)

Max was justly proud of a score that surpassed *Symphony of Six Million* in scope and complexity. That fact was not lost on a risk-taking producer whom Selznick had brought with him to RKO—and who soon would change Steiner's destiny.

BY AGE 38, MERIAN C. COOPER had lived the life of a dozen boys' adventure novels. The Florida native had volunteered as a WWI bomber pilot; in 1918, he was shot down in a near-fatal crash. A year later, the fervent anti-Communist enlisted as an aviator in the Polish-Soviet war. Again he was shot down, spending nine months in a POW camp before escaping. After travels to Africa, Cooper teamed with another restless American, photographer Ernest Schoedsack—a lanky 6-foot-6 to Cooper's stocky 5-foot-8t.

Together, they tried a new career: filmmaking. After semi-scripted nature documentaries, Paramount engaged the duo for their first dramatic feature, *The Four Feathers*, starring Fay Wray. Enter David O. Selznick with an offer to Cooper to produce for RKO.

Wray recalled Merian as "a fascinating combination of high imagination, an implicitly rebellious nature . . . an adventurer, and a visionary."[31]

The description also fit Steiner. Add Cooper's love of classical music and it shouldn't surprise that the two became fast friends. "Maxie and I fought the Depression together," Cooper said in 1971. "I loved to see him conduct with that firm but gentle manner of his. And what sweetness he had as a human being."[32]

Cooper was planning an epic screen fantasy so expensive that, with Selznick's blessing, some of its costs were being quietly funneled on to other RKO titles. To help finance that epic—known as Production #601, and mostly set on a mysterious island—Cooper and Schoedsack also produced a tightly budgeted thriller that would share sets, crew, and cast members with #601.

This side-project, *The Most Dangerous Game,* was the first of countless screen versions of Richard Connell's 1924 short story. Joel McCrea starred as Bob Rainsford, a huntsman who finds himself shipwrecked on an island by a sadistic Russian, Count Zaroff (Leslie Banks). There, Zaroff hunts to the death "the most dangerous game"—man. Bob becomes his latest would-be trophy, forced to outwit Zaroff's guns, arrows, and hounds, with help from another shipwreck survivor, Eve Trowbridge (Fay Wray).

Schoedsack and Cooper knew the movie needed an original score; but Max, their first choice, was too busy. Instead, Steiner hired W. Franke Harling, probably feeling he owed Harling a break after his scoring of *Bird of Paradise* fell through.[33] Harling wrote and recorded a full orchestral score for *Game.*

Cooper listened and held his nose.

Too lightweight, too "Broadway," he complained.[34] Instead, he wanted music like *Bird of Paradise*—exoticism mixed with danger. Despite Max's workload, Cooper implored Steiner to write a new score in two weeks' time. Max was incapable of saying no to a friend; besides, he was excited by the movie's originality, its long stretches without dialogue, and its fever-pitch emotion perfect for musical enhancement.

In days, Steiner wrote 32 minutes of new music. He reviewed Harling's tossed score, and felt that its opening three notes—E–G–E, a minor-third interval—had potential.[35] He retained those three notes and changed their time signature, from a stern $\frac{4}{4}$ to waltz time. From there, he spun a haunting new melody: the darkly seductive "Russian Waltz," played on piano in the film by Zaroff as he banters with his unwitting prisoners.

To play the actual piano part, Max chose a musician who became a friend and his longest musical collaborator, Norma Drury. She would be present for some of the happiest moments of Steiner's life, and one of the most terrible.

RATHER THAN BEGIN *The Most Dangerous Game* with cymbal-clashing force, Steiner matches the movie's enigmatic first image—a closed door—with a solo horn playing a two-note hunting call. Its notes, E-flat down to C, have the same minor-third interval as the "Russian Waltz," only turned upside down. Subliminally, Steiner is linking two key themes.

Only as the door swings open do we hear the "Russian Waltz," played in a bracing fortissimo. Then the screen dips to black as music fades out, unresolved. Steiner has given us the musical equivalent of Cooper's filmmaking philosophy: "Keep it Distant, Difficult, and Dangerous."[36]

Game's first scene—Rainsford and friends chatting on their doomed yacht—is unscored. "This world is divided into two kinds of people," Rainsford says, "the hunter and the hunted. Luckily I'm a hunter, and nothing can ever change that!" Bob's words tempt fate: with a boom, the ship careens and sinks quickly (Zaroff uses lights to lead boats *toward* shoals). Steiner subtly reintroduces music *"after last explosion."*[37] The "real" world, represented by the opening dialogue scene, did not need music. Now, the score guides us into a realm of fantasy and nightmare.

Bob swims ashore and walks the seven steps up to the castle door. Steiner precisely matches each step with an ascending note for solo bass clarinet. This technique, soon known as "mickey-mousing," was so named for the split-second matching of music and movement a la Disney cartoons. When applied to Steiner, the phrase was usually meant as a dismissal, a way to describe his approach as crude and overly literal.

Was Max offended by the phrase? Surprisingly, no. "I like to term my method—facetiously, of course—the 'Mickey Mouse' type," he wrote in 1940. "That is, I permit myself to be dominated by the story and the characters, and synchronize the music to them."[38]

As Steiner knew, the term might equally be called "Wagnerian." In the opera *The Flying Dutchman*, the title character's steps on shore are matched with the same musical exactness that Steiner uses in *Game*. The technique strikes many viewers today as dated—and by definition, it is. As movies became more realistic, so did their music, and such specific underscoring of movement would seem absurd in a modern-day drama. But even today, horror films, fantasy, and comedies still use "mickey-mousing" because their stylized worlds permit it.

The larger-than-life drama of *Game* demanded larger-than-life underscoring. Some choices now seem extreme—one dissonant chord is held for *eight seconds* to match a florid close-up of Zaroff—but most of the score employs subtleties that few viewers could catch on a single viewing. Zaroff is linked not only with the two-note "hunt" call, and the waltz that evokes his Russian background, but with a third theme. As he glares at Eve with undisguised lust, we hear a loping, syncopated motif that implies his true barbarism. *"THE COUNT'S THEME ... (KIND OF 'SAFTIG'?) [Juicy]."* Steiner will often use slow syncopations to convey decadence in characters.

The composer mostly avoids fast tempos until the movie's third act: the hunt to which the story has led. Zaroff releases Bob and Eve into his jungle. If they elude him until sunrise, he promises them freedom. Steiner pulls fragments from his established themes to build new suspense effects. For example, the first three notes of the "Russian Waltz" become a "stalking" ostinato (a repeated musical pattern) for Zaroff.

Especially effective is the scoring of Rainsford's first mantrap for the Count: a tree rigged to fall on him. As Zaroff moves toward the trap, there are no sound effects—only timpani, playing a heartbeat-like rhythm over a sustained chord for low brass, celli, and winds. Every four beats, Steiner adds a new note to the chord, each note half a step above the one before it. The growing sound cluster, with notes ascending higher and higher over an unchanging foundation, and the soft, relentless beat of the timpani, create a

Fay Wray and Joel McCrea in a publicity still from *The Most Dangerous Game.*

tension that must eventually snap. It does, when Zaroff spots the trap and fires an arrow at Eve and Bob nearby, narrowly missing them.

Bob and Eve weren't alone in feeling a rising panic. *"Bernard: Help this if you can! It's now 4 a.m. and I can't think anymore. Worked since 8 this morning!"* Steiner's S.O.S. may have been inspired by what came next: seven and a half minutes of nonstop action music.

After the costly discarding of Harling's score, Max knew he had to deliver.

In the story, 30 minutes remain before sunrise and Bob and Eve's salvation. Zaroff raises his hunting horn and blares the two-note "hunt" motif—the first sounds we heard in the film, bringing us full circle. Cut to the exterior of Zaroff's kennel. Growls from starving hounds within. A servant flings open the door, the dogs charge out, and *"The chase begins."*

A breathless $\frac{6}{8}$ rhythm powers a ferocious new ostinato, suggesting the *Allegro* of Rimsky Korsakov's *Scheherazade* crossed with a Cossack raid. Every previous theme in the score is now "swept up in this headlong orchestral on-slaught," writer Bill Whitaker noted.[39] Steiner modulates his keys higher and higher, with the "Russian Waltz" now a wild chase motto driven by thunderous timpani. (*"This is right! I want discords!"*) The two-note hunt call resurfaces throughout the demonic scherzo, played in its own key: Steiner had the horn recorded separately and superimposed over the chase cue.

Ultimately, Rainsford and Eve triumph over Zaroff, who falls to his death into a pit of his starving hounds. The castle door that began the film now closes, as Steiner juxtaposes the "Russian Waltz" and Zaroff's theme in a celebratory *major* key for the first time. *"Make this as nice as you can, it's 5:30 [a.m.] and I am dying! Dein [a pun on the German word "Your"] Max."*

Just two weeks after the rejection of Harling's score, Steiner conducted the first of four marathon sessions, with a maximum of 31 musicians.[40] Murray Spivack tried to head off executive displeasure over costs with a note. "There were a great many individual mistakes in the orchestra . . . unavoidable, inasmuch as the musicians were working from 10:00 a.m. to 6:00 a.m., and the music was extremely difficult."[41] Max put it more succinctly. Parodying the phrase *Poco piu mosso* (play faster) he jotted on his sketch, *"Poco piu pfui! Diese modern Musik!"*

Score had been budgeted at $5,900. Its final cost was $13,720.54—more than the combined salaries of McCrea, Banks, Wray, and supporting player Robert Armstrong.[42] But Cooper believed the result was worth every penny, and so did critics. *Hollywood Daily Citizen* spoke for many: "Everyone is raving over the musical background . . . Fully half the power of this film is credited to the music."[43]

IN EIGHT MONTHS, with three milestone scores, Steiner had made the leap from journeyman to pioneer of a new art form. And before the end of 1932, RKO gave him other chances to shine.

Max was "too busy"[44] to score *A Bill of Divorcement*, a drama marking Katharine Hepburn's screen debut. He assigned the film to Roy Webb, whose score was rejected—probably by director George Cukor, who was less fond of underscoring than Selznick. But *Bill* required an original piano sonata, supposedly written by a mentally ill composer (John Barrymore) and performed in the final scene. Hired to write the sonata, plus a main and end title, was W. Franke Harling—who achieved an unprecedented trifecta with his third firing from an RKO movie that year.[45]

Inevitably, Max jumped in to write the Tchaikovsky-esque piece later published as the "Unfinished Sonata." Its grandiose emotion helped make *A Bill of Divorcement* Radio's second biggest grosser of the year.

THE FILM SCORES OF MAX STEINER

1932 Releases

Ladies of the Jury (11/31–12/31)

The Lost Squadron (11/31–2/32)

Girl Crazy (12/31–3/32)

Symphony of Six Million (1/32–3/32)

State's Attorney (2/32–4/32)

Westward Passage (3/32–4/32)

Is My Face Red? (4/32–5/32)

What Price Hollywood? (4/32–5/32)

Roar of the Dragon (4/32–5/32). An exciting Steiner prelude foreshadows action scores to come.

Bird of Paradise (1/32–7/32)

The Most Dangerous Game (8/32)

Thirteen Women (7/32–8/32). Selznick tried to salvage this supernatural thriller starring Myrna Loy with a last-minute score from Max. A campy misfire, it has become a cult favorite.

A Bill of Divorcement (9/32). At *Bill*'s premiere, on 10/21/32 at RKO's Hillstreet Theatre in Los Angeles, Steiner conducted the "RKO Studio Orchestra" assisted by "Sol Hoopii's Hawaiian Chorus" in a suite of music from *Bird of Paradise*.

The Phantom of Crestwood (9/32). Steiner repurposed many of his
best RKO cues to date into this clever mystery thriller.
The Sport Parade (8/32–9/32)
The Conquerors (7/32–10/32)
Little Orphan Annie (10/32)
Secrets of the French Police (8/32–10/32)
Rockabye (10/32–11/32)
The Half-Naked Truth (10/32–11/32)
The Animal Kingdom (11/32)

The most delightful of Max's 1932 titles was the proto-screwball comedy *The Half-Naked Truth*. Lee Tracy headlined as a motor-mouthed publicist who convinces New Yorkers that his hooch dancer girlfriend (Lupe Velez) is a Turkish princess. Director Gregory La Cava needed someone to portray a Broadway orchestra conductor, for a scene in which Velez turns a sedate stage dance into a raunchy burlesque. Who better for the conductor role than Steiner?

That October, "Max Steiner, Radio music chief, put his pan in front of the camera . . . without lines, but with closeups," a trade item reported. "He's now referring to himself as 'Clark' Steiner, and says if he gets any offers to play in westerns, he's going to change his name to 'Hoot' Steiner."[46] Onscreen, Max not only conducts, but shows a hint of his mischievous personality as he mugs with surprise, shrugs, and beats a jazzy tempo as Velez's dance goes blue.

Somehow, Steiner found time for a side venture close to David Sarnoff's heart: the mixing of movies and radio. *Hollywood on the Air* was a live weekly radio series, with a goal ahead of its time—to deliver a 30-minute infomercial for RKO product. For the series debut, Selznick "contributed a nice speechlet," one critic reported. "Followed Max Steiner with a medley of picture song themes, and then to sound stage No. 8 for a re-enactment of *What Price Hollywood*," RKO's latest A-picture. "If this is a sample of the pro-film plug idea . . . it's a winner."[47]

Max enjoyed the energy of a live broadcast and the informality of a radio studio—Broadway minus the tuxedo. Whenever the pressures of film composing became too great, he dreamed of radio work as an enticing escape.

IN LESS THAN A YEAR, Steiner's reputation in Hollywood had soared, and other studios were imitating his approach. Musical underscoring grew increasingly common; and as a result, Steiner would be credited—then and for years thereafter—as the "father" of film music.

Such attribution is only partly correct. It is more accurate to compare Steiner's pioneering work to that of D. W. Griffith, who did not invent the close-up or other techniques often credited to him. But Griffith was the great synthesizer of those tools, just as Orson Welles blended overlapping dialogue, deep-focus photography, and other existing concepts into a single motion picture that changed cinema.

Steiner employed leitmotivs with unprecedented subtlety and psycho-logical complexity, used orchestration as a tool to convey character and mood, and connected music to specific screen action with more precision than anyone before him. "Real film music began with Max," composer Hugo Friedhofer observed in the 1970s. "His is true mood music, unobtrusive back-ground that is also connective tissue, subtle and sensitive."[48]

But Max's slate of achievements in 1932 wasn't yet complete. By December, Merian C. Cooper's top-secret "Production #601" was ready for scoring.

What happened next would change Max Steiner's future, and the history of RKO, in ways that neither could have imagined.

8

Startling, Unusual Sensation

BY DECEMBER 1932, the animated beeping of RKO's "radio tower" logo must have sounded like a distress call to many at the cash-strapped studio. The Great Depression had worsened, and five thousand movie theaters closed,[1] as unemployed Americans bypassed film in favor of radio's free entertainment.

For RKO, bankruptcy loomed. Its front office pressured David O. Selznick to work faster—an order he resented, having given Radio its best slate of pictures since the studio opened. When David's father-in-law, Louis B. Mayer, offered him a production unit of his own at MGM, Selznick accepted.[2]

Taking his place as RKO production chief was Merian C. Cooper. Dogfighting in WWI, escaping from a Russian prison, and filming tigers in Africa seemed a fitting resumé for the job of running Hollywood's most troubled studio, and Cooper tackled the task with gusto.

He had reason to be enthusiastic. By February, he had completed the movie that was an obsession for him—a project so risky, and so expensive, that it stayed tightly under wraps during all of 1932.

KING KONG OWES ITS ORIGINS to a book Cooper received at age six: *Explorations and Adventures in Equatorial Africa* (1861). Cooper never forgot its description of "the fierce, untamable gorilla . . . the terror of the bravest native hunters."[3] Encountering apes in Africa "led him to conceive a gigantic, semi-human gorilla being pitted against modern civilization with a 'Beauty and the Beast' premise," wrote historian Rudy Behlmer.[4]

In 1930, Cooper was leaving his New York office when he heard the sound of an engine above him. "He reflexively looked up just as the sun flinted off the wings of a plane flying extremely close to the tallest building in the city, the New York Life Insurance Building," Ronald Haver wrote. "He realized that if he placed the giant gorilla on top of the tallest building in the world and had him shot down by the most modern of weapons, the armed airplane, he would have the story of the primitive doomed by modern civilization."[5]

Cooper joined RKO partly to access the resources he and Ernest Schoedsack needed to make their epic adventure.[6] *How* they would film an oversized gorilla, plus assorted dinosaurs, was solved when Selznick introduced them to stop motion genius Willis O'Brien. "The whole secret of successful productions of this type is startling, unusual sensation," Cooper wrote Selznick. "One animal should have a really big character part in the picture . . . a creature of nightmare horror and drama."[7]

Schoedsack's wife, Ruth Rose, penned the final script, following Cooper's edict to "Put us in it. Give it the spirit of a real Cooper-Schoedsack expedition."[8] By December 1932, principal photography was complete—but RKO was now a different studio. Selznick had given notice. Support for extra funding of *Kong* had evaporated, and Cooper knew that the movie needed thousands of dollars for one more element.

Music.

According to Max, studio executives panicked when they saw O'Brien's "jittery"[9] animation of Kong: "They thought he looked pretty phony."[10] Steiner claimed that RKO ordered him not to "spend any additional money on music," but that "Cooper said to me, 'Maxie, go ahead and score the picture to the best of your ability, and don't worry about the cost because I will pay for the orchestra.'"[11]

Executives' nerves were indeed on edge. But documents show that prior to *Kong*'s release, RKO sensed it had a hit on its hands.[12] As for the studio's supposed unwillingness to pay for a score, four months earlier, for *The Most Dangerous Game*, Radio recorded *two* complete scores before Cooper was satisfied. Given that *Kong* needed to be a success, and Cooper was now in charge of the studio, he would not have to reach for his own pocketbook—although the producer may have told Max he'd pay if necessary, to ensure that Steiner gave his all.

MAX HAD LITTLE INTEREST in tales of fantasy and horror, but he knew that *Kong* was special. When he saw the work in progress, "I thought it was just great. It was made for music. It was the kind of film that allowed you to do anything and everything, from weird chords and dissonances to pretty melodies."[13]

He understood that Kong was both antagonist and, by film's end, its tragic hero. A musical language began forming in Steiner's imagination: one that would be "impressionistic and terrifying."[14] He would use the largest orchestra possible, employ the sensual colors of Debussy and Ravel for early scenes at

Publicity still from *King Kong*.

sea, use the most modern harmonic language, heavy on dissonance, for scenes of action, and anchor the score around a Wagnerian leitmotiv for Kong—one that could signal ferocity or vulnerability, depending on its harmonization, dynamics, and orchestration.

As for when score would first be heard in the film, to Cooper's surprise Max proposed that they leave unscored the movie's first 18 minutes, set in the concrete jungle of Manhattan. "The beginning of the film is realistic, showing the Depression," John Morgan recalled. "Max told me he wanted to save the music until the fantasy part of the film begins, when it becomes like a dream. 'Get to the island, then I'll bring in the music.'"[15]

In more than two hundred surviving manuscripts of film scores, Steiner seldom gives a date for the start of composition. *Kong* was an exception. His pencil sketch begins with a cover page filled with information: "KONG / Reel 3 . . . Music by Max Steiner / Began 9th December 1932."[16] As he embarked on the highest-stakes project of his life, he sensed a moment of importance.

The first music heard after *Kong's* main title has a cue name fitting its impressionistic mystery. "A Boat in the Fog" starts with liquescent arpeggios for harp, suggesting the ripples of the sea. A soft, sustained chord for strings evokes the fog that puts filmmaker-adventurer Carl Denham (Robert Armstrong) and his fellow explorers aboard the *Venture* in a ghostly state of suspension—the beginning of their journey into the unknown. Over harp and strings, a solo English horn plays three descending notes that seem to float from a distance.

They are the theme for Kong.

IMAGINE THAT YOU ARE CLIMBING UP a tall ladder and reach the top. Your ascent was not difficult: each step was clear in front of you, and you probably felt a sense of relief as you reached the top. To descend, you are more cautious. Carefully, you place one foot on the step below—a tentative move, since you cannot clearly see the step. As you search for the next step below, your foot hesitates. If the ladder is high, it's a process fraught with tension.

Musical chromaticism—central to the music of *Kong*, and all Steiner scores—works in a similar way. Play the key of middle C on a piano. Now play the key above it: C-sharp. You just played the interval of a semitone, or half-tone. This is known as a *chromatic interval*, because C-sharp is the nearest pitch to C (in Western music).

Put another way, C-sharp is the closest "step" on our musical ladder, followed by D above it, then D-sharp and so on. Playing these ascending notes suggests a geographical climb upward, like the trip up our imaginary ladder— a pattern that creates an emotional lift, which grows as notes go higher. But if you descend from middle C, the psychological effect is the opposite: a downward chromatic pattern suggests falling, and even takes on an ominous sound as you reach the lowest notes on a piano.

Steiner would use ascending and descending chromatics throughout his career to trigger feelings of exultation, anxiety, or menace. No score uses this device more brilliantly than *Kong*. The ape's theme consists of three notes, descending chromatically. This theme is heard forcefully in the opening bar of the main title, then mysteriously in "A Boat in the Fog." Max tells us that even when offscreen, Kong is the driving force of the story.

"Listen!" shouts first mate Jack Driscoll (Bruce Cabot) during the scene "A Boat in the Fog" accompanies. "That's not breakers. That's drums!" Together, dialogue and music create a gateway between the film's separate worlds of reality and fantasy. Tom-toms are heard by the characters, but enhanced with orchestral instruments that only we the audience hear.

The score's second cue, "The Forgotten Island," is a miniature tutorial in scoring. A hypnotic ostinato for tom-toms plays softly from start to finish; over those drums, trombones play an ominous low chord. Triadic (three notes) in form, the chord is sustained as we see Skull Island's great wall. The music is its sonic match: imposing, impenetrable. The trombone chord is repeated three times. Then its notes take one full step upwards, while an un-changing "root" chord in low horns plays under it. The rise of the trombones creates the feeling that we are cautiously climbing upward—a subliminal link with the towering wall.

Carl Denham asks the ship's captain, "Have you got a good man with those gas bombs?" He's answered by one of the score's most important themes: a four-note, questioning figure. Throughout the film it will represent danger. On shore, the travelers hear chanting voices and a dance-like rhythm, played not just by drums, but strings. It is another blend of diegetic music and dra-matic underscoring.

Natives dance a sacrificial ritual at the foot of the great wall. Music explodes on the soundtrack, as trumpets blast the frenzied "Aboriginal Sacrifice Dance" over full orchestra. The dance is a variation on "The Forgotten Island"; played *"fff—molto marcato"*—very, very loud, with much force—it gives us the an-swer to the cryptic version of the theme heard earlier as the ship approached the island.

The wild music comes to a halt when the native chief spots the intruders. Then comes the most famous mickey-mousing in Steiner's career: each of the chief's steps toward Denham is accompanied by a descending musical note played by solo sousaphone. Steiner repeats the effect as the chief takes three steps toward Denham and his leading lady, Ann Darrow (Fay Wray).

A relief from this intensity comes in the quiet scene that follows. As Driscoll and Ann meet on deck at night, Steiner cleverly uses his four-note "Danger" theme in a new way. When Driscoll tells Ann "I'm scared for you," the ominous motif is heard in its usual minor key. But as Jack admits "I'm sorta scared *of* you, too," violins play the Danger theme in a *major* key (*"Dolce"*)—a wry Steiner comment on the perils of romance.

Jack's halting admission—"Say . . . I guess I love you!"—leads to *Kong's* most lyrical passage: Ann's theme. An unabashed Viennese waltz, it begins with a descending phrase that mirrors Kong's theme; Max is linking the two characters. Steiner rarely indulged his fondness for puns when naming cues, but Ann's theme is an exception: "Stolen Love" is the perfect title for a piece that begins with a clandestine ("stolen") meeting, and ends with Ann's abduc-tion by natives. She is about to become a sacrifice to Kong.

Thirty-eight minutes into the film, as natives dance before the wall, *Kong's* tempo shifts from a steady *moderato* to a breathless allegro furioso. For the next hour, it scarcely pauses. No sound film before it dared to create so much dialogue-free action. None relied so much on music to achieve its impact.

Close-ups of the terrified "bride of Kong" are accompanied by Ann's theme, no longer a waltz but a screaming figure for high strings. The great gates open; Ann is tied to a post, as a battalion of brass climbs higher. *"FURIOSO . . . THE ORCHESTRA SHOULD GO 'NUTS' HERE!"*

Natives strike a giant gong. Thirteen seconds of silence. Then there rises a slow, thumping rhythm of quarter notes—a "footstep" pattern for low brass. From offscreen, a lion-like roar. The musical "footsteps" grow louder. Finally, he appears—Kong, parting tree branches like a curtain. His arrival is heralded with the fiercest version yet of his three-note motif.

As Ann stares up at the ape, percussion pounds like a soon-to-burst heart, as the first four notes of her theme cry out over and over in high strings. No film music would capture terror more viscerally until Herrmann's shower music for *Psycho*. If Kong's first appearance triggered audience laughter, the movie would fail. In scoring Kong's entrance with such intensity, one imagines Steiner saying *I dare you to laugh now*.

The sailors race to the gate, inspiring an important new theme: a fast, staccato march, heroic and exciting. The theme returns moments later as a slow jungle march, accompanied by a rising/falling pattern for low winds—an orchestral "left right, left right." Ray Bradbury, one of *Kong*'s greatest fans, never forgot the thrill it elicited: "Play me a few bars of Steiner's background theme for Carl Denham and his chums lurking through dinosaur country, and there it is, inside my suddenly turned-back-to-thirteen [year old] head. Primitive stuff? Yep. Powerful stuff? The proof and the power are still there."[17]

A stegosaurus charges the men, but is taken down by Denham's bombs. The serpentine shake of its tail is matched by timpani roll (*"FRANK: WATCH PICTURE"*—Max is writing for specific musicians). But a dissonant triad, with G-natural clashing against its closest neighbor, A-flat, announces a new antagonist: a brontosaurus, rising Loch Ness–style from a swamp.

Rite of Spring–like dissonances find a cinematic cousin in this, the second half of *Kong*'s score. "Max had a great affinity for Russian music," John Morgan recalled. "He loved Prokofiev. And in Prokofiev's score for *Alexander Nevsky* [1938] in the 'Battle on the Ice' sequence, you hear the three-note Kong theme! Not that Prokofiev necessarily knew *King Kong*; it might be a wonderful coincidence."[18]

STEINER REALIZED THAT HIS SCORE would lose effectiveness if it did not stop at some point. *"LOG SEQUENCE (no music)"* reads his first sketch for Reel 7. Ultimately, he and Cooper decided that score would help the scene in which Kong shakes all but two of Ann's rescuers off a log high above a cavern. This cacophonous allegro reinforces the destructive power of Kong and heightens our identification with the doomed men.

Originally, sailors who survived the fall to the cavern's floor were devoured by giant spiders. A preview screening convinced Cooper to cut the grisly scene; Max never scored it.[19] In the final film, the sequence continues with Kong searching for Driscoll, hiding on a ravine below the ape. As Kong swings his arm down toward Jack, Steiner mickey-mouses Driscoll's defensive knife jabs into Kong's hand.

And then, something extraordinary happens. Kong lifts his bloodied palm to his face. His eyes soften into an expression of wounded curiosity. "*Kong looks at his wound—Dolce [tender]—strings glissando*"—a downward sliding effect for violins, sounding here like a sigh.

The evolution of Kong from monster into sympathetic victim has begun.

Steiner finds the perfect place to halt music as Kong fights a T. rex threatening Ann. Instead, the soundtrack showcases *Kong*'s other "composer," Murray Spivack. The sound recordist manipulated real animal sounds, changing their speeds, overlapping them, and playing them backward to create the voices of Skull Island's denizens.[20]

Kong takes Ann to a high cliff. There, he brushes his captive with a single finger, disrobing her. The ape's grunts soften. The "Danger" motif resurfaces, but it is played gently by harp and celeste, as Kong sniffs the tiny skirt in his hand. Danger indeed; Kong is holding the very thing that will lead to his destruction. Music here could have emphasized Ann's fear. Instead, it has shifted into a subjective portrait of Kong's curiosity.

Then, unexpectedly, Kong *tickles* Ann, as fluttering woodwinds mimic his wiggling finger. In a gesture Max must have loved, a puzzled Kong sniffs his finger, as solo contra bassoon imitates his childlike act. "*Kong tickles . . . WATCH PICTURE—STINK FINGER.*" Kong will remain a figure of terror; but thanks to this scene and Steiner's scoring, he will now be more complex and worthy of our pity.

During Kong's last creature fight, with a pterodactyl, Jack runs to Ann and the two descend the cliff on a vine. Fight and flight are evoked simultaneously in music: low brass intone Kong's theme, while violin triplets swirl in their highest register, suggesting the pterodactyl's flapping wings and the humans' peril as they climb down the vine.

Then, a musical coup de grâce: the scene shifts to Denham and the surviving sailors waiting outside the gate, despondent. Their march theme is slowly, cautiously played by solo harp. Suddenly, a hard cut throws us into a tight two-shot of Ann and Jack, running for their lives toward camera. The sailors' march flips from languid reverie to a heart-pounding *"ALLEGRO"* of the same notes. Steiner grafts Kong's theme over it: the unseen ape is gaining on Ann and Jack. The two themes modulate upward . . . again . . . then again, in terror and desperation, as the pair approach the gate, until: *"Grandioso— Sweepingly—THEY ARRIVE!"* Ann's theme, in a triumphant major key, finally breaks the musical tension.

Kong's destruction of the gate separating him from Ann, and his obliteration of the native village, is another dissonant nightmare. *"This should sound like a House on Fire! . . . EVERY INSTRUMENT WITHIN THE REGISTER SHOULD PLAY . . . KONG THROWS MAN TO GROUND: ADD HARP . . . [KONG] WITH MAN IN MOUTH—Trumpets Flutter."* But as Kong is brought down by Denham's gas bombs, Steiner plays the moment not as a victory but as fatalistic grand opera. *"Timpani roll . . . [Kong] FALLS . . . This entire page should sound very full and sustained a la Wagner!"* Music is guiding our sympathies toward Kong.

Denham's euphoria—"We're millionaires, boys!"—segues movie and music into a brighter color. "KONG: THE EIGHTH WONDER OF THE WORLD" shouts a Broadway marquee, as we enter the theater on opening night and hear Max's exuberant "King Kong March." Steiner is paying homage to his years on Broadway. The march's jaunty, minor-key melody, played by pit-band orchestra, is a witty pop variation on the Kong motif: the ape's descending chromatic motto is flipped here so that the notes ascend, in another clever variation.

Onstage, Kong is enraged by flashbulbs and the sight of Driscoll embracing Ann and breaks from his chains. The return of Steiner's score creates a chilling rumble: the ape's growls are joined by timpani, basses tremolo, and spiraling violins. As Kong begins his rampage in the streets of Manhattan, Steiner repeats past motifs to remind us of horrors being relived. Kong gnaws on a screaming man; we hear the same semitone dissonance that accompanied monster meals on Skull Island. Searching for Ann, Kong climbs a building and pulls a sleeping woman from her bed. "Stolen Love" tells us who he is looking for—just as a F-sharp/G-natural dissonance seals the poor brunette's fate, as Kong realizes his mistake and lets her drop to the pavement far below.

Eventually the ape finds the real Ann. As he dangles her above the city, Steiner captures Ann's terror, and her Skull Island déjà vu, by reprising the music from Kong's first appearance: *"FURIOSO—Strings 8va [an octave higher than written] . . . as in Reel 5."*

Publicity still from *King Kong*.

WHILE STEINER WAS COMPOSING, Cooper decided the movie needed one more spectacular set piece. *"ELEVATED TRAIN SEQUENCE (about 2 minutes),"* Max notes. *"Not finished yet—will see it tomorrow."*

That scene inspired one of the score's best-loved cues. Strings swoop down an octave into a chugging imitation of the train we see approaching. *"NOT TOO FAST—sempre crescendo / Whistle"*—the latter evoked by a jazzy two-note "wah-wah" for trumpets. Steiner's train ostinato modulates upward, giving us an adrenaline jolt as we see the train's oblivious passengers inside. Another pulse-quickening modulation upward of the *chugga-chugga* rhythm as Kong finishes smashing the track ahead of the locomotive. Brass and winds growl Kong's theme over the train rhythm, suggesting their intertwined destinies.

The trumpets' "train whistle" repeats incessantly, now a wail of panic. From the train conductor's POV, we see Kong's head rise in the stretch of broken track; then *"THE CRASH—sforzando."* He pulls the train off its track, bashing its cars like matchsticks, as Steiner revives a surprising theme: that of Skull Island's natives. Last heard as the ape smashed native huts, its use here links "savage" and "civilized" worlds, both unable to defend themselves from Kong.

THE GORILLA'S CLIMB TO THE TOP of the Empire State Building is accompanied by the most vertigo-inducing film music pre-Hitchcock and Herrmann: ascending chromatic chords, and an upward-spiraling figuration for strings, as a dreamlike wash of harp arpeggios suggest the dizzying impact of the height.

Cut to the iconic image of Kong holding Ann at the skyscraper's top. Cymbals crash and strings play an operatic statement of his theme. With three notes, Steiner restores Kong's identity as tragic figure. His theme repeats over and over as a whirling triplet, making us feel his confusion and entrapment.

Score works seamlessly with the sound of the attacking airplanes, whose drone Max imitates with a tremolo chord. The perfect blend of music and effects was no accident. Recalled Murray Spivack, "I wanted to make damn sure that we could hear the airplane, but I didn't want to sacrifice the music to the noise of the airplane. So I would put the slow speed on the airplane and either pitch it higher or pitch it lower, depending upon where the music was playing, so that we could hear both the orchestra and we could hear the airplane."[21]

Steiner uses the biplanes' gunfire to sneak out his score. For two minutes, we hear only Kong and his attackers. Finally, Kong touches his bleeding chest, uncomprehending. His legs tremble. *"Kong slides down wounded—Heart*

Publicity still from *King Kong*.

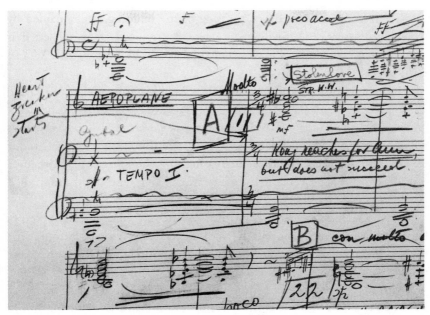

Kong's finale, original pencil sketch. As he would for decades, Max includes notes on orchestral color, screen action, and emotional intent.

breaker starts." His theme is now a gasp of defeat. "*Kong reaches for Ann, but does not succeed.*" We hear the first two notes of Ann's theme, now indistinguishable from Kong's, as a dying sigh.

"*HE PICKS ANN UP FOR THE LAST TIME—con molto espressione— Lots of Harp Bitte!* Kong strokes her ... This should sound almost like the Miserere from* Trovatore." Author Nathan Platte explains this note: "Steiner paraphrases the end of Leonora's exclamation from the Miserere Chorus in Act IV of Verdi's *Il Trovatore*. The text is also applicable to Kong, who stands besieged not by the sound of prayers, but by the roar of airplanes. . . . 'The distress that fills me almost deprives my lips of her breath, my heart of its beating!' "[22]

A plane fires a lethal blast into Kong's neck, a cymbal crash denoting impact. Kong looks skyward, as his theme is played with *bel canto* lyricism by trumpets ("*SLOWER—HEARTBREAKER*"). A final round of bullets. The ape swings his arm back in a gesture of surrender . . . and Steiner gives the fallen King a fortissimo, Valkyrian statement of his motif: "*Good Bass [line] here—To hell with the airplane imitation!*"

---

* German for "please."

Kong's body bounces down the side of the building, accompanied by shrieking dissonance. Visually we are spared the moment of impact: it is music—an accented chord for low brass—that tells us "*KONG HITS THE GROUND.*"

The final two minutes of score are among Steiner's most moving. "*STREET WITH KONG'S BODY—ANDANTE (Triste).*" A policeman pushes back crowds from the dead giant. As Denham appears, Max plays Kong's theme as a requiem, answered by an exquisitely tender version of the "Danger" motif for solo violin, harp, and celesta. Steiner may be reminding us of the theme's only other quiet appearance in the score: when Kong gently held and studied Ann on the island.

"Well, Denham," says the cop, "the airplanes got him." Denham knows better, and so do we. Music tells us his thoughts with a quotation from Ann's theme, "*dolce, slowly.*" Then the film's famous curtain line: "Oh, no. It wasn't the airplanes. It was *beauty* killed the beast."

"*Picture begins to fade out. GRANDIOSO. GIVE BERNARD!*" Steiner is allotted a full twenty seconds after the fade-out to play Kong's theme, in a *fff* symphonic re-statement. Then, in a last nod to *Kong's* visual and musical verticality, an ascending triplet figure lifts us to a triumphant D-major chord—the final notes in Max Steiner's first immortal film score.

MAX WROTE THE MAIN TITLE LAST. With *Kong's* themes now deep in his DNA, he created a thrilling two-minute overture using Kong's motif, "Stolen Love," and the natives' Sacrificial Dance. On the score's final page, six lines say it all: "*Fine [End] / Hurrah! / Thank God! / Ich bin glucklich! [I am happy!] / NUTS! / NÜSSE!*"

Steiner's early involvement in the film gave him a generous eight weeks to write the music. It is doubtful that he could have created such an intricate work in less time.

He did not do it alone. In Bernhard Kaun, Max had a perfect collaborator who did much to make *Kong's* orchestra sound larger than it actually was. Some film music histories list the number of players as "an 80-piece orchestra" or larger. In fact, the ensemble at its biggest was only 46 musicians.[23] To create a fuller sound, Steiner and Kaun used stratagems Max learned in his theater years.

Violinists quickly put down their instruments to play a viola passage. According to John Morgan, who later restored the score for re-recording, six musicians "played virtually every woodwind instrument in existence and in combination; thus individual cues could have sections utilizing

Recording *Kong*. Note inscription at top. (MS Papers; L. Tom Perry Special Collections, Harold B. Lee Library, Brigham Young University)

three bass clarinets, or four B-flat clarinets, or four saxophones. . . . The brass was fairly large, including (at their largest) three trumpets, four trombones, and two tubas."[24] (Alas, the condenser microphones of 1933 could capture only a fraction of the music's richness.) Max often conducted a full reel of film without stopping, then used the best sections from different takes.[25]

For years, reports differed on the score's cost. According to a letter to Cooper, the total amount was $30,603.48—more than double the price for the wall-to-wall music of *Bird of Paradise*. It nearly matched the cost for *Kong*'s actors ($35,956), and swelled the budget to $672,155.[26] The expenditure is all the more impressive given the fact that by the time of recording, RKO had entered receivership, after defaulting on $3.5 million.[27]

"We literally had no money," recalled Cooper, by now RKO's production chief. "And here's what a devoted friend [Max] was. Three times I was told to close down the studio by the board of directors in New York. And each time, Maxie came to me and said, 'Coop! Merian! I'll work for nothing. Don't close her down.' And I never did."[28]

FEW MONTHS IN PEACETIME American history were more tumultuous than March 1933. The Great Depression had hit new lows. A third of the nation's labor force was unemployed.[29] On March 6, newly elected President Franklin D. Roosevelt ordered the closure of all U.S. banks for four days, after a month of panicked withdrawals. On March 9, Congress passed the Emergency Banking Act, which led to the start of the New Deal.

That same week, Hollywood studios announced 50 percent salary cuts for two months.[30] Then, on March 10 at 5:54 p.m., nerves were further rattled when a massive earthquake centered in Long Beach caused $50 million in damage and 120 deaths. Max described it in a story with an unlikely but telling punchline: "I was walking down the plaza in front of the [RKO] Administration Building to go home. I heard a terrific rumble. Then people started running out of doors and jumping out of windows. Some of them were screaming. I just stood there, mystified. 'What is this?' I asked. 'My God' [a coworker replied], 'Don't you know? It's an earthquake!' 'Oh,' I said, much relieved. 'I just thought another administration was coming in.' "[31]

THE FOLLOWING DAY, a different kind of jolt hit the nation, as Warner Bros. released its gritty backstage musical *42nd Street*. Filled with songs that became standards, and featuring the camera innovations of dance director Busby Berkeley, *42nd Street* launched a new era of movie musicals which, unlike their 1929–1930 predecessors, took full advantage of cinema techniques.

And then there was *King Kong*. The success of RKO's most expensive project was critical to the studio's future. If *Kong* flopped, Radio might simply have closed.

But Cooper and Steiner had reason to be optimistic. "They previewed this picture in one of our adjacent towns [San Bernardino]," Max wrote music publisher Sam Fox. "From all indications, it is going over very big. Everyone says that it is the most colossal production that has ever been screened."[32]

There was still reason to worry. *King Kong*'s premiere date of March 2 would be four days before Roosevelt's bank shutdown. The film was booked in not one but two of Manhattan's most cavernous theaters: Radio City Music Hall and the RKO Roxy.

That week, 180,000 moviegoers dared to deplete their reserve savings to see *King Kong*.[33]

Among those attending the Hollywood premiere at Grauman's Chinese Theatre was an awestruck 12-year-old named Ray Harryhausen. "When we went into the cinema," he recalled, "they had a half-hour prologue show with live performers on stage dressed in native costume and flying trapezes over the audience. Then the picture opened with Max Steiner's Wagnerian-type score. . . . [34] It was just overwhelming [and] did for me what my music appreciation classes in high school failed to do. It stimulated a very strong desire to explore the wonders of the classical world of music[35] . . . I haven't been the same since I came out of that cinema. It changed my life."*[36]

In Tucson, 12-year-old Ray Bradbury had a similar epiphany. "It was Steiner's *King Kong* score, when I was on the exhilarating/excruciating rim of puberty in 1933, that made me realize there was a vast, puzzling and unknown art-form out there in the world inside the silver screen that was capable of summoning up images, within the instant of hearing, a week, a month, or a year later. . . . It was a beginning for me and thousands like me, an invitation to listen as well as look."[37] When Bradbury and Harryhausen became friends years later, "one of the things that drew us together was our love of Steiner. . . . We went off to see many films not just because we were attracted by the stories, but because Steiner was behind the scenes setting the mood."[38]

At a time when every household dime counted, *King Kong* grossed an astounding $2 million. But contrary to legend, it did not pull RKO out of bankruptcy. The film's net in 1933 was $650,000—huge, but not enough to erase the studio's debts.[39] Re-releases of *Kong* during healthier economic times would be more profitable. But its success "convinced the world that the beeping-tower studio still belonged in the movie business," Richard B. Jewell noted.[40]

Surprisingly, few reviewers singled out Steiner's music. So much of *Kong* was a shock of the new that professional critics focused on more obvious aspects. Those who did mention the score did so haltingly, or even negatively. Columnist Louella Parsons described it as "curiously appropriate,"[41] while another wrote that *Kong*'s "musical effects . . . became a bit comic at times, for instance, when we hear a full symphony orchestra in the heart of the dangerous Kong country when there should have been nothing but tom-toms."[42]

One exception was the *Hollywood Herald*. "Max Steiner deserves a special paragraph for his musical score . . . [it] definitely helps to make *King Kong* a big picture."[43] RKO was well aware of the music's power: the studio reused

---

* The live stage prologues in Los Angeles and New York did not use any Steiner music.

portions of it in such movies as *Double Harness, The Silver Streak, The Last Days of Pompeii, The Last of the Mohicans*, and *Back to Bataan*.

Over the years, as *Kong* evolved from success to phenomenon, more writers recognized Steiner as a major contributor. As early as February 1934, a *Variety* columnist noted, "Going back over recent months . . . the picture which seems to be a shining example for its music score is *King Kong* . . . no regular release has contained a more expert emotional buildup via music than *Kong* did for the introduction of the giant gorilla. This was truly a fine piece of work . . . and undoubtedly was responsible to a definite degree for that picture's box office success."[44]

Kong's premiere was commemorated with a large souvenir program encased in metal. Inside were profiles of the creative team, including a full page about Steiner and Spivack. It reflected Cooper's gratitude for a score that exceeded his highest expectations. "[*Kong*] has played continuously, so far as I know, on a screen somewhere in the world for 39 years," he said in 1971. "Much of the reason for this is because Maxie Steiner was able to create what no other man that I knew of in Hollywood at that time could."[45]

Generations of film composers have agreed. Jerry Goldsmith remarked in 1993 that "the techniques developed by Steiner for *Kong* are basically the same techniques we use today. . . . I'm doing what I'm doing because of it."[46] For Danny Elfman, "the entire concept of a full-blown, synchronized film score was really defined by *King Kong*. . . . It is big and bold and ambitious . . . it clearly defines the personality of Kong and his world, bringing the audiences into an alternate reality. And, as with all great film music, it is so well integrated that it's almost impossible to imagine so many of the scenes without it . . . I owe Max Steiner and the score to *King Kong* a great personal debt."[47] Even a frequent Steiner critic, musicologist Christopher Palmer, described *Kong* as "a landmark; it showed the basic power of music to terrorize and to humanize."[48]

To humanize. Steiner gave an imaginary giant gorilla a soul. But was he merely responding to a well-told story, or is there another reason his score breathes with such emotion? In his best work, there is an element of identification, and *Kong* was no exception. All three of Steiner's most famous films—*King Kong, Gone with the Wind*, and *Casablanca*—feature heroes or heroines forced to leave their homes, and made vulnerable by their love for another. In music, Max would write his truest autobiography.

Steiner and Spivack get their due in *Kong*'s opening night program.

THE FILM SCORES OF MAX STEINER

1933 Releases

The Monkey's Paw (9/32–10/32). Just before scoring a bigger simian, Max wrote bookend cues for this supernatural thriller (and RKO's worst-reviewed release of the year). The film is considered lost, although a truncated, dubbed French version survives. Steiner kept an acetate recording of his main title, which presages *Kong* with brassy dissonances, sinister chromatic descents, and an early draft of *Kong*'s theme for Ann Darrow. (Author's collection.)

The Cheyenne Kid (1/33)

King Kong (12/32–1 or early 2/1933)

The Son of Kong (10/33)

Other 1933 titles are included in the sidebar of Chapter 9.

AMONG THE FIRST PROJECTS Merian C. Cooper greenlit at RKO was an obvious sequel. "Make *Son of Kong*," Coop instructed Schoedsack, "and I don't care what you make, because anything called *Son of Kong* will make money."[49] He then left for a much-needed vacation.

Assembled on the cheap and just 70 minutes long, *The Son of Kong* abandoned its parent's grandeur and pathos, in favor of plot clichés (a search for hidden treasure) and slapstick comedy. But take *Son* on its own modest terms and there are pleasures to be had: a clever premise (Carl Denham needs a fortune to pay off New York bill collectors, in the wake of Kong's destruction); Willis O'Brien's stop-motion work; and a Steiner score that finds fresh variations on his *Kong* themes while adding new ideas.

Max had just over two weeks to write almost 45 minutes of score, to be recorded with a small orchestra (28 players).[50] Fortunately, he was tickled by *The Son of Kong*'s playful tone.[51] His theme for "little Kong," heard at the start of the main title, expresses befuddlement, not terror, even if its last three notes share the same rhythm as Papa Kong's motif. When 25-foot Junior makes his first appearance on Skull Island, music tells us that he's really an overgrown child ("*SCREWY*," Max notes of a muted trumpet solo—an early use of a favorite word).[52]

A comic high (or low) point comes at the end of Kong's brawl with an oversized bear, when a soprano sax plays a dazed version of the "Son" theme as "Kong looks cross-eyed." Later, the ape even scratches his head, Stan Laurel–style, and shrugs in "a classic *Oy vey* gesture," Bill Whitaker observes. "This prompts from Steiner a [passage] conjuring up . . . the Klezmermusik of Jewish musical theater of Eastern Europe."[53] When the ape plays with one of Denham's rifles, Max indulges in musical punning by quoting George M. Cohan's *Over There*—specifically the phrase *Johnny, get your gun . . .* And as Kong shakes coconuts from a tree, Steiner mickey-mouses the act with a giddy flutter-tremolo for woodwinds, harp, and strings pizzicato.

In the film's less jokey first half, Steiner elicits maximum emotion for scenes in which Denham, en route to Skull Island, bonds with another lost soul: Hilda (Helen Mack), daughter of an alcoholic entertainer. We meet her as she sings, with touching inadequacy, a torchy melody that conveys her mood and Denham's: *Oh, I've got the runaway blues / I want to wander away / Oh, I've got the runaway blues today . . .*

Lyrics were by an uncredited Edward Eliscu; the melody is a Steiner original. A lightly syncopated tune over steady quarter notes, its shifting minor-to-major chords convey a lovely, Depression-era sense of longing. Its description of rootlessness, and dreams of a better place, probably struck a nerve in Max, who felt the same pangs after leaving Vienna and London. If used in a better movie, the song might have been a hit. Instead, it serves as *Son of Kong*'s "Stolen Love"—a dolce melody that later becomes a frenzied allegro when the heroine is in peril. Its title even has a double meaning a la "Stolen Love": as Hilda and Denham flee various dangers, the playing of "Runaway Blues" is Max's subtlest joke in the film.

For most moviegoers, *The Son of Kong* had all the appeal of undercooked hash after a sumptuous gourmet feast. Still, its failure couldn't tarnish the reputation of *Son*'s famous father, or that of the composer who gave him a soul. If 1932 was the year Max Steiner found his voice as a composer, 1933 was the year he used those skills to create his first masterwork.

And before year's end, Steiner had forged innovations in another genre—the musical—in partnership with the greatest dance duo in screen history.

9

Orchids in the Moonlight

ON JUNE 22, 1933, as *King Kong*'s grosses sparked a burst of hope at RKO, 45-year-old Max Steiner signed a new one-year contract with the studio. His salary was $750 a week (more than $14,000 today) for the first three months, climbing to $800 for the rest.[1] But the deal's signing was not a given. By June Steiner was exhausted; and in a burst of temperament, he announced that he was leaving RKO, citing an untenable work schedule.[2] Twelve days later, probably after talking with Merian C. Cooper, Max signed the contract.

There was another reason for Steiner's dissatisfaction. Max had hoped the songs he wrote for movies would generate extra income, through royalties collected by ASCAP—the American Society of Composers, Authors and Publishers. Formed in 1914, ASCAP annually distributed thousands of dollars to top songwriters like Berlin, Kern, and the Gershwins. By 1933, Max desperately wanted to be a member, confident that film music would fall under its provisions.

That April, Steiner sent a cheery letter to membership chairman Raymond Hubbell, a songwriter Max greeted as an "old friend."[3] Hubbell's reply was several degrees cooler. He informed Steiner that "this society has nothing to do with the synchronization of numbers"[4]—in other words, film music. (ASCAP did siphon to composers a portion of film music royalties collected abroad, but the amount was negligible.)

In October, Max learned he had been elected to the lowest ASCAP rank: Non-Participating Membership.[5] Convinced that a fortune was being denied him, Steiner set his sights on full membership, and on convincing the group that domestic royalties on film music should fall under its purview. But a plan of action would have to wait: more than 30 RKO releases required his scoring or supervision, during another year of experimentation.

MERIAN C. COOPER CONTINUED the Selznick model of producing sophisticated comedies and literate dramas. *Sweepings* was the downbeat tale of Daniel Pardway, a self-made department store tycoon (Lionel Barrymore) whose spoiled children squander his fortune during the Roaring Twenties. The multi-decade drama inspired Steiner to write another "American pioneer" march a la *Cimarron*.[6] But *Sweepings'* melody, "The Store," is different. It transforms across the movie from an upbeat theme of success to a poignant elegy of loss. Steiner's message is clear: no matter what happens in Pardway's life, it is seen through the prism of "The Store."

RKO's fastest-rising star, Katharine Hepburn, benefited greatly from Steiner's attention. He composed a haunting minor-key tango for her second film, *Christopher Strong*, and a glittering full score for her third, *Morning Glory*. The story of an aspiring actress who makes good on Broadway, *Glory* was shot in a quick 18 days.[7] After seeing a cut without music, Hepburn's agent told her to buy the film and destroy it. But the actress disagreed, especially after Max contributed what Hepburn described fifty years later as "a wonderful score."[8]

Music gave the film scope and heightened empathy for Hepburn's naïve, ambitious Eva Lovelace. Max's main theme begins with the same musical phrase Richard Rodgers would use as the first ten notes of "Blue Moon"— a melody written the same year. Rodgers spent 1933 in Los Angeles; did he see *Morning Glory*, a movie about his home turf of Broadway, and did Max's theme stick in his subconscious? Either way, Steiner's fanfare-like motif grandly evokes the brass ring of fame Eva hopes to catch, just as the waltz theme that follows captures her allure.

The score's highpoint comes in a party scene where Eva gives a room-silencing read of "To be or not to be." Hepburn's performance is accompanied by a sighing, small-group ensemble of harp, woodwinds, and low strings. Its writing must have taken Max back to his days in London with Sir Herbert Beerbohm Tree. Eva follows *Hamlet* with *Romeo and Juliet's* balcony scene; here, Steiner uses violins that stay above Hepburn's purring speech by half an octave. "I make it my business when I start on a picture to ascertain the pitch of the voices of the different principals," he explained. "When I write my music I try to keep away from their pitch because, when the music is dubbed, if the music is in the same register as the talk, it is lost."[9]

By now, the composer had created an efficient process for scoring. He resisted reading a movie's screenplay: "I may read [a script] that I like very much, and then when I see the picture I'm terribly disappointed. On the other hand, I may read a script which I don't like at all. Then when I see the picture, I am impressed because it is so much better than the script. I prefer, therefore, to approach the picture without any prejudice."[10] Instead, he began by viewing a film's rough cut, which was usually ready days after shooting was completed. During that viewing, "In my mind's eye I create themes for the principal characters," he explained.[11]

> Do you realize that every [character] has a tempo, an individual timing, to which his actions are always attuned? I have to match my themes to the tempo of the actor.[12]
>
> The director and perhaps the producer may tell me their ideas of what should be done. Their ideas do not always coincide. In this event, I try to persuade them to swing over to my ideas—or it may be that I like their ideas better than my own.[13]
>
> Then I time it . . . I have the film put through a special measuring machine and then a cue sheet created which gives me the exact time, to a split second, in which an action takes place, or a word is spoken. The music for each cue is timed exactly by the number of feet and extra frames and by the number of minutes and seconds each cue runs.[14]
>
> For instance, let's say the actor walks in at the beginning. This is 00. He sits down in six seconds, starts, to talk. Ten seconds. His first line might be at 20 seconds. Then he gets up at 23 seconds, walks out of the house at 40 seconds, comes back at 50 seconds and so on.[15]
>
> While these cue sheets are being made, I try to digest what I have seen and try to plan the music for this picture. There may be a scene that is played a shade too slowly, which I might be able to quicken with a little animated music, or to a scene that is too fast I may be able to give a little more feeling by using slower music. Or perhaps the music can clarify a character's emotion, such as intense suffering, which is not demanded or fully revealed by a silent close-up.
>
> After my themes are set and my timing is completed, I begin to work. I run the picture reel by reel again to refresh my memory. Then I put my stopwatch on the piano and try to compose the music . . . allowed by this timing. Once all my themes are set, I am apt to discard them and compose others, because frequently, after I have worked on a picture for a little while, my feeling towards it changes.
>
> Having finally set my themes, I begin the actual and tedious work of composing. The great difficulty lies in the many cuts which make up a modern motion picture. I write my music to split seconds. I have

written music for 1/3 of a second or eight frames; 1/4 of a second or six frames; or 1/2 second which is twelve frames.

There is nothing more effective in motion picture music than sudden changes of mood cleverly handled, providing, of course, they are consistent with the story. [In an imaginary scene of a cabaret singer who, mid-performance, learns that her father is dead], it would be absolutely wrong to change from the hot tune in progress to music appropriate to her mood. We must consider the jazz orchestra as actual music, not as underscoring . . . and, second, no greater counterpoint has ever been found than gay music underlying a tragic scene.[16]

That, of course, is the great problem of composing for the films— to give the score continuity, to keep the audience unconscious of any break, yet to make the music perform its function of sustaining each mood and scene. Of course, some scenes are more effective without music. I am the first to admit that, and when I feel that music can add nothing to a scene, I refuse to try to find a way to make it do so.[17]

The task of presenting memorable themes in a near-subliminal way required more ingenuity than most critics would admit. "Concert music is full of secrets," observed Franz Waxman, the German-born composer who came to Hollywood in 1934. "Film music must make its point immediately, because it is heard only once by an audience that is unprepared and didn't come to the theater to hear music anyway. I believe in strong themes that are easily recognizable and can be repeated and varied according to the film's needs. But the variations must be expressive and not complicated."[18]

It was a philosophy Max shared. "A filmgoer sees the picture with his eyes, and his ears are devoted to the dialogue," he told a reporter. "The sound of the music seems to penetrate to him through a different sense entirely: it registers an immediate emotional reaction, but it lingers in the subconscious a while before its presence is fully realized in the conscious mind."[19]

IN MARCH 1933, RKO took another adventurous step by returning to a genre that had previously brought both triumph and disaster: the musical.

Melody Cruise was the offshoot of an Oscar-winning RKO short subject, *So This Is Harris!*, starring bandleader Phil Harris. Its director was 32-year-old Mark Sandrich, who had overseen dozens of shorts that showed a gift for pacing and comedy. Eager to move on to features, he turned *Harris!* into a stylish audition. Packed with flashy optical wipes and double exposures, it synchronized screen action to music beats, using rhyming dialogue and song to freshen a standard mistaken-identity plot.

Accolades for *Harris* convinced RKO to give Sandrich a feature—one that let his imagination run as wild as a meager $153,000 would allow.[20] Fortunately, *Melody Cruise*'s stars came cheap: Phil Harris, *Son of Kong* ingénue Helen Mack, and scene-stealing farceur Charlie Ruggles. The setting was a liner bound for Panama, stocked with double entendrés, scantily clad party girls, and infectiously catchy songs by Will Jason and Val Burton.

Its thin plot was typical for producer Lou Brock, who prized snappy individual scenes over story. The movie's cohesion came from a team that would soon weave its art deco magic on bigger RKO musicals: director Sandrich, set designer Van Nest Polglase, costume designer Walter Plunkett, and musical director Steiner. For RKO, *Melody Cruise* was the singing canary in the coal mine that paved the way for Fred and Ginger.

For a year, Max had been telling his bosses that audiences were hungry for a well-made musical. Now he had the chance to prove it. Besides scoring *Cruise*'s opening sequence and various others, he oversaw a team of orchestrators to ensure consistency of style.

So eager is *Melody Cruise* to tell its story through music that it even turns RKO's beeping logo into the first bar of score. Its rhythm and pitch are continued by the orchestra, which segues into a bouncy rendition of the film's standout song, "Isn't This a Night for Love?" From there, we're launched into a witty visual tone poem about the miseries of winter. Synched to the beats of Steiner's score, we see swinging store signs, crunching snow shovels, a street cop flapping his arms like a bird. When characters speak inside a travel agency, they do so in rhyme. At a train station, rhythmic exclamations come from the hissing wheels of a locomotive ("Let'ssss go, let'ssss go!"). Like a live action cartoon, this prelude sets the tone for a breezy screen bonbon that jumps from "normal" scenes to full-blown surrealism.

Transitions are embellished with kaleidoscopic effects: a "propeller" spin changes one scene to a new one; an image "explodes" into optical confetti to reveal another. During the singing of "Isn't This a Night for Love?" a starry constellation reforms itself into a treble clef and music notes. The film's message is clear: see how *fun* a movie musical can be?

In its recording of songs, *Cruise* was a turning point for RKO. Until 1933, most songs in films were performed live by vocalists, with an orchestra providing on-set accompaniment. During filming, Murray Spivack recalled, "We'd get a good take for sound and it was bad for the camera. The camera would get a good take and it was bad for sound."[21] Recording an orchestra on location was especially impractical. For *So This is Harris!* the music department made a record of the needed accompaniment, using what Steiner described as "a soft piano, i.e., a piano with a muffler on it, which was used to keep the principals in tempo and on pitch."[22] The recording was played on set to keep time, after which it was covered "by the proper orchestra accompaniment, the conductor listening through earphones to both voice and soft piano."[23]

The *Melody Cruise* number "He's Not the Marrying Kind" was filmed partly on an actual ship. During the song, the camera cuts among a bevy of femmes in separate locations, speak-singing their frustration over Phil Harris's commitment issues. Recording each girl live, while playing a "soft piano" track to guide them, allowed Sandrich to cut effortlessly among 16 performers. It also simplified filming in locations as varied as a promenade deck and the ladder on a smokestack.

Released in June 1933, *Melody Cruise* returned a respectable gross of $150,000.[24] More important, it established Mark Sandrich as a director to watch—and it convinced RKO that musicals were once again a safe port for profit.

A rare moment of relaxation, ca. 1933. (MS Papers; L. Tom Perry Special Collections, Brigham Young University)

TWO MONTHS AFTER THE RELEASE of *Melody Cruise*, cameras rolled at Radio on a lavish follow-up. *Flying Down to Rio* began during the RKO-Selznick era, as a vague concept in search of a story. Cooper approved the project after producer Lou Brock pitched a flying scene—something he knew that Coop, a pilot, would love.[25]

Dolores del Rio signed on to star. Gus Kahn and Edward Eliscu were hired as lyricists, and for composer, Brock chose Vincent Youmans. Max was elated: not only did he revere Vincent as a songwriter, but their all-night sprees in Manhattan were some of his happiest memories. Now, Steiner anticipated a West Coast sequel on a Hollywood budget.

All of which made Youmans' arrival the more shocking. The 34-year-old was frail from tuberculosis and alcoholism and looked "as though this was his swan song," Eliscu recalled. "It was pathetic, because he had been a very lively, vigorous man."[26]

While at RKO, Selznick had signed another Broadway talent for yet-to-be-determined screen work. The 34-year-old Fred Astaire was a logical addition to *Rio*, although his part was a supporting one. Chosen as his dance partner was an RKO regular Fred knew from Broadway—22-year-old Ginger Rogers.

Steiner was thrilled to reunite with Astaire nine years after *Lady, Be Good!* As *Rio's* musical director, he took part in many of Astaire's meetings with dance director Dave Gould and Gould's 23-year-old assistant, Hermes Pan. Astaire and Pan were soon finishing each other's sentences, and a 40-year partnership was born.

Vincent Youmans belied his failing health by composing songs as fine as his work on Broadway: "The Carioca," "Orchids in the Moonlight," and *Rio's* title tune. Steiner's orchestra sometimes played live on set; an upside of that approach was a spontaneity in playing.

On September 7, 1933, cameras rolled on Astaire's first movie dance solo, "Music Makes Me." Onscreen musicians seem to be accompanying him, but the sextet of real players was out of frame. They included some of Max's favorite musicians: saxophonist Eddie Sharpe, also one of *Rio's* orchestrators; tuba player Jack Barsby, prominently heard throughout *King Kong*; and Hal Findlay, who also made Steiner's cue sheets.[27]

Findlay did triple duty as Astaire's rehearsal pianist, during which the dancer worked out each step. Steiner's role was supervisory: he hired the pianists and occasional drummer, who "collaborated with Astaire and his dance assistants on the musical arrangement," explained author Todd Decker. Once the dance was set, the team "wrote out a short score indicating all the important musical points of emphasis for the arrangers and orchestrators in the music department."[28]

At this point, Steiner became essential, as he assigned and critiqued the orchestrators' work. Astaire "would suggest tempo and key changes," John Morgan recalled, "and he used a work sheet that described a dance number with beats notated like a click track. He would suggest a special musical effect to Max, and if it was agreed upon, it was included in the arrangement."[29]

Steiner introduced Fred to the pianist who on later films would be the dancer's closest creative partner next to Hermes Pan. Classically trained in Chicago, 21-year-old Hal Borne moved to L.A. to work in movies, but California's union required him to wait twelve months before he could become a session musician. In 1986, Borne recounted what happened next.

There was a very exclusive club on Sunset Boulevard called the Colony Club. In one of their side rooms they had gambling. I worked with Lou Kosloff, a great fiddle player, and a drummer, in an intimate room that sat about forty people.

One evening a short fellow came in with a couple of people. Lou said to me, "Max Steiner just walked in." Well, I played while the violinist and drummer took a break. I did lots of Gershwin, early Kern, and I'd never play it the same way twice. Mr. Steiner was delighted. He said, "How much longer do you have to go before your year is up that you can work in the studios?" I said, "Almost three months." He said, "Come to the studio."

I went to his building. He shook hands with me, this little man with glasses and a wonderful sense of humor. He said, "I think I have a job for you where you will be a rehearsal pianist with Fred Astaire, and there might be some original composition you have to do." Here's a 21-year-old kid standing there in shock. He took me to one of the stages, and Mr. Fred Astaire was sitting there and Miss Ginger Rogers.

Mr. Steiner said to Fred, "This is Hal Borne, the gentleman I was telling you about." Fred said, "Why don't you play something for me?" So I played a little Gershwin in my own style. Fred turned to Max and said, "I have a pianist." Just like that.

Max said, "I thought you would. I'm going to use him on the recordings, too. We don't have a guy like this here, we have a classical pianist [Max Rabinowitch] but he can't play jazz. This boy plays everything, so I'm going to use him on some of Hepburn's pictures—I'm going to make him work!"[30]

In the meantime, Borne worked on *Rio* as a "sideline" musician—a player seen onscreen but not actually performing.

ON SEPTEMBER 21, AT 9 a.m., Astaire and Rogers reported to Stage #8 to rehearse their first screen dance together. That night, from 8 p.m. until 12:15 a.m., 14 musicians performed a "Test Track" recording of the dance music: an instrumental of "The Carioca." The recording was probably used as a guide track the following morning, when filming of Fred and Ginger's dance—their only one in the film—began at 9 a.m. On September 26, after four days of shooting, their two-minute segment of the "Carioca" sequence was complete.[31]

Flying Down to Rio's title song showcased Hollywood's strangest (only?) aerial ballet, performed by chorines on the wings of biplanes. For its orchestration, "Steiner had devised some tremolos in the violas, cellos, and basses, simulating the noise of an airplane motor," Spivack remembered.[32] Max viewed such mimicry not as a cheap effect but as legitimate composition. That November, a reporter quoted his belief that "songs of great cities, harbors, factories, and railroads will be turned into imitative melody. 'Movies have made such a symphony possible in the near future,' he says, 'by proving that most of the world's material sounds can be musically imitated.'"[33] One of Steiner's mentors, Richard Strauss, would have applauded the idea, having remarked that he could musically delineate a knife from a fork.[34]

Max's simpatico work with Astaire contrasted sharply with the helterskelter shooting of *Rio*'s nonmusical scenes. Producer Lou Brock was so obsessed with secrecy—or so unprepared—that according to co-star Gene Raymond, script pages were distributed on the day of shooting. "When we finished the picture we thought, 'This is going to be the bomb of all bombs.'"[35]

Two months later, *Flying Down to Rio* was previewed in Los Angeles. After Fred and Ginger danced "The Carioca," "The audience cheered," Hermes Pan recalled. "Right away, the studio knew: we've got something big."[36] On December 22, *Rio* opened at New York's capacious Radio City Music Hall. Gene Raymond, passing in a cab, was agog to see a ticket line that "went all around the block."[37]

Max hoped that *Rio* would be the first of many screen teamings with Vincent Youmans; but the songwriter's half-hearted efforts to beat tuberculosis were sabotaged by heavy drinking. Steiner did his best to keep his friend active. He urged RKO to buy Youmans a home recording system, to allow him to compose in bed: "He could even write a picture for us with these records, and I would know exactly what he is thinking about," Steiner wrote his bosses.[38]

Ginger Rogers and Fred Astaire dancing "The Carioca," in a publicity still from *Flying Down to Rio*.

Youmans got his recording machine, but never completed another score. He died, age 47, in 1946.

FLYING DOWN TO RIO GENERATED nearly half a million dollars in profit for its desperate studio.[39] But Max had other reasons to remember the film.

Since 1930 the composer had virtually lived at RKO; but in fall 1933, he stopped at his Beachwood Drive home long enough to review a phone bill. Noticing expensive calls to and from Paris, Max had them traced. His worst fears were confirmed: his wife, Aubry, was having an affair with a purported

Russian prince she met during a recent trip to France. Despite Steiner's neglect of her, "he was devastated," a friend recalled.[40]

In November, the gossipy press reported details of the divorce suit filed by Aubry. She cited "mental cruelty,"[41] the most common grounds of the day at a time before no-fault divorce in California. "Mrs. Steiner complained that her husband often refused to speak to her, left her alone nights, and did not take her to places of amusement," wrote the *Daily News*.[42] The *Examiner* added that "Constant calling of the gas man, the light man, and the phone man to collect unpaid bills made married life unbearable."[43]

This claim marks the first recorded instance of a Steiner weakness that worsened over time. Despite a salary of $41,600 a year (more than $780,000 today), Max seemed incapable of living within his means. Gabor's bankruptcies had taught him nothing—except, perhaps, to live well in the present and let tomorrow take care of itself. Steiner's woes grew when Aubry was granted monthly alimony of $100, an eighth of his salary.[44] Distracted by film projects, Max left details of their financial separation to his lawyers.

He would live to regret it.

FLYING DOWN TO RIO'S ROMANTIC GLOW may have helped inspire what happened next. During a recording of "The Carioca," Max called the usual meal break. He then approached his harpist, Louise Klos, and asked her to join him for dinner. The 27-year-old musician had been playing RKO sessions since 1931. Eighteen years Steiner's junior, she was surprised by his offer.

But "that night, his friend and agent, Charles Beyer, happened to be present," Louise recalled. "According to Max, Charlie said to him, 'You fool, have you noticed the beautiful harpist that's sitting there in the orchestra?' Max's chauffeur was waiting outside, and drove us to a lovely, very swank restaurant called the Vendome on Sunset Boulevard. We then returned to the studio to continue the recording. This was the beginning of our dating."[45]

Unlike Beatrice and Aubry, Martha Mary Louise Klos was about to assume a co-starring role in Max's life. She was striking in appearance—"slim and very glamorous," according to a colleague, with "very white skin and pitch black hair, which she always wore parted in the middle and straight back. . . . Her face was soft and round with full lips and slightly hooded eyes."[46]

For once, Max was attracted by more than physical attributes. Louise's background suggests why.

Born in 1906 in St. Joseph, Missouri, the daughter of a businessman and an artistic mother, Louise was taken to concerts at age three. After hearing Verdi's opera *Rigoletto*, "there was never a question as to my ambition to be

Louise. (Louise Steiner Elian papers; L. Tom Perry Special Collections, Brigham Young University)

a great musician, and especially a great opera singer."[47] At age five, she began studying piano; at age fifteen, voice.

But it was another instrument that set Louise on her professional path. "One day my mother Mary Francis and I passed a music store where there was a display of harps in the windows. Mother had always loved the harp, so for Christmas that year she gave me an Irish harp." By age 16, Louise was earning money as a harpist in women's hotels and other venues.

In 1916 her parents divorced, and three years later Louise and her mother moved to Los Angeles. When Mary Francis's second marriage ended in 1924, Louise abandoned dreams of college and devoted herself to supporting the family. A year later, she and five girlfriends were hired by the ocean liner *S.S. Lurline*, where their ensemble played during trips to and from Hawaii. In 1926, she had her first brush with Hollywood, playing in the orchestra that accompanied silent films at Grauman's Million Dollar Theatre.

When talkies began their dominance, Louise appeared onscreen with two other musicians in the Warner Bros. short *The Colonial Girls*. Months later, she booked her first job as a Hollywood session musician. A gifted sight-reader, Louise became the industry's busiest harpist, toting her instrument to Paramount (*The Love Parade, Love Me Tonight*), MGM (*Hollywood Revue of 1929, The Rogue Song*), and RKO.

"I fell in love with Max's music right from the first time I worked with him," she later said.

> The harp parts were so beautiful. A lot of composers don't know how to write for the harp. Just a glissando or a chord. But Max *knew*, and it was such a pleasure to play for him.[48]

Louise, ca. 1926. (Louise Steiner Elian Papers; L. Tom Perry Special Collections, Brigham Young University)

He had a great sense of humor, so we looked forward to sessions with him. We had to be fine sight-readers, because we only saw the music for the first time at the sessions.

We worked unbelievable hours. Many times we would start at 9 a.m., break for lunch (one hour), then to dinner (one or two hours). At midnight, the studio would send out for lunch for us, then back again to work until 6 or 7 a.m. After going home for a few hours, we would start again at 12 or 1 p.m. The union scale was three hours a session for $30—a double session was six hours. Most first-chair people made their own arrangements for double or triple pay.

Louise soon realized that she and Max had different attitudes toward money. "He loved to play roulette. The first date we had after the dinner, he took me up to the Clover Club. People from the picture industry and society belonged to it. We went into the casino and he said, 'Give this young lady twenty-five dollars' worth of chips.' I'd only seen roulette in movies. I said, 'How do you play?' He said, 'If you have a favorite number, just put the chip on the number. If anybody really knew they would break the bank over time!' He said [gambling] relaxed him. He wanted to get away from sitting at the piano and writing. Well, I won sixty dollars and I gave it to him. He said, 'Oh no, this is yours. Just buy yourself something nice with it.' He loved playing cards also. He and the boys would play a fancy type of gin rummy. Sometimes they'd play all night."[49]

THE FILM SCORES OF MAX STEINER

1933 Releases (continued)

So This Is Harris! (10/32)
Our Betters (1/33)
Christopher Strong (1/33–2/33)
Sweepings (2/33)
Diplomaniacs (2/33–3/33). Wheeler and Woolsey's best comedy, this surreal political satire, co-written by Joseph L. Mankiewicz, contains some of Steiner's liveliest musical supervision.
Melody Cruise (3/33–5/33)
One Man's Journey (6/33)
Double Harness (6/33)

Morning Glory (7/33)

Midshipman Jack (7/33)

Ann Vickers (8/33)

Chance at Heaven (8/33)

The Right to Romance (8/33–10/33)

If I Were Free (8/33). Additional music.

Little Women (6/33–11/33)

Aggie Appleby: Maker of Men (9/33–10/33)

Rafter Romance (9/33)

After Tonight (10/33). Contains the Steiner song "Buy a Kiss."

Flying Down to Rio (8/33–12/33)

AS MAX EMBARKED on a new love affair, he was also scoring what became the most surprising RKO release of 1933.

Little Women starred an ideally cast Katharine Hepburn as impetuous would-be novelist Jo March. Director George Cukor aimed for naturalism, abandoning elegant costume sketches for Jo, her sisters, and mother Marmee in favor of simple calico dresses more reflective of 1860s fashion.[50]

In case the period story failed to resonate with jazz-age viewers, RKO imposed restrictions.[51] Cukor was limited to two printed takes per shot, while Steiner crafted an intimate score for 21 musicians that he intended to be "quaint and old-fashioned."[52] *Little Women*'s main title is unique among his work: as we see a Currier and Ives–style drawing of a snow-covered home, a solo spinet piano (similar to a harpsichord) plays what sounds like an authentic Victorian lullaby. Nostalgic and reflective, this original theme avoids sentimentality, thanks to the beauty of its simple melody, supported by chamber-like strings and harp. In 60 seconds, the main title transports viewers to a bygone time. Later, the theme will be linked specifically to Jo. Like Steiner's best motifs, it is malleable, conveying tenderness, defiance, disappointment, or comedy, depending on its arrangement.[53]

For the theme of Beth, Steiner uses the period song "Bloom, My Tiny Violet," a fragment of which Beth sings in her first scene. Max may have suggested its usage, with its lyrics' apt references to "my dear sister" who will be "ever near." Steiner's touching variations on the theme suggest Beth's kindness, her love of birds (evoked in graceful woodwinds), and her frailty. Her death scene blends orchestra and a wordless female chorus, an effect Max usually reserved for scenes involving the mysteries of the afterlife.

He seamlessly incorporates period music, most memorably when the sisters stage their overwrought performance of "Miss Josephine March's Most Hair-rising yet Melodious Operatic Tragedy 'The Witch's Curse.'" Steiner accompanies their melodrama with solo piano and strings—music that sounds intimate enough to be played by the March family, but recorded with a slightly bigger ensemble than Jo could have mustered. (Steiner excelled at this trick of using multiple musicians to match a smaller onscreen group.) The music here is an intentional hodge-podge of familiar classical themes: Schubert's "Der Erlkönig," Rossini's "William Tell Overture"—music the sisters would have known. They also were favorites of silent movie accompanists, allowing Max to parody the one-size-fits-all film music of the recent past, before his own exacting method made the practice obsolete.

Expectations for *Little Women* were modest . . . which made its release, on November 16, 1933, all the more astounding. Booked for seven days at Radio City Music Hall, it played to packed houses for three weeks. Its uplifting portrait of a family pulling together to survive economic hardship was exactly what Depression audiences craved. *Little Women* became RKO's most successful release to date, grossing $2 million.[54] And although George Cukor was not a fan of Steiner's heart-on-sleeve music,[55] Hepburn later called Max's work "a brilliant score."[56]

WITHIN THE INDUSTRY, Steiner's reputation was growing rapidly, thanks to music that enhanced everything from a monster blockbuster to sparkling musicals to period Americana.

But after four years of nonstop work, and a second divorce, the composer was on the verge of physical collapse. And his state of anxiety would only be worsened by events near his parents' home in Austria—in neighboring Germany.

10

Working Night and Day

FOR RKO, 1933 HAD BEEN A YEAR of promising strides—but that October, Merian C. Cooper disappeared from the lot amid rumors of a heart attack. He would make occasional returns to the studio, but by May 1934, he had officially stepped down.[1]

Fortunately, an ideal successor was ready to replace him. Pandro S. Berman, age 29, was Radio's most sophisticated producer—commercially savvy, and drawn to stories with provocative adult content. His first duties as studio head included finishing a film begun by his predecessor. Cooper had made a two-picture deal with his friend, director John Ford, who was still in the journeyman stage of his career.

Recalled Coop's wife Dorothy, "Merian said to Ford, 'You choose one [picture] and I'll choose one. Ford chose *The Informer*. Merian wanted to get a picture made quickly, and he chose *The Lost Patrol*.'"[2] Both were tightly budgeted, and both were ideal for a director drawn to tales of men tested by outside forces, and their own flaws of character.

Patrol was made first. It told the bleak story of a garrison of British soldiers in WWI, stranded in the Mesopotamian Desert where they are killed, one by one, by unseen Arabs. The movie ran just 74 minutes, but as RKO discovered after a preview, the unremitting slaughter of a sympathetic cast was too much for audiences.[3] And with most of its action set at one location, a fort under siege, the film seemed static in rhythm.

Ford did not plan for the movie to be scored; his budget includes just $30 for a bugler.[4] But Cooper, while recovering from his heart attack, overruled his friend and assigned Steiner. Max would score only *Patrol*'s first reel—then a determination would be made whether music helped the movie.

On December 13, 1933, 31 musicians recorded 11 minutes of score under Steiner's direction.[5] Days later, it was decided: Max would score the entire film.

His enthusiasm for *Patrol* ("an excellent picture")[6] helped mitigate the fact that RKO wanted the movie finished, and fast. Steiner later claimed to have written the nearly wall-to-wall soundtrack in eight days.[7] In fact, he had from early December to January 18, 1934, the day of the final session.[8] But given the quantity and complexity of his work, the timeline must have felt shorter. (Max may also have been recalling the time he had to score Reel One.)

AGAINST THE IMAGE of an empty desert, *The Lost Patrol* opens with the sound Ford had wanted: a solo bugle. But as a title card appears, the bugle's major-third fanfare is answered by a grim, suspended F-minor chord, played by orchestra with sforzando punch. Steiner has told us in five seconds what the film is about: heroism in the face of death. A brisk, minor-key "Arab" dance begins; its first four notes—a serpentine, falling pattern—are based on intervals in the Persian scale. These notes will be linked throughout the movie with the invisible Arabs lying in wait.

The main title ends with a montage of featured cast, as we hear a new theme: a stately British "cavalry" march that evokes the men's humanity, with a mix of stoicism and heart that was becoming a Steiner specialty. This music initially describes a larger group, before it is attached to a single character— Victor McLaglen's Sergeant, the lone survivor.

Steiner gives each soldier a defining theme, intensifying our attachment to them and making each of their deaths a heartbreaking experience. If the Sergeant's motto embodies stiff-upper-lip dedication, the theme for 19-year-old, idealistic Pearson offers a more vulnerable iteration of that idea. Just before his death, Pearson articulates the story's themes of brotherhood, as he tells the Sergeant of his pride in serving among such men. Many composers could have written a touching theme for him; Max's music conveys nothing less than love.

The religious zealotry of Sanders (Boris Karloff) is captured in a deliberately heavy-handed hymn (*"a sort of organ effect with Harp"*).[9] By film's end, as Sanders, now insane, staggers across the sands carrying a cross, his theme has metastasized into a lumbering death march. For a sandstorm at night, Steiner creates a chillingly beautiful soundscape by blending a humming, wordless chorus of 30 with high harmonics in violins. *"ADAGIO—The Wind starts— Soprano, Alto, Basses SING IN CUPPED HANDS."*

The cultural identities of two quarreling-but-close soldiers permits flashes of humor. *"The Scotchman and Irishman are ARGUING, therefore the two themes [are played] together. They are in two keys, but they fit!"* Bitonal writing recurs throughout: bugle calls or character themes are juxtaposed softly against slow-moving chords in another key, creating a queasy sense of danger.

Character themes also take us to places beyond those we see, reducing the film's visual monotony. As Brown (Reginald Denny) recalls past erotic adventures with "dark" women, Steiner gives us the aural equivalent of a flashback. *"I'd like it to sound somewhat like Wagner's 'Dreams' . . . He talks about the girls. I'd like this to be somewhat 'eerie' (mysterioso)."*

Max repeats the strategy as Morelli (Wallace Ford) remembers circus performing days with a lost love, musically transporting us to that place and time: *"Tempo di Valse (delicate—Trapeze Waltz). A little Vaudeville color wouldn't hurt."* When the Sergeant describes his own loss—his wife's death in childbirth, the son he doesn't know—his march theme becomes tender. *"Add Celeste. Work a little Music Box into this. He's talking about his baby!"* Here and in other scores, Steiner redefines our expectations of a march, proving that the form can be as emotionally expressive as any other.

Twice, Steiner daringly plays *against* the visuals, writing music that reflects the optimism of a character, versus the disaster we know is imminent. When a Cockney soldier climbs a tree for a better view, Max plays a sprightly version of the WWI tune "Pack Up Your Troubles." (*"Happily . . . aren't I cute??"*) Its rickety-tum cheer continues until a gunshot kills the soldier instantly.

Later, a circling pilot spots the surviving men and lands, unaware that snipers surround him. As the Sergeant and Morelli frantically try to wave him away, the pilot—misinterpreting their gestures—grins, waves, and exits his plane, his step accompanied by a jaunty, spit-and-polish march. This cheery music seems doubly incongruous as the film cross-cuts to the warning screams of the soldiers, but Steiner's nervy disconnect between what we see and what we hear creates a tension unlike any normal suspense cue. Again, a gunshot stops the music—and pilot—dead. Silence, then a sforzando minor chord. The Sergeant and Morelli stare at the body, their hopelessness becoming ours, like a flood of depression following a manic burst of joy.

Max's contribution is most heart-wrenching in the penultimate scene, as the Sergeant—now alone—reflects on the row of graves he has dug for his comrades. Against a weary version of the Sergeant's march, Steiner interweaves in succession each of the dead men's themes as countermelodies. Only the most inattentive viewer can fail to picture each fallen soldier—an effect nonexistent without score. Steiner's final cue is a hushed restatement of the "Arab" theme. One man has survived, but the desert has won, in what may be the most pessimistic coda the composer ever wrote.

For the film's UK release, RKO replaced this haunting finale with the upbeat 17th-century fife and drum tune "British Grenadiers." Unfortunately, this version of *Patrol* is now the one most widely available. Its musically bland coda, although okayed by Steiner, was not intended to be heard outside Britain.[10]

As usual, Max became giddy as his latest marathon neared an end. Reel 5: *"Bernard: This is the Jewish soldier, who is delirious! (just as I am all the time—or maybe drunk!)"* Recording of the final score was finished at 4:30 a.m. on January 19.[11]

Just one day later, RKO began its promotion of *Patrol* with a live one-hour radio dramatization, complete with Steiner score, and probably conducted by the sleep-deprived Max. "Exceptionally fine background music from the film," *Variety* opined, "is almost in itself a satisfactory program."[12]

That sentiment was echoed in review after review when *The Lost Patrol* opened on February 16. "Steiner must be credited with a large contribution to the success of the venture," *Hollywood Spectator* observed. "He composed a score that gives the whole production life. Without music *The Lost Patrol* would have been a picture of unrelieved anguish, one that would have been too harrowing for any audience."[13] In his scrapbook, Steiner underlined this in red, along with encomiums in other reviews, one of which compared him to Shostakovich.[14]

THE LOST PATROL MARKED A TIPPING POINT in the perception of film music. Few critics or producers would again question the inclusion of a score, and when the Motion Picture Academy added a music category to the Oscars in 1935, *The Lost Patrol* became the first dramatic title to be nominated. (A Columbia musical, *One Night of Love*, took home the trophy.)

A grim thriller that once seemed unreleasable was now a hit. After that, Louise Klos recalled, RKO "left [Max] alone completely."[15]

But Steiner hardly had time to celebrate; more than three dozen scoring and supervisory jobs awaited his attention. The best was a pet project of Pandro Berman that has lost little of its power. *Of Human Bondage* was an unflinching adaptation of British author W. Somerset Maugham's novel. Lester Cohen's script telescoped the book's 30-year timeline, focusing on its hero Philip Carey's relationship with Mildred Rogers, a crude waitress who exploits his devotion.

For his leads, Berman hired international star Leslie Howard, pairing him with an ambitious but largely unproven actress borrowed from Warner Bros. The 25-year-old Bette Davis knew that the showy, unsympathetic role of Mildred was her ticket to stardom, and attacked the part with a ferocity that made Leslie Howard sit up and fight for every scene.[16] Under John Cromwell's direction, the movie crackled with carnal, sado-masochistic tension.

(MS Papers; L. Tom Perry Special Collections, Brigham Young University)

"It will probably be one of the best pictures we have ever made," Berman wrote his bosses. "Its box-office I cannot vouch for as it will depend upon whether the public will accept a fine realistic picture."[17] His concerns were confirmed at a preview that April. "It was a total disaster," Berman said decades later. "The audience would not accept the character of this girl, nor the fact that the man tolerated her character with as much patience as he displayed. . . . By the time it was over at least half of the audience had left the theater. Naturally we were very depressed."[18]

The film's release was delayed, and a now-familiar process of musical triage began. "*Of Human Bondage* is to be run for you tomorrow at 10:30 a.m. in Room 2," editorial head James Wilkinson wrote Max on April 30. "Mr. Cromwell is especially anxious that you attend."[19]

Steiner loved the film. In Philip, he recognized himself as a youth, yearning to be an artist and foolishly, obsessively, in love. In Max's case, it was not with a Mildred but with a Mabel—Funston, the actress he followed from Vienna to London, only to learn she had married another. *Bondage* became "my favorite story, being somewhat related to an actual happening in my life," he wrote in a 1934 article.

Steiner's new score was less complex than *The Lost Patrol* but just as effective. Credits introduces his main theme: an intoxicating waltz, playfully titled in his score "Valse Louise" (*"Appassionato . . . make this as romantic as possible"*).*[20] The tune's opening phrase climbs ecstatically from a low A-flat to a plaintive G-natural above, then takes two chromatic steps down before resting on C. In its swoony lyricism it represents the Mildred that Philip imagines, not the reality. Steiner's intent is to take us inside Philip's mind, beyond rationality, to make us feel his *idée fixe* and to explain "the power that is holding him to her," he wrote. "That her physical charm has created in his mind a spiritual loveliness with which he endows her."[21] By 1934, Max was a confident and often insightful writer in his second language of English.

While Philip struggles to read a school book in his noisy flat, he sees a vision of Mildred and hears her waltz. This leads to a striking effect: as Philip snaps out of his dream, the waltz suddenly stops with an editorial hard cut mid-note. Steiner's pleasure in such experimentation is palpable, as he tests how far he can go in using music and sound for psychological effect.

Another bold choice would be the score's most talked-about element. Philip has a clubfoot, the inward turning of one of his feet. It cripples him psychologically as well as physically. Close-ups of his limping walk are a visual leitmotif; Steiner intensifies Philip's self-consciousness with a two-note pattern, softly dissonant, that mirrors, but does not precisely "mickey-mouse," his steps.

The composer is equally attuned to Mildred. *"Through this entire scene, Bette Davis walks like a cat! (noiseless) . . . This is a sort of seduction scene! Only the girl is a 'bastard' and doesn't mean it!"* Davis had played a small role in an earlier Steiner-scored film, 1931's *Way Back Home*. On *Bondage*, he was inspired by her electrifying presence, and also attracted. Being seduced by his leading ladies—at least by their celluloid forms—was a regular part of his creative process.

Predictably, Max's sketches are filled with flippant comments (*"French horn or Trader Horn [a hit MGM movie]—I feel horny today!"*). But some of

---

* On another score that year, Max wrote a private dedication to Louise "with love and lots of arpeggios, her composer conductor pianist cat catcher drunkard Gentile." (Inscription on sheet music, "I Wish I Were a Fisherman," written for 1934 film *Stingaree*, LSE, Box 2.)

Bette Davis and Leslie Howard in a publicity still from *Of Human Bondage*.

Bondage's "jokes" reflect a new preoccupation. *"End of Reel and segue to next part . . . Adolf Hitler." "Scene about Mildred's Tuberculosis. Note: This is a very cheerful picture—Hitler!"* In January 1933, Adolf Hitler had been appointed chancellor of Germany. By 1934, he had begun filling concentration camps with political dissidents and Jews.

Only 325 miles separated Berlin from Vienna, where Gabor, Mitzi, and other family members lived. The specter of an anti-Semitic dictator close to his parents' home joined a growing list of stresses in Max's life. None was more debilitating than his round-the-clock work schedule. *"It's now 3:45 A.M. and*

I don't give a damn if I ever see Gower Street again! How are you, Papa? [Kaun had become a father.] *I am too tired to try to become one tonight! Some other time, maybe . . . "*

Reviews of *Bondage* vindicated Berman's faith in the project, earning raves for Davis and Steiner—with some exceptions. In his book *Our New Music*, Aaron Copland bemoaned Max's "unfortunate idea of making his music limp whenever the club-footed hero walked across the scene, with a very obvious and, it seemed to me, vulgarizing effect."[22]

The criticism smarted. Years later, Steiner addressed it in an interview: "The 'sick' music for the lame man . . . has been criticized as bad taste musically, but it fits the picture. Walking must have a musical accompaniment—low perhaps. The regular symphonic writers are unwilling to follow the play in this matter, and so are unwilling to do this work. But there is a unity in my music, exactly similar to the unity in Wagner's operas."[23]

Steiner preferred the review he received from conductor Leopold Stokowski, who wrote a letter "telling me that the scoring of this limping walk was a stroke of genius. . . . I greatly treasure this tribute and still have it framed and hanging on the wall in my home."[24]

As Berman predicted, *Of Human Bondage* was a drama of quality—and of limited box office appeal.[25] Berman soon resigned as studio production chief, resuming his role as RKO's finest maker of individual films.

The paths of Steiner and Davis would not cross again until 1937. In the meantime, Max served as the musical voice for another blonde actress who specialized in tales of passion and self-sacrifice. Patrician in look, measured in vocal cadence, Ann Harding excelled at portraying women who thought and felt more than they said.

Harding's career reached its apex in 1934, with a pair of dramas that elicited two of Steiner's most tender scores. In *The Life of Vergie Winters*, the actress portrayed a milliner from the wrong side of the tracks whose two-decade affair with a politician (John Boles) results in a child she must give away. Later she is wrongfully imprisoned for her lover's murder. Banal in its plot, *Winters* surprises in its telling: during scenes showing townspeople gathered for communal events—a political rally, a funeral—we hear the characters' private thoughts, spoken on the soundtrack, setting up the dichotomy between their public faces and true feelings.

Steiner builds most of his score on a single theme. Like Vergie herself, it is unpretentious and exquisite. One can picture Max sitting in the glow of a screening room, transfixed by Harding's radiant close-ups—then writing her a musical love letter, in support of her calm, contralto voice.

Two sequences stand out. The opening scene is a flash-forward, in which citizens fill the streets for politician John Shadwell's funeral. A band plays Mendelssohn's doleful Op. 62, No. 3 (Funeral March). The camera lifts us from street level to an overlooking prison cell. Inside is Vergie, haggard and silently weeping. Steiner's orchestra subtly joins in with the diegetic street band, adding soaring string countermelodies to the Mendelssohn. Score has become a brilliantly orchestrated requiem, expressing what Vergie cannot, and placing our sympathy with her before she has even spoken.

Later, Vergie sits alone picturing the wedding of her daughter, which takes place that day and which she cannot attend. As she imagines the ceremony, Steiner's delicate theme for Vergie wafts in and out of Wagner's wedding march, sometimes playing as countermelody, sometimes subtly replacing it. In the early 1930s, only RKO created such scenes in which dialogue vanished for minutes, and a fusion of music and image drove the narrative. The studio knew it could count on Steiner.

Vergie Winters marked the first collaboration of Max and Louis Kaufman, a 29-year-old violinist from Oregon who would balance a three-decade concert career with Hollywood sessions.* "I always enjoyed working with him," Louis said of Steiner. "He was invariably polite and good-natured, exceedingly meticulous, and knew exactly what orchestral color fitted each scene. . . . If [orchestrators] did not achieve the effects that Max envisioned, he would call out corrections on the recording stage, such as 'Woodwinds play at bar B to D, horns tacet.' Or 'Flutes play that phrase instead of oboes.' Orchestrators and copyists on the set hurriedly copied out parts for waiting players."[26]

Kaufman's violin is prominent in *Vergie*, although "Max didn't use solos" often, observed Louis's wife Annette. "He preferred a less obtrusive 'section' sound."[27] The composer soon counted the Kaufmans among his closest friends. "You have to imagine Max's charming soft voice," Annette recalled, "the charm, wit and warmth of Max's lovable personality. He had a slight accent, like all the Viennese—Lotte Lehmann, Luise Rainer, Anton Walbrook. He was a perfectionist in his composition and conducting."[28] But unlike another friend of the Kaufmans, Bernard Herrmann, Max "never became cross in conducting."[29]

Two months after *Vergie Winters*'s release, another Harding vehicle, *The Fountain*, reached theaters. Its story may sound familiar: during wartime, two

---

* In 1947, Kaufman made history with the first recording of Vivaldi's *The Four Seasons*, an award-winning album that helped spark renewed interest in the composer.

men love the same woman. One is the husband she admires. The other has her heart, but gives her up for a larger ideal. The action mostly takes place in one location, and the lovers are haunted by a tune played on solo piano. But there, similarities to *Casablanca* end. *The Fountain* is set during World War I; it has no hissable villains; and surprisingly, the male rivals form a strong bond of friendship. In the face of war, the film suggests, humanity's only hope is in forgiveness and love.

Its melancholy tone is crystalized in Steiner's main theme, a minor-key waltz of rare beauty and sadness. Nearly an hour into the movie a new theme is heard, evoking the spiritual love felt by Julie (Harding) for her dying husband, Rupert (Paul Lukas). Later, Julie plays this "spiritual" melody on the piano as her husband listens. After several seconds, she pauses, then plays the waltz, which by now is linked to her lover (Brian Aherne). Rupert's expression shows that he understands the change. Without a word of dialogue, music has advanced the story.

By summer 1934, Steiner had worked on more than one hundred films— and to his mounting frustration, the amount he had earned in ASCAP royalties was less than $20.[30] Max sent the group a series of pleading letters. The only reply he received was from a secretary, informing him that a recently issued royalty check of $1.32 was a mistake.[31]

The message was clear: as far as ASCAP was concerned, Max wasn't worth $1.32.

He also was disappointed by the commercial failure of his movie songs and themes published as sheet music. In 1934, Max wrote several tunes that he hoped would be used in RKO's *Stingaree*, a bizarre operetta-western starring Richard Dix as a heroic bandit who kidnaps and falls in love with a singer (Irene Dunne). All but two of his songs were rejected.[32] Inevitably, his sketches for *Stingaree*'s underscore re-christened the film *Stinkaree*.*[33]

It was in this aggravated, overworked mindset that RKO's music chief began work on what would be the studio's biggest production of the year.

Pandro S. Berman was eager to capitalize on the success of *Flying Down to Rio* by casting Astaire and Rogers in a movie of their own. On a trip to London, Berman saw Fred onstage in Cole Porter's *Gay Divorce*, which Berman "thought would be an ideal vehicle."[34] The project moved ahead, now titled *The Gay Divorcee*—the extra "e" due to censors who would not

---

* Alert viewers will spot Steiner conducting the concert hall finale, shot on Universal's *Phantom of the Opera* stage.

condone the idea of a gay (happy) divorce.[35] Berman assigned Mark Sandrich to direct, and commissioned songs from two teams—Con Conrad and Herb Magidson, and Mack Gordon and Harry Revel—retaining only "Night and Day" from Porter's stage score.

Max was tasked with providing Astaire with musicians during rehearsals, composing some of the underscore, supervising the orchestration of songs and dances, and conducting recording sessions. One of his first actions was hiring Hal Borne, the pianist who by now was a member of the local musicians union. Along with Hermes Pan, Borne would "lay out their dances," the pianist recalled. "I'd play and Fred would say, 'Now the second chorus, can you make an improvisation?' And I said, 'Sure, and I'll improvise around the melody . . . "[36]

Once the piano score of a dance was approved, Steiner assigned the music to an orchestrator—or two, or three—until he and Astaire were satisfied. Then Max conducted a playback recording for filming. Astaire often came to sessions to discuss tempos and other details. "He would ask for particular orchestral effects under the dancing," Arlene Croce wrote. "Drums were never loud enough for film in a jazz number, and he liked sudden alternations of *pp* and *ff*."[37]

Louise recalled with delight days when Fred and Ginger visited the orchestra, to compare dance steps with the music being recorded.[38] During an arrangement, Astaire and Steiner often stopped the orchestra to showcase the taps, percussive instruments of their own.

Most of *The Gay Divorcee*'s songs were sung live on set. The most charming example is Astaire's "A Needle in a Haystack." The shifting distance of his voice in relation to an overhead microphone reveals the live-on-set capture. In tandem with the dance he performs in a single take, the scene offers a simulacrum of Astaire's live stage performances.

The "soft piano" method of recording a guide track, then adding orchestra later, was used for most scenes. An exception was Astaire's tap dance to the movie's first song, "Don't Let It Bother You." The use of live orchestra on set, Steiner wrote, was "a very difficult procedure . . . because of the camera set-ups my orchestra and I were sometimes as far as a hundred feet away from [Astaire]. On a big stage where sound might have traveled at a rate of ¾ [of a] second, I had to be a little ahead of Mr. Astaire's taps . . . to offset this so-called sound lag."[39]

No such challenge occurred during the filming on July 3 of *Divorcee*'s most famous sequence: Astaire and Rogers's "courtship" dance to "Night and Day," shot using a prerecorded guide track.[40] By then, excitement about the movie

Max confers with Fred Astaire and director Mark Sandrich. (MS Papers; L. Tom Perry Special Collections, Brigham Young University)

was spreading at the studio, and as expectations climbed, *Divorcee*'s dance finale "The Continental" expanded to a record 17-1/2 minutes.

Max and team were under the gun, and Steiner grew defensive. Scribbled notes on the score of "The Continental" exude tension. On a section blending orchestrations by Bernhard Kaun, Clifford Vaughan, and Eddie Sharpe: *"Do these over as Max thinks they smell!"*[41]

Music costs nearly doubled, from $24,753.95 to $46,333.49.[42] Overage reports exude passive-aggressive frustration. "It was necessary to remake guide track for the CONTINENTAL Dance Number due to the metronome being inaccurate." "This overage is due to the extreme difficulty in scoring the CONTINENTAL and the inadequate time we had to prepare same." Handed one such report for his signature, Max exploded. In oversized handwriting, he wrote, "I resent this as a slur on my unimpeachable integrity for the last five years. We can easily offset this overage by cutting 'The Continental' number out entirely. Max R. W. Steiner, Head of Department."[43]

Max's burst of temperament may have had another cause. Days after his "signing" of the overage report, he made a conciliatory visit to the office of

Fred Astaire and Ginger Rogers in a publicity still from *The Gay Divorcee*. "The Continental."

studio executive Frank O'Heron. Steiner, O'Heron wrote RKO president B. B. Kahane, was distressed over "the Nazi situation in Vienna, which . . . is involving [his mother] in probable loss of her property unless she gets immediate relief from Max. . . . He would like a loan from us of $3,500. . . . I recommend that we make this advance and I am sure we will get it back many times over. Max is not a person who will be outdone in generosity and I think it is distinctly to the company's advantage to do this."[44]

By 1934, Austria's democracy had given way to dictatorship. Chancellor Engelbert Dollfuss's policy of "Austrofascism" reflected growing national sympathy with Germany's Nazi leaders. On July 25, Dollfuss was assassinated by Nazis in an attempted government takeover. His successor, Chancellor Kurt Schuschnigg, described the country as a "German state." For Max's parents, now separated, and his other family, Austria was a dangerous place to live.

Whatever the exact details of Mitzi's financial woes, the crisis was resolved when Steiner signed a new contract with RKO. A $300 portion of his weekly $850 salary was subtracted to repay the loan.[45] But Max's resentment over the new contract festered; and after three draining months on *The Gay Divorcee*, with some recording sessions lasting until 3:30 a.m., Steiner snapped.

THE DAY WAS SATURDAY, SEPTEMBER 29. With *Divorcee* finally complete, B. B. Kahane probably looked forward to a weekend of relative calm, as the film's negative traveled to New York. A studio memo was delivered to the RKO president's attention—but it was not the shipping confirmation he expected.

> From: Max Steiner
> Subject: Office Hours
>
> TO ALL LOVERS OF NIGHT SHIFTS!
>
> Effective Monday morning, October First, I can be found at the Studio during the hours: 9:00 am to 12:30 pm; and from 1:30 pm to 6:00 pm, every day except Sundays and Holidays. However, I WILL NOT be found, any longer, during the hours from 6:00pm to 9:00am next morning, as in the past.
>
> Should this not be satisfactory to anyone, I shall be only too happy to cancel my contract.
>
> Furthermore, I just received an offer from the President of the May Company, Eighth at Broadway, Los Angeles, California, who wants to obtain my services, on a long term contract, as a "BED-TRYER" and that looks awfully good to me.[46]

By the time his memo was delivered, Max was en route to Mexico for a weekend of gambling at Agua Caliente, Hollywood's favorite south-of-the-border resort. If he meant his note to inspire a sympathetic chuckle from the boss, he grossly miscalculated. B. B. Kahane wanted Steiner's head—and after that, a new musical director.

For years Murray Spivack had done his best to shield Max from his own worst instincts. Ironically, Spivack was returning that weekend from his own trip to Mexico:

When I got [back] to the studio, I read Kahane's answer to Steiner's letter. He said, "I did not like your letter, and it only remains for you to set the date that your resignation becomes effective."

I didn't know what the devil to do. I wanted to save Max's job, because I knew he was a very fine composer and a good conductor. And Kahane had an assistant by the name of Joe Nolan, who knew nothing about the motion picture business, and he kept saying, "What does that crazy fiddle player think he's doing? We're getting [conductor] Nat Shilkret!" I said, "I've worked with Shilkret. He's not a composer."[47]

Fast forward to Thursday, October 4, and the arrival of another memo:

Dear Mr. Kahane,
Forgive me for not answering your note before this, but I have been away from the studio for three days sick and exhausted from the terrific hours I had put in on "Gay Divorce." [sic]

If my note has offended you, I am sincerely sorry. Believe me, it was not intended to be offensive and should never have been sent to you personally at all. I simply told my girl to send it to all departments like all the regular inter-office correspondence, and I thought everyone would get as big a laugh out of it as Eddie Eckles got . . .

Please set the date as soon as you see fit for my resignation to become effective, as I have no intention whatsoever of embarrassing the company in any way.

Thanking you for your kindness and good-will in the past, I remain,
Respectfully yours,
Max Steiner[48]

The memo saved his job. But according to Spivack, Max had not written it. *He* had.

"I dictated a letter to [Max's secretary] stating, 'I'm sorry that you read my joking letter of a serious nature, and since you apparently are dissatisfied with my work, it now remains for you to set the date that my resignation is to become effective.' So in other words, I passed the buck to him."[49] Spivack's memory of the memo's content, nearly 50 years later, supports his claim of authorship.

Whatever the case, Steiner returned from Mexico a chastened employee— but his relationship with the studio was permanently damaged. The incident also inspired RKO to hire an additional music director: Alberto Colombo, a former arranger for Paul Whiteman.

THE FILM SCORES OF MAX STEINER

1934 Releases

The Meanest Gal in Town (12/33)
The Lost Patrol (12/33–1/34). AAN.
Stingaree (1/34–4/34)
Strictly Dynamite (2/34–3/34)
Keep 'Em Rolling (3/34)
Finishing School (5/34)
Murder on the Blackboard (5/34)
The Life of Vergie Winters (4/34–6/34)
We're Rich Again (4/34–5/34)
Of Human Bondage (5/34–6/34)
Down to Their Last Yacht (2/34–6/34) Often cited as RKO's worst release, this incoherent musical comedy led to the firing of producer Lou Brock (*Flying Down to Rio*). Steiner contributed one song and served as musical director, but emerged unscathed.
The Age of Innocence (6/34–8/34)
The Fountain (7/34–8/34)
The Richest Girl in the World (8/34)
The Gay Divorcee (5/34–10/34). AAN.
The Little Minister (9/34–12/34). Max's chamber-like score for this J. M. Barrie adaptation starring Katharine Hepburn is among his most winsome of the 1930s.

Spivack became convinced that by championing Steiner, he had written his own pink slip. "I could read the handwriting on the wall . . . I thought, 'Okay, now I'm going to look for another job.'"[50] Like many graduates of RKO, the sound recordist went on to greater glory, winning an Oscar in 1970 after decades of acclaim for such films as *Spartacus, West Side Story, My Fair Lady*, and *The Sound of Music*. But his relationship with Steiner had a sad coda. "I didn't find out until three or four years later from [Louise] that he was very jealous of me. And I said, 'I can't understand why. I didn't write music, I was just trying to help him as much as I could.' That's when I vowed I would never 'marry' another music director."[51]

In later years, Steiner spoke of Spivack as one of his favorite collaborators at RKO. Max's "jealousy" was probably a passing mood, triggered by anger at a studio that considered him replaceable with a conductor like Nat Shilkret.

But for the time being, Steiner's frustrations were patched over. *The Gay Divorcee* was the triumph its studio prayed for, earning a staggering $584,000 in profit.[52] It received five Academy Award nominations, taking home one for "The Continental"—the first Best Song winner. *Hollywood Reporter* swooned over cast, songs, and "the excellent arrangements of all the music as conceived by Max Steiner."[53]

The makers of *The Gay Divorcee* had cracked a musical code that, for a time, would generate RKO's most reliable money-earners. And for Max, the months ahead would bring not only choruses of acclaim, but also the highest honor Hollywood could bestow.

PART FOUR

Emperor

11

Monarch of Sound

DESPITE SIMMERING TENSIONS between Steiner and the front office, RKO's musical director achieved his highest public profile yet in 1935.

By now, the 47-year-old had many friends among the press, who profiled him in articles that ranged from insightful to absurd. "Today, Max Steiner, the RKO generalissimo of music, is hailed as a foremost composer for the screen," proclaimed the *Illustrated Daily News* of the "Little Monarch of Sound."[1] "His face furrowed with concentration, he arises hurriedly, as if startled.... He is business-like and alert, but when he speaks about music the inflection changes . . . to that emotional intensity which the greatest of the arts calls for."

Perhaps the most reliable picture of Steiner at work was written for the magazine *Author and Composer*, whose writer was told by Max:

> I read almost all leading newspapers, as a composer must be well informed. I get newspapers from New York, Vienna, and other metropolitan cities throughout the world. Then, too, I'm buying new records all the time.... For here in Hollywood I feel isolated, and as a consequence must keep in touch with the trend of the times . . .
>
> I'm never convinced that any song [of mine] is good until somebody else tells me it is good. I think over a theme song for some time. Sometimes I'm convinced that it's good, and in that event, I'm usually right. But at previews of my music I'm usually scared stiff!
>
> I'm interested in the opinion of everyone on the lot. If the carpenter tells me it's wrong, I don't pass it off lightly, but immediately ask him just why he thinks it's wrong. In the final analysis we must compose music for the millions of people who attend picture houses throughout the country, and not for professional musicians.[2]

Trade journals quoted his witticisms ("He's every other inch a gentleman," Max supposedly said of a colleague).[3] He was even made a Kentucky Colonel by that state's governor, Ruby Laffoon—a commission that the composer, still infatuated with all things military, viewed with pride.[4]

Most risible was an RKO press release describing the "oddest fan letter" Steiner received. It came from an 80-year-old woman in South Carolina who "had seen the picture *Break of Hearts*," a turgid Katharine Hepburn–Charles Boyer romance brightened by Max's Schumann-esque love theme. Supposedly, the fan "had tried everywhere to purchase a copy of the theme song . . . 'And unless I get one within the next week I shall commit suicide.' Steiner promptly . . . dispatched it to the woman by airmail."[5]

Hyperbole aside, Max was generous to his fans. Around 1932, he began keeping discs of many of his scores. These were made on acetate for instant playback at recording sessions, since the soundtrack to be used in the movie was captured on film that required developing. At his own expense, Steiner made copies of these acetates, distributing them to friends and industry colleagues.[6]

DURING A FILM'S SHOOTING, it was rare for a director to solicit Steiner's input—which made it doubly gratifying when John Ford contacted Max *before* making his second movie for RKO. *The Informer*, based on Liam O'Flaherty's novel, was tightly budgeted at $243,000. The front office had little faith in the film,[7] which followed the long last night of Gypo Nolan (Victor McLaglen), a revolutionary in 1922 Dublin who sells out his friend, a wanted IRA agent, to British soldiers. Guilt slowly consumes the "gutter Judas,"[8] who is killed before sunrise by his former friends.

Ford eschewed his usual lean style, giving *The Informer* the look of a German expressionist nightmare. He filled street scenes with fog—a perfect metaphor for the brutish Gypo's confusion (and a good way to hide a scarcity of sets). Ford had never made such a stylized sound film, which may explain why he was solicitous of Steiner's involvement. Max's operatic scoring, and his fondness for catching visual action, could help put viewers inside the mind of the hyper-sensitized, increasingly paranoid Gypo.

Before screenwriter Dudley Nichols began work, he and Ford "had one fruitful session together with Max Steiner, who was to write the music; Van Nest Polglase, who was to do the sets; Joe August, the cameraman; and a couple of technicians. This, to my mind, is the proper way to approach a film production—and it is, alas, the only time in twenty-five years I have known it to be done: a group discussion before a line of the script is written."[9]

Two sides of Max: proud Kentucky Colonel and RKO jester, abetted by assistant director Freddie Fleck. (MS Papers; L. Tom Perry Special Collections, Brigham Young University)

That meeting gave Steiner time to ensure legal clearance of Irish folk tunes he would use. Before Gypo betrays Frankie (Wallace Ford), the men share a lusty chorus of "The Wearing of the Green." Later, as Nolan contemplates Frankie's "Wanted" poster—and as his act of betrayal haunts him—Steiner revives the song in ghostly variations for horns. As a street balladeer sings the sentimental "Rose of Tralee," Steiner adds a soft wash of dissonance, as Frankie's crumpled "Wanted" poster wafts through the air and sticks to Gypo's leg like a phantom.

Max's original themes show how much he had matured since 1932. True, his "Gypo" motif—the score's central motto—is a march; but unlike its predecessors, it could represent no other character than Nolan. Its relentless quarter-note rhythm suggests the military force hovering over Gypo, as well as the footsteps of the imaginary nemesis that follows him (*"Timpani on beats—very heavy"*).[10] Over this rhythm, Steiner introduces a sharply accented, minor-key melody—one made "Irish" by the syncopated snap in the last two notes of its phrases. (It is a rhythm common in Irish and Scottish folk songs like "Comin' Thro' the Rye": *Gin a bo-dee / Meets a bo-dee . . .*) Composed during filming, the theme was played for Victor McLaglen, who reportedly adjusted Gypo's lumbering walk to match the music's rhythms.[11]

The motif for Katie, the prostitute Gypo hopes to flee with to America, is rhythmically related to Nolan's theme, proof of their intimacy; but its tempo is slow and defeated, like Katie. Played with sighing *portamento*, its *doloroso* melody is almost a blues aria. The most effective use of it is during a scene in which she does not appear: as Gypo stares at Frankie's poster and decides to inform, Kate's motif returns on the soundtrack. It tells us why Nolan will betray his comrade for 20 pounds—the price of two boat tickets to America.

For most of *The Informer*, temptation is evoked by another theme. As a British soldier pushes money across a table to Gypo, we hear four shimmery descending notes (B-flat–E–C–A-flat) against a dissonant chord (E–D–B-flat). The first "fall" in the four-note theme, from B-flat to E, is a *tritone*—a dissonance sometimes called "the devil's interval" due to the unsettling mood it creates. The fall from E to C to A-flat creates a chord one half-tone away from a comfortable harmony, creating a sense of irresolution and unease.

The idea of a four-note "coin" theme was likely inspired by an image 28 minutes into the movie: after Gypo has begun spending his blood money, four sparkling coins drop from his pocket at Frankie's wake, triggering suspicion. The "coin" motif also links the music to the biblical quote that begins the film: "Then Judas repented himself—and cast down the thirty pieces of silver."

Steiner synchronizes *The Informer*'s music to physical movement with balletic precision. The striking of a match on a lamppost; the flight of a burning "Wanted" poster up a chimney . . . Never again would the composer be so overt in his Wagnerian technique—or, as his detractors would put it, so heavy-handed in his mickey-mousing.

But while his literalness in *The Informer* can grow tiresome, many effects retain their power. One stands out. After being tried and found guilty by his peers, Gypo waits in a barnlike cell, water dripping from above, as his captors outside draw lots to choose his executioner. "I wanted to catch each one of these drops musically," Max recalled. "The property man and I worked for days trying to regulate the water tank so it dripped in tempo and I could accompany it."[12] Steiner deliberately slows the scene's rhythm, heightening tension with a variation on his four-note "coins" theme. This ostinato repeats with deliberate monotony for more than two-and-a-half minutes, growing in volume as Gypo seeks a way to break free. Music does not exactly copy the dripping water; rather, it uses the visual as a jumping-off point to thrilling effect.

During Gypo's final escape attempt, music explodes with Kong-like violence—or as Max facetiously requests: *"95 Drums, 18 Trumpets, 208 Violins, 49 Cellos, 4 Trombones, 1 Harp, 1 Flute . . . S.O.S. HELP!!!!!!"* Then

Victor McLaglen in a publicity still from *The Informer*.

a sudden silence, as four shots are fired into Gypo on the street. Dying, he staggers toward a church, the "coins" motif now a thunderous death march. "I tried out many different effects attending those slow, faltering footsteps," Max wrote. "Matching step to musical note would have been either funny or distorted . . . so I used a hit-and-miss system, timing the footsteps perfectly and then *avoiding* them in the music so that the beat notes of the theme did not coincide with the fall of each footstep."[13]

As Gypo shoves the church doors open, a startling *ff* chord banishes the "coins" motif: Nolan has rejected greed. The church's sole occupant is Mrs. McPhillip, Frankie's mother. Gypo's theme becomes a plaintive query for violin, as he crawls toward the woman. "'Twas I that informed on your son, Mrs. McPhillip. Forgive me." As Frankie's mother speaks—"You didn't know what you were doing"—her forgiveness is reinforced by a wordless choir, as Gypo stretches his arms, Christ-like, and proclaims, "Frankie! Your mother forgives me!"

This finale has not aged well. Its exaggerated tableau is accompanied by a benedictory "Amen," which critic Christopher Palmer called "the score's only calamity . . . bereft of any true sense of spiritual ecstasy."[14] This finale for organ, chimes, and choir is far from Steiner's best "spiritual" music; but nothing short of Bach's *St. Matthew Passion* could add a truly redemptive lift to such an artificial scene.

As Max finished his work, expectations for *The Informer* remained dire at RKO. "Who wants to look at a picture that is always in the fog?" B. B. Kahane groused.[15]

The answer came in May 1935, and it astonished the studio.

"This is not entertainment, this is life," declared the *Detroit Evening Times*. "Thanks to the writing of O'Flaherty, the direction of John Ford, the music of Max Steiner. . . . It towers above the average movie like Gibraltar above the sea."[16] *Hollywood Citizen-News* proclaimed that "Without the masterful musical genius of Max Steiner the picture would not be one-third the picture it now is."[17]

Virtually every major review was a rave, and nearly all praised Max. Richard Watts, critic for the *L.A. Herald Tribune*, took time to see *The Informer* with and without music, then penned a second evaluation: "With a really stirring score . . . the picture is even finer than it seemed to me on first sight."[18] The *New York Times* asked Steiner to pen an article dissecting his approach. He also heard from friends old and new. Wrote Gus Kahn—lyricist of "Pretty Baby," "It Had to Be You," and other standards—"This is my first 'fan' letter.[19] I think your score for 'The Informer' is the finest that has ever been written for any picture." And from Frank Capra, a telegram: "DEAR MAX YOUR SCORING ON THE INFORMER WAS THE BEST I HAVE EVER HEARD. MAZELTOFF."[20]

The year 1935's most surprising hit earned RKO a hefty profit of $325,000.[21] And on March 5, 1936, *The Informer* took home four Academy Awards—for Best Director, John Ford; Best Actor, Victor McLaglen; Best Adaptation writer, Dudley Nichols; and for Best Scoring, Max Steiner. It was Max's first win, in a category just two years old. For Steiner, whose occasional boastfulness masked a constant need for approval, the Oscar confirmed that he had reached the peak of his profession.

That *The Informer* feels less compelling today does not undercut its significance. The movie elevated John Ford from a jobbing director to a revered poet of the cinema. And it confirmed Steiner's reputation as Hollywood's most innovative composer.

In 1939, Max was asked by the Academy to name "pictures, which, in Mr. Steiner's personal opinion, were milestones in the progress of screen music." He selected six: *The Jazz Singer; The King of Jazz,* Universal's epic Paul Whiteman revue; *100 Men and a Girl,* a Deanna Durbin comedy featuring conductor Leopold Stokowski; and three scores of his own: *Bird of Paradise, The Lost Patrol,* and *The Informer.*[22] In 1948, a radio adaptation of the film on *Ford Theater* broke with its usual format by using Steiner's score versus in-house music. Explained its producer, "We feel that in the case of the magnificent, history-making score you wrote for *The Informer,* it would be sacrilege for us to attempt to write new music."[23]

In time, even Steiner tired of such kudos. Recalled his friend Hugo Friedhofer, "Everybody would come to him years later and say, 'God, *The Informer.* That was a great score.' And Max would sort of break down and weep, that is to me, and say, 'I've done so many things since that I like so much better.'"[24]

IN 1935, WHAT FRUSTRATIONS HE FELT were not due to *The Informer.* After six years at RKO, Steiner was eager for a break and frustrated by his meager bank account. He was sending weekly checks to Gabor, alimony to Beatrice and Aubry, and spending lavishly on alcohol, cigars, gambling, and Louise.

As he would for decades, he ignored problems by immersing himself in work. Fortunately, 1935—his last full year at RKO—would be his most varied.

The Paris-set musical *Roberta,* based on Jerome Kern and Otto Harbach's Broadway hit, reunited Astaire and Rogers. It also gave Max a chance to redeem himself in the eyes of Kern, after his disappointing musical direction on *Sitting*

Pretty. Kern's enthusiasm for the resulting movie encouraged Steiner to ask the Broadway giant for a favor. As a "Non-Participating" member of ASCAP, "I haven't one cent of foreign royalties so far," he wrote Kern,[25] who replied the next day: "Your request for my intervention has received immediate attention."[26]

One month later, Max was elated to learn that ASCAP had elevated his status to Active. However, his earnings did not change; ASCAP still refused to recognize film scores as music eligible for domestic royalties.

BEFORE CAMERAS ROLLED ON *ROBERTA*, Pandro S. Berman was already planning the next Fred and Ginger extravaganza. In November 1934, he convinced America's most popular songwriter, Irving Berlin, to write music and lyrics for *Top Hat*.

Steiner and the wiry, intense Berlin worked together closely and well. They met often with the screenwriters and Mark Sandrich; the result was a silk-smooth integration of story, song, and dance. That cohesion is reflected in Dwight Taylor and Allan Scott's script. Their introduction to "Isn't This a Lovely Day (To Be Caught in the Rain)" notes that "The thunder is really a tympani effect and the lightning is a glissando which starts the music."[27]

Max's one preserved anecdote about the film's making typically involves panic:

> While recording *Top Hat,* one morning I overslept. I knew the orchestra was waiting for me, so I drove like a madman down Beachwood Avenue. I was stopped by a policeman who wanted to know where the fire was. When he examined my license he said, "Max Steiner? Are you the musician and composer?" I admitted that I was. "I'm so glad to meet you," he said shaking my hand, "but why were you driving so fast?" I explained, and he smiled. "I'm also a musician. I belong to the union and I'm the piccolo player for the Police Band. I play D-flat piccolo. What part for piccolo do you like best?" "[Sousa's] *Stars and Stripes,*" I answered. "Me, too," he said. "Come on. Never mind the ticket, I'll escort you to the studio."
>
> We went to Gower Street at what seemed like 90 miles an hour. When we arrived at the studio, the officer asked, "May I come in and listen a few minutes?" "Sure," I said gratefully. He parked his motorcycle outside of the stage, came in and listened for awhile.
>
> When I had a five-minute rest, he came over to me. "This was a wonderful experience. I must get back on duty, but please think of me sometime. Maybe you'll have an extra piccolo part, but don't forget to

Publicity stills from *Top Hat*. "The Piccolino."

write it in D-flat." I took his name and phone number, and shortly after that had something with a lot of piccolo runs in it. I put him on as an extra man. He was pretty good, and we remained friends.[28]

For Louise, the year of *Top Hat* would be what she often recalled as "the happiest part of my life."[29] True, Max squirmed whenever marriage was discussed: he "had a funny idea, maybe not so funny, that when one had the license that somehow romance flew out the window."[30] But they were seldom apart, during marathon sessions of composing and recording, and during weekend escapes for extravagant play.

Louise's 1935 diary gives a shorthand look at their life together: trips to the resort towns La Quinta, Coronado, Palm Springs, and Agua Caliente; gambling at the Clover Club and the racetrack; cocktails with songwriters Dorothy Fields and Jimmy McHugh; dinner parties with the Alfred Newmans.[31]

"Newman I had known as far back as World War One," Max later recalled.[32]

His wife Beth was a dear girl and very ambitious for her husband. One day I received a letter from her. It read, "Dear Max: Please do not call Alfred Al anymore. It sounds so Jewish and so unimportant, so please call him Alfred." I replied: "My dear Beth: I agree Al is very bad and always ruins everybody. Look at Al Jolson, a complete failure. Also Al Smith, governor of New York, another no good bum. I will also write to the governor of California requesting that he change the name of Alcatraz to Alfred-catraz, so people won't think it's a Jewish prison."

While I'm on the subject of Alfred Newman, I must tell you about one of his and Beth's parties. It was a masquerade party, and Al had a seven or eight piece orchestra playing Mozart. He was dressed as Mozart and conducted *Eine Kleine Nachtmusik*. My costume was simply a full dress suit with a red ambassadorial ribbon across my shirt. When I arrived the party was already in full swing, and one of [the musicians] was already stretched out on the floor in his Mozart suit.

As a gag, Alfred had Edward Everett Horton dressed as a butler announcing each guest as he arrived. He would call out: "Mr. Fredric March, a $50,000-a-picture man." "Miss Tallulah Bankhead, a $75,000-a-picture woman." When Tallulah was thus announced, she gave out with an enormous belch and remarked: "Oh, I beg your pardon. Somebody I ate, no doubt."

On safari with Louise—in La Quinta, California, 1934. (MS Papers; L. Tom Perry Special Collections, Brigham Young University)

By the end of 1935, RKO was miraculously showing a profit for the first time since 1931.[33] Steiner continued to pick and choose what films he would score, resulting in one missed opportunity: George Stevens's directorial breakthrough *Alice Adams*. It gave Katharine Hepburn her best role since

Little Women, and although Max assigned the score to Roy Webb, Steiner contributed a bittersweet waltz theme, "I Can't Dance Alone." Dorothy Fields wrote lyrics for a sheet music version, which sadly went unnoticed despite *Alice Adams*'s success.

One filmmaker to whom Steiner could never say no was Merian C. Cooper. In 1935 Coop and Schoedsack fulfilled another of their ambitions: a lush adaptation of H. Rider Haggard's fantasy novel *She*. RKO was less enthused about a tale involving a lost civilization, ruled by a beauteous but cruel queen who never grows old (Helen Gahagan). But the success of *King Kong* convinced Radio to roll the dice.

Steiner had barely a month to write more than 75 minutes of music, which demanded the scope and color of *Kong*. Fortunately, he was intrigued by the character of "a woman who lived fantastically, two hundred years after her time."[34] His theme for the Queen of Kor—"She Who Must Be Obeyed"— begins with three notes of musical *déjà vu*: a chromatic descent of G-flat to F to E that is identical to King Kong's theme. But for She (the character), the theme continues for another six notes, sliding sinuously downward before leaping up magisterially to C, then dropping an octave. Emotionally, the effect is one of mystery, followed by grandeur, followed by resignation—the Queen's character arc in nine notes.

She's secret world is discovered by a troupe of explorers, among them hero Leo Vincey (Randolph Scott) and Tanya, a Russian orphan (Helen Mack). Tanya inspires another melancholy "Russian" waltz; but this Tchaikovskian tune surpasses its predecessors in lyric expressiveness. When the Queen recognizes Tanya as her rival for Vincey, Max artfully interweaves their motifs. *"The Conflict! Queen's theme and Tanya's theme together as counterpoint. Kollossal!!!"*[35]

Kaleidoscopic harp glissandos evoke the supernatural Flame of Life responsible for *She*'s agelessness. Steady, heartbeat-like quarter notes suggest her obsession with time—a rhythmic idea Steiner sets up in the film's first shot, as the "ticking" rhythm of harp and winds matches the swinging hands of a clock.

The Queen may have been impervious to time's passage, but Steiner had no such luxury. *"Page 5 to follow—So God wills!"* Assigning some cues to Bernhard Kaun allowed him to focus on *She*'s musical showpiece: the climactic Hall of Kings ceremony, during which the Queen plans to execute Tanya. Steiner attacked with glee the composition of a pagan ballet—one whose dissonances and thunderous percussion nod to *The Rite of Spring*, but whose pulse-quickening modulations, reptilian woodwind snarls, and core theme—the She motif—are pure Steiner.

Ultimately, the Flame of Life betrays the Queen, changing her from beauty to desiccated corpse, as harp and tremolo strings create Wagnerian fire music. Back in England, beside a glowing hearth fire, Leo and Tanya reflect on the real "flame of life": love—an idea Steiner reinforces by gracefully intertwining the Flame theme with Tanya's.

Ecstatic to have met his deadline, Steiner's last sketch page explodes in an orgy of punnery. *"Hurrah! . . . I guess we're all full of 'She' now! Winnie 'Shee'han* [a Fox executive] *will love this!!!"*

She's aspirations toward mythic grandeur are undercut by its juvenile plot and stiff performances. But the movie has moments of otherworldly magic, and Steiner rightly valued his contribution highly. "This is probably the best music I ever wrote," he remarked in 1944, "although the picture was not a success. It is very symphonic and very modern."[36] Eleven years later, he called it "my best job to date."[37] And not long before his death, Steiner told a friend "that it was more advanced than *The Informer*, and it should have won the Oscar."[38]

On July 25, RKO hosted an unusual preview of *She*, held only for music critics. "All were very enthusiastic about the score," a studio memo reported, "and said it was an opera without arias."[39] One attendee wrote, "Most who will see the film will not realize the psychological changes of mood secured through musical effects, nor appreciate the ingenious craftsmanship. . . . But musicians should realize that in [film scores] there lies a field of tremendous potentiality."[40]

THE YEAR 1935 PRESENTED MAX with one more chance to demonstrate that "tremendous potentiality" with a score as invigorating as the movie it accompanied was misconceived.

Imagine making a film of *The Three Musketeers* in Hollywood, 1935. If the studio was Warner Bros., the movie would cast itself: Errol Flynn as dashing would-be musketeer D'Artagnan; Olivia de Havilland as Constance; Miriam Hopkins as scheming Milady DeWinter; Basil Rathbone as her ruthless enforcer Rochefort; Alan Hale, Patric Knowles, and Ian Hunter in the title roles.

Alas, RKO had no such bench to draw from. Promising early cast announcements (Laurence Olivier, Alan Hale) gave way to B-list actors (Walter Abel as D'Artagnan, Paul Lukas as Athos), and a director, Rowland V. Lee, utterly lacking panache.

Steiner proved the truest musketeer of all, creating an Oscar-worthy score that evokes the exuberant spirit of Dumas's immortal guardsmen in a way the actors cannot. By now, Max was attuned not only to a movie's

strengths but, more importantly, to its weaknesses. No other score of his works harder (without appearing to doing so) to raise the quality of the film it accompanies.

"I spent months of research in an old music library, studied all the old songs, but didn't use them. . . . I wrote new music, trying to make it suggestive of this period. . . . The dialogue was modern. Music that was too similar to that period, therefore, would have been dull."[41] Steiner struck a perfect balance: his score sounds baroque/classical when establishing the Paris of 1625, but it expands into thunderous orchestral Technicolor for action scenes.

To disguise the film's plodding pace, Max infuses it with buoyant melody. Its opening minutes could be a movie musical: as the title card appears, a drum corps beats a rousing march rhythm, joined by lively piccolo obbligato. Our mental picture of guardsmen on parade is heightened by the sound of a male chorus; they declaim Max's anthemic "Song of the Musketeers," with its boisterous call to *"Drink! Drink! Drink! To the Mus-ke-TEEEERS . . ."* The theme is the score's heart, a stirring call to arms and an affecting statement of brotherhood. (No film composer has surpassed Steiner's gift at evoking the fraternal love between men.)

Steiner responds strongly to the contrasting personalities of the heroines: the French Queen Anne, strong, yet compromised by a secret affair; and her delicate lady in waiting, Constance. Anne's theme is played by celli and violins, the lower strings' color giving her motif a maturity (*"Dignified"*)[42]. Constance's theme is written from the POV of her besotted admirer, D'Artagnan. Introduced by celeste and harp (*"a Harpsichord imitation"*), its first two notes jump an octave, like a soaring leap of the heart, then continue with a lyricism that now was second nature for a composer always inspired by the sight of a beautiful woman.

The outdoor "Fencing Drill" is shot and scored like a dance, with each lunge and parry timed to accented quarter notes. Above the pulse of drums, a clarion trumpet theme filled with octave leaps and martial triplets bracingly captures the force of these battle-tested men. (*"Old-fashioned Military Band—but mit 'guts'!"*). For its recording, Max tried an experiment. "He wanted to have an outdoor ambience to the sound of the music," a friend recalled. "So the recording was done outside. They went out at around midnight on the RKO lot, and they had to stop if an airplane went by or a car honked. Sure enough, if you listen to it on the acetate, it does have a different ambient quality about it."[43]

For chase scenes, the clip-clop rhythm of horses—from Milady de Winter's carriage to the Musketeers' racing steeds—motivates Steiner to write arguably the most exhilarating music of his RKO career. Reel 7: De Winter's minions attack the Musketeers. *"I want this whole thing to sound like hell let loose!"* Reel 10: Milady's race to Paris, with the Musketeers in pursuit. *"Coach galloping FURIOSO."* Steiner's musicians are now playing an astonishing 195 beats a minute—almost as fast as a metronome can click. This sequence "is the climax of the score," author J. B. Kaufman observed, "and Steiner unleashes a mighty torrent of music that sweeps away everything in its path . . . character themes reappear in turn, riding above this onrushing fury like pennants fluttering above a stampeding cavalry."[44]

King Kong's pencil sketch ran 114 pages. As Kaufman notes, the "*Musketeers*" sketch runs to a staggering 284 pages."[45]

In September 1935 a *New York Times* reporter was present, as Max struggled to record his most demanding work to date:

Steiner is feverishly trying to get the score written and recorded to meet an arbitrary release date set by an optimistic sales department . . .

His orchestra—there were thirty-six pieces—was assembled in the room. . . . His assistant was conducting. The rehearsal over, the composer put his head out of the monitor room, high up over the stage. He ordered changes in the seating of the musicians [and listened] through the recording channels to learn how it would sound coming from the screen. It seemed to satisfy him, for he emerged and relieved his assistant.

"Now," he said, "I want a little more fanfare in that part that goes ta-de-ta-ta-ta. That's where the Musketeers are kicking the hell out of the other guys. Give them a song of victory!" He always talked in plain language to his musicians. . . . On another occasion, he said, "When D'Artagnan raises his hand a second time, in the place where he looks like a producer turning down an option, give it a longer note."

. . . A bell rang, the lights were turned out, all but those on the stands and a small spotlight high in the rafters that shone down on the conductor's music. The scenes being scored were projected above the heads of the orchestra. Steiner led the musicians with his baton, one eye always on the screen to see how he was synchronizing. The first time he was a little fast and finished too soon. He slowed it down for the next take.[46]

The final recording is a testament to the exceptional quality of musicians Steiner had assembled—an ensemble now capable of sight-reading a score that would take many symphony orchestras days to rehearse.

THE FILM SCORES OF MAX STEINER

1935 Releases

Roberta (11/34–2/35)

Star of Midnight (1/35–3/35). William Powell and Ginger Rogers starred in this stylish *Thin Man* imitation, in which Max's song "Midnight in Manhattan" becomes a key plot point.

The Informer (2/35–4/35). AA.

Break of Hearts (3/35–5/35) The tale of an amorous symphony conductor (Charles Boyer) allowed Steiner to skillfully lead excerpts from Tchaikovsky's Fifth Symphony, Schubert's "Unfinished" Symphony, and other concert hall staples on the soundtrack.

Top Hat (4/35–7/35)

Alice Adams (5/35–6/35)

She (6/35)

Metropolitan Nocturne (6/35). Max served as musical director for this acclaimed musical short built around Louis Alter's concert piece of the same name.

The Three Musketeers (6/35–10/35)

I Dream Too Much (8/35–11/35)

As with *She*, most critical praise for the film went to Steiner, whose music at the climax generated applause during a press screening.[47] RKO executives were also appreciative: for the first time, the words "Music by Max Steiner" appeared on its own separate title card.

Nonetheless, Radio's star composer was increasingly bitter. He stewed over the fact that his $850 a week salary—$500 after debt repayment—was below market value, at a time when film music was growing in importance. In the wake of Max's trailblazing, other studios had expanded their music departments, and they followed the Steiner scoring template with hires like Franz Waxman and Erich Wolfgang Korngold, both of whom made their Hollywood bows that year.

By fall 1935, Max had another reason to be strategizing a move away from RKO: David O. Selznick was establishing a studio of his own. It promised to deliver a jolt of innovation to the industry, in its choice of material and its rejection of assembly-line production.

And when it came to the post of musical director, Steiner and Selznick had the same man in mind.

12

Exodus

BY 1935, DAVID O. SELZNICK was ready to escape his gilded cage.

Two years of producing at MGM had yielded elegant hits like *Dinner at Eight* and *David Copperfield*. But they also fed his desire to escape the factory system MGM symbolized, to become his own boss. By October, as Hollywood business began to rebound, the 33-year-old had left Metro and was well on his way to realizing his dream. He announced the formation of Selznick International Pictures, a studio co-funded by businessman John "Jock" Whitney.

"The day of mass production has ended," Selznick told reporters. "It has become ... so essential for a producer to collaborate on every inch of script, to be available for every conference and go over all details of production that it is physically impossible for him to give his best efforts to more than a limited number of pictures."[1]

His studio was based in Culver City, on Los Angeles's west side. Its administration building was a white colonnaded structure whose plantation-like façade would appear in the logo of each Selznick feature. Jock Whitney would be chairman of the board; and for music director ...

The choice seemed as obvious as it was problematic.

"Max Steiner was thrilled to know you want to talk to him before he makes any other deals," an underling wrote Selznick on August 22. "His contract with RKO doesn't expire until June. However, he says he wouldn't dream of signing with them or anyone else, if there were a chance of going with you."[2]

For Max, serving as music director for the visionary producer would be far more prestigious, and lucrative, than the same job at RKO. David aspired to make only exceptional films—the kind likely to get special attention from audiences and Academy voters. And although Max was temporarily stuck at

RKO, Selznick would not need a composer until his first movie was well into production.

The prospect of a fresh start with Selznick, and his belief that he had found his soulmate in Louise, convinced Steiner to set up permanent roots. Since 1930 he had lived in a rented house; now he tasked Louise, who had a freer schedule, to find them a home. Ultimately, "we decided to buy a lot and build," Louise recalled.

> I went to an agent in Beverly Hills and was shown a lot on Cove Way. It was an acre, and the adjoining lot of one acre was also available, which we bought later. I came back to the studio and told Max the location. It happened to be across the street from where Selznick lived.
>
> Max was so busy that he asked me to go ahead and buy it since he respected my judgment. I put a deposit down and got an architect, builder, contractor, etc. Max didn't see the location for about a week. When we drove by, he seemed delighted.
>
> In the meantime, he had seen Selznick and told him we would be neighbors. David asked Max where the location of our lot was, who our builder was and so forth, and Max said, "I don't know. Louise is looking after everything because I'm so busy getting this picture out." Selznick jokingly replied, "You're not only a great musician, you're crazy, too."[3]

Impatient to leave RKO, Max decided to force the issue. He demanded his immediate release . . . an edict the front office ignored, except for their hiring of an additional music director, Nathaniel Shilkret.[4] Seething, Steiner continued talks with Selznick, and on December 5 David gave Jock Whitney an update. "I think he is going to be an enormous asset . . . there is, in my opinion, no one in the entire field within miles of Max. . . . I feel there is little or no gamble in signing him up for 52 weeks because we can dish him out to other producers and receive favors in return."[5]

Back at RKO, Steiner became the squeakiest wheel. Presented with a new contract to sign, "Max stormed in on Kahane and turned it down flat and asked for his release," a Selznick staffer told his boss.[6] But RKO again refused. "He must continue until June," Selznick was told, but "he knows of no reason why he can't be borrowed if you ask Kahane for him." As for his becoming Selznick's music director, "This is what Max wants."[7]

STEINER'S FINAL PICTURE at RKO was a classy farewell. *Follow the Fleet* was the fourth Astaire-Rogers-starring vehicle. Amid several soon-to-be standards by Irving Berlin, the highlight was "Let's Face the Music and Dance," performed within a supposed stage show, which begins with a nearly four-minute pantomime by Fred and Ginger. The sequence, author Todd Decker noted, "can be read as a miniature Astaire and Rogers film—the melodrama they never made—complete with dramatic underscoring by Max Steiner."[8]

Its setting is a gleaming Art Deco casino where, in the pre-song pantomime, gambling losses drive Fred to the brink of suicide (did Max feel a pang of recognition?). He is stopped by the sight of Ginger, also contemplating self-destruction. Maurice de Packh orchestrated the number, including Steiner's musical prologue; he was guided by copious notes from Max:

"Curtains open [on rooftop set]—Fred enters—Violins (schmalzo) . . . Murray—do your best!! It should tear your heart out! He reaches for the gun—mysterioso, no tremolo . . . I'd like a feeling of Drama but still keeping a little rhythm going—my idea is to have this somewhat like a symphonic 'Paul Whiteman' arrangement. [He] puts gun to head—he sees Ginger—roll on cymbal—FRED RUNS TO HER . . . Ginger spins around—FURIOSO. Ginger & Fred closeup—E-flat horn, dolce . . . Harp arpeggios—Freddie sings . . . "[9]

The sequence characterizes what Steiner brought to the Astaire-Rogers series as a whole. Seldom did he arrange or orchestrate their dances (although main titles and underscoring were often his). But as supervisor, editor, and conductor of the numbers, he left his mark by encouraging his team to create subtle orchestral fills, strong dynamic changes, and, where appropriate, drama—like the high, sustained line for strings playing over the title tune in *Top Hat*, which adds an electric charge to the start of the song.

Steiner was proud of his work on the series, whose entries were now international events. But by December 1935, with two months of work left on *Fleet,* he was desperate to move on.

David O. Selznick had finished shooting his first independent production.

LITTLE LORD FAUNTLEROY WAS BASED ON Frances Hodgson Burnett's 1886 novel about a poor American child who learns he is actually an English lord. The gentle story of family division and reconciliation had been a childhood favorite of Selznick,[10] who was eager for Max to write the score.

By January 2, 1936, a loan-out deal with RKO was reached. Selznick paid "twice Mr. Steiner's weekly salary"[11] for the loan, and everyone was a winner—except Max. That same day, he reluctantly signed a new two-year contract with RKO,[12] probably as a condition of his loan-out, and certainly in bad faith since he still planned on leaving. To make matters worse, he couldn't start composing on *Fauntleroy* due to work on *Follow the Fleet*. "I have developed a sort of stomach trouble, probably due to extreme nervousness," he wrote a friend, "and this is evidently what affects my eyes as well. I am on a strict diet, and imagine—I have stopped smoking and cut down drinking to one highball a day. What a life!!! I would rather be dead. If they stop 'something else' that I like to do as well, I will damn well shoot myself."[13]

RKO work dragged into late January—and *Fauntleroy* had to be completed by February 15 for tax reasons. With the deadline just three weeks away, Selznick's studio manager Phil Ryan urged the hiring of composer Herbert Stothart, with whom Selznick enjoyed working at MGM. Max himself doubted he would have enough time. But David ignored him, suggesting to his staff that Steiner record *Fauntleroy* at RKO if he wished to, in deference to his "peculiar temperament."[14]

A fair description? Probably. But it was also the pot calling the kettle black, given Selznick's manic personality and his growing penchant to focus on the most minute details of production.

By the last week of January, *Follow the Fleet* finally docked—and like a champion racehorse making up for a late start, Steiner proceeded to break his own speed records. He completed the entire *Fauntleroy* score—47 minutes of music—in slightly over *one week*.[15]

Max's oft-repeated claim of writing day and night on a project must be true in this case. Even so, he could not have pulled off such a miracle without the assist of RKO's music staff, particularly orchestrator Bernhard Kaun. Selznick also helped by writing detailed instructions on the type of music he wanted, along with "spotting" notes about its placement ("Start music on Ceddie's and Havisham's arrival at Castle, and stop on Interior Library as Ceddie starts to shake hands with Earl").[16]

The final score fulfilled Selznick's directive of "utter simplicity."[17] Steiner wrote no music for the story's villains, thus contrasting their mercenary schemes with the goodness of our hero, Ceddie (Freddie Bartholomew); his mother, "Dearest" (Dolores Costello); and the gruff Earl of Dorincourt (C. Aubrey Smith), who comes to love his American grandson and his long-estranged daughter-in-law.

The Mozartean delicacy of the score belied the haste of its writing. Probably recalling his own princely childhood, Max translated the generous soul of Ceddie into music; his theme does not imitate youthful innocence but becomes it. As usual, the timbre of an actor's voice was factored into writing: "I used low notes and soft, deep woodwinds to back the childish treble of Freddie Bartholomew."[18]

His theme for "Dearest" illustrates another frequent device: translating a character's name into notes. The two syllables of "Dearest" become the sunny, perfect-fifth interval of B down to E, followed by a climbing triplet (F-sharp, G-sharp and A) before the B–E "Dearest" interval repeats. (*"I'd like it to 'sing'!"*)[19] Many of Steiner's best-known themes would have a song-like correspondence between their rhythm and the name of a film title or main character.

Max understood the essence of what Selznick wanted: emotion aimed directly at the heart. (*"With all the schmaltz you've got,"* he notes at the climax.) But that February, he discovered that Selznick's views on film music had changed since 1932. MGM's Herbert Stothart had persuaded the producer that moviegoers enjoyed hearing music already familiar to them.

That notion was anathema to Steiner, who preferred original themes. (His brief quotations from famous tunes to convey a location—e.g., "Rule Britannia" or "La Marseillaise"—were another matter.) For 1935's *David Copperfield*, Selznick and Stothart had scored a farewell scene with "Auld Lang Syne." For a similar scene in *Fauntleroy*, Selznick wanted the same melody.[20] Max complied, with a note to Kaun: *"Ultra Schmaltzig and delicatessen."*

For the film's many scenes of carriage rides, Steiner employed his technique of mirroring but not exactly matching screen action. "Hoofbeats are not identically synchronized but the melody is in time with their trotting. At the last, when the horses draw up to the castle entrance and stop, I allow my notes to fall exactly with each hoofbeat, even to a little backward step a horse takes when it comes to a standstill."[21] Equally true to form were Max's mix of jokes and panic as he raced toward the finish line. Regarding a mild dissonance: *"This is correct—believe it or not, sweetheart!" "S.O.S. Help! It's 1:15 and the orchestra is called for 2 o'clock!"* And finally: *"Thanks, Bernard, for everything! XXX Love and Kisses, Max."*

The score was recorded at RKO, with Steiner capturing as much as 7-1/2 minutes in a single take.[22] In a hopeful sign for his future with Selznick, Max not only made the deadline but brought music in under the $15,000 budget. "Even the mechanics and employees are astounded at what he has done," Phil Ryan wrote Selznick. At the same time, Ryan pointed out how they could use Steiner's achievement *against* him in future. "He has established a record that . . . we can always point at, when arguing with him, as it concerns time necessary to prepare and score a picture."[23]

For now, there were only smiles and sighs of relief. Max put his emotions into a telegram on February 19: "DEAR BOSS MANY MANY THANKS FOR HAVING GIVEN ME THE OPPORTUNITY TO SCORE LITTLE LORD FAUN-TLEROY. IT FELT JUST LIKE OLD TIMES AND I HOPE AND PRAY THAT YOU WILL FORGIVE ME FOR WHATEVER MISTAKES I MIGHT HAVE MADE CON-SIDERING THE SHORT TIME I HAD. I KNOW YOU HAVE A GREAT PICTURE AND I WISH YOU THE GRANDEST SUCCESS YOU HAVE EVER HAD. SHOULD THE MUSIC HELP A LITTLE IT WILL MAKE ME VERY HAPPY. MAXIE."[24]

Selznick replied: "DEAR MAX AM MOST GRATEFUL FOR YOUR TEL-EGRAM AND EVEN MORE GRATEFUL FOR THE SUPERMAN JOB YOU DID . . . AFFECTIONATE THANKS AND REGARDS—DAVID SELZNICK."[25]

Released two months later on April 2, *Fauntleroy* launched Selznick's studio on a note of triumph. *Variety* accurately predicted "a box office knockout"[26]— its profit was nearly half a million dollars—while *Hollywood Screen World* observed that "the beautiful and appropriate music score . . . contributes considerably."[27]

Max, full of confidence, ca. 1936.

Its producer agreed. Two days after scoring was finished, David initiated a contract "between Selznick International Pictures and MAX STEINER, on the following terms and conditions: He is to be musical director and supervisor. Principal period: one year, starting with expiration of his present RKO contract."[28]

RKO's B. B. Kahane had grown sufficiently weary of Steiner's tantrums that he was ready to sever ties. On April 16 it was official. "Max Steiner, musical director of Radio Pictures, has signed a deal with Selznick International to function in the same capacity," *Hollywood Reporter* noted.[29] The composer eagerly looked forward to a new chapter in his life—one in which scores would be written in a supportive atmosphere, for a producer who appreciated music's importance—and who would pay him an industry-high salary of $1,250 a week ($23,000 today).[30]

On May 2, Steiner's six-and-a-half year association with RKO ended. He was flooded with affectionate farewells from colleagues, including a studio vice president who cautioned him to "stay away from the tables in the anteroom at the Clover Club."[31] It was advice Max ignored.

Steiner's exit was perfectly timed. After a year of soaring box office, RKO cratered in 1936 with a string of theater-emptying flops. Its misjudgments were recapped in an article Max kept; enthusiastically underlined is one sentence: "And to think RKO traded Max Steiner for Shilkret!"[32]

In a sense, Steiner would never really leave RKO. His music for *King Kong, The Most Dangerous Game,* and other pioneering scores was re-used in dozens of Radio releases well into the 1940s. The continuing viability of his work reflected the fact that Steiner had not only transformed film music but had written some of its most enduring examples. As author J. B. Kaufman observed, "The RKO films of Max Steiner are not merely the prelude to a great film career; they represent, collectively and sometimes individually, one of its highlights."[33]

AS MAX MOVED HIS OFFICE to Selznick International, his sense of accomplishment was whetted by two unexpected honors. First came word of a World Cinema Congress Medal in Venice.[34] Next was a bronze medal awarded by the king of Belgium, at a Cinema Exhibition in Brussels.[35] On May 16, Bernhard Kaun—who followed Steiner to Selznick—conducted a symphony concert in Los Angeles, its program consisting mostly of Mozart and Max. That night, a lucky audience heard what would be the only public performance during Steiner's lifetime of music from *King Kong, Bird of Paradise*, and *Symphony of Six Million.*

In later years, classical critics usually viewed film music with dripping contempt. Which makes the *Los Angeles Evening News*'s review of
the concert worth quoting: "Steiner has an extraordinary command of the
orchestra.... He is distinctly not derivative. On the contrary, his idiom is contemporary and highly individual. He is a master of descriptive composition
and while he frequently reaches his effects by highly unorthodox methods, he
does reach them."[36]

Those words just as accurately described Max's next project for Selznick—
one that reveled in coloristic effect like a cinematic *Scheherazade*.

The Garden of Allah paired two of the most carnal actors in Hollywood,
Marlene Dietrich and Charles Boyer, and photographed them in the luxuriant
new process of three-strip Technicolor. Arizona locations stood in for the Sahara,
and today, *Allah*'s stunning images of winding caravans, swirling sandstorms, and
Dietrich dressed as a silk-chiffon goddess still draw gasps from viewers.

Steiner's music followed suit, combining European romanticism with
pagan sensuality. With its ravishing soundtrack and a visual symphony of
color, *Allah* offers everything—everything, that is, except a compelling story
or dialogue that doesn't elicit eye rolls. "This script—you know it is *twash*,"
Dietrich sighed to dialogue director Joshua Logan.[37] Many on Selznick's
staff had urged their boss not to film Robert Hitchens's 1904 novel, about
a Russian monk who flees his monastery, taking its secret formula for wine,
only to fall in love with a beautiful heiress in the North African desert.

Casting Boyer as a celibate monk, and Dietrich as a devout ex-convent
girl, sounds like something out of *The Producers*. But if one views *Allah*'s vo-
luptuous images with its surviving "music and effects" track, which has no dialogue (to simplify foreign dubbing), the movie becomes a prime, pleasurable
slice of Hollywood exoticism.

When Steiner arrived in Culver City, he found a production at war—with
the elements, and with Selznick. 130-degree temperatures in Arizona melted
the film stock, adding to the misery of director Richard Boleslawski, husband
of Max's favorite pianist Norma Drury.* The stars were on strike for a better
script. That April, Selznick recalled the entire production to Culver City,
where the Sahara was recreated with sand trucked back from Arizona.[38]

L.A.'s cooler temperatures and Selznick's charm quelled much of the tension. "There was a little restaurant on Washington Boulevard opposite the

---

* Boleslawski died two months after the film's release, age 47. "We all should have died after
The Garden of Allah," Dietrich mused. "But he should have died *before* the film." (Maria Riva,
Marlene Dietrich by Her Daughter [New York: Random House, 1992], 383–89.)

studio," Max recalled.[39] "After the day's work, Marlene Dietrich, a wonderful cook, used to go over there and cook dinner for David and me and herself. She made us goulash, wiener schnitzel, and all her wonderful specialties. She was a darling woman and I shall always love her, not just for her skill with a skillet."

Max saved a party invitation from Boleslawski—sent, it said, "with a modicum of misgiving"—to a "mild binge" on Pathé Stage 14 to celebrate the end of filming. Menu items included Jellied Chicken Leg Consommé a la Dietrich, Steamed Bloater Boleslawski, and "Alka-Selznicks (listen to it fizz)."[40]

The latter would come in handy. By the time a rough cut was assembled, *Allah* was $250,000 over budget.[41] To reduce the film's many longueurs, its run time was shortened from nearly two hours to 78 minutes. Much music disappeared along the way; and unlike *Fauntleroy*, Selznick conveyed most of his requests while Steiner was writing instead of before. Typical was one directive: "Mr. Selznick hopes that we won't go overboard on Oriental music, as there is a danger of the picture being monotonous anyway—and more romantic and European music may help."[42]

Since Dietrich's maidenly Domini hails from a town "near a certain capital in Europe," Steiner filled his score with a waltz-style theme to describe her. It ascends a full octave in its first phrase, then whirls in dance-like triplets to a high G above middle C as if intoxicated by her beauty. *"With all the Schmaltz—Bernard, this whole strain should be 'pulsating.'"*[43]

Allah's score begins as we see a silhouetted Bedouin against an orange-blue sunset. *Tutti* (unison) orchestra proclaims a musical grabber, a minor-key "call of the desert." Throughout the story it will serve as a sonic hammer of fate, in contrast to Domini's gossamer theme. Other dichotomies fill the score. Its juxtaposition of a Christian "Amen" against the Arabian desert call in the film's final seconds summarizes the story's core conflict, between spirituality and desire.

Max was also inspired by the one scene of unabashed eroticism: the Salome-style dance of a dagger-wielding market girl (Viennese ballet star Tilly Losch). A press release gushed that an "orchestra of Arabians furnishing native instruments was obtained."[44] In fact, Steiner used Western instruments, combined with cimbalom (a Hungarian dulcimer), balalaikas, zither, and other percussion. Max's own score notes are less suited for publication. *"KOOTCH DANCE . . . Orgasm music!! (Verstehst? Ich habe schon vergessen! [You know? I have already forgotten!] Die audience soll 'Kommen'! [The audience should 'come'!]"*

Other notes in Max's score suggest the second-guessing he was forced to do in lieu of clear direction from Selznick. *"DAGGER DANCE . . . They might want it to sound 'menacing' (I don't!). I hear a melody, almost all woodwind! What will Selznick say?"*

Steiner uses a wordless chorus to turn wind and sand into a supernatural presence. In 1915, Richard Strauss musicalized the whirling snow of a mountain peak in *An Alpine Symphony*. Here, Steiner pays homage with an eerily beautiful blend of voices, brass, organ, and percussion. *"CARAVAN . . . Wind through WIRES sounds like that."*

STEINER HAD HOPED that the slower production pace of Selznick International would lead to a less stressful scoring process. He was mistaken. Recutting of the film led to last-minute rescoring. More ominously, Max fielded several requests from his boss to incorporate well-worn classical themes into the score, thematic consistency be damned. His heart must have sunk as he read orders to use Wagner's "Liebestod" from *Tristan und Isolde* as Boris tells Domini he is a monk. Steiner persuaded Selznick otherwise,[45] but in future he would not be so fortunate.

Since Selznick's studio did not have a full music department, recording was done at United Artists. Fortunately, the UA stage was among Hollywood's best. Bassoonist Don Christlieb remembered *Allah* as "a big orchestra and a great sound, with the cream of top players. Max looked like the perfect prototype of a businessman, but that was in looks only. His first read-through of a cue . . . was invariably followed by verbal whining, but not against the players, for he was not abusive. It was a result of his disappointment in what he was not hearing. He would immediately begin rearranging the percussion, drums, harp, celeste, bells, xylophone, and piano. He did this not only for balance but for notes, interchanging them from one instrument to another. . . . This could go on and on, but somehow when he rehearsed the percussion in its new setting it sounded well enough to serve as a score without the rest of the orchestra, and with the orchestra it sounded sensational."[46]

The lack of a recording studio and full music staff meant that Selznick paid premium for the services of others. *Allah* was an early casualty. Max had drafted a preliminary music budget of $27,722.50, but the final cost—$54,817.41—was nearly double.[47] Still, Selznick seemed unfazed, focused only on the end result. "Dear Maxie, Just a word to tell you how delighted I am with the final music of 'Allah,'" he wrote on October 26. "I am still your leading fan."[48] A relieved Max telegrammed back: "DEAR MR. SELZNICK I AM WISHING YOU A WELL DESERVED TREMENDOUS SUCCESS . . . I THINK YOU ARE PRETTY GOOD TOO. AFFECTIONATELY MAXIE.[49]"

Hopes were high after the press screening, held at Grauman's Chinese on October 30. Audiences were wowed by two elements: the soon-to-be-Oscar-winning cinematography, and a soundtrack innovation that marked a turning point in audio clarity. The new "Push-Pull" recording system captured a much wider dynamic range, resulting in cleaner voice and music presentation. Background clicks and hiss were now a thing of the past.

"For Max, the improvement of the push-pull soundtrack was as important as stereo later in the '50s," his friend John Morgan recalled. "You could hear a true pianissimo, and then a fortissimo right after it."[50] The improvement was evident to first-nighters: "The Hollywood preview audience cheered the musical accompaniment by Max Steiner," observed *Literary Digest*.[51]

That night, music was showcased almost as much as the film, as Steiner led an orchestra and chorus before the screening, in what *Hollywood Reporter* called a "prelude of operatic dimensions."[52] After the movie, industry elite traveled to the Trocadero nightclub on the Sunset Strip. There, Max had another chance to promote his work. "Everybody came up and asked me whether [bandleader] Phil Ohman could play Marlene's theme," he wrote a colleague. "I went downstairs and made an orchestration, working about an hour on it. . . . I played it with the orchestra in fox-trot form. Everybody from [Twentieth Century Fox co-founder] Joe Schenck to Lubitsch . . . asked to have it played again and again."[53]

As for the movie, *Variety*'s London critic spoke for many: "*Garden of Allah* . . . impresses as the last word in color production, but a pretty dull affair. Max Steiner's score is second only to the gorgeous color cameraing."[54] The score was Oscar-nominated but lost to *Anthony Adverse*—the first win by fellow Austrian Erich Wolfgang Korngold. By then, *The Garden of Allah* had vanished from screens like a Technicolor mirage. Despite decent box office, its cost made profit impossible, leaving Selznick $300,000 in the red.[55]

Fortunately he had other projects in the pipeline. And for Max, no period of his life would be happier than the fall of 1936. The same week that critics raved about his *Allah* score, he received a telegram from the government of France: "Pleased to announce your decoration as Officer, Academy Ministerial Decree, diploma signed yesterday."[56] Steiner accepted a blue ribbon decoration from Los Angeles's French consulate.[57] Hollywood's "little monarch" had achieved an honor worthy of Debussy or Ravel.

THE FILM SCORES OF MAX STEINER

1936 Releases (continued in Chapter 13)

Follow the Fleet (10/35–2/36)
Little Lord Fauntleroy (2/36). Selznick International.
The Garden of Allah (8/36–10/36). Selznick International. AAN.

Between January and July 1935, Max had worked on nine titles at RKO. In the first seven months of 1936, he had scored precisely . . . two. Selznick's next film would not finish shooting until early 1937; in the meantime, his music director was too expensive to keep idle. But just as David had predicted, rival studios were eager to borrow Steiner.

What happened next, neither man could have foreseen.

"David came to me one day and asked, 'Max, do you want to save me some money?' I replied that of course I did. 'Well, they want you over at Warner Bros. to score a picture called *The Charge of the Light Brigade*. Will you go over on a loan-out and help take the financial load off of me?'"[58]

With that brief conversation, Steiner's future was set on a new course . . . and one of the most prolific, exasperating, and memorable associations in film music history was about to begin.

13

Battles Won and Lost

FOR AS LONG AS THERE HAD BEEN Warner Bros. productions, movies and music were inseparable.

That union of sight and sound began early in the twentieth century, when carnival-goers in Ohio and Pennsylvania stared at the flickering screen of a small Kinetoscope theater. The film was 1903's *The Great Train Robbery*, presented under the aegis of Abe and Sam Warner. The siblings, ages 19 and 16, had bought a print of Edwin S. Porter's wildly popular western, and probably screened it with music from the cheapest piano player they could find.[1]

Their success launched a career joined by two of their brothers: Jack, the youngest, born 1892 in Ontario, Canada; and Harry, born 1881 in the family's native Krasnosielc, Poland. In America, their father worked as a shoemaker—a trade that the sober Harry followed. Decades later, Harry would roam his multi-million-dollar studio, searching for dropped nails and popping them in his mouth as he had as a boy, to avoid a penny of wasted product.[2]

At age 13, Jack displayed what would be a lifetime supply of ham by leading audiences in sing-alongs, while film reels were being changed at the Warners' first theater in New Castle, Pennsylvania. Jack's tenor solos also worked brilliantly at sending patrons running for the exits after a show, hastening the brothers' ability to bring in a new crowd.[3]

For all that could be said against him—and many would say a great deal—no one doubted that Jack Warner loved music. "Films are fantasy," he was quoted as saying. "And fantasy needs music."[4]

The importance of music grew as the brothers branched into production. By 1925, Warner Bros. owned a studio on the West Coast and a Brooklyn company called Vitagraph. Sam signed a deal with Western Electric that added a new ingredient to their movies: sound.

The 1927 premiere of *The Jazz Singer* sealed the studio's technological dominance. Among the conductors of its "Vitaphone Orchestra" was a St. Louis–born veteran of Broadway—Leo F. Forbstein, who by 1931 at age 38 was the studio's music director. That year, Warners consolidated operations, moving its main studio to Burbank in California's San Fernando Valley.

Jack succeeded Sam (who died in 1927) as the family's driving force, relishing his position as vice president in charge of production. Abe stayed east, acting as treasurer. Harry, the president, also handled business from New York, as his relationship with the self-aggrandizing Jack took on the dynamics of a jazz-age Cain and Abel.

In 1933, Warners kicked off a glorious renaissance of movie musicals with *42nd Street*. Its soundtrack featured an orchestra of mostly jazz musicians, many hired from the bands of Jimmie Grier and Gus Arnheim.[5] Another turning point came in 1934 with the arrival of Erich Wolfgang Korngold, who would write 17 scores for the studio. His work led Forbstein to increase the orchestra's classical bona fides by hiring several symphony players. By 1935, Warner Bros.' orchestra could deliver scintillating performances of everything from Wagner to Harry Warren.

BY 1936, FORBSTEIN AND STEINER had moved in the same circles long enough to form a friendship. That February they collaborated on planning music for the Academy Awards. A related note from Max to Leo is signed "Love," and closes with a P.S.: "Don't forget pinochle Sunday. . . . See you tomorrow at the races."[6] Forbstein's admiration for Steiner was both personal and professional. "Warner Bros. was after Max when he was at RKO," Louise Klos recalled. "We would run across Leo many times at the Clover Club, and he would say 'Jack wants you, you've got to come over to us.'"[7]

The movie that finally brought Max to Warners was tailor-made for the studio's hottest new star, Errol Flynn. *The Charge of the Light Brigade* was loosely inspired by Alfred, Lord Tennyson's poem—an ode to British cavalrymen in the Crimean War who, despite knowing of a strategic error by senior command, bravely rode to certain death. Hardly a viable plot for a would-be blockbuster. So with blithe disregard for history—and the commercial savvy that kept it profitable during the Depression—the studio engineered a plot that turned the slaughter into a sacrificial victory. Warners also moved the story's setting from Russia to the more exotic India.

The film's prime mover was a producer who combined sophistication with an ice-cold business sense. The 36-year-old Hal B. Wallis had been part of the Warner machine since 1923.[8] By 1933, the former traveling salesman

Olivia de Havilland and Errol Flynn in a publicity still from *The Charge of the Light Brigade*.

and publicist had risen to the rank of executive producer, overseeing most of Warner's A-projects. And although he seldom raised his voice, his chilly eviscerations of a subordinate's shortcomings could be devastating. "He was stern," recalled Art Silver, a trailer editor. "I waited at his desk, and he would look up and say, 'I am not impressed.' He was never a very pat-on-the-back kind of guy. He was an I-am-not-impressed kind of guy."[9]

His criticism was all the harder to take because he was usually right. "Wallis was an S.O.B. and a tyrant, but the most expertised man I ever met," said director Irving Rapper. "His day-to-day judgment was excellent."[10]

During three months of shooting Wallis fought with *Light Brigade*'s director, Hungarian-born Michael Curtiz, who lived for little else but making movies.[11] Curtiz would direct more than 160 films, as he pushed himself and others to capture the most thrilling footage possible.

Like Curtiz, Wallis possessed a genius for pacing. During shooting, he intervened if the rushes seemed too fast or too slow. After filming, he oversaw the refining of the rough cut with the precision of a composer, dictating memos that detailed the exact length of footage to be trimmed or added. He also knew the value of music. Drawn, as he later wrote, to "strong orchestral scores,"[12] Wallis's gold standard was Korngold. Unfortunately, there was only one of him, and having just scored the Warners epic *Anthony Adverse*, Korngold spent that spring visiting his hometown, Vienna.[13]

BY THE TIME *LIGHT BRIGADE'S* SHOOT ended in July, the job of composer remained unfilled. A new arrival in Hollywood from Berlin, Ernst Toch, viewed a rough cut with Wallis, and by July 10 it appeared he had the job—but weeks later, Toch was out of the picture.

His early sketches may have disappointed. Or Forbstein may have heard over a hand of pinochle that Steiner was available. Whatever the case, by August 17 the job belonged to Max.[14]

Steiner knew that if he passed this unofficial audition, other work at Warners would follow. "Max loved the film and he put everything he could into it," his friend John Morgan recalled. "He had, as he described it, the best orchestra he had up to that time, and the biggest."[15]

For Steiner, the film's reverential depiction of soldiery and empire tapped into fond memories of Austria-Hungary. There was just one problem: *Light Brigade* required over 90 minutes of music, and had a completion date of October 7.[16] That left about five weeks for composition. On average, Max would have to write three minutes of score a day. That totaled roughly 120,000 notes—about 300 on each of the sketch's 400-plus pages.

Max needed a new orchestrator, and fast: Bernhard Kaun had chosen not to follow him to Warner. Luckily, Forbstein knew just the man.

In all of Hollywood, no one moved between composition and orchestrating for others with less ego than Hugo Friedhofer. He was classically trained by a student of Ottorino Respighi. As a cellist in his native San Francisco, Hugo had "discovered the advantage of sitting in the middle of the orchestra, where he could hear what the other instruments were doing around him," wrote historian Linda Danly.[17]

"If he's good enough for Korngold," Max told Leo, "he's good enough for me."[18]

Steiner by nature was effusive and gregarious. The 35-year-old Friedhofer "was a curmudgeon, albeit a rather warm and kindly one," recalled author Tony Thomas.[19] Hugo's impeccable craftsmanship earned him a reputation as "the most learned of us all and often the most subtle," according to *Laura* composer David Raksin.[20]

For the next decade, Friedhofer was Steiner's closest collaborator. It didn't hurt that each had the constitution of a workhorse, a jaded view of Hollywood, and a deep knowledge of symphonic music. (Hugo spoke fluid German, too.)

On *Light Brigade*, they hit the ground running. Most of their discussion, Hugo recalled, was "confined to telephone conversations. And we never saw each other from the day we ran the picture until the time that we went on the stage. We used to have these wild telephone conversations, sometimes at two, three, four o'clock in the morning . . . the hours that we used to put in were simply fabulous."[21]

"WHO SHALL EXCEL THEM," proclaims the laurel-leafed text as *The Charge of the Light Brigade* begins. Steiner's explosive first notes echo that challenge with a maestoso fanfare backed by thunderous timpani. This fanfare modulates upwards no fewer than six times, finally releasing the tension of its ascent with a shimmering statement of "Rule, Britannia." During additional onscreen text, music modulates six more times into the stratosphere, until—at last—*Charge*'s title card inspires an exultant *sffz* release.

After a daring juxtaposition of dissonant trumpet calls, Max introduces the heart of his score: a march for the Lancers that he titled "Forward, the Light Brigade." The march proves elastic throughout the film, conveying pride, danger, and finally eulogization. Its first measures convey the quiet anxiety at the start of a perilous journey: trumpets play a questioning "herald" theme over a strict quarter-note rhythm that summons images of shining uniforms and trotting horses. This accented rhythm dominates the score, suggesting the forward march and determination of Tennyson's brigade ("Theirs not to reason why, Theirs but to do or die"). Part two of the march is a burst of major-key sunlight, daring us not to be swept up in its jaunty pride—despite brief shifts into the minor, presaging danger ahead.

Errol Flynn plays Major Geoffrey Vickers, who leads the 27th Lancers' final charge after losing the heart of his fiancée Elsa (Olivia de Havilland) to his brother Perry (Patric Knowles). In his first musical theme for de Havilland, Steiner pens his most mature waltz to date. Its melody, in the bright key of A-major, uses a favorite device of Vincent Youmans: repeating a musical cell (here, four notes) and returning over and over to the note that begins the phrase.

The theme also conveys Elsa's secret love for Perry. When she reluctantly dances with fiancée Geoffrey, Steiner tellingly gives the two a blander tune: a second-hand pastiche of *The Blue Danube*. In what may have been a subtle rebuke of Selznick, Steiner would often use pre-existing music to represent a relationship in which one person does not love the other.

For villainous rajah Surat Khan, Max uses the "Eastern" intervals of the pentatonic scale to craft a motif for low brass, piano, harp, and bells. The theme suggests Khan's menace even when he is offscreen—most memorably when Geoffrey reflects on Khan's treacheries, and decides to lead the Lancers into their suicidal battle against him.

Looking at Steiner's pencil sketches, one would assume that he and Friedhofer had worked together for years. Only occasionally do his remarks suggest a process of training. *"Hugo: no celeste! It bothers the dialogue. Mostly strings and woodwind and a little . . . "* Here he draws a tiny harp and harpist.[22]

"Steiner's sketches were so complete, they looked like a road map," Friedhofer recalled.[23] The clarity of Max's notations was enhanced by his system of using colored pencils, to distinguish melody lines from supporting figurations. But all of the voices served a purpose. "He was insistent that parts deep in the harmonic progressions had an interesting musical line," John Morgan observed. "I think that is why musicians enjoy playing Steiner— because their parts always make them feel they are playing an important part in the fabric of the music."[24]

The first action scene in *Light Brigade* inspires comments that convey se-rious intent with typical low humor: *"The whole page lacks inner harmonies (Violas—douchebags, organs—jockstraps)" "3 Trombones, Basses, 8 Tubas, 4 Kitchen stoves, 1 cliteris with mute."* Friedhofer amends the latter: *"Spell it with an 'O' Maxie."*

When a musical phrase modulates upward, Steiner economically writes *"one tone up," "half tone up"* or *"a third higher"* rather than write out the phrase in its new key. He would use this time-saving device for the next three decades (*"I haven't enough lives to write it all out,"* he noted on a later film).[25] The score is also filled with a phrase that proved essential for meeting deadlines: *"Come Sopra"*—Italian for "as above." When a theme or its accompaniment was to be played without change for several measures, Steiner wrote *Come Sopra* to indicate a continuation of what came before, saving him from having to write every note again.

Light Brigade's sketches are filled with other shorthand that Hugo learned. *"They kiss . . . Himmel [Heaven] music." "HEARTBREAK!! A la Tosca—only better!" "ES SOLL SAFTIG [Juicy—i.e., full.]"* By Reel 7, as action scenes pile on, the density of Steiner's writing grows—and so does his agitation. *"INDIANS WITH LADDERS . . . Knock Knock—Who's there? Ladders! Ladders-who? Ladders-pray we'll finish this picture!" "INDIANS AGAIN (I wish my stocks would climb like these INDIANS)." "4000 Violins, 75 Basses, 22 Trombones, 14 Tubas, 11 Toilet plungers . . . These BASTARDS never stop climbing walls!!"*

BEHIND THE JOKES WAS GENUINE DESPERATION. "I understand that [Steiner] may not finish the scoring of the picture for a week or ten days," Wallis wrote Forbstein on September 19.[26] "I must have the picture ready for preview October first." Around that date, fresh urgency seeped into Max's pencil sketches. *"Dead man hanging by his feet. Hugo: I need help! for this whole sequence. I smell bad!! But I can't help it!"*

These anxieties were mere preamble to scoring the final charge, in which the "noble six hundred" are killed along with Surat Khan. The sequence accelerates visually from *moderato* to *allegro furioso*, with nearly ten minutes of score following suit. Musically, "It was murder," Friedhofer said.[27]

Steiner conceived the scoring as separate internal "movements," each faster than the one before. *"THE BEGINNING OF THE CHARGE—AND OUR END."* Blending his original march themes with "Rule, Britannia," the Russian Imperial anthem and frantic bugle calls, Steiner concocted a dissonance-filled tour de force. The result catches the constantly changing visuals without sounding like a quilt of random phrases. It was an exhausting exercise he would face, with grim determination, on many films to come.

Fortunately Max found inspiration in the expert timing of the charge, as edited by George Amy and conceived by Wallis and Curtiz. The highest compliment Steiner could pay a film was that it was "made for music": *The Charge of the Light Brigade* was the first of several Curtiz titles to earn that appellation.[28]

IN ITS ORCHESTRATED FORM, the score totaled over one thousand pages. Friedhofer doodled a piquant cartoon on its last page: standing over two graves marked "Max" and "Hugo," Leo Forbstein muses, "A couple of swell fellows. I wonder who we can get . . . "[29]

The score that Steiner called with anxious humor *The Charge of the May Company*[30] was recorded from September 24 to October 6.[31] Hal Wallis's frostiness thawed as he listened to music as stirring as Korngold's best work to date. The film's shipping date was pushed out a few days.[32]

But Steiner was still under the gun. Recalled John Morgan, "One of Max's gripes was that Jack Warner loved music so much that he insisted that the score be put to the film before it was shown for a preview audience. Normally, a studio will track a film with anything, because they know that after a preview they'll make cuts and changes. A lot of the time, after a preview they wouldn't let him re-record something that changed. If they cut a section out of the movie, they would just make a cut in the music. There are a couple of bad music edits in *Light Brigade* because of this."[33]

It was a practice that frustrated Max for the rest of his career. "I'm still fighting this," he wrote in 1964, "but it seems that nothing can be done about it."[34]

BY OCTOBER 1936 it was evident to all at the studio that Steiner had arrived and conquered. Jack Warner loved the score, which was not only featured in the movie's trailer (standard practice at the studio),* but in a special behind-the-scenes short.

Two weeks after music's completion, *The Charge of the Light Brigade* opened on October 20, 1936. It grossed a stellar $2.7 million,[35] and nearly all reviewers surrendered to its bravura and galvanizing score. "Max Steiner has never done a finer job," *Variety* wrote, "sonorous, appropriately militant, splendidly adapted to and fulfilling the various moods."[36]

BY THEN, STEINER WAS WORKING ON another loan-out. It would be a fascinating anomaly, both for him and its director, Frank Capra.

Lost Horizon, based on James Hilton's bestseller, followed a group of disparate Westerners who are spirited to the Himalayan village of Shangri-La, where people are at peace and never grow old. By 1936, as the Depression dragged on and as fascism spread across Europe, a fantasy set in an idyllic land without war had obvious appeal.

Its cost of $2.6 million, the most Columbia Pictures had ever spent, meant that the film had to be a smash.[37] Columbia's bullheaded president, Harry

---

* For the rest of his career at Warner Bros., Steiner wrote bespoke music for his films' trailers, based on that film's principal themes. Pencil sketches for these scores can be found at MSS 1547.

Cohn, wasn't reassured when Capra announced that he wanted a little-known friend to write the score. Dimitri Tiomkin was a Russian-born concert pianist and composer who had been kicking around Hollywood since 1929.

To win Cohn's approval, Capra came up with a compromise: Max would be musical director and conductor of Tiomkin's work. "I knew that if wise old Steiner thought the score was inadequate, he himself would step in to rewrite it—fast," Capra later acknowledged.[38]

Max was happy to team with one of Hollywood's most successful directors. Tiomkin was happy to have Max as his protector and partner. "Composers are usually jealous of each other, but Steiner had only one idea—to get the best out of the score. If I made a suggestion, he wanted to find out what was in my mind and do it that way."[39]

Nine orchestrators made instrumental parts from Tiomkin's rough sketches, while Max made further adjustments as he conducted an orchestra and chorus of up to 96 musicians.[40] "Mr. Cohn was having a heart attack about the size," recalled Louise, who played on the sessions.[41]

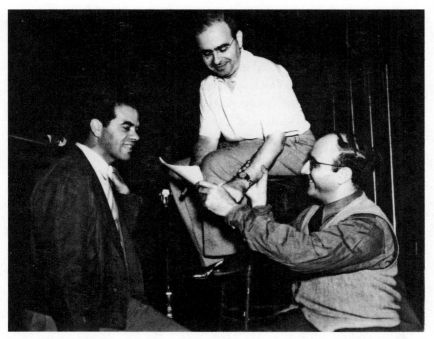

Frank Capra (left), Max, and Dimitri Tiomkin are in accord during the scoring of *Lost Horizon*, 1936. (MS Papers; L. Tom Perry Special Collections, Brigham Young University)

Capra arrived one day to listen and "left with stars in my eyes." But what seemed like a simple job took five months to complete. On November 20, a three-hour cut was previewed in Santa Barbara. Viewers laughed, yawned, and walked out in droves.[42]

As Harry Cohn sputtered, Capra put the film back into production, re-shooting scenes and cutting others. With each edit, music changed. Max conducted every session, working as hard as he would on his own scores to make Tiomkin's music a success. "We would start to record about eight at night and seldom finished until six or seven in the morning," Steiner wrote in 1964.[43]

About midnight, Capra, Tiomkin, and I went to Chasen's for supper. One night, Harry Cohn came in with a party of people from the Clover Club to hear some of our music. We had the Hall-Johnson Choir of fifty voices. Cohn sat down and looked around. Ten minutes later, he got up. He was red in the face and so mad he was shaking.

He stalked off the stage and slammed the door. We worked until about seven in the morning. I had just gotten into bed and was falling asleep when the phone rang. It was Cohn's secretary: "Mr. Cohn wants you in his office right away."

While I was parking my car outside the studio, I could hear Cohn screaming upstairs. I walked into his office. He was sitting behind his desk and had Tiomkin and Capra there and was bawling them out but good. To me, he yelled: "And you, you German Schweinhund! You German louse! You German S.O.B.!"

I resented this very much. For one thing I'm an Austrian, not a German. Then he proceeded to tell me that he was going to run me out of the picture business; he was going to go to Jack Warner, he was going to call Selznick; he was going to call everybody he could think of to have me thrown out for having [so many] people recording for one sequence. He got so mad he threatened to kill me.

He jumped from his desk and ran after me. I ran to the door. He caught me and said, "Max, who's that beautiful blonde sitting in the front row of the cellos?"

I broke into laughter as I told him, "Joan Gilbert."

Although initially a box office disappointment (re-releases softened the blow), *Lost Horizon* earned critical hosannas and an Oscar nomination for Tiomkin, launching a career that encompassed 22 nominations, four wins, and celebrity unprecedented for a film composer. In his autobiography, Tiomkin looked back on *Lost Horizon* as a project that "spoiled me completely." As for Steiner, "He was responsible for much of the musical success of the film."[44]

IN THE MIDDLE OF HIS FIVE-MONTH TRIP to Shangri-La, Max's life underwent a monumental change: he and Louise married.

The event almost took place earlier that year during a trip to Baja, California, with Charles Previn, a musical director at Universal. Driving through Tijuana, "There were signs on some buildings saying Weddings, Divorces," Louise recalled. "Charlie suggested that we get married then and he would be our best man. Max went in to arrange everything, but he came out looking very perturbed. It seems the cost of a marriage license in Mexico had been raised to around $20, and since we had bought some gifts at Caliente, we didn't have enough cash."[45]

Midway through *Lost Horizon*, the 48-year-old composer and his 30-year-old fiancée returned to Tijuana. On October 31—Halloween—they tied the knot.[46] "I thought of the Spanish tune which the orchestra played the evening that we got down to Ensenada," Louise wrote Max years later. "Remember they came to our table and played it?"[47]

Music was never far from either of their lives.

Two days later, the pair moved into their home at 1012 Cove Way, Beverly Hills. For the first time since Vienna, Max Steiner had a home of his own. Its two-plus acres accommodated a gated driveway, a large back yard shaded by tall trees, a three-car garage, and a sprawling, two-story white house. Its neo-Colonial entrance led visitors into a sunlit entryway. The living room contained "fine pieces of furniture," musician Aida Mulieri Dagort recalled. "I noticed a beautiful, rare giraffe-style piano."[48] It was the instrument given to Max by Johann Strauss.

Asian-themed furniture filled Louise's music room. A covered outdoor patio allowed the pair to enjoy the California sun while feeding their pet dogs. In their elegant dining room, the Steiners were served by a mostly African American staff. (A valet, cook, and chauffeur were mainstays.) And of course, there was a well-stocked bar.[49]

In a sign of the affection he had earned from coworkers, "The musicians that make up Max Steiner's studio recording band gave him a 'lawn shower' for his new home," *Hollywood Reporter* noted.[50] "The brass section gave him an oak tree, the strings an entire lawn, the reeds his spring flowers and the drummer sent a lawnmower."

Cove Way allowed Max to indulge in two favorite hobbies: photography and gardening. "When not playing farmer he loves to dig little ponds, canals, and water falls lined with stones over which lead some safe (and also unsafe) rustic bridges," journalist Bruno David Ussher wrote.[51]

> His workroom is fairly shut off from the rest of the house. It is a long, low-ceilinged apartment finished with sound absorbing wall covering. At one end is a superlative phonograph, at the other a built-in loud-speaker so that Steiner can test his recordings. Of course there is a grand piano, also a writing table, shelf space to spread music manuscripts and a couch bed, for the times when "Maxie" works double and triple eight hour shifts . . .
>
> Wall and floor space is crowded with a most diversified collection of weapons, from short hunting knives to sabers, from old pocket derringers to good sized replicas of cannons. Incidentally the affable composer is proud of being a keen rifle shot. [By 1937, Steiner was an honorary member of the L.A. County Sheriff's Department.][52]

During the previous ten months, Steiner had married the woman he loved and who helped bring his music to life. He had moved into a perfect home, won his first Academy Award, earned acclaim as music director for Selznick, and launched a promising side-career at Warner Bros.

Cove Way, exterior and Louise's music room. (Louise Steiner Elian Papers; L. Tom Perry Special Collections, Brigham Young University)

(Louise Steiner Elian Papers; L. Tom Perry Special Collections, Brigham Young University)

He was also returning to the old, frenetic work pace that he claimed to despise but also thrived on. While supervising *Lost Horizon*, Steiner wrote two scores on loan-out to Warner Bros. *God's Country and the Woman* was noteworthy only as the first Warner feature in Technicolor. But director Frank Borzage's *Green Light*, starring Errol Flynn, inspired a moving, underrated score.

As 1936 came to an end, only one shadow hovered over Steiner: once again, he was in debt. On December 18, he signed a promissory note to Selznick International Pictures, for a loan of $4,000.[53] The amount was substantial, but Max was unfazed. After all, his position with David O. Selznick—his "leading fan"—would probably last for years.

Instead, it lasted barely four more months.

THERE WAS EVERY REASON TO THINK that *A Star Is Born* would be another happy collaboration. A cynical-romantic look at Hollywood, it explored the industry's toll on two married stars: Vicki Lester, née Esther Blodgett, an actress on the rise (Janet Gaynor), and Norman Maine, a Barrymore-like alcoholic (Fredric March). In 1932, Max and David had teamed on *Star*'s unofficial first draft at RKO, *What Price Hollywood?* Both films tapped into viewers' desire to project themselves into the lives of celebrities, while also suggesting that the cost of fame was too high.

But even before Max began work on *Star*, trouble brewed. Selznick was increasingly anxiety-ridden, and his criticisms extended to Max. "The idea that he cannot compose until the picture is cut is nonsense," David wrote general manager Henry Ginsberg, "because all his themes can be set and all his music selected and composed, in general, and changes made later if the scene is ten or fifteen feet longer or shorter."[54]

Two days later, Selznick backtracked. Memo to Ginsberg: "We criticize and ride Max Steiner a great deal and no doubt will have to continue to do so in the future, so it might not be amiss to pat him on the back on the fast job he did of composing, arranging, and the actual scoring of *Star Is Born*."[55]

Three days later, Selznick watched *Star* with music—and his promised pat on the back became a kick, as he tore into Steiner's work as never before. An assistant recorded David's on-the-fly reactions. "Music spoils flow of scene—too many changes, no emotional quality." A later cue: "Dead." Esther's trip to central casting: "Too slow."

From there, it only got worse.

"Worthless."

"??????"

And most insultingly, a long list with the same two letters: "N.G." No Good.[56]

Selznick's comments enraged Steiner. David wanted most of the score changed or rewritten, with many cues to be replaced with music from *Little Lord Fauntleroy*.

For the composer, it was bad enough that old music was being used to dramatize the emotions of new characters. Even worse were instances when Selznick removed a cue and replaced it with . . . nothing.

Early in *A Star Is Born*, Esther is hired to serve hors d'oeuvres at a swank Hollywood party. There, she pauses at guests' tables to show off her impressions of actual movie stars. Steiner's cue for the scene begins as elegant source music, then subtly morphs into action-specific commentary during Esther's impressions. As she imitates Mae West's drawl, a hot clarinet plays the saloon standard "Frankie and Johnny." When she switches to the brittle cadences of Katharine Hepburn, Max wittily plays the spinet-solo theme for Hepburn's "Jo" from *Little Women*, a score he knew Selznick loved.

Inexplicably, his boss removed the entire cue. The scene as scored by Max can be seen on the Internet: with music, it is breezy and charming,

An early example of Selznick exploiting score: piano sheet music for a theme from *A Star Is Born*.

putting us on Esther's side even as we recognize the absurdity of her imitations. Without music, as presented in the final film, the scene comes off as badly edited, with dead air between dialogue. Worse, we now cringe at Esther's imitations, performed in silence, as we wonder whether to laugh with her or at her.

One good thing came from the rescoring: a new theme Max called "Janet's Waltz," after Esther's portrayer, Janet Gaynor. Its wistful beauty shows that even when frustrated, Steiner could write first-rate music. Its opening phrase of four descending notes is repeated a fifth higher, then a third higher, before unspooling a long, flowing continuation of melody. Again, the composer uses a musical "climb" to create a sense of emotional uplift, with a carefully timed release at its emotional peak.

"Janet's Waltz" strengthened the score, but the damage was done. Steiner considered the final score a ruination. And on April 8, he sat down to write one of the most painful letters of his life.

My dear Mr. Selznick,

After thinking and thinking it over, I have come to the conclusion that it would be best for all concerned if you would permit me to resign.

I would not know <u>what</u> to compose for your next picture! I <u>can</u> not and do not <u>want</u> to change my technique of writing, not because I am stubborn but because I am <u>afraid</u> to do so, having always been most successful in my way of scoring up to the, for me, so unpleasant advent of *A Star Is Born*!*

I have made all the changes you ordered and am most unhappy. I only wish it were possible to remove my credit from the screen.

You surely know of my strong affection and friendship for you. Therefore, in order to preserve this, to me so enviable friendship, it is absolutely imperative that our contract be nullified.[57]

THE FILM SCORES OF MAX STEINER

1936 Releases (continued)

The Charge of the Light Brigade (9/36–10/36). Warner Bros.
Lost Horizon (10/36–2/37). Columbia. Score by Dimitri Tiomkin; musical supervision by Steiner.
God's Country and the Woman (11/36). Warner Bros.
Green Light (11/36–12/36). Warner Bros.

1937 Releases (continued in Chapter 14)

A Star Is Born (3/37–4/37). Selznick International.
Nothing Sacred. Selznick International. Uncredited; additional music only.

Selznick agreed. But what the producer later called their "divorce" became more of a separation with benefits. After David listened to Oscar Levant's

---

* Writing to a friend, Max was less humble: "I am conceited enough to believe that I am a pioneer in that field and know something about it; besides, my music has always been successful." (MS to Frederick Day, May 13, 1937, MSS 1547, Box 2, Folder 13.)

bluesy score for 1937's *Nothing Sacred*, the producer demanded changes due to "too many discords."[58] Steiner provided uncredited rewrites and new orchestrations, free of charge, alongside Selznick's new music director Lou Forbes—the brother of Leo Forbstein, and a recommendation of Max's.

There was another reason Steiner made return visits to Selznick. In 1936, David had purchased a new novel for $50,000—a record payment for a first-time author. By April 1937, Margaret Mitchell's *Gone with the Wind* had become a million-seller, and with each passing month, expectations rose over Selznick's screen adaptation.

According to Steiner, the producer promised that he would bring Max back to score the Civil War epic.[59] If such an agreement was made, it was not put in writing. Nevertheless, Steiner believed with a certainty worthy of Scarlett O'Hara that nothing would stop him from scoring what promised to be the most important motion picture of his life.

14

The Right Place to Be

ON APRIL 14, 1937, IT WAS OFFICIAL: Max Steiner and David O. Selznick had parted ways.[1] But the same industry reports announcing the break had other news to share. On April 12, four days after his resignation letter to David, Max had become a Warner Bros. staff composer.

After Steiner left Selznick, his agent, Charles Feldman, had urged Max to beg for his job back, since there were no openings in town. "I told him, 'Why don't you try Warners'?" Steiner recalled in a private letter.[2] "I had already talked with Forbstein the day before I resigned from Selznick. 'Selznick paid me $1,250.00 [a week] and you ask Mr. Warner for $1,500.' Feldman fainted. . . . [He] talked with Warner, and Warner said he wouldn't pay that kind of salary . . . I thereupon called Leo Forbstein and told him that I was sorry but that Feldman had told me that the deal was off, and Leo answered . . . 'The deal is not off, because I just left Warner and I got you the $1,500 plus a two year contract with a two year option.'"

Max had brokered his highest salary to date, plus mention in publicity ads for a film, and solo screen credit in the main titles.

No longer a musical director, Max could focus solely on composing, and soon felt "thoroughly relaxed and more than satisfied with my new job," he wrote a friend.[3] "I believe that this is the right place for me to be. It is a very big organization; they leave me completely alone and consider everything that I write 'colossal.'" Even at an annual $78,000 (more than $1.3 million today), Steiner was a bargain. For the next decade he worked on an average of six films a year—a record 12 in 1939. If Max scored ten films over 12 months, as he would in 1937, his cost per picture was $7,800, below the price of an A-list freelancer.

And in a studio of workaholics, he was probably the most tireless of all.

WARNERS WAS INDEED A BIG ORGANIZATION. At 135 acres in size, the Burbank studio operated "somewhat like a moated feudal city," *Fortune* observed in 1937.[4] "By never buying unnecessary stories, rarely making retakes, and always knocking temperament on the head when they can, the Warners probably get more production money onto the screen than any other studio." Its films were shown mostly in Warner-owned theaters. And unlike RKO, the studio would end fiscal year 1937 with a gross consolidated income of about $100 million.[5]

Fortune credited much of that success to Jack's tight-fisted supervision, remarking that his "bargain-counter dictatorship has produced some excellent pictures. . . . If he does not allow much liberty of temperament on his lot, he is very far from discouraging liberty of imagination." Emphasis on frugality led some to call Warners the "San Quentin of studios."[6] Yet it made films as handsomely produced as its rivals, and often more adult.

"Jack was a showman who played his hunches," Hal Wallis recalled.[7] "Just from glancing at a title or riffling through a few pages, he could sense whether a property would interest millions of people. . . . He was usually right." Observed director Irving Rapper, "People were always feuding and getting suspensions—I had ten." But "if Warner liked you, he'd let you do anything you wanted."[8]

Steiner's arrival could not have been better timed. The studio had entered the 1930s cranking out gangster tales and sex comedies that outraged censors. After the enforcement of the Production Code in 1934, Warners made more prestigious features—while still grinding out comedies, musicals, and crime dramas for the masses. Uniting all its product was a vivid house style: photography that embraced deep shadows while rejecting gloss; a brisk editorial tempo; and a high-volume soundtrack with bold, brassy music.

The music department housed offices for each staff composer, two of whom were especially helpful to Max: Heinz Roemheld and Adolph Deutsch, a London native who composed and also orchestrated. Steiner's office was big enough to include a mahogany desk, a grand piano, a wall of autographed photos, and framed testimonials.[9] The space was shared with his loyal secretary since 1930, Marie Teller.

Freelancer Erich Wolfgang Korngold also had an office. According to producer Henry Blanke, "When he heard something that sounded like his music, he opened his door and said, 'Why do you steal from me? Why don't you steal from the man I steal from, Richard Strauss?'"[10] Max clearly wasn't the only composer at Warners with a sharp wit. However, "I don't think there was any jealousy between the two at all," Louise recalled.[11] "They admired each other.

One time I was with Max and we'd had a session. Korngold came on stage for something, and Max said to Erich, 'I should be jealous, my wife likes your music too!' "

Privately, Steiner did have one criticism of Korngold's approach. "He thought it was often too much for the scene," recalled a friend.[12] "Max said it was like a Christmas tree with too much tinsel and too many ornaments. Korngold did counterpoint on top of counterpoint. But Max also said, 'He's a fine composer.' "

The most versatile staffer was 28-year-old arranger-conductor Ray Heindorf, who excelled at everything from Busby Berkeley musicals to the idiom of Korngold. Heindorf was also "largely responsible for what is instantly recognizable as 'the Warners sound,'" observed music producer Ray Faiola.[13] "Partly a by-product of the acoustics in the recording stage, its origin was primarily that of orchestral balance, with jointly pronounced string and horn sections that produced an enveloping sound heard in films as early as *42nd Street* and as late as *The Music Man*."

Warners' recording stage was an acoustical marvel, despite its modest appearance. "It looked more like a huge two-story barn," recalled harpist Aida Mulieri Dagort.[14] "The walls were supported by exposed 2x4s . . . and the spaces in-between were stuffed with asbestos. By the 1940s they had become black from years of accumulated dirt. . . . During working hours the air became filled with rosin dust from the bows of the string players. . . . The soundproofed control booth and the projection booth were in second floor rooms built into one side of the stage. The whole arrangement was dominated by an oversized screen behind the orchestra."

MIXING OF A SCORE WAS DONE LIVE during a recording. Recalled Arthur Piantadosi, an assistant mixer, "I'd read the score and when they rehearsed, [chief mixer Dave Forrest] would give me signals. 'At bar 22, favor the flute solo with the woodwind mike, and at bar 48 favor the violas over the cellos.' I wore gum-soled shoes, so very quietly I went all around the different microphones, waited until the designated bar, and moved the microphone. You had to rehearse every cue. In those days they spent time—you didn't treat Max Steiner like garbage."[15]

In hiring Steiner, the studio also inherited key members of his team. Hal Findlay still created his cue sheets, which broke down screen action to the split-second. Pianists Max Rabinowitch and Norma Drury joined the orchestra. Drury "was a tall, full-figured woman," recalled Aida Mulieri Dagort, "striking in appearance. She had a high cheekboned Slavic face and straight black hair pulled back into a knot. Norma was always full of good humor and pep and had a great infectious laugh."[16]

Louis Kaufman was the orchestra's concertmaster when not touring as a soloist. And of course, Louise was Max's principal harpist.

Working with first-rate musicians who were also friends meant an atmosphere of camaraderie. "Max was very down-to-earth and friendly, not at all the usual haughty, lecherous, Hollywood character," recalled Dagort.[17] Now 49, he had "thinning black hair that was beginning to gray at the temples. In spite of glasses, I saw two sparkling black eyes and a pleasant, almost pixie-like face. . . . He was a wonderful, sweet gentleman, who shifted from one foot to the other, and chewed on his cigar when someone came up to talk with him."

Steiner was unusual in his hiring of several women. Observed Louise, "Max was one of two conductors in Hollywood who didn't care about the sex of the people in his orchestra. [Korngold was the other.] In all the major studio orchestras, the musicians were primarily men. Max had the idea that only ability mattered."[18]

Paving each step of the way was Leo Forbstein. Although some of his duties seemed designed to raise Steiner's blood pressure—like hounding him to meet a release date—"We became bosom pals," Max recalled.[19] Ever sensitive to language, Steiner was amused by Leo's "peculiar vernacular regarding the orchestra. He would always say, 'I would like to go with you tomorrow.' This meant that he wanted to record the next day."[20]

After Selznick's denigrations, Warners must have felt like a trip to Shangri-La. Of course, Max was not entirely left alone. A film's producer—usually Wallis or Henry Blanke, who trained under Lubitsch—often gave Steiner "spotting notes" indicating the desired start and stopping point of music. But Max was allowed input on these choices. Recalled Wallis, "If there was time, Max played themes for my consideration on the piano in my office. He hummed and moved his tiny body up and down the keyboard with tremendous energy. I always looked forward to these sessions. Steiner and I decided whether it should be a heavy score or a light score. . . . Often, he wrote the entire score without our first hearing anything but the theme."[21]

For Jack Warner, there seemed no such thing as too much music. "Max said that he thought Warner would have been happy if Max wrote from the first frame to the last," a friend recalled. "That way, in places where they felt they didn't need it, they could just dial it out."[22]

EVERYTHING AT THE STUDIO WAS PERFECT for Steiner. Everything, that is, except his assignments.

After Selznick's A-pictures, Max was frustrated to learn that his first Warner titles were hardly the stuff of Academy Awards. Things started passably with *Kid Galahad*, a boxing drama starring Edward G. Robinson and Bette Davis. But days after completing it, Steiner sulked when assigned to *Slim*.[23] The slight, entertaining drama starred Pat O'Brien and Henry Fonda as power line repairmen Red and Slim, competitive best pals in love with the same dame.

Surliness faded when composing began. Steiner's title theme is unusually swingy, and the film's literally charged content gave him new chances to turn technology into music. For the main title: *"ELECTRIC TOWER... Telegraph imitation by Steiner... somewhat like the R.K.O. trademark."*[24] As for a later comment, *"Hugo dear... This whole last part smells from herring,"* it is unclear if he means the music, the movie, or both.

Max felt a wave of déjà vu that October: *Submarine D-1* was a slight, entertaining drama starring Pat O'Brien and Wayne Morris as U.S. Navy tars Butch and Sock, competitive best pals in love with the same dame. What Max couldn't have foreseen is that his patriotic score for this paean to the navy would bail him out of tight deadlines for years to come. Its brawny main march (*"a la Sousa"*)[25] and several other cues—like a bitonal, comic riff on "What Can You Do With a Drunken Sailor?"—would be lifted intact by Steiner for many later flag-wavers, including *Dive Bomber, Fighter Squadron* and *Operation Pacific*.

MAX'S PASSION AND VERSATILITY soon won over even Hal Wallis. The producer who sent pages of blistering criticism to top directors wrote Steiner many notes of praise, and regarded him as a friend.

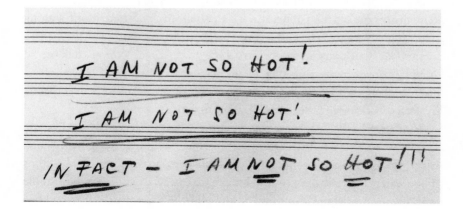

"Steiner was as much a part of Warner pictures as our stock company," Wallis recalled.[26] "A tiny, fast-talking, hypersensitive gnome with great wit and a strong streak of schmaltz, he received visitors at his home on Sundays in white pajamas, smoking a large cigar, with rich strains of his latest score as background music. The only time I saw him ill-tempered was when I suggested bringing in an outside composer to help him. Although his work load was heavy, Max wanted to do everything himself. Had he been able, I think he would have composed music for every picture we made. . . . He was impassioned, wholehearted in everything. And it showed in his work . . . [Steiner and Korngold] were both indispensable to the success of our pictures in the thirties."

IN LATE APRIL, Wallis and Henry Blanke assigned Max to a project he felt was worthy of his stature. *The Life of Emile Zola*, starring Paul Muni, chronicled the 19th-century novelist's rise, and his role in exonerating Alfred Dreyfus, a military captain whose imprisonment was driven by anti-Semitism. It was the first of many Warner fusillades against the growing threat of Nazism abroad, and the anti-Semitism all too prevalent in 1930s America.

Zola's death from smoke inhalation is foreshadowed in the first scene. It is a deceptively light-hearted glimpse of the struggling young Emile burning his work in a faulty stove, with the friend who shares his loft, Paul Cézanne. The scene is cribbed from Puccini's *La Bohème*, which introduces its hero in near-identical fashion. Steiner plays up the similarity with an *Allegro giocoso*[27] scherzo; but in a nod at tragedy to come, he includes a *"smoke effect"* for *"low flutes, harp, celeste, piano, vibraphone . . . quasi-mysterioso."* A joke earlier in his sketch sums up this canny blend of darkness and light: *"A terrific trick—I studied with Schoenberg and Romberg."*

When Zola meets the prostitute who inspires his first book success, *Nana*, Steiner turns the syllables of her name into a plaintive two-note motif, sighing from a high G down to C, and setting them against a minor-key *Valse lente*— a weary Parisian cousin to Sibelius's *Valse triste*. Zola's famous defense of Dreyfus, *J'Accuse*, is given its own triumphant three-note motif. This perfect-fifth leap from two Gs up to C is an inversion of the doomed Nana's theme. Musically, justice is literally the reversal of injustice.

The Life of Emile Zola received a standing ovation at its preview.[28] Ecstatic reviews were followed by ten Oscar nominations, including Best Music Score. And although Steiner was not a winner, *Zola* became the second of his films to be named Best Picture. To Max's delight, Jack Warner "took the trouble to write me and tell me how good he thought the score was."[29] It would not be the last time. The studio chief saw most of his product with and without music; the frequent agony of the former taught him never to take a Steiner score for granted.

AMID MAX'S PLAYFUL COMMENTS on *Zola*'s sketches, there is one unusual note of caution. After decorating a Wagnerian phrase with swastikas—for Max, Wagner was both a genius and "the first Nazi"—he adds, *"DON'T LET LEO SEE THIS!!!"* But by Reel 12, swastikas once again fill its pages, taking the place of asterisks.

Max's reason wasn't flippancy. It was fear.

By April 1937, Germany was rearming for war. Its Austrian-born dictator had spoken only privately of plans to annex his homeland; but many, including Max, worried that an Anschluss was imminent. Hitler had been a shadow in Steiner's life as early as 1905. Both men were devotees of Lehar's *The Merry Widow*, and both likely attended the same performances of the operetta during its premiere engagement, at Vienna's Theater an der Wien.[30]

By 1937, Hitler was threatening the existence of Steiner's family in Austria. Max feared that his own success might add to their danger.

After he received a request for his biography from *Who's Who in American Jewry*, Marie Teller replied, "Mr. Steiner is not of the Jewish faith, inasmuch

Paul Muni in a publicity still from *The Life of Emile Zola*.

as his father is a Protestant and his mother is Catholic."[31] Editor John Simons persisted, replying that *Who's Who* would include "all notable men and women whose racial descent is Jewish." Again, Steiner demurred. Again, Simons persisted. "We are publishing an article in any event on your career" that would include "the names of your father and mother."[32]

Despite legal threats, Simons included Max in his publication. But by then, Steiner's mother was beyond even Hitler's reach. In October 1937, the composer received a letter from Felix Zipser, a Viennese physician, informing him that 67-year-old Mitzi was "gravely ill" with stomach cancer. Only her stubbornness was unchanged.

"I couldn't initiate any kind of aggressive therapy sooner because your mother resolutely refused to undergo a thorough exam. . . . Back when I treated her for a heart condition, your mother already caused me the greatest of difficulties, as she repeatedly quit therapeutic treatments under the pretext that she had no money to pay for them. . . . I believe that the time she has left will be short and painful and would like to do whatever I can to make the time she has left bearable."[33]

Max was stunned and wracked with guilt. Fighting multiple deadlines, he realized he would never see his mother again. "PLEASE DO EVERYTHING NECESSARY IN TERMS OF TREATMENTS AND HEART THERAPY," he wired. "SEND BILLS DIRECTLY TO ME."[34]

On October 31, Louise and Max celebrated their first wedding anniversary. Seven days later, they received word that Mitzi was dead.

That Christmas was Steiner's most melancholy since coming to America. On December 23 he sent two telegrams to his father. The first read: "JUST SENT FLOWERS FOR MAMA'S GRAVE." The second: "MERRY CHRISTMAS—MAX."[35]

STEINER'S MOST ENDURING CONTRIBUTION to Warner Bros. in 1937 was not a score, but a fanfare.

That year, the studio's triangle-shield logo become uniform in its appearance onscreen. As Max began *Tovarich* starring Claudette Colbert, he decided that the new logo deserved a distinctive accompaniment. He revised a brassy opening he wrote that summer for the comedy *First Lady*, and crafted what became the second most famous studio fanfare in cinema history (after Alfred Newman's 20th Century Fox theme).

Jack Warner loved it and insisted it be used on all Warner titles unless an exception was granted.[36] Neither Korngold nor in later years Franz Waxman was required to use it; and Max omitted it if a film's opening music was so similar in mood that the fanfare seemed redundant.[37]

That December, Steiner refined the fanfare in what would be its definitive version, for *Gold Is Where You Find It*. He raised its key from B-flat to the brighter sound of C major, and turned four measures of ascending triplets, written in the time signature of $\frac{4}{4}$, into two measures of triplets written in $\frac{12}{8}$. The reason: $\frac{12}{8}$ has 12 beats to a measure, versus four beats a measure in $\frac{4}{4}$. Steiner could now conduct the climbing phrase more precisely with 12 beats of the baton, controlling its ritard (slowing down) as the triplets reached their climax.

Since the fanfare's ending has no resolution, it was re-recorded each time it was used. The reader is invited to listen to the first seconds of Warner Bros. movies from 1938 to the early '50s with fresh ears: note the ingenuity with which Steiner segues from the fanfare's close into a range of moods, from screwball comedy (*The Bride Came C.O.D.*) to bleak social drama (*Caged*).

EVEN AT HIS BUSIEST, Max couldn't turn a deaf ear to David O. Selznick. In September 1937, the producer considered borrowing Steiner for *The Adventures of Tom Sawyer*—but only "if certain conditions were agreed to by Warners and by Maxie—first, that he start preparing now; second, that he forget the 'Mickey Mouse' scoring, and for all his pleas to the contrary he knows just what I'm talking about; and third, that he operates on a set budget."[38] Never mind that by the time his Technicolor cameras stopped rolling, Selznick had hired three directors and replaced multiple actors during a shoot that, despite an absence of stars, exceeded a million dollars.[39]

Selznick's music director, Lou Forbes, enlisted Franz Waxman to write several original cues, and licensed existing music by Newman, Steiner, and others.[40] Inevitably, Selznick borrowed Max to score a few key scenes, three of which stand out. Tom and pals' midnight trip to a graveyard, ending in their witnessing a murder, is scored with hushed ghost-story intensity: *"Large gong, pp—basses and celli, timpani roll—vibraphone . . . Hammond organ overtone."*[41] Steiner intensifies that mood at the film's climax, when Tom and Becky realize they are lost and alone in a giant cave. The sequence, opined writer Joseph D'Onofrio, "takes on the look and feel of a claustrophobic nightmare, aided considerably by Max Steiner's evocative score."[42]

Best of all is the sequence's climax. Searching for a way out, Tom climbs the cave's shadowy rocks alone. His candle is suddenly extinguished by a breeze that is given voice in a shimmering, major-key chord (*"FASTER . . . Timpani, make crescendo"*). Harps, celesta and vibraphone (*"ethereal"*) follow Tom as he ascends. Music modulates upward with him, building into a soaring hymn for full orchestra, a la Strauss's *Alpine Symphony*, as Tom reaches the pinnacle and faces a godlike shaft of light. *"Heaven music—Ecstatic—'Becky, there's light!'"*

WHILE MAX WAS SETTING MARK TWAIN to music, Warner contract player Bette Davis was enjoying the fruits of victory, after a year of battling Jack Warner for better roles.

The part of 1850s southern belle Julie Marsden, the title character of *Jezebel*, was perfect for Bette's fire. And thanks to an excellent script and William Wyler's painstaking direction, *Jezebel* also launched a new epoch at Warners, making Davis its top female star.

Steiner had scored her previous drama, *That Certain Woman*. Its music—jazzy-defiant one moment, Puccini-esque the next—led Hal Wallis to recognize another of Max's specialties: enriching the psychology of a complex heroine. With *Jezebel*, the Steiner-Davis partnership flowered into full maturity. Max would go on to score 15 more films in which she appeared, and enjoy a friendship with the actress who proudly called him *"my* composer."[43]

In *Jezebel's* early scenes, music suggests both Julie's coquettish charm and the ego that will be her undoing. *"[Julie] throws umbrella . . . molto grazioso but she is a bitch!! [Music] should show her temper!"*[44] Steiner ensures that instruments never fight her vocal timbre or her New Orleans accent: regarding the line "Am I?" he notes, *"She says Am ah—in this pitch, between E and F."*

Quarrels with her fiancé, Preston Dillard (Henry Fonda), lead Julie to defy her beau—and society—by wearing a scandalous red dress to an all-white formal ball. (The film is black and white, but Ernest Haller's cinematography convinces us that we see Julie in scarlet red.) "Pres" calls her bluff, spinning her on the ballroom floor in a waltz as others dancers exit in shock, and Julie pleads for her furious partner to stop.

Jezebel's script details each beat of this, the film's centerpiece.[45] But it was Wyler who made the scene unforgettable, in partnership with the finest waltz that Steiner wrote in his 68 years of exploring the form. Its opening three notes—three F-naturals—match the syllables of "Jezebel," the term Julie soon will be branded with. A rising triplet (G–A–B-flat) leads us to a repetition of the opening three-note phrase; then another triplet lifts us higher into the firmament. Steiner combines the intoxicating swirl of a Johann Strauss waltz with a melody whose "grave, dignified beauty,"[46] to quote Philip J. S. Hammond, hints at disaster to follow.

Max had a model for the music's controlled tension: Ravel's *La Valse*, which starts with seductive beauty, then escalates into an arrhythmic maelstrom.

Bette Davis and Henry Fonda in a publicity still from *Jezebel*.

Steiner does not go as far as Ravel's climactic violation of tempo and melody (it would not fit the action) but few who see *Jezebel* forget the scene's almost wordless intensity, in which music is a character.

The threat of yellow fever has been planted early in the film. Pres becomes its victim, and the moment of his infection is captured with chilling subtlety, as a plantation guest plays Chopin's E-major Etude while Pres strolls outside. "A blurred dissonance occurs, timed precisely to Pres's slapping of a mosquito on his wrist," authors William DuBois and Jack Darby noted.[47] "The ominous dissonance of Steiner's harmonic touch [played by nondiegetic orchestra against the diegetic Chopin] signifies something more than mickey-mousing."

At film's end Julie holds Pres, near death, on a wagon carrying them to exile on a quarantined island. Their fate is left to our imagination; but the movie's last seconds deliver a grim apotheosis, as hellish street bonfires and cannon blasts create a crescendo to match a swelling rumble of drums, harp, and orchestra. *"My idea (however lousy) is to keep the tempo slow but work up the orchestra just the same . . . Symphonically."* A mood of apocalyptic dread may have come naturally. *"Hugo: Please help this as much as you can. It is now 6:20 A.M. And I am called for 9:30 with the orchestra—I can't think any more."*

Jezebel earned Bette Davis her second Academy Award. For a time, it seemed as if a second Oscar would adorn Max's music room. But curiously, the Academy placed *Jezebel* in the category of Best Scoring, a hodgepodge of musicals, comedy, and dramatic scores. (The winner was Newman for *Alexander's Ragtime Band*.) In the separate category of Best Original Score, *The Adventures of Robin Hood* earned Korngold a second Oscar, for his greatest cinematic work.

Korngold had initially turned down *Robin Hood*;[48] and briefly, it looked as if the film would be Max's. The fact that Warners insisted on Korngold fed Steiner's suspicion that he was seen, in 1938 parlance, as the studio's War Admiral, running second to Korngold's Seabiscuit.

For each *Jezebel*, Max felt he was unfairly saddled with two or three programmers like the gangster tale *The Amazing Dr. Clitterhouse*. Oscar Levant, ever ready to stab the hand that helped him, smirked in print that Steiner was "an excellent man on prison-break fogs, and also does a good job of industrial noises. Do you recall the whistles, bells, clanging of doors and other institutional sounds for *Crime School*? . . . They were all part of Steiner's scores for these films, and enormously effective."[49]

Max's resentment verged on paranoia. "People in the industry all give me 'the works,'" he wrote Hal Wallis, "telling me that Warners think I am only good for action pictures, and when pictures like *Juarez* and *Robin Hood* come along, they give them to someone else."[50] One score page for *Each Dawn I Die*, a James Cagney prison drama, is ornamented with a drawing of three sobbing faces. Its caption: *"The audience."*[51] An illustration on the last page needs no text: carefully drawn in red and black pencil, it shows a boy in profile producing a fountain of urine.

But even Max had to acknowledge the excellence of *Angels with Dirty Faces*. Directed by Michael Curtiz—by now Steiner's favorite director—the drama starred Cagney and Pat O'Brien as childhood friends whose paths take a familiar diversion: Cagney's Rocky Sullivan becomes a hoodlum, O'Brien a priest unable to keep his pal from ending up in the electric chair. *Angels'* finale became movie lore: in Rocky's prison cell, Father Connolly urges his friend to feign cowardice as he walks to the chair. That way, the street kids who idolize him won't follow his criminal path. Rocky refuses, but during his death march, he breaks down into hysterics.

In scoring the scene, filmed and edited as a slow, suspenseful crescendo, Steiner faced a delicate balancing act, as he told an interviewer:

As the procession of officers, priests and the condemned man goes toward the execution chamber, they, of course, were not marching in military order and therefore not all "in step." Steiner said he composed some half dozen scores for this scene, none of which was satisfactory and were discarded.

He finally got a theme that suited him, but he was confronted with the problem of the rhythm, since it accompanied a group of men marching. It couldn't be definitely rhythmic; it couldn't well be long sustained chords with slow-moving harmonies, so he finally hit upon the idea of having the "undercover" rhythm follow the cadence of the individual in the group which the audience likely would be watching.

As you watch the scene and listen to the scoring, you realize that the cadence changes from one individual in the group to another, as his particular prominence at the moment calls for.[52]

Steiner scores the movie's final cast list with a favorite device, his musical equivalent of a story extension. By playing Father Connolly's religioso theme, instead of the leaping, flame-like octaves that define Rocky, the composer suggests that Sullivan's dangerous charm has lost its influence on the boys who worshipped him, and that they will avoid his fate.

FOR MAX, 1938 WOULD LIVE IN MEMORY not for its scores but for the arrival of a disaster he had long feared. On March 12, Hitler's army marched into Austria. The Anschluss had begun.

For months, Max had tried to expedite his father's emigration. Now, he "pulled every string at the state department," Louise recalled.[53] Those efforts paid off. In a letter stamped with an official swastika, Steiner was informed that 80-year-old Gabor could leave Vienna.

Max booked passage for his father via liner to New York, where he arranged to have him met by a friend, journalist Arthur Faltin. "He does not speak English," Steiner told Faltin, "and I am afraid he might get into trouble. . . . Also this beautiful Hitler regime allows a traveler for America to take only 20 marks ($4.00). . . . I haven't heard from him when he can come [but] expect to hear any day. . . . Please don't advertise to anyone in New York that he is coming, as he does not wish to meet any relatives for reasons best known to himself."[54]

Gabor Steiner. (MS Papers; L. Tom Perry Special Collections, Brigham Young University)

Preparing to leave a city run by Nazis, Gabor seemed just as anxious about meeting relatives in New York—probably due to his outstanding debts. But fear of creditors was replaced by a greater worry, as weeks passed with no update on his departure. Max was near-hysterical. Hal Wallis did what little he could.

Steiner to Faltin: "Warners are giving me two weeks vacation. I am, therefore (believe it or not) taking my first trip out of California in seven years and I'm going to Honolulu."[55]

ON MAY 28, 18 DAYS AFTER his 50th birthday, he and Louise departed for Hawaii aboard the S.S. *Lurline*. Their two-week stay at the Royal Hawaiian Hotel seemed like an escape to paradise. "It is so glorious here," Louise wrote her mother.[56] "We swim every day, practically spend all day on the beach . . . this vacation is doing him just worlds of good. . . . You should see the full moon on the water."

It was the last truly carefree time in Max Steiner's life.

THE FILM SCORES OF MAX STEINER

All films listed in this and subsequent chapters are Warner Bros. releases unless otherwise noted.

1937 Releases (continued)

Kid Galahad (4/37)

Slim (4/37)

The Life of Emile Zola (5/37–6/37). AAN.

That Certain Woman (6/37–7/37)

First Lady (7/37)

Submarine D-1 (10/37)

Tovarich (10/37/–11/37)

1938 Releases

Gold Is Where You Find It (12/37–1/38)

Jezebel (1/38–2/38). AAN.

The Adventures of Tom Sawyer (2/38). Selznick International. Additional music only.

Crime School (4/38)

White Banners (4/38–5/38). This moving drama, starring Claude Rains, features one of Steiner's most underrated scores.

The Amazing Dr. Clitterhouse (5/38–6/38)

Four Daughters (7/38)

The Sisters (8/38–9/38)

Angels with Dirty Faces (9/38–10/38)

The Dawn Patrol (10/38–11/38)

They Made Me a Criminal (11/38)

IN SEPTEMBER, GABOR'S NINE-MONTH VIGIL finally ended: he could leave Austria in a matter of days. As he began his journey west, a *Hollywood Reporter* item captured the stakes, noting that Gabor "was one of the last to get out . . . days before the border was closed."[57]

On September 15 Max received the news he'd waited for. "Your dear pop 'came, saw and conquered,'" Arthur Faltin wrote from New York. Gabor "is younger than the two of us put together. . . . I hope you enjoy with him 20 more years in the land where the milk and honey flows."[58] (Years later, Max repaid the favor by helping Faltin find work.)

Gabor arrived in Los Angeles on September 19 "in first-class condition," Max wrote Faltin, "and he loves it out here. . . . The gardener had put 'Welcome Papa' in roses on the door; and, of course, you can imagine his feelings."[59]

Louise had carefully prepared Gabor's new home, in Cove Way's guest apartment over their garage. "We also engaged a chauffeur, George, who spoke German"[60]—which Louise did not. But despite that divide, Gabor's first meeting with his daughter-in-law was a warm one. Later, he gave her a gold bracelet: it contained miniature medals representing the many honors Gabor received in his glory days, from Italy, Persia, Montenegro, Tunisia, Russia—and from Emperor Franz Joseph of Austria.[61]

GABOR'S SAFE ARRIVAL MARKED THE END of what had been, for Max, a nightmare of near-unbearable stress. Almost certainly he had saved his father's life.

But in the months to come, as events unfolded that he seemed unable to control, Steiner's sense of relief, and his domestic happiness, would be as distant a memory as his days spent with Louise on the sleepy beaches of Honolulu.

Fighting for Steiner

SINCE LEAVING AUSTRIA, Max Steiner had not only mastered the English language but could easily switch from the latest American slang to the tone of an erudite professor. On December 13, 1938, he shared that gift during a one-hour talk for members of the Music Clubs and Professional Women Musicians group, who assembled in a Warner Bros. screening room for a memorable show and tell.

Max proved an insightful speaker. "There must be an intelligent and intelligible reason" for the presence of underscoring, he began.[1] "You'll never know how I love the slamming of doors or the dropping of a book or any impact that will give me a cue on which to introduce the music for a given scene." Sequences from recent Warner titles were shown without, then with, his music. They included 1938's *The Sisters*, whose events are set in motion when Bette Davis's Louise Elliott elopes with a ne'er-do-well reporter (Errol Flynn). A real-life journalist captured Steiner's analysis of the scene:

> "It was simply useless to bother only about the hurry of the characters . . . there was plenty of natural sound—running horses, carriage wheels, footsteps on stairs and the like—to keep the scene from seeming empty. So I set about to compose a sequence which would foretell something of the uncertainty and final collapse of the marriage that was to follow the elopement. How well I succeeded I will leave you to judge."

He then had a projectionist throw on the screen this elopement scene, first without the music and then with the underscoring. The difference was a revelation! The whole meaning of the sequence was brought out in highlight to a degree that no other medium could accomplish. Not only was the scene heightened in artistic content . . . with the application of the musical soundtrack there was a smoothness about the dialogue, a sort of toning down and weaving together of all the sound that rid the sequence of startling and crude effects.[2]

Steiner would give similar lectures in 1939, 1940, and 1941. Surviving excerpts from the talks overlap with his contemporary comments in interviews, so it is possible to give an approximation of his introductory remarks.

The hardest thing in scoring is to know when to start and when to stop. Music can slow up an action that should not be slowed up and quicken a scene that shouldn't be. Knowing the difference is what makes a film composer.

Some composers get carried away with their own skill—they take a melody and embellish it with harmonies and counterpoints. If you get too decorative, you lose your appeal to the emotions. My theory is that music should be felt rather than heard.[3]

Many so-called serious composers are still unwilling to give serious attention to film music. They insist on weighing it against the symphonic music of the classicists and find it wanting. In the first place, their intent and function are entirely different. Good film music is written for a specific purpose and if the film composer refuses to recognize the dictates of the picture, he may write a great symphony but it will serve the film badly.[4]

Steiner received dozens of enthusiastic thank-yous from his audience, many praising his sincerity and warmth. Wrote one, "It wasn't the fine demonstration you gave us, not the concert of fine music (and it was fine music) that prompted this letter. It was the personality behind the demonstration. . . . The fact that he is one of the top Hollywood composers is beside the point. He would have been equally as interesting as a personality if he were a baker in his native Austria."[5]

FOR MAX, THE LECTURES OFFERED pleasant relief from a growing frustration.

On the chilly night of December 10, 1938, David O. Selznick and a crowd of invited guests watched as Culver City firemen ignited a wall of flames on the RKO Pathé backlot. The burning of Atlanta was underway, as the first night of shooting began on *Gone with the Wind*.

Steiner had heard nothing from his former boss confirming that he would score the film. Privately, Selznick was waffling, and as newspapers chronicled each day of production, Max grew anxious.

His five-year impasse with ASCAP was also about to erupt again. Although now a full member, Steiner received virtually none of the foreign royalties that he believed should be netting him a small fortune—and ASCAP still refused to collect domestic royalties for film scores. Meanwhile, attempts to convince publishers to issue his themes as sheet music fell on deaf ears. "I cannot understand how a man that has composed as many musical scores for pictures as I have, with letters from all over the world asking for my compositions, records, etc., might not be a fair bet for you," he wrote to one. "It is a hell of a feeling for a composer of my standing and reputation and success, to know automatically while I am writing, that all of the music I am putting on paper is dead."[6]

After 50 weeks of frequent all-night work, and months of stress over his father's safety, Steiner approached the Christmas holidays on the verge of a meltdown. It arrived on December 31.

The ostensible cause was anger at his agents, Charles Feldman and Ralph Blum. Another possible trigger was a note he received from Selznick, thanking him for a seasonal gift of flowers. There was no mention of *Gone with the Wind*. Fueled perhaps by too many holiday spirits, Steiner fired off a letter to his attorney, Louis Minter, in which he announced that "it was imperative for me to get into the radio field," since he "did not and do not trust the future of pictures."[7] This even though "[I] am probably today the foremost composer in motion pictures.

I have had all kinds of calls for loan outs to other studios; like, for instance, *Gunga Din* at RKO . . . but Feldman-Blum don't even know that any of the studios want me. . . . I have made up my mind to resign from Warners in any case, on the expiration of my present contract [in 1939]. . . . The Warners have been very kind to me, and I am extremely fond of everybody on the lot . . . but I have got the radio bug and I have decided to go to New York early in May and take a small radio job at very little money. I have an offer of ten broadcasts from New York for a certain sponsor, at 500 dollars a broadcast; each broadcast to take place every two weeks, out of which, however, I shall have to pay for all the orchestrations. My actual salary, therefore, would be around 150 dollars for each two weeks, which would be just enough to pay my hotel bill . . .

[My agents] will probably ask you: "Well, how is he going to live in New York during those twenty weeks?" And you say: "The 75 dollars a week that he will actually be making will pay for his hotel bill and all he will have to pay is for his food and cigars . . . his wife makes enough money to keep on going by herself. You know how screwy Steiner is. . . . He doesn't care about money anymore."

Writing the fusillade seemed to cool his temper; and in years to come, he acknowledged his irrational mood swings. "I have to be half nuts," he told a reporter.[8] "If I wasn't, I couldn't live this kind of life . . . I don't have any birthday, I don't have any Fourth of July, I don't have any Sunday. I don't have anything! . . . On Christmas Day I had just one hour with my family."

With growing frequency, he took his complaints—about deadlines, about critics—to the press. "I'm not just fighting for Steiner. We're all alike, all of us that write music for movies. Maybe I have only two, three, or four weeks to write the music for a picture. It goes 60 minutes. That's about as long as two symphonies. . . . When I'm writing for a picture I sometimes don't sleep more than two or three hours a day. I get all nerved up. I resign three or four times a day. But they don't pay any attention to me. After it's all over I recover fast."[9]

MAX'S INTENSITY MAY HAVE HELPED that December, as he tackled the scoring of his most emotionally charged Bette Davis film to date. Its story of a strong-willed woman dying of cancer surely resonated with him months after the passing of his mother.

In *Dark Victory*, Davis starred as Judith Traherne, a self-centered socialite who finds love and purpose as she faces a diagnosis of brain cancer. Director Edmund Goulding encouraged his star to suppress any pull toward sentimentality.[10] Tears for Judith would be shed by her best friend, Ann (Geraldine Fitzgerald).

Other emotional commentary came from Steiner's music. Max had already scored six Davis features; by then, the genre known as the "women's picture" had become his favorite. He told a friend that on action movies, "after writing all those notes, they often got lost in the final sound mix. But with the Davis films, he got the opportunity of writing music for character development and psychological motivations, where virtually every note is heard and contributes to the drama."[11]

The movie's early scenes—as Judith tries to ignore mysterious headaches—are scored from her point of view: light-hearted, with a trace of unease. A cheery allegretto becomes a soft, swimming blur of descending chromatics—*"a sort of*

Bette Davis and George Brent in a publicity still from *Dark Victory*.

6/8 blues. She is faking a hangover—doesn't want her friend to know."[12] When Judith takes a ride on her beloved horse, the music is initially *"almost a comedy scene."* Harp glissandos make tactile the wind blowing in her face. But Judith's double vision, as the horse is about to jump, sparks panicked dissonances. *"HER MIND WANDERS (Hence the screwy harmonies—1/2 tone off)."*

Just as Judith tries to ignore her illness with flippancy, Max accompanies his score's most moving passages with quips seemingly intended to distance himself from a (too revealing?) emotional connection. When Dr. Frederick Steele (George Brent) recognizes Judith's illness during examination: *"Heartbreak—screwy—and hopes for screwing!"* (Max probably knew that Davis and Brent were lovers during filming.) As Judith faces her condition: *"This is known as 'psychological Music'! MOLTO ODOROSO!"*

But behind the wisecracks, his attention to detail is precise. To evoke Judith's head pain, he asks harp, piano, and celesta to create the orchestral version of an impressionist painter's blur. *"Piano with pedal down— SWIMMY—UNREAL."* Judith's recognition that she is seriously ill is scored with tamped-down passion: *"HIDDEN TEARS—VERY DELICATE please!"*

Two themes dominate the score. A slow, minor-key waltz is played by muted strings, vibraphone, celesta, and harp, evoking with seductive melancholy the specter of death. Steiner pares down his orchestration further to create a "veiled" effect when referencing Judith's imminent loss of sight, which will come shortly before her passing.

Balancing Judith's music is the life-affirming theme for Dr. Steele. Songlike and simple, this major-key motif is among Steiner's purest depictions of decency. Step-like quarter notes mirror Steele's calm and reliability; its swoop up from B-flat to E-flat, then down an octave, creates a melody evoking his optimism—a quality that guides Judith to a place of acceptance. During the final cast list, Max plays a grandioso version of Steele's motto—Steiner's way of observing that although Judith is gone, the doctor's work will continue.

No sequence in a Davis-Steiner film would elicit more anecdotes than Judith's preparation for death. Blindness has set in; she hides it from Steele, now her husband, as he leaves home for a work trip. Judith is now alone. She moves calmly up a staircase to her bedroom. She lies down. A closeup of her face, resting on a pillow, slowly drifts out of focus. Fade to black.

Geraldine Fitzgerald often recalled the sequence's filming with audience-pleasing detail. The set "had been beautifully lit with a kind of heavenly glow shining on Bette as she slowly climbed the stairs. Suddenly she stopped . . . and said to Eddie Goulding, 'Is Max Steiner going to underscore this scene?' 'Oh, no,' said Goulding. 'Of course not! We all know how you feel about that!' '*Good*,' said Bette, 'because either I'm going up the stairs or Max Steiner is going up the stairs, but we're goddamn well not going up together!' "[13]

In fact, Bette and Max were friends. And while she may have made a sharp remark about too much underscore—few colleagues were spared her tongue-lashes—it is equally possible that Davis asked Goulding if the scene would be scored to help calibrate her timing and movement.

A studio press release offers another account of the scene's filming. "Goulding wanted mood music before shooting it. There was a radio in Miss

Davis's station wagon. So the car was driven onto the set and Goulding dialed it until he got a program of organ music."[14]

Geraldine Fitzgerald also claimed, "I think . . . [Bette] had the Vienna Boys Choir accompanying her."[15] In fact, the ensemble was a modestly sized chorus directed by Dudley Chambers, a favorite collaborator of Max's since RKO. And Steiner's music is actually a restrained *Liebestod*. *"Pianissimo. Very light—I want to leave a sort of suspense."* Only in the film's final seconds does a wordless chorus join the ensemble. *"Chorus humming . . . Heaven music . . . Hugo: Make this such a beautiful heaven that no supervisor can ever get there!"*

How Bette actually felt about the scene is implied in two of her later interviews. "There was really no need for Judith to die," she told David Frost, "because my beautiful Max Steiner did it for me. Even before I got on the bed, the angels were singing."[16] And to biographer Charlotte Chandler: "Dear old Max Steiner. I'm glad we went up those stairs together."[17]

The completion of *Dark Victory* in January 1939 ushered in a year whose workload verified Max's claim that only someone "half-nuts" would tackle it. First came a film that raised his ire while inspiring one of his freshest scores. *The Oklahoma Kid* took Cagney and Bogart out of their usual gangster trappings and transported them to the Old West, where Cagney's giant sombrero made him look, according to Bogey, like an oversized mushroom.[18] Viewed on its own terms, *Kid* is mostly a breezy lark, with Cagney infusing his one-note character with energetic improvisation. "Feel the air, just feel it!" his cowboy Jim Kinkaid grins, sniffing and pinching the space around him.

Steiner approached his first real western with no affinity for the genre— but once at the piano, he relished the film's possibilities. It allowed him to create strong dramatic cues for scenes of injustice (one of its heroes is lynched), while encouraging playful scoring for Cagney's comic performance.

Steiner's anthemic main theme, in square $\frac{4}{4}$, begins with sonorous triads and a heroic perfect fifth (*"'Cagney' Family Theme . . . Pioneer like"*).[19] This diatonic fortitude is a contrast to Jim's theme, a quicksilver chromatic figure that spirals upward (*"will o' the wisp . . . dissonances intentional"*). It has more than a whiff of Richard Strauss's *Till Eulenspiegel's Merry Pranks*; Max is telling us that Jim is an elusive trickster. The motif is usually played by piccolo and oboes; Steiner will often use the reedy astringency of woodwinds for characters who stand outside the social norm, whether good (Philip Marlowe) or bad (Veda Pierce).

Trilling bassoons echo snores from a room of salesmen. As Jim carries out a drunk, a dainty wind arrangement of the Civil War–era "Marching to Georgia" suggests that Max could have moonlighted on Warners' *Merrie Melodies* cartoons. *"Hugo! They'll probably fire me for this—but I think it's funny!"*

Steiner emphasizes the fluidity of Cagney's dance-like motion: *"Mozart-ish"* is a frequent notation. When the star is not onscreen, Steiner steps in to goose the tempo. *"A horribly slow scene. I am trying to help!"* And as the finale nears, jokes become rapid-fire. A fermata (long pause, or *lunga*) is noted *"LUNGA-DIN!"* For a burst of action: *"Agitato con fuoco (yourself)!"*

Such comments show why author Kate Daubney considered Steiner's sketches to be the text in which he "is most clearly seen: witty, versatile, shrewd, lewd, completely conversant with his environment and the social and political dynamics of the studio, alert to the ironies and truths of the characterizations he was expressing. . . . The most striking feature of the [sketches] is the enormous energy which they convey. The flamboyance of the notation, with copious underlining, long sweeping slurs, the thickness of note beams, the string, harp, and piano glissandi in different colors, reflects in the written score much of the animation it would feature in performance."[20]

By the time Max completed *The Oklahoma Kid*, another western had arrived. *"Now—for Dodge City!"* he notes on *Kid*'s last page. *"Goody-goody! Can't we Dodge it?"*

The answer, of course, was no. *Dodge City* would debut just ahead of *Stagecoach* and other titles that made 1939 a turning point in the western's evolution. (As war clouds amassed in Europe, a surge in American patriotism revived the genre's popularity.) Warner Bros. surrounded *Dodge*'s Tasmanian-born star Errol Flynn with a corral of contract players (Olivia de Havilland, Ann Sheridan, Alan Hale) under the two-fisted direction of Michael Curtiz. The movie's set-pieces ranged from the biggest saloon brawl in Hollywood history to a bullet-riddled climax aboard a train on fire. Slim on substance, *Dodge City* delivers popcorn-ready cliffhangers by the barrel.

The studio scheduled a gala premiere for their epic, to be held on April 1 in Dodge City, Kansas. Steiner had less than three weeks to compose an almost wall-to-wall score for the 104-minute film. *"MAESTOSO,"* Max writes on Bar One the pioneer march that opens the movie, with enough thunder and uplift to silence a theater. *"Strong melody—an EPIC picture promise! Which they don't get! A NEBICH [Yiddish for "poor thing"], not an EPICH!"*[21]

Steiner withholds his love theme for Flynn's Wade Hatton and de Havilland's Abbie Irving, another beauty of a melody, until well into the story. Wade's smitten attitude inspires Max to fill his sketches with the most elaborate and surreal genitalia in his oeuvre. *"Love's Awakening . . . A German Siege Gun,"* he writes above a pink-and-purple appendage pointing north, as a human-faced heart floats nearby. *"This is supposed to be a six shooter. At least I'm satisfied with once!"*

When spotting the picture with Henry Blanke, the pair agreed to have no music in the burning train climax. Amid thundering wheels, gunfire and other effects, "music wouldn't have been heard," Max told a reporter months later.[22]

> Well, I finished the music one noon after working fifty hours without sleep. At 12:15 what happens? Somebody calls up and says they have decided they absolutely have to have music for the train fight.
>
> "When?" I says.
>
> "Today."
>
> So there I am, with no sleep, and I got to write music for a train fight. The orchestra was already ordered for that night at 6 o'clock. I moved them to 10:30. By 6 o'clock the music was written. By 10:30 it was arranged and the parts were copied, and by 6 the next morning we were recording it.
>
> Suppose the big critics say, "That's awful. Mr. Steiner ought not to have to compose that way." Let them go and tell that to Mr. Warner. You know what would happen? Two cops would take them by the arm and that would be the last time they would be seen.

Warners' costliest title of 1939 was finished on-schedule. Blockbuster business followed, and Flynn would go on to star in seven more westerns, most of them scored by Steiner.

Musically, *Dodge City* revitalized the sound of the Hollywood western, becoming "a template for western scores," John Morgan observed.[23] "Max defined what you think of as an Indian theme or a cattle theme. Newman had scored a few westerns before that and they sounded like traditional film music in their harmonic language. *Dodge City* had a modern American feel of the kind that [concert composer] Virgil Thomson and others would be writing."

WHAT LITTLE TIME MAX SPENT away from composing he devoted to his father. Gabor Steiner had lived for almost six months in Cove Way. He still spoke almost no English, and as he and his son grew close once more, Louise felt increasingly alienated.

The couple's five-year relationship had been surprisingly harmonious, given Max's focus on work and his occasional bursts of anger. Louise herself was not without temperament. But their life was mostly convivial "until his father came to live with us," Louise recalled.[24] "Papa and Max would speak German at the dining table, and I was left out of the conversation many times. Then suddenly Max would realize and apologize. We'd find that if we didn't include Papa in everything he would become upset. . . . When people [have] to work out their little problems, a mother or a father taking sides only fuels the fire."

There were other problems in the marriage. "Max was a very generous person, taken advantage of by certain people. A soft touch when he played cards with his friends. He paid up when he lost, but when the others lost to him, he wouldn't accept their money. Many times we would dine with friends and he wouldn't let them pay. Max loved roulette, and sometimes he wound up paying heavy losses. After a while, I didn't even want to go with him . . . to throw away hard-earned money didn't make much sense to me."[25]

As tempers frayed at home, Max wrote his "Schnooky" a playful note, hoping to revive memories of their idyll in Hawaii the previous year:

> To my LOUISE—
> NOT because she never fought with me—
> NOT because she has been a very bad–bad–bad tempered girl
> NOT because she is a damn good "lay"—
> BUT because she has been so sweet and kind to my poor old father!
> Her "poui poui" boy
> Max—Known to everybody as "THE LAY OF WAIKIKI"[26]

But teasing puns couldn't ease domestic tension, or erase the fact that Max's money woes were worsening. Gabor was a full-time dependent. Monthly alimony checks still went to Max's first wife, Beatrice. And ASCAP paid him virtually nothing.

Meanwhile, his negligence on other financial fronts was having serious consequences. He had entrusted his money, including tax payments, to attorneys whose carelessness—or worse—had placed him in a growing state of debt.[27] Gently refusing a touch for cash from an old friend, he wrote, "I am more than sorry that I cannot help you. . . . You see, thru my divorce from Audree, I got into a terrible mess with the state income tax people who are making me pay the entire taxes for two years for her as well. . . . On top of which, I just brought my father over from Austria, and you can easily imagine how much money that cost . . . I am absolutely flat."[28]

ON MARCH 15, 1939, STEINER'S SPIRITS SANK as Nazi troops marched into Czechoslovakia. Another European war seemed imminent. U.S. resolve to stay out of the conflict extended to Hollywood, where censors banned criticism of foreign governments—even Hitler's Germany.[29]

It was an edict every studio followed—with one exception.

Perhaps only Hitler could bring Harry and Jack Warner into agreement. The two sparring brothers were united in their belief that Nazism threatened not just Europe but the future of America. In 1934 Warner Bros. became the first Hollywood company to close its operations in Germany.[30] In 1938, the conviction of four German agents operating in America gave Jack and Harry a chance to bring their defiance to the screen.

Confessions of a Nazi Spy was a documentary-style drama based on the writing of ex-FBI agent Leon G. Turrou, to be played by Edward G. Robinson. Franklin Roosevelt gave his blessing to the project, recognizing it as a valuable weapon in his stealth battle against Hitler.[31] But when Hal Wallis asked Steiner to score the film, Max refused. His reason was simple: he still had family in Austria. When Wallis assured him that he would not be credited on the movie, Steiner agreed.[32]

His music, like the film, was uninspired and often strident; but U.S. moviegoers had never seen a drama so direct in its assertion that Hitler's violence could cross to U.S. shores. *Confessions*, a box office hit, marked the first of many Steiner scorings of the Nazi menace.

The presence of Gabor—"the poor old man," Max wrote a friend[33]—even led Steiner to contemplate "a little tone poem called 'The Exile.' It is quite Jewish in character, extremely modern, and has a super-structure of rigid, dissonant music. A few musicians who have heard what I have finished to date have told me that one can almost hear the 'swastika.' "[34]

But Max abandoned the piece, confining his anti-Nazi music to the cinema.

AS LATE AS MARCH 1939—three months into the filming of *Gone with the Wind*—David O. Selznick still could not bring himself to choose a composer. But that month, he finally shared his pick in a memo to studio general manager Henry Ginsberg.

"My first choice for the job is Max Steiner, and I am sure that Max would give anything in the world to do it."[35]

Word reached the ecstatic composer by March 29. "I would love to see you one evening," Steiner wrote Hal Wallis, "as I want to ask your advice regarding a very personal matter.... I do not want to borrow any money."[36] After their talk,

Wallis give Max his approval—but there was one more boss to convince. And on April 5, Steiner sat down to write one of the most important letters of his life.

My dear Mr. Warner:

. . . When I came over to work at Warners, I had an understanding with Leo that whatever happened I was to do GONE WITH THE WIND. . . . In fact, the only way I could get my release from Mr. Selznick was with that promise.

I know, Mr. Warner, that you are friendly toward me and you have no idea how much I appreciated your so very nice letter than you sent before you left for the east.

Therefore, I am taking the liberty of writing and explaining to you what GONE WITH THE WIND means to me. As you well know, I have worked day and night, Sundays, holidays, Xmas, etc. to get your pictures out on time for release dates and as fast and as cheaply as possible, and nothing that you have ever asked me has been too much for me to do. It was, therefore, a great shock to me when a different composer [Korngold] was assigned to JUAREZ . . .

I must tell you frankly that I am upset and rather hurt, and you have no idea the amount of kidding I have taken on that account. Not only by musicians but by producers and other people in the industry. They all kid me about Warners having demoted me to westerns and prison pictures, and in order to regain the prestige and standing that I had before the JUAREZ incident, it is absolutely necessary that I do a top picture of the type of JUAREZ, ROBIN HOOD and GONE WITH THE WIND with their vast opportunity for music. After all, I am sure you will agree—one cannot win Academy Awards with THEY MADE ME A CRIMINAL, CRIME SCHOOL, ANGELS WITH DIRTY FACES, OKLAHOMA KID, etc. . . .

You have never had a letter from me, nor a complaint, nor have I ever been in your office, or had any reason to go there until now; but this is so serious a matter to my peace of mind that I decided to take a chance and write you. I haven't slept for days. . . .

I am counting on you, because I know you to be fair and a friend of mine. Therefore, will you please give your consent . . . should [Selznick] find it necessary to get someone else, I would never get over it.

You probably will think me crazy and eccentric; but, Mr. Warner, if I wasn't "just a little off," I couldn't do the kind of work that I am doing. You see it isn't always money with a musician. I'm not asking for any raise, or bonus, but am perfectly willing to do GONE WITH THE WIND either on leave of absence or under my contract--any way you want; but, it is necessary for me, my pride, my standing and my future activity to do GONE WITH THE WIND, as it is necessary for an actor to get a <u>break</u> once in awhile.

Will you please write me a short note, giving me your okay.

Many, many thanks in advance, and with kindest regards, I remain,

Most sincerely yours,
Max Steiner[37]

He received a reply the following day.

Dear Max:
. . . First I want to say that irrespective of what pictures you score, you are the best musical composer in the industry.

[Regarding] GONE WITH THE WIND. I have told Leo and Hal Wallis that this is satisfactory and that you can do it.

. . . Just want to add that while I realize we have brought another composer in to do certain pictures from time to time, it is with great pride that we can point to the important music in pictures such as ANGELS WITH DIRTY FACES, DODGE CITY, OKLAHOMA KID, FOUR DAUGHTERS, CRIME SCHOOL and JEZEBEL and I am sure that the important music you have placed in these and many other films, have contributed much to their success, and I assure you it isn't the bigness of the picture that counts . . . for you won an Academy Award for doing a picture no one ever heard of, THE INFORMER.

However, I do hope that with GONE WITH THE WIND you will not only win the Academy Award, but the plaudits of the public, who are after all, our most important judges.

Yours for more work and longer hours.
Sincerely,
Jack Warner
P.S. Keep away from the Hollywood Turf Club . . . because I am going to be there every Saturday.[38]

The studio boss's motives weren't based on kindness. Warner knew that Selznick would pay his studio a rate far above Steiner's weekly salary–and that any composing time beyond their agreement would come at an even higher cost.

In the meantime, Jack wanted as much music as possible from Max before his mind turned to Tara. Recalled Hugo Friedhofer, "By 1939 Steiner was Jack Warner's favorite for almost every kind of film . . . at one time it created a great deal of dissension among the music staff. The boys were all called in and a couple of Steiner's films were run for them and Leo Forbstein announced, 'Now fellows, Jack Warner wants you to write as close to what Max is doing as you possibly can.' "[39]

THE FILM SCORES OF MAX STEINER

1939 Releases (continued in Chapter 16)

Dark Victory (12/38–1/39). AAN.
The Oklahoma Kid (1/39–2/39)
Dodge City (2/39)
Confessions of a Nazi Spy (4/39)
Daughters Courageous (4/39–5/39)
Each Dawn I Die (5/39)
The Old Maid (6/39)
Dust Be My Destiny (4/39–7/39). Max wrote a haunting title song for this lovers-on-the-run drama starring John Garfield. The theme was issued as sheet music but attracted little notice.

As Steiner waited for orders from Selznick, Warner Bros. assigned him to no fewer than four films. He completed them all between April and July. They included *The Old Maid*, a Civil War drama that served as a warm-up for *GWTW*. During the shoot, Edmund Goulding served more as referee than director for his stars, Bette Davis and Miriam Hopkins. Soured by filming's end, his feelings changed after hearing Steiner's tender score. "I am sincerely grateful to you for the musical treatment," he wrote.[40] "I was very unhappy about the picture when I went away. . . . I felt it was over-played and jerky and that I had missed. On seeing the picture with the music it told a different story, thanks to you. Again I say, I am deeply grateful to you."

ON JUNE 27, PRINCIPAL PHOTOGRAPHY ended on *Gone with the Wind* after five months of shooting. There remained half a year of re-shoots, editing, visual effects . . . and of course, music.

Steiner would be loaned to David for specific blocks of time, and he was needed at his home studio through July. In the meantime, Max steeled himself for the project that would require every musical and organizational skill he had acquired over three decades.

But not even a lifetime of experience, and the stamina of a man much younger than his 51 years, would be enough for *Gone with the Wind*.

To beat the ticking clock, and the relentless, shifting demands of David O. Selznick, he would need an army.

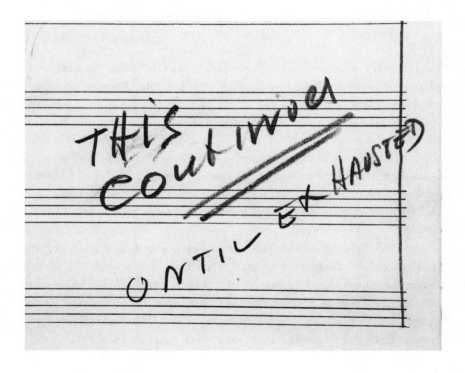

16

The South Is Dead

ON A SUNDAY MORNING IN OCTOBER 1939, violinist Louis Kaufman was relaxing at home in West Los Angeles with his wife, Annette, when the telephone rang.

It was Max. "Louis, are you free today? Come right over with your violin. I have some themes to submit to Selznick for *Gone with the Wind*. It's not very interesting with just piano." Louis made the ten-minute drive to Cove Way, where Steiner "had set up a small recording machine," Kaufman recalled. "Max and I played over the themes for Scarlett, Rhett, Melanie, Tara, etc." After hearing the recording, "Selznick enthusiastically approved these samples."[1]

David O. Selznick seldom lacked enthusiasm that fall, as his four-hour opus entered its final phase of post-production. But enthusiasm seldom equaled happiness. A small library is necessary to chart *GWTW*'s agonizing creation: the firing of director George Cukor, who was replaced by Victor Fleming, whose breakdown led to the hiring of Sam Wood, after the firing of cinematographer Lee Garmes, after two years of script drafts, after . . .

Leslie Howard, miserable playing the passive Ashley Wilkes, summed things up in a letter. "Fleming takes four shots of something a day to keep him going. . . . Selznick is bent double with permanent, and I should think, chronic indigestion. Half the staff look, talk, and behave as though they were on the verge of breakdowns."[2] A Selznick assistant described the shoot as "utter chaos . . . [Vivien] Leigh hated Fleming . . . Fleming hated her. Clark Gable hated David . . . Everybody hated David. He interfered in everything."[3]

Selznick's attention to detail had become obsession by the time Max was put on the payroll in August 1939. Now, David had a new production element to micromanage. "I should appreciate it if Mr. Steiner would adapt whatever his plans are for the score to use, instead of two or three hours of original music, little original music and a score based on the great music of the world and of the South in particular."[4]

Selznick was fixed in his belief that existing music was more effective than score written specifically for a film. Max disagreed, but found a compromise. Period tunes, many of them referenced in the novel, would be woven into an original score, which used the harmonic language of the classical repertoire without quoting from it.

That process began with Steiner's first viewing of the movie in August. *GWTW*, he told Jerome Kern days later, "will be the most outstanding picture ever produced in the history of the film industry."[5] To the long list of men seduced by Scarlett O'Hara, as embodied by Vivien Leigh, add the name of Steiner: Max was besotted by the actress's beauty and vitality. "What Gable looked like or what Vivien looked like . . . sure, it influenced me," he said in 1967. He then sighed and added that Leigh "was a darling girl."[6]

But Steiner moved beyond the male gaze to identify with Scarlett's psychology and ambition. Unrequited love, the devastation of one's home, the desire to restore the family name—Atlanta and Vienna may have been five thousand miles apart, but for Max, the O'Hara story was also his own.

For two years, Steiner had toyed with a four-note musical fragment in his Warner Bros. scores—a pattern that leaped a full octave from its first note to its second, then descended with a syncopation. Used in *The Amazing Dr. Clitterhouse*, it resurfaced in *They Made Me a Criminal*, two minor programmers.[7] Did Max realize that this musical cell had greater power he was trying to unlock? Was his mind already drifting to Tara? (Say the words *Gone with the Wind* with these four notes. They match.) That August he returned to the pattern, shifted it into a major key, and expanded it into the single most famous melody of his career.

"I can grasp that feeling for Tara," he later said, "which is one of the finest instincts in her, that love for the soil where she had been born, love of the life before her own. . . . That is why the Tara theme begins and ends the picture and permeates the entire score . . . Tara is a living thing."[8]

But is the Tara theme also Scarlett's? No—and yes. Max composed a motif for the heroine to suggest her calculating nature; a slow version of it is heard in the film as we see a cat sleeping by a sundial (*"Mr. Selznick wants a synonym between 'The Cat' and Scarlett 'The Cat'!"*).[9] This phrase's often staccato rise and fall suggests Scarlett's moments of "Fiddle-dee-dee" indifference; but in a rare miss for the composer, it fails to capture Scarlett herself. "It doesn't come off," Steiner admitted.[10] But he also saw the reason: Scarlett's obsession with

Publicity still from *Gone with the Wind*.

Tara made its theme her theme as well. "Tara's the whole story . . . It was her whole life."[11]

For a motif reflecting the love between Ashley Wilkes and his gentle wife, Melanie (Olivia de Havilland), Max found the perfect corollary in a theme he had written for 1934's *The Fountain*. Spiritual and calm, it originally defined the idealistic love between Ann Harding and Paul Lukas's characters. The theme works beautifully in counterpoint with a separate motto for Melanie herself, which reflects kindness without treacle—a Steiner hallmark.

Swooning and deliberately extreme in emotion ("*TRAGICO*"), Steiner's theme for Ashley Wilkes doesn't really depict the man; it is Scarlett's romanticized vision of him. Its legato, "feminine" phrasing was deliberate: "Even if he did go to war," Max said, "Ashley was a weakling. Why Scarlett was so anxious to sleep with him, no one will ever know. . . . Ashley was to me a softie, and that is why the music is like that."[12]

Rhett's theme is a stolid march with a touch of ruefulness. One of the score's most underused themes (for more on this, read on), it is first heard prominently as Butler gazes up at Scarlett at the Wilkes party. Scarlett's father Gerald is defined by his Irish heritage, his theme dominated by a lilting triplet rhythm and a trilling mordent—an ornament on a note that quickly steps above the main note before dropping down again. Intriguingly, the third note of Gerald's motif drops an octave from the first; it is Gerald who teaches Scarlett the importance of Tara, and as we know, "Tara's Theme" is also characterized by a full-octave interval.

Max's approach to house slave Mammy sounds on paper like a stereotype of its era: a sprightly, neo-folk tune doubled on banjo. In fact, it transcends *GWTW*'s indefensible view of slaves-as-extended-family to create a musical portrait as memorable as Hattie McDaniel's Oscar-winning performance. The bridge of Mammy's theme includes a paraphrase of the Tara motif; Max is telling us that the estate cannot function without her, and that she is its heart.

STEINER'S CREATIVITY THAT SUMMER AND FALL was protean. Between August 21, his start date on *GWTW*, and the October afternoon that he auditioned themes for Selznick, Max wrote two other film scores—and finished half of another.

The half was Warner Bros.' *Four Wives*, a sequel to the smash *Four Daughters*. *Daughters* told the mostly sunny story of an all-American family whose clashes (two sisters want the same man) are overcome thanks to sibling loyalty and a joy in playing music together. The film's most charismatic figure was Mickey Borden, a brooding pianist played by John Garfield. In one scene, Mickey plays a fragment of a Gershwinesque tune he's written; it was actually composed by Max Rabinowitch, a Warner session pianist. Steiner incorporated the theme into *Daughters*' underscore.

Mickey dies in *Daughters*, but in *Four Wives* his melody lives on: his friend Felix uses it as centerpiece of a symphonic work performed at the climax. Behind the scenes, Steiner was tasked to expand Rabinowitch's melodic fragment into a seven-minute concert work—one that had to be finished before its onscreen performance was filmed in September.

Finding inspiration under pressure, 1939. (MS Papers; L. Tom Perry Special Collections, Brigham Young University)

(Writing *Wives'* underscore would come later.) Max finished the work he called *Symphonie Moderne* in time for its opulent, three-day filming under Michael Curtiz's direction.[13]

STEINER ALSO WAS DIVERTED FROM *GWTW* by another project that August—this time by none other than David O. Selznick.

Intermezzo is rightly remembered as the Hollywood debut of Ingrid Bergman, in a remake of a film she made in Sweden. Under contract to Selznick, the 28-year-old starred with Leslie Howard in the story of the brief, passionate affair between a concert pianist (Bergman) and a married violinist. Its score was written in less than two weeks and is based mostly on classical melodies, along with a Korngold-style theme by Heinz Provost from the original Swedish film. The unifying musical voice of *GWTW* is absent; instead, leitmotivs come from Beethoven, Grieg, and others.

"Steiner and [music director Lou] Forbes . . . will have one week from the time we turn the picture over to them to do the scoring," Selznick wrote in July. "There is no reason on earth why the entire score of the picture cannot be done from orchestrations already in existence, both of classical and motion picture music."[14]

Publicity still from *Intermezzo*.

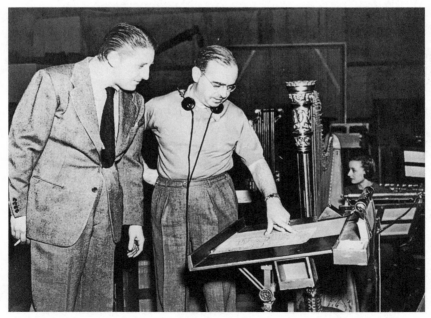

With Selznick music director and close friend Lou Forbes, 1939. (MS Papers; L. Tom Perry Special Collections, Brigham Young University)

Forbes and Steiner became senior partners on a team of celebrity composer-orchestrators: Friedhofer, Russell Bennett, and—via cues from earlier movies—Waxman and Newman. Steiner's sketches wryly note the many chefs at work: *"Beethoven/Steiner/Grieg." "Steiner x Tchaikovsky not to speak of Friedhofer."* And simply: *"Steiner et al."*[15]

Selznick considered the result as an ideal template for assembly-line scoring. For Max it was a nightmare, minus the sleep. "I would start to work at nine o'clock in the morning, lie down about midnight for a few hours, I'd be awakened by my butler at five a.m. and then I'd go back to work. The doctor would give me an injection to keep me awake, and I'd keep going."[16] That ritual injection, which continued through *GWTW*, contained Selznick's drug of choice: Benzedrine. Remarkably, with the exception of 1939, Steiner needed no pharmaceuticals to make a deadline. Besides, "my doctor told me I had to stop. It was gonna affect my heart."[17]

Intermezzo's piecemeal score would receive an Oscar nomination. Days after the movie's release, Selznick expressed his satisfaction to Steiner and Forbes in a memo that flipped from praise to implicit admonition. "The outstanding point that has been commented on by so many . . . is its use of classical music to such a great extent instead of original music hastily written. This is a point on which I have been fighting for years, with little success."[18]

Max would never agree. And he would show his own preferred method of using existing themes in his next project—another side-trip away from *GWTW*, preapproved by Selznick.

WE ARE NOT ALONE IS THE BEST Max Steiner film you've never heard of.

Based on a novel by James Hilton, who co-authored the script, the Warner Bros. drama tells with slow-burning power the story of a good man's death, as he and an equally kind young woman are destroyed by events beyond their control on the eve of World War I. The *New York Times*'s Frank Nugent spoke for many in calling it "a film of rare tenderness and beauty, compassionate and grave."[19]

As David Newcome, a village doctor in Britain, Paul Muni is unusually still and soft-spoken—a hollow-cheeked, mustachioed cousin to another Hilton character, Mr. Chips. Resigned to the criticisms of his cold wife, Jessica (Flora Robson), David pours adoration on their son, Gerald. David also performs quiet acts of rebellion, like aiding Leni, an Austrian immigrant (Jane Bryan), who becomes Gerald's governess and surrogate mother. Leni and David fall in love, but their chaste bond, developed over violin-piano duets, is recognized only by the viewer. As Britain plunges into war, with foreigners under attack, David tries to arrange an escape for Leni, now an enemy alien, with tragic results.

Steiner did not have to imagine Leni's panic as an Austrian in England at the start of the Great War. It was his story as well, and he responded with the most heartbreaking score of his career.

Prior to filming, Steiner met with Muni, Forbstein, and director Edmund Goulding to choose the pieces David and Leni would play onscreen, and that David would whistle as he walks through town.[20] During this process, Max found the central idea of his score. David's "whistle" tune became his motif; it is the opening theme of Josef Haydn's 1791 "Surprise" Symphony, which earned its nickname thanks to a musical joke. After seven whispery measures, the last chord in its eighth bar is an exploding fortissimo, which has launched sleeping concertgoers out of chairs for more than two hundred years. (Max uses the theme without the fortissimo jump.)

Steiner's choice was an intuitive masterstroke. Haydn's simple melody is based on the C–E–G notes of a C-major chord. Its construction is childlike, like the over-trusting David. And in a pun Steiner no doubt relished, the idea of "Surprise" is central to the story's end. David's wife dies after accidentally taking the wrong medicine, and David and Leni—caught fleeing the town for Leni's safety—are arrested and tried for what is misconstrued as Jessica's murder. When David is asked by the prosecutor if he is in love with Leni, realization—*surprise*—strikes him. "I hadn't thought of it," he says softly, before admitting that he is. His words liberate him emotionally—and condemn him and Leni to death. The Haydn "Surprise" theme now becomes beatific, in the style of Wagner's *Lohengrin* Prelude.

In a private letter, Steiner noted that he "wrote and recorded *We Are Not Alone*, [a] score of one hour and ten minutes, in six days. During these six days, I slept eighteen hours at most. This is a terrific strain on the eyes and the heart."[21] He was rewarded with a rare honor: praise from Hal Wallis. "Just to tell you that I did like the score on WE ARE NOT ALONE very much. I thought it was a beautiful job."[22]

That opinion was echoed by another tough critic, Hugo Friedhofer. A "standout of Max's for me was *We Are Not Alone*," he said in the 1970s. "It was a very sad picture . . . but beautifully made. And Max did a lovely score for it."[23]

BY THE TIME OF THE RELEASE of *We Are Not Alone*, audiences were not thinking about World War I but about a new and terrifying conflict. On September 3, hours after Hitler's invasion of Poland, Great Britain announced that it was at war with Germany—and with Max's Austrian homeland.

For Steiner, the news was devastating, especially since his beloved Aunt Ida remained in Austria. But his anxiety was tempered by joyous news at home.

Louise was pregnant.

Their child was due in March 1940; and while few women at the time worked during pregnancy, Louise played harp on all of her husband's scores until shortly before her delivery. For Max, the Steiner family dynasty was an almost mythic concept. He celebrated with an affectionate piece of doggerel attached to Louise's presents that Christmas: *"To 'Ma' Louise / I hope they'll not use a chisel / To get little Louisel / Out of big Swisel / And that it [won't] "drizzle" / On the day when my Louisel / Presents the little Weasel / Which was made thru Daddy's grizzle— / Pop goes Louisel! / Love & kisses Your daddy."*[24]

ON SEPTEMBER 9, lucky residents of Riverside, an L.A. suburb, became the first to see a rough cut of *Gone with the Wind* at a surprise preview. Even with a temporary music track, *GWTW* was greeted at its conclusion with a long, loud ovation.[25]

But Selznick's relief soon shifted to alarm. Much work still had to be done, and the film's December 15 premiere in Atlanta could not be moved.

Nothing worried David more than the score. In October, as Max finally began focused work on the film, Selznick told staff that "I am very serious about wanting the whole score of 'Gone with the Wind' played for me before it is recorded, by as small an orchestra as is practicable . . . if it will help avoid any arguments or waste of time later, perhaps two or three musicians could be gotten in to play the themes for me before we go into the expense of arrangements."[26]

When Steiner played the recordings of his themes, featuring Louis Kaufman's violin and Max on piano, Selznick's "enthusiasm" (per Louis) was tempered by some disappointment. "Crazy about the Melanie theme, the Mammy theme, and the Tara theme," D.O.S. wrote, "but Max has failed terribly with the Scarlett theme and the Rhett theme."[27] The latter two would not be prominent in the film.

As early as April, Selznick had begun dictating thoughts about the score— many of them contradictory. For the early, pivotal scene in which Gerald O'Hara tells Scarlett, as they stand outside Tara, "land is the only thing in the world worth workin' for, worth fightin' for," Selznick first imagined "light and gay music." By September he wanted "no music under entire Gerald-Scarlett scene" until the camera's dramatic pull-back, at which time a "negro spir-itual" would be heard. Until he decided on "symphonic music over pull-back shot . . . "[28]

On November 6, all of Selznick's musical ideas were combined into one document for Steiner.[29] It was as dense as it was confusing. A day later, David tried to distill his thoughts into a 12-page memo. Many more would follow.

Max did not go into battle alone. He assembled a team of all-star orchestrators—at least 13, led by Friedhofer, Heinz Roemheld, and Adolph Deutsch.[30] Dudley Chambers handled chorus chores. As Steiner divided up tasks it became clear that, due to limited time, his ideas often would have to be executed by the others, to a degree he avoided in the past.

Making the job harder were constant new instructions from the boss. According to Louise, Selznick "would sometimes call Max at 2 o'clock in the morning if he wanted to play something for him at that hour. He had a pro-jection machine in his home, and we lived across the street, so Max would go over."[31] Discussions grew increasingly one-sided. When Steiner suggested pe-riod music to use, Selznick overruled him. When Steiner proposed placement of his own themes, Selznick overruled him. "This is Georgia, not Ireland," he snapped when Max proposed a use of Gerald O'Hara's theme.[32]

By November 8, Steiner had one month left to write about half of a roughly three hour score, for the most eagerly anticipated title in movie history, for the industry's most demanding producer.

That day, a festering doubt hit him with alarming certainty.

He couldn't do it. He could not finish the score on time.

Fortunately, Selznick didn't panic. "Steiner has again told us he cannot meet the date," he wrote John Hay Whitney on November 9.[33]

We discount this very largely because Steiner is notorious for such statements and works well under pressure, and I am inclined to take the chance that we can drive him through. . . . Tomorrow, Friday, he is recording the first several reels. If quality is disappointing, this, to-gether with his pessimistic statements, would warrant pulling him off, particularly in view of [the] fact that Herbert Stothart is dying to do the job . . .

Stothart was my second choice for the job, and it is my regret now of course that he was not first choice . . . secretly we ran the picture for him today, and he is simply frantic with eagerness and enthusiasm to do it . . .

What I would like to do is to start Stothart selecting and writing in the morning with his full knowledge that he may not go ahead if we decide to proceed with Steiner Sunday or Monday. Or it might be desirable to have him go ahead and write those reels Steiner is not working on, in case of further trouble with Max . . .

As a third alternative, we might have him collaborate with Steiner on the score, although not at all certain this would work out. In any event, I would be relieved of my depression about the quality of the score . . . if Stothart could start to work with us in the morning.

But nothing stays secret in Hollywood. That weekend, news of Selznick's dealings with Stothart reached Max, who flew into a predictable fury.

It was the best thing that could have happened.

"Stothart had a few drinks on Saturday night, apparently, and did a lot of loose talking about how he was going to fix up Max's work," Selznick told Whitney on Monday.[34] "The result was that within ten minutes it was back to Max, and he was in a rage. . . . However, Max spurred on by the Stothart episode, really went to town, and the result is that by tomorrow we will have considerably more than half the picture scored. And it looks as though we are going to be okay without Stothart. I am sure that in any case we can credit all our attempts to get Stothart with leading Max to faster and greater efforts."

"FASTER AND GREATER" WAS ACHIEVED in the usual way: more hands on deck. Orchestrators Friedhofer, Deutsch, Roemheld, and Joseph Nussbaum composed music for scenes that Max would have preferred to write himself. At least his collaborator wasn't Stothart; it was the hand-picked team of "Steiner & Co.," as many score pages are puckishly credited.[35]

Steiner reserved for himself the major character scenes and most of the movie's first half: idyllic plantation life, war, Scarlett's return to a ravaged Tara. Music was essential for these, while *GWTW*'s second half—especially its early scenes of Reconstruction, Tara's rebuilding, and Scarlett's marriage to Frank Kennedy—were less score-dependent. Steiner did write most of the final hour, as Scarlett and Rhett's marriage collapses and tragedy follows tragedy.

Knowing that action scenes took longest to compose, Max assigned some of these to associates. Heinz Roemheld was given the escape from Atlanta, reworking a cue from his 1930 score for *White Hell of Pitz Palu*. The result—a leaping scherzo, punctuated with Valkyrie-like horns—delivered excitement, but Roemheld's bland use of "Dixie" and "The Battle Hymn of the Republic" was less inspired than Max's period interpolations.

Friedhofer composed several scenes in the film's second half, most notably Scarlett's shooting of a Yankee deserter. "But the score . . . the material . . . was all Max's, really," Friedhofer insisted. "What I wrote, with a few minor exceptions, was based on Max's material."[36]

Steiner was no longer alive at the time of these comments. Had Hugo believed that the score heavily drew on the ideas of others, he was free to say so. Instead he stressed the opposite: although other composers scored scenes, it was usually with Steiner's themes, and under his supervision. Recall Friedhofer's description of their working relationship at Warners: "A great deal of our conversation . . . was entirely confined to telephone."[37] Many cues in the *GWTW* sketches are not in Max's hand. But knowing the system he used for time-strapped scores, he almost certainly outlined verbally the approach for scenes that he did not write, and which themes to use.

Take the main title. Its pencil sketch is written by Friedhofer; but Steiner would never have allowed anyone else to compose the opening minutes of his most important score. The main title is mostly a statement of the "Tara" theme, which he had written by October. It would have taken him only minutes to dictate to Hugo the cue's opening burst of "Dixie" (six bars), followed by Mammy's motif (two); the thrilling modulation that lifts this D-major opening up to F major for 'Tara's Theme"; and so on. As this theme's bold first statement softens, the score asks for *"A GRADUAL DIMINUENDO OF KOLOSSAL PROPORTIONS."* The handwriting is Hugo's, but the joking-serious phrase is Max's.

OUR FIRST SIGHT OF SCARLETT O'HARA, flirting with the Tarleton twins at Tara, is described as *"Easy—Flowing—a la Selznick."* Most noteworthy is the scene's musical definition of Scarlett: a coquettish, skipping tune for ascending eighth notes, played by celesta. The melody sounds so much like Steiner that few listeners recognize it as "Katy Bell," an 1863 song by Stephen Foster.

In choosing the tune, Steiner not only addressed Selznick's wish to have music of the time; he captures the spirit of naive Scarlett before the war. "Sometimes Max gets criticized for using popular music of the day," his friend John Morgan observed. "But as Friedhofer said, 'Max always makes them his own.' He wove them into the total scoring and harmonized them so that it sounded like Steiner."[38]

All of Reel 2 is in Steiner's writing, including Gerald's sermon about land to Scarlett. In its final version, a soft introduction of the Tara theme crescendos into a hymn-like maestoso so stirring that not even Selznick could criticize it.

As Scarlett is corseted in her bedroom, Mammy's theme adds warmth and humor as we observe the slave's skill at manipulating her mistress. The Wilkes barbecue gives Steiner & Co. a showcase for period tunes: Foster's "Lou'siana Belle," "Dolly Day," and "Ring de Banjo," arranged with 1860s color that separates them from score. After Rhett cautions his hosts about the risks of war, Steiner scores his exit with the 1861 tune "Ye Cavaliers of Dixie" ("*with Dignity*"). But the reel's best music is original: the introduction of Melanie's theme; the Melanie-Ashley love theme, first heard as the silhouetted pair step out of a dark room into the light of the party; Scarlett's confession of love to Ashley, ending in rejection ("*She gets mad! Remember Jezebel—a similar idea!*"); and the announcement of war, in which Max's party music turns rigidly militaristic.

Within minutes, Scarlett is married to Melanie's brother Charles, and just as quickly widowed. As she sullenly dresses in black, eager to forget Charles, Max insolently quotes the spiritual "Massa's in de Cold, Cold Ground," daintily played on celesta.

The Confederate dance that follows is logically filled with period tunes, some from Mitchell's novel: "Maryland, My Maryland" (better known as the melody of "O Tannenbaum"); "Dixie"; and "Lorena," a melancholy song of loss later prominent in Steiner's score for *The Searchers*. But when Rhett and Scarlett dance, Steiner's writing takes over with an original, Viennese-style waltz, its romanticism heightened by sighing *divisi* strings. Max knew that an existing theme wouldn't serve the drama's needs: Rhett's love for Scarlett will become as strong a part of the narrative as Scarlett's love for Tara.

NO SCENE WAS MORE OF A MUSICAL MINEFIELD than Scarlett's walk through hundreds of wounded soldiers at the Atlanta train station. Selznick's directions were intricate. "Score the square with a pathetic medley of Southern songs to give the impression of the South bleeding to death . . . Suggest off-key [dissonant] 'Dixie' in funereal tempo with 'Taps,' etc., and perhaps 'Maryland, My Maryland,' 'My Old Kentucky Home,' 'Swanee River,' etc . . . No original music at all."[39]

Steiner rose to the challenge. As Scarlett is walking among the men, "Dixie" is played laboriously in B-minor. The camera rises, revealing the scene's epic scale. Max matches the camera move with an upward modulation, allowing a subtle change into a major-key rendition of "Maryland, My Maryland," as

Publicity stills from *Gone with the Wind*.

trumpets intone "Taps" as countermelody. As the crane shot nears its zenith, Foster's "Old Folks at Home" (aka "Swanee River") dominates, an ironic counterpoint to the carnage of dead and dying. The mood becomes plangent, as "Taps" returns in final, forceful counterpoint, just as the billowing Confederate flag is revealed above the panorama.

Steiner has included everything on Selznick's list except "My Old Kentucky Home." And while there was "no original music" per request, his use of the many melodic cells—their arrangement and harmonization—puts the cue in Steiner's voice.

"THE SOUTH IS DEAD. And so am I!" Max writes pages later. But he summoned the energy to spar with Selznick, over the scoring of Scarlett's discovery at Tara that her mother is dead.

For the preview, Selznick temp-tracked the scene with two Waxman cues from the movie *His Brother's Wife.* The second employed a hypnotic, heartbeat-like rhythm for timpani, similar to Waxman's classic "creation music" for *The Bride of Frankenstein.* Steiner's scoring for the scene used a quietly suspenseful variant of the Tara theme, tying music to the larger narrative.

When Selznick chose to use Waxman, Max pleaded his case in a letter. "While I do not question or criticize your liking that piece of preview track, I do strongly object to it on account of bad modulation, different type recording, different orchestra, and improper ending under [Scarlett's] scream.... Why have such glaring imperfections in what may prove to be the best picture to date? ... Please excuse my rotten typing, but I am extremely nervous and worried."[40]

Selznick was unmoved.

The rest of the Act One finale stayed as Steiner planned. Gerald O'Hara's theme returns, shadowed by whispering dissonances as Scarlett realizes he has lost his mind. *"Now we know he's NUTS ... just even as you and I!"*

At the close of the film's first half—Scarlett's speech "As God is my witness, I'll never be hungry again!"—Steiner's mastery of Wagnerian music-drama is fully utilized. The finale begins with the Tara theme presented as swirling musical question; then builds into a defiant statement of Tara for orchestra and chorus. As Scarlett slowly rises from the ground, climbing key modulations match her. *"Grandioso ... a tone higher ... [then] a major third higher."* They culminate in a two-note brass punctuation that prepares us for her speech: *"FULL BRASS fortissimo ... also Organ, Timpani ... As God is my witness—all the strings ..."*

Then, at the apex of *GWTW*'s drama, Steiner's frustration takes over. *"I'll never be humping again! Molto crescendo . . . I don't know what D.O.S. likes—as usual—probably a guitar will play this [scene] finally?"*

MAX'S "HUMPING" JOKE WAS MORE than schoolboy irreverence. As Steiner worked around the clock, his sublimated sex drive was channeled into the score. During Ashley's confession that he loves Scarlett: *"ECSTATIC . . . This is unadulterated screwing music! . . . maybe 3 Trombones . . . added to portray Ashley's Balls!"* And while scoring the birth of Melanie's son: *"This might be too screwy! But after all, the Baby always comes after screwing! . . . Change anything you want—even your underwear! I don't care!! My sex life has Gone With the Wind!"*

According to Louise, Max was now sleeping two hours a night. His worsening temper was aimed at an easy target: her. One day, she recalled,

> We had a little misunderstanding, and didn't speak for a day or two. In the morning of the third day, I happened to come out of our bedroom, and Max—his was right across the way—we both happened to open our doors at the same time.
>
> I said "Hello." He looked rather sheepish and he said, "Hello. Come in, I want to play this for you. This is for Melanie's death." So I went in and listened, and was very affected by it, and everything was forgotten, and we were great friends again. He said, "What are you doing for lunch?" We went out and had lunch together and were happy as could be.
>
> On our way back as we were coming into our driveway, one of our butlers came running out and said "Oh, Mr. Steiner, your father is very upset at you. You went away without telling him anything, without taking him." Max immediately was very upset, and dashed in the house.[41]

Steiner's rift with Louise came just as he was scoring the collapse of Rhett and Scarlett's marriage. This aspect of the story inspires one last great motif in the score: the "Butler Love Theme." Steiner's sympathies may have been shifting from Scarlett to Rhett, whose efforts to please his partner—often without success—resonated each time a memo arrived from Selznick.

Max was justly proud of his transcendent scoring of the death of Melanie. *"Lohengrin x Tristan together are a louse by comparison!"* Rhett's farewell to Scarlett is another superb example of restrained but powerful emotion.

"*Tenderly—Cello, with much expression. This should sound very serious—He does not love her any longer.*" As Rhett recounts his failed attempts to win her affection, the Butler love theme returns: "*I want to make the saddest tune possible (in a major key).*" As Rhett leaves Scarlett, his seldom-heard theme gets its most effective statement. "*He walks out—RHYTHMIC . . . FULL . . . He turns into his old self—An Adventurer . . . A sort of 'heartbreaking' MARCH.*"

Now alone, Scarlett recalls the words of Gerald and others, reminding her of Tara. The scene lets Steiner recap his motifs during "*GHOST VOICES . . . This is the FATHER'S IRISH THEME . . . She looks up . . . The TARA Theme must get stronger and stronger.*" The final image—a dolly back from Scarlett, silhouetted under the great tree—echoes the film's first half visually and musically; in fact, this final cue was written first, then adapted for the end of the film's first half.

AS STEINER & CO. RACED TOWARD THE FINISH LINE, Selznick's attitude toward his frazzled composer swung from support to hostility.

November 17: "I think the score is coming along fine, and if you will just go mad with schmaltz in the last three reels I will undoubtedly be as happy through the years with the memory of a great Steiner score as has always been the case in the past."[42]

But that same month, Selznick flew into a rage, after learning that Steiner had spent part of October writing underscore for *Four Wives*—something David had forbidden in his loan-out deal with Warners. "Steiner and Warner Brothers jointly double-crossed us," he fumed. "The result is that he is now rushing like mad to do the *Wind* score and at best the score is going to be a disappointment. . . . I do not see how we can get out even a bad score in the time remaining."[43]

DOS memo, November 23: "Thanks to a new demonstration of the failure and refusal of Mr. Forbes and Mr. Steiner to cooperate, this reel calls for a new scoring job on the finish . . . "[44]

November 28: "Once again Mr. Forbes and Mr. Steiner have let slide an opportunity. . . . If ever a piece of film is screaming for a particular piece of music, it is this one for 'Marching Through Georgia,' but even this wasn't enough to overcome the egotism that demands original compositions."

December 1, 14 days before the premiere: "Stop throwing music off-key and doing tricks with it. . . . Stop having the music try to tell the dialogue, and use music for what it's supposed to be used for, which is mood."[45]

December 6, nine days before the premiere: "Step by step we are getting closer to the truth: Max Steiner admitted last night that the score he did for Warners took a week. First it was a day, then three days, then a week, and God only knows what the truth is."[46]

Meanwhile, Max and his team were in a hell of their own. Recalled Hugo, "We were recording and dubbing practically simultaneously . . . that whole thing had a nightmare quality, because we were really under pressure. We never started recording until after dinner, and we'd record until two, sometimes three in the morning. . . . Then we would go home, grab a couple of hours' sleep, get up, and write, with orchestrators and copyists breathing down our necks, and grab a bite before recording, and then start the whole thing all over again . . . it was touch and go as far as making the Atlanta premiere was concerned."[47]

Most of the orchestra came from Warner Bros., adding a measure of comfort despite all-night recording at United Artists. Surviving outtakes capture Max in a range of moods: tense ("No no, you're not *playing* it, boys!"), resigned ("Nobody will ever hear this probably") and self-critical, as he tries to sync shifting tempos with screen action ("Stick to me, boys, and everything will go wrong"). Serving as concertmaster was Louis Kaufman. Louise, six months pregnant, was first harpist.[48]

The final session was completed on December 6, nine days before the premiere.[49] Few of Selznick's sound mixers slept for the next week, as reels of optical film containing the score were developed, then combined with *GWTW*'s dialogue and effects tracks.

A typical Steiner pencil sketch score ran between 90 and 250 pages. *Gone with the Wind* set a career record: 457 pages.[50]

As Selznick departed for the Atlanta premiere, he left behind him a cloud of rancor. Steiner was frustrated, convinced that David "went haywire."[51] Selznick believed that Max had betrayed him by doing secret work for Warners. But in calmer moments, the producer recognized the worth of Steiner's labor. On December 6, David wrote William S. Paley, CBS founder and owner of Columbia Records. "You might like to have one of your record companies get out one or more records of the musical score of *Gone with the Wind*. I know that under ordinary circumstances the musical score of a picture couldn't be expected to sell records, but . . . this may be the exception. And incidentally, the score is quite beautiful."[52]

Paley declined.

Keeping time while racing against it: the recording of *Gone with the Wind*. (MS Papers; L. Tom Perry Special Collections, Brigham Young University)

In the months ahead, consumers were flooded with *GWTW* merchandise: dolls, cookbooks, puzzles, nail polish. But no commercial recording of Steiner's score was issued until 1954.

THE FILM SCORES OF MAX STEINER

1939 Releases (continued)

Intermezzo (8/39). Selznick International. AAN (music supervisor Lou Forbes was the sole credited Oscar nominee).
Four Wives (8/39–11/39)
We Are Not Alone (10/39)
Gone with the Wind (10/39–12/39). Selznick International/ MGM. AAN.

On the night of December 15, 1939, Selznick joined Gable, Leigh, Margaret Mitchell, and other luminaries inside Loew's Grand Theatre for *GWTW*'s triumphant premiere in Atlanta. The stars were serenaded on arrival by an African American chorus (none of the music was Steiner's). According to author Michael Sragow, "Ten-year-old Martin Luther King Jr., son of the pastor of Ebenezer Baptist Church, sang spirituals as part of a choir clothed in slave garb."[53]

No African Americans, including Hattie McDaniel, were invited to the screening.

Since 1939, the motion picture celebrated that night has drifted slowly away from the cultural mainstream. A growing number of viewers cringe at its blinkered view of the old South as a "pretty world" of "gallantry" filled with childlike, grateful slaves.

Yet in spite of this, *Gone with the Wind* remains one of the most compelling products of Hollywood's golden age. Audiences still respond to its timeless emotional truths: the yearning for home, the pain of unreciprocated love, the tragedy of missed emotional connections, the devastating death of a child. It is this story that Max Steiner set to music, with both intimacy and the sweep of grand opera.

He received sole composing credit for the film, a fact that "Steiner & Co." accepted with equanimity; his cowriters could use their participation to get more work. The credit was not unjust. The music of *Gone with the Wind* reflected the singular vision of Steiner, who now hoped that it would restore his standing as Hollywood's most important composer.

In the weeks ahead, he would get his answer—one that would be accompanied by the most crushing disappointment of his career.

Breaking Point

AMERICA'S RESPONSE TO *GONE WITH THE WIND* was no less rapturous than that of Atlantans. " 'It' has arrived at last," Frank Nugent wrote in the *New York Times*, "and we cannot get over the shock of not being disappointed."[1]

Variety singled out Steiner in the same sentence as Victor Fleming and screenwriter Sidney Howard.[2] Other critics praised "a thrillingly sustained music score"[3] and a main theme that "drags at the heart and becomes an integral part of Scarlett's longing."[4] A note Steiner received after the L.A. premiere was especially gratifying. "Dear Max," Jack Warner wrote, "Your score for GONE WITH THE WIND, which I saw last night, was really wonderful. You have done a great job for a great picture."[5]

The epic was expected to sweep the Oscars, and in January 1940, Steiner received two of the Academy's 11 Best Original Score nominations—for *Dark Victory* and *Gone with the Wind*. Bizarrely, the Academy also featured a separate, near-identical category: Best Score. Both categories contained scores from movie musicals as well as original dramatic scores.

On February 29, Hollywood gathered at the Cocoanut Grove as Bob Hope presided over his first Academy Awards ceremony. But within minutes of its 8:30 p.m. start, murmurs of surprise spread across the room, prompted by the first major blunder in Oscar history.

Since 1930, the Academy had kept winners' names secret until their announcement. Those names were given in advance to major news outlets, to ensure quick publication after the program. The media kept its pledge of secrecy—until 1940. At 8:45 p.m., the *Los Angeles Times* broke the embargo, printing all of the winners in its evening edition. Late arrivals to the awards like Clark Gable learned moments before entering that they had lost.[6]

With the birth of their child days away, Max and Louise did not attend. Their absence proved a blessing. Waiting anxiously at home, Steiner either read or heard on radio the winner for Best Original Score. It was Herbert Stothart, for *The Wizard of Oz*.

Somehow, Max had lost the Academy Award for a score already recognized as a film music landmark. It was "absolutely heartrending," Louise said in 1996.[7] "He was upset, naturally so. We couldn't believe it." Max was further angered when the Best Score Oscar went to *Stagecoach*, a musical patchwork with multiple composers, lacking the cohesion of *GWTW*'s team efforts. For the rest of his life, Max confused the results of that admittedly confusing night, saying he was beaten by *Stagecoach*, not *The Wizard of Oz*.[8]

So how did *Gone with the Wind* lose for its iconic score?

With the film a lock in most categories, it is likely that the Academy saw a way to honor *The Wizard of Oz*, with its incomparable songs by Harold Arlen and Yip Harburg, by giving it two music honors: Best Song ("Over the Rainbow") and Best Original Score. But since *Oz*'s underscore was based mostly on the movie's songs, it truly belonged in a separate category from *GWTW*. (*Oz* also had the advantage of having its songs played on radio and issued as records.)

Whatever the reason, the damage was done. Awards mattered deeply to Max: his hunger for recognition reflected unhealed wounds dating back to the collapse of his family's empire.

After the 1940 Oscars, Steiner's comments about his most famous work were often qualified with disappointment. "I'm glad you liked *Gone with the Wind*," he wrote a fan that year. "It was a job. Clark Gable and I were the only ones connected with the picture who lost in the Academy Awards."[9]

Nevertheless, his contribution to the most successful motion picture in history (in modern dollars, more than $3 billion gross)[10] brought him enhanced industry prestige, and a breakthrough at his home studio. By the end of 1940, Steiner had written seven full scores for Warners—all of them major releases.

The year began auspiciously with ringing box office for *Four Wives*, featuring Max's *Symphonie Moderne*. For the first time, a Steiner work found some life outside the movies, thanks to radio broadcasts, a 1943 recording, and a few concert performances. As *Four Wives* played to full houses, Max was finishing another biopic a la *Emile Zola*, but with a juicier subject. *Dr. Ehrlich's Magic Bullet* starred Edward G. Robinson as the real-life German Jew who devised the first effective treatment of syphilis in 1909. Any studio but Warners would have deemed the subject unfilmable; but Hal Wallis won over censors by emphasizing scientific progress in the script.[11]

The best passages in Steiner's score contrast declamatory power with restraint. Scenes of Ehrlich studying bacteria through a microscope are quietly intense, even mystical, thanks to Steiner's impressionistic soundscapes, which make the tiny microbes a tangible nemesis. A chord bracketed by a dissonant second (C-natural against C-sharp) represents the mystery Ehrlich hopes to solve: *"The Nuclei . . . a SORT OF PROPHECY,"*[12] conveyed with celesta, harp, and other "swimmy" percussion.

The chance to score a film about syphilis also was sure to bring out the schoolboy in Max. *"Don't you think Clapholz should do the copying?"* And after Ehrlich's advice to a patient, "You must come twice a week," *"A nice picture with nice dialogue: I can't even come once a year!"* There was also a hint of discord at home. After a syphilis victim is told he cannot marry: *"The sucker: He doesn't know how lucky he is."*

Steiner next dove into another giant western—one he despised. *Virginia City* doubled down on *Dodge City*'s noisy action, reuniting Errol Flynn with Michael Curtiz. But unlike *Dodge*, *Virginia City* was a production teetering on collapse. Rewrites lasted through filming, and Flynn loathed his leading lady, the temperamental Miriam Hopkins.[13]

The film was a mess, which meant one thing: Max was expected to fix it. Anxiety and anger fill his sketches. The Academy Awards were days away, and he was seething after reading Oscar Levant's book *A Smattering of Ignorance*, filled with sarcastic jabs at him. *"Hugo! I know I won't win the Academy Award with this music!! Because it smells! But I don't really care!! As you know they give 'Oscars' away as the symbol of achievement! And I'm afraid they might give me 'Levant.'"* *"Chet North is dubbing this—hence nothing matters! Just a wasted effort! I am writing without any ambition!! HELP! I STINK! MAX STINKER!! I can't think'er no more. This picture is horrible!! Curtiz must have been drunk!"*[14]

Yet the score contains superb passages that Steiner would self-borrow for years: another grand "pioneer" theme; a rollicking stagecoach gallop; and an exquisite, minuet-like theme for Hopkins's Southern spy-turned-heroine, Julia Hayne. Its cantabile (songlike) feel reflects Max's attention to story: Julia's ambition is to become a singer. But the composer was not inspired by Hopkins herself. Her low, drawling speech earns her the epithet *"Slabmouth"* throughout Max's sketches.

ABSENT FROM *VIRGINIA CITY*'S recording was Max's favorite harpist.

On March 2, 1940, Louise and Max celebrated the arrival of Ronald Lawrence Maximilian Steiner, born at Good Samaritan Hospital. "That was the happiest day of my life," Louise recalled.[15] In Ronald's baby book, his proud parents wrote that his name signified a person "worthy of admiration, victorious, a leader."[16]

An extra wing was added to Cove Way, with the Steiners' main bedroom converted to a nursery. "Max didn't have any routine of attending church," Louise remembered, "so when Ron was born, Max asked me regarding baptizing him in my church, St. Paul's Episcopal. That was the only time Max and I were in a church together."[17]

After nursing Ronnie for a month, Louise returned to recording, leaving her baby in the hands of a nurse and household staff. As with Max, the need for creative expression was too strong to ignore.

HER RETURN COINCIDED WITH the recording of Steiner's richest score of 1940. *All This, and Heaven Too* "was a very appropriate title," Louise recalled. "Max said that was how he felt about the birth of our son and our life together."[18] Bette Davis and Charles Boyer headlined a sumptuous adaptation

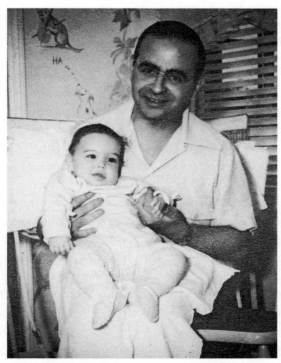

Introducing Ronald Steiner. (Louise Steiner Elian Papers;
L. Tom Perry Special Collections, Brigham Young University)

of Rachel Field's bestseller. Davis played Henriette Deluzy Desportes, a governess in 1847 France. Her unspoken love for her employer, the brooding Duc de Praslin, ends in murder (his wife's), suicide (the Duc's), trial (Henriette's), and exoneration. It was melodrama of the highest order, and nearly the highest cost. A budget of $1.4 million was steep for Warners, and a sign of how *GWTW* had fed Hollywood's appetite for super-productions.[19]

For Steiner, its story of unconsummated but passionate love was just the kind of film he had been begging to score. From its first seconds, his music overflows with melody and color, starting with an explosive quote of the mad Duchess's thunderous theme (*"BITCH MUSIC . . . ACID"*).[20] Steiner then switches to a contrasting burst of sunlight with one of his loveliest creations: an *appassionato* waltz, to be linked to Henriette. Its opening five notes are repeated higher, then soar upward into a dancing, stratospheric continuation of the melody. "The haunting beauty of this warm-hearted and very hummable tune, reprised in mostly tender and sad harmonies, shines brightly throughout the film," wrote Philip J. S. Hammond.[21]

Common throughout the score are instructions like *"Delicato, dolce, Tranquillo, molto expressivo e charmante"*—a reminder that just outside Max's study was the nursery of his son. Ronnie even made a musical cameo of sorts. Max had his boy in mind as he wrote the theme for kind-hearted preacher Mr. Field, who tells Henriette that "no matter what our despair, there is a heaven for us on this earth if we can only find it."[22] In parenthood, Max believed he had found his.

By 1940 Jack Warner so trusted his top composer that, according to Max, he issued an edict that "no directors or producers were to be allowed in on the stage where I was recording or when we were dubbing."[23] But on *Heaven*, director/producer Anatole Litvak wanted more input.

During dubbing, he asked Max if he could hear some of the music. Anatole "was a close friend of mine, so I told him I'd sneak him in," Steiner recalled.[24] "We listened to a couple of reels. Then he put his arms around me and said, 'Maxie, it's the greatest.' Fifteen minutes later I had a call from Jack Warner: 'Haven't I told you not to let anybody in while you're dubbing? You disobeyed me. And now Litvak wants me to take you off the picture. He thinks the music will ruin it. So it just serves you right!'"

It is equally likely that Litvak liked what he heard, but that Warner, eager to keep directors at a distance, put the fear of God into Max to teach him a lesson.

Warner himself loved what he called "the important music score,"[25] and his verdict was echoed by another producer Steiner was thrilled to have as a fan. "Your score is outstanding," wrote Samuel Goldwyn, "one of the best jobs you have ever done."[26] Friedhofer ranked it among Max's finest; and even Bernard Herrmann, who seldom praised colleagues, was impressed. When Herrmann later called his own romantically charged music for *The Ghost and Mrs. Muir* his "Max Steiner score," he was alluding to *All This, and Heaven Too*, according to Friedhofer.[27]

PROFESSIONALLY, STEINER WAS BACK ON TOP. On June 21, a month after his 52nd birthday, he was deemed famous enough to be profiled on a radio show produced by the American Legion. A newspaper ad offers the only record of what must have been a fascinating program. "The dramatized life story of Max Steiner . . . will be presented tomorrow night over station KMPC from 9:00 to 9:30 in the new radio feature 'A Citizen is Born.' Each week this program presents the life story of one of America's 'adopted sons' with the 'son' himself enacting the leading role and supported by a studio cast."[28]

But privately, Steiner's troubles were mounting. Inattention to his finances had resulted in mounting debts. Steiner owed thousands in back taxes. And although Gabor's flight to America saved him from Hitler, it did not protect him from his own creditors. "These people are very demanding with respect to the full amount of the obligation . . . your father promised to pay," lawyer Louis Minter wrote.[29] If repayment was ever made, it came from Max's pocket.

Steiner's own debt to Minter was climbing, although the attorney bore much of the blame for his client's tangled finances. Yet when Minter recommended that he take over the handling of Max and Louise's expenses, they agreed.[30] Now, even a request from Steiner to buy new furniture received a stern response. Instead of chairs, Minter wrote, perhaps guests "would all have more fun sitting on the beautiful carpeting than fancy chairs."[31]

Imagine the reaction of Hollywood's highest paid composer, and probably its proudest, to news that he could not afford chairs.

IN OCTOBER 1940, 82-YEAR-OLD GABOR surprised his son by marrying Erna Mundelius, a German-born secretary Max hired to handle correspondence to Vienna. "She was 78 years old and had only one eye, but she was a darling woman," Max recalled.[32] "They took a furnished apartment down on Swall Drive, not very far from us. Papa called me and asked me to come and visit them. I went over about 11 o'clock one morning and there was Erna in bed. She was all made up and had a frilly net cap on and wore a pretty bedjacket. Papa was walking around, smoking a big cigar and dressed in a handsome robe. I went over and kissed Erna and inquired: 'Well, how was the honeymoon?' Papa answered for her: 'You may not believe this, son, but she's still a virgin!'"

She was also in failing health. Max made weekly payments for an in-house nurse, gave the pair a weekly allowance, and paid their monthly rent.

Thank God there was work to offer escape.

David O. Selznick had forbidden Max from mickey-mousing. In the Warner melodrama *City for Conquest*, composer Eddie Kenny (Arthur Kennedy) demands it from the screen. Auditioning his symphony-in-progress for brother Danny (James Cagney), Eddie plays a Gershwinesque melody—the "part that I call East River. The rumbling of the El over Allen street." Upward progressions. "The story of all those who tried to scale their dizzy heights"—a downward glissando on the piano—"but crash, frustrated and broken to the concrete pavements. And then of those few who finally reach the top"—twinkling chords in high octaves—"only to find out that above them are still the unattainable stars"—even higher chords.

As such literalism suggests, Eddie's "Magic Isle Symphony," written by Steiner, is hardly a piece for the ages—"another big symphonic hunk," to quote Friedhofer.[33] Max loved translating the mechanistic bleats of city life into music. But while his pastiches of Gershwin in earlier scores were effective for a main title or a brief city montage, his *City* symphony is terminally derivative of *Rhapsody in Blue*, from its solo yawning woodwind opening, to its "East River" melody that is a re-harmonized soundalike of *Rhapsody*'s slow, central tune. When Max got the chance to write a concert work within a film, the result, ironically, is some of his least personal music.

Max talked up the piece to his friend Victor Blau of Music Publishers Holding Corporation, a Warner publishing arm, claiming that his bosses "think it is the best thing I have ever written."[34] Steiner often used that phrase for his latest work—a tic that reflects not just show biz hyperbole, but the manic state in which he usually wrote. It is far from the only indication that Steiner may have suffered from bipolar disorder (formerly known as manic depression), typified by exaggerated highs and equally depressive lows. It would help explain his ability to work for days with little or no sleep, his addiction to adrenalin-rush activity like gambling, and also his erratic behavior in the months ahead.

To Steiner's frustration, Warners elected not to publish *City*'s "Magic Isle Symphony." And six years later, when an original cello concerto was needed for *Devotion*, the studio hired Korngold. That choice suggests that while Jack

Warner's support for Steiner never wavered in the 1940s, the studio boss decided that his talents were best applied to underscoring.

It's hard to disagree.

FAR MORE INVENTIVE WAS THE SCORE he tackled next. *The Letter* reunited Bette Davis and director William Wyler, for a superlative film of Somerset Maugham's 1927 play. Davis embodied with animal ferocity its protagonist, the wife of a rubber plantation owner in the tropics who shoots her lover, pleads attempted rape and self-defense, but after her acquittal, admits to her husband that "With all my heart I still love the man I killed."

The Letter's opening sequence is a long tracking shot through the plantation at night—calm, almost silent. Soft percussion, including harps, bells, and celesta, echo the drip of rubber from a tree. Then music stops as a gunshot explodes on the soundtrack. Cut to Leslie Crosbie's lover, staggering out of the Crosbie home. He collapses as Leslie fires five more shots into his body, her face an implacable mask.

According to screenwriter Howard Koch, Wyler wanted "a fundamental image—something that by its recurrence would reveal the woman's suppressed guilt. . . . We decided to have a full moon the night she did the shooting. . . . From then on, starting with that night, she would draw away from the moonlight to avoid the memory of what she'd done."[35]

That metaphor proved a springboard for Steiner. Unusually, his music centers on a single motif, evoking the retribution Leslie tries to avoid. The theme is a musical lightning bolt, its first three notes of D–B–D played in sharply accented octaves. That same minor-third triad is repeated in triplets as the phrase is repeated again and again; its hammer-like repetition is a perfect match for the image of the looming moon, which stares down on Leslie like a celestial judge.

Steiner always looked forward to a Davis performance, knowing it would invite layers of musical psychology. On *The Letter*, he reveled in the chance to give counterpoint to Leslie's mendacity. *"Should not sound too Kosher—she's lying like Hell!" "Two harps (BIG)—Throws herself on bed. Hugo! She's acting! She wants to 'chisel' the lawyer into saving her!"*[36]

For the quietly charged confrontation between Leslie and her lover's Eurasian wife (Gale Sondergaard) in a Chinese shop, the composer pushed his team to create a sound unlike any he had attempted before—one anticipating the experimental percussion of John Cage and Philip Glass. "Max persuaded the sound effects department to eliminate all this physical beaded curtain noise," Friedhofer said, "and then we proceeded to make a loop. . . . We used something like eighteen percussion instruments on it."[37]

Steiner's score includes a separate "effect sheet" for the scene, with parts listed for first and second celeste, first and second piano, plus *"Bali Bells . . . Small Bells . . . Vibraphone (Hard stick) . . . 2nd Vibraphone (Soft Sticks)."*

"We worked several hours to get just the right balance of sound on it," Hugo recalled.[38] "Somebody said, 'That's like Max, that here he could have done the same thing with a small electric fan and a set of Japanese wind bells. Instead he spends three hours with an eighteen-piece percussion section, getting the same effect.' . . . But it was very, very effective in the picture. And that's one of the many things about Max that was delightful, and instructive."

The Letter's score won Steiner his eighth Oscar nomination. It lost—to Leigh Harline and *Pinocchio*, in a likely replay of the *GWTW* versus *Oz* confusion between underscoring and songs.

WITH MAX'S LATEST WARNER CONTRACT set to expire the following April, the composer again grew restless. He was disappointed when one of the studio's most anticipated productions, *Kings Row*, was given to Korngold.[39] It earned Max's rival more accolades around the globe.

He fumed over a stalled deal to issue sheet music for *Gone with the Wind*. "I cannot begin to tell you how upset I am that nothing has been done," he wrote the publishers.[40] A book of ten *GWTW* themes in simplified piano arrangements was finally issued in 1941.

Between worry about relatives in Vienna and another year of nonstop work, Max was desperate for a break. Fortunately, Wallis and Jack Warner agreed, permitting the Steiners to visit New York in December 1940.

The trip was a happy one. Its highlight was dinner with RCA founder David Sarnoff and his guest, Arturo Toscanini, during which the maestro asked a delighted Max about the process of writing film music.[41] During the trip, Steiner also pitched a curious project to his bosses. Max, the *Seattle Times* reported, was "trying to talk the Warner Brothers into letting him film the [Wagner] opera 'Siegfried,' and with 'real opera stars . . . I can film "Siegfried" and show a profit,' Steiner insisted cryptically. 'I've worked out a plan to make opera palatable . . . even fans who like the Lone Ranger will beat a path to the box office.'"[42]

Whatever his formula was, it had no takers.

MAX FOUND BETTER USE for his Wagnerian erudition in a movie released shortly before his trip. The least pretentious of Warner biopics, *A Dispatch from Reuters* starred Edward G. Robinson as Julius Reuter, German-born founder of the international news agency.

Scenes of Reuter's early success using carrier pigeons inspired music of charm and cleverness. As Julius haltingly converses with future wife Ida in his pigeon loft, Steiner unspools a Fritz Kreisler–like waltz theme of ineffable loveliness; he then enhances it with ornamentations by fluttering woodwinds. They mirror the scene's avian co-stars, as well as Julius and Ida's shy courtship. *"Hugo—I am trying to keep the pigeons 'talking' thruout!"*[43]

The score's Wagnerian connection comes minutes later. Reuter has promised his clients, a group of wealthy bankers, that his pigeons will return at a specific time with stock quotes attached to their legs. When the birds do not appear, the bankers start to exit. Suddenly, the winged messengers arrive, in a triumph that sparked an opera association for Steiner: *"Pigeon a la Lohengrin!"*

Wagner expert David Neumeyer explains. "The joking avian reference is to Lohengrin's arrival borne by a swan. More than that, however, the immediate dramatic situation is parallel: in Act 1, Scene 2 of Lohengrin, trumpets are sounded, everyone awaits the arrival of Elsa's champion, and tension is palpable at the passage of time; suddenly he appears . . . and a noble and celebratory choral music follows on a brief polyphonic display of wonder. In *A Dispatch from Reuters*, Steiner inserts a trumpet call as the pigeons are sighted and a triumphant, *tutti* presentation of the film's main theme . . . accompanies the arrival of the first pigeon."[44]

As such a sequence proved, movies made the best use of Steiner's knowledge and dramatic sensitivity. It was a fact he acknowledged in April of 1941, a month before his 53rd birthday: facing a mountain of debt, he signed a new four-year contract with Warner Bros.[45]

He also kept spending with reckless disregard. One-year-old Ronnie was the main beneficiary. As the boy grew, "Max, being an elderly father, adored him and spoiled him rotten," recalled harpist Aida Mulieri Dagort, "giving him, among other things, a real miniature automobile that he could drive around their property. . . . Louise often brought him to work with her, where he would run among the instrumentalists and often sit between us. He was a handsome child and resembled her, with dark hair and white skin."[46]

The sight of Ronnie among the musicians must have delighted his father.

THE IMPACT OF A MOTION PICTURE depends not only on its quality, but on the timing of its release. Take *Sergeant York,* starring Gary Cooper as the real-life Alvin York, who became the most decorated soldier of World War I. In 1941, it was beloved by audiences and critics, and its box office take of $6 million made it Hollywood's third highest grosser of the era, behind only *Gone with the Wind* and *Snow White and the Seven Dwarfs.*[47]

Today, it is difficult to get past the film's broad depiction of backwoods life in Tennessee; past Cooper's self-conscious "simplicity" and *Li'l Abner*–style dialogue ("I'm a-knowing where there's a piece of bottom lands to be had, and I'm a-going to get it"); and past its unsubtle propaganda. (Jack and Harry Warner intended *York* to prepare America for its inevitable role in the European war.)

For the purposes of our story, *Sergeant York* marks the last joyous experience for Max, during a time soon to reach a disastrous end.

Producer/director Howard Hawks loved popular songs, and suggested 20 folk tunes and church hymns to be used in the story and Steiner's score.[48] Max employed several, including "Frog Went a'Courting," "Old Time Religion," and most appealingly "I Got a Gal at the Head of the Holler." That melody skips playfully in whole steps up the tonic scale, then reverses its path as if returning home, in a sort of pastoral "Twinkle, Twinkle Little Star." The tune became a Steiner favorite; after its use for York's bride Gracie (*"Will O' The Wisp idea"*),[49] it accompanies other winsome country girls in 1952's *The Lion and the Horse* and 1956's *Come Next Spring*.

Not on Hawks's list was the folk tune Max used as Alvin's motif: "Wild Horse." Its punchy syncopation captures York's hell-raising youth and the fast-trigger heroism of his war service.

Steiner's original music blends beautifully with its folk sources, most notably a *delicato* piece of Americana for Mother York. Ever-sensitive to the timbre of actors' voices, he would never give "Cooper's low voice, for instance, a cello accompaniment," he told a reporter.[50] Max's high spirits while writing are clear from his notations, imitating York's twangy drawl: *"Hugo! This whole thing very light . . . I'll be a'thankin' you! MAW-X."* And noting the absence of music during war scenes: *"Dearest Hugo! We shall meet again in Reel 13 . . . Love, Schmuck."*

But whenever he wasn't composing—and often when he was—Max was a nervous wreck. Although Gabor no longer lived at Cove Way, his nearby home and his wife's poor health kept him a constant presence in Max and Louise's lives. As the latter would recall, conflict between the couple grew.

When Max was upset over something really trivial, he would lose his temper and be abusive. Max was very difficult to live with—a genius whose music I loved. A good person. However, he could be unreasonable as time went on.

He never enjoyed going with me to concerts or operas. Usually there was an excuse, that he had a certain assignment to do. He would suggest taking my mother or some of my friends. However, he had time to gamble, either at the Clover Club or gin rummy with his men friends.

He had been spoiled by his family and practically everyone around him (including myself). He was hard to talk with about anything other than his own work. He had a very authoritarian attitude; he was always right. And he was married to the piano, where he did all his composing. When we'd go to a vacation in Agua Caliente or Palm Springs, he'd have a piano installed so he could do some work.

There was not the camaraderie and communication necessary to make for a successful marriage.[51]

Warner Bros. was pushing Max harder than ever. "One day there was a picture to be gotten out in a hurry," he would recall. "I had written the music and was all finished, but I had caught the flu and was home in bed. I had a 104 degree fever and my doctor (also Forbstein's) happened to be with me when the phone by my bedside rang. It was Leo. 'Maxie,' he said, 'I want to go with you [record the score] at nine o'clock tomorrow morning.' The doctor grabbed the phone. 'Leo,' he said, 'You're out of your mind. I won't let Max even go to the bathroom. This is a sick man and I don't want him out of bed.' He handed the phone back to me. There was silence for a moment, then Leo's voice came back: 'How about 1 o'clock?' I 'went' with him at 1 o'clock. My doctor swore he'd never take either of us as a patient again."[52]

Recalled Louise, "They always put too much on him. And when he'd complain, Jack Warner would say, 'But Max, you're the only one who can save this picture.'"[53]

THE FILM SCORES OF MAX STEINER

1940 Releases

Dr. Ehrlich's Magic Bullet (1/40)
Virginia City (2/40)
All This, and Heaven Too (4/40–5/40)
A Dispatch from Reuters (7/40–8/40)
City for Conquest (8/40)
The Letter (9/40). AAN.
Santa Fe Trail (11/40)

1941 Releases (continued in Chapter 18)

The Great Lie (1/41–2/41). Mary Astor won a Supporting Actress Oscar, playing a Tchaikovsky-specializing concert pianist. Max incorporates the Russian composer's music throughout the score, which also includes the Steiner song "I Have So Much More."

Shining Victory (3/41)

The Bride Came C.O.D. (4/41). Max's swingy main title was a favorite of Hugo Friedhofer: "Only Max could take the Wagner *Bridal Chorus* and make it a side-theme in his own melody. [Steiner:] 'BA-da, BA-da, BA- [Wagner] dum-DA-DA-DA . . .' He was so clever, it became a bridge within his own theme."[54]

Sergeant York (5/11–6/11). AAN.

Dive Bomber (7/41)

For Steiner, there was another, frightening source of anxiety. His vision was failing.

"You asked whether I am happy?" he wrote ex-wife Beatrice.[55] "I am as happy as anyone can who works day and night and is half cripple as far as my eyesight is concerned. [My doctor] told me frankly that I could never be cured, as the tissues of the pupils are eaten away to a certain extent. I am stone blind at night; cannot drive a car or even cross the street alone, and it has been like that for the past two or three years . . . The peculiarity of my ailment is this: whenever I get very worried about anything or excited about anything, my eyesight, what I have left of it, gets worse."

Max's hypertension was evident to both friends and outsiders. "Steiner shows that strain that working for movies puts on a man," wrote a journalist.[56] "He talks rapidly and incessantly, chews nervously on a cigar and paces up and down."

Although he was prone to verbal outbursts, he had never been violent. But according to Louise, in July 1941, this changed.

I had worked all day at 20th Century Fox with Al Newman. When I came home, I noticed the car of our friend Norma [Drury] in the driveway. Norma had worked with Max at Warners and she drove him home.

We had a couple of drinks, and Max asked Norma, "Would you like something to eat?" She said yes. I didn't jump immediately, but Max looked at me and said, "I want you to go and fix Norma a sandwich." Norma said, "Never mind, Max, I know the kitchen, I'll go down and I'll fix it for myself."

Norma had gone down, and Max started yelling at me, ordering me to go downstairs to fix something for Norma. I said, "In a few minutes." He yelled at me, saying to go at once, and threw a glass ashtray, which hit my head.

After the ashtray broke, he put his hands on my head and slammed me into the wall. I was terrified, and finally got away from him and went downstairs.

Norma was in the kitchen. Her eyes got as big as saucers and she said, "My God, what happened?" I was wearing a white slack suit, and it was covered with blood. Immediately she tried to see Max, and then she called the doctor, and probably at 2:30 to 3:00 in the morning, the doctor came. He shaved part of my head—the glass had broken—and he took stitches. I had to wear a turban to cover that up.

It was a terrible thing. It instilled in me fear, which I had never felt before. It made me very much afraid of Max.

He was very apologetic and I put off any action about separation, because I wanted to be fair to him and our son and myself. I still loved Max and I tried to carry on. However, the atmosphere was increasingly tense. The feeling of fear never quite left me.[57]

Louise had often second-guessed her career path, wishing at times that she had pursued her childhood dream of a singing career.[58] Steiner's actions convinced her it was time to find out. That summer, she moved out of Cove Way, left Los Angeles, and at age 35 embarked on a new life of vocal studies in New York. Ronnie would stay with Max, at least for the time being.

Louise's departure was the first act in a decades-long tragedy that consumed much of the rest of Steiner's life. And as events worsened, the composer increasingly buried himself in work, as he channeled his loneliness and romantic longing into some of the greatest music of his career.

18

Voyage into Fog

AFTER LOUISE'S DEPARTURE, Max tried to pretend that little had changed in their relationship. But in the letters he wrote her almost daily, Steiner's upbeat reports of his latest score's success invariably gave way to anger.

Typical is a note in which he refers to himself as "your <u>old</u> gentleman from Vienna"—a pun on his 53 years, and an attempt to say that he is his old, loving self. "I miss you a lot—funny thing—I never thought I would until after you had left. Do you miss me a little bit? Like hell you do! I don't think you love me anymore, but then that's life! You are young, vivacious and beautiful—and I—a broken down decrepit organ grinder—in the last stage of senility!"[1]

On another day, he appealed to her instincts as a mother. "Ronnie is perfect and beautiful. . . . He calls for . . . his <u>Mamma</u> all the time—you better come home or he'll be sore at you. He won't play with his aeroplanes—cries Mamma—and throws them away."[2]

Steiner rarely offered hope that he would be more sensitive to Louise's needs. He seemed incapable of acknowledging the root problems in their marriage: his obsession with work and his withholding of the emotional support she needed. Instead, he preferred to channel his feelings into music—as he did with his latest assignment at Warner Bros.

The list of Hollywood "religious" films is one that most secular movie lovers avoid, with few exceptions. But in 1941, Warner Bros. produced a drama that transcends its religious trappings, offering a quietly moving story of service amid sacrifice. *One Foot in Heaven* starred Fredric March and Martha Scott in the fact-based story of Methodist minister William Spence, his long-suffering wife, Hope, and their two children. Together they travel from parish to parish across early 20th-century America, facing endless obstacles: budget shortages, poor lodging, hypocrisy from city leaders who pay obsequy to Christianity while neglecting the local poor.

The film explores the toll William's cause takes on his family, from the pressures on his children to Hope's never having the permanent home she longs for. In its most charming vignette, it also celebrates cinema as a force for social good. After William condemns movies as a sin without ever having seen one, he is persuaded to attend a showing of the 1917 western *The Silent Man*, starring William S. Hart. Captivated by its message of good defeating evil, Spence reverses his stand against movies on the pulpit the following Sunday.

While arranging the piano music for this sequence, Steiner must have recalled his own first movie scoring, for the 1916 silent *The Bondman*. In other ways, the story of the Spences also hit close to home. William's passion for work borders on obsession, and his family is expected to follow him unquestioningly. The resulting tension is a recurring theme—one reinforced in Steiner's moving score.

Unlike the ersatz religioso that ends *The Informer*, *Heaven*'s main theme is persuasively spiritual: a three-note phrase repeated higher, then higher again, before its next iteration is lower on the scale—the musical equivalent of two steps forward, one step back on a quest. Steiner's own predisposition toward helping others also finds an alter ego in William Spence. The faith that drives the minister is symbolized in the iconic Methodist hymn "The Church's One Foundation." Steiner's instinct for drama turns the familiar tune into an *Ode to Joy*–like hymn of humanity, and its use in the final scene is towering. The aging Spence is about to leave a community that loves him, uprooting his family yet again to help another troubled parish. As townspeople gather outside their church, drawn by music, Spence plays the hymn on a majestic organ. Gradually the organ is supported by full orchestra, as the theme thrillingly modulates upward: *"Add Vibraphone to chimes . . . Bells . . . 2nd set of Chimes—VOICES . . ."*[3]

Norman Vincent Peale, a consultant on the film, attended a preview and watched as a restless audience gradually settled into the story. "Finally at the end a great hymn was sung, built up in soaring music of organ, orchestra and chorus. . . . They were moved by the spell of it and burst into a great ovation."[4] *Hollywood Reporter* echoed his account. "The glorious musical score by Max Steiner . . . is a masterwork that does humble one with the simple beauty of its quality. His music for the final scene . . . must send any audience out of the theater exalted and reborn."[5]

Max gave Louise many reports of *Heaven*'s warm reception, before diving into a more epic endeavor—one offering an even greater opportunity to channel his longings into the language he spoke best.

FACED WITH THE TASK OF VALORIZING George Armstrong Custer, the arrogant general who led his troops to their death at Little Big Horn, the writers of *They Died with Their Boots On* chose the only path possible: they fictionalized his story almost beyond recognition. Their success must be seen to be believed; *Boots* is the most affecting drama in the Errol Flynn–Olivia de Havilland canon.

An air of parting hangs over the film, as if its makers realized that it would be the last Errol–Olivia teaming, and the last period-adventure classic to star Flynn, whose career soon would fade amid his increasing reliance on drink and drugs.

Its director was Raoul Walsh, a rugged, eyepatch-wearing filmmaker who "saw more with one eye than I did with two," Irving Rapper recalled.[6] Walsh valued Steiner's contribution, and the two enjoyed a friendship for 25 years.

For once, Max was thrilled to be assigned to a western, describing it to Louise as "a wonderful picture and as good for me as *Sgt York* . . . I feel all hopped up about it."[7] He began work on September 29, 1941.[8] By now, Franklin Roosevelt had re-imposed the draft. America's entry into war was two months away. That grim national mood is mirrored in the film, and Steiner responded strongly to its spirit of fatalism and duty.

For its opening titles, Max abandons his usual Warners fanfare in favor of a pounding "Indian" theme for low brass and percussion: the theme for Crazy Horse of the Sioux Indians. It is followed—chased?—by the score's recurring motif for military heroism: "Garry Owen," a rousing Irish march used by the real General Custer's Seventh Cavalry.[9] In the movie's first seconds, Steiner foreshadows the famous battle that closes the drama.

The score's grand scope is achieved partly with a sharp musical contrast between expansiveness, in the form of wide note intervals, and narrowness, evoked by close and often dissonant ones. Custer's theme starts with the cheerful leap of a perfect fifth, accompanied by a quietly loping march rhythm. The motto is flexible enough to capture Custer's early fecklessness and (onscreen at least) his final nobility. Chromaticism, less attractive to the ear, "becomes associated with quirkiness, personalities at odds with the norm," author Kate Daubney observed.[10] "The difference between Custer's blunt openness and [his foe, Lieutenant] Sharp's deviousness is captured in the difference between the large open intervals of the former theme and the stepwise motion of the latter. However, the military backgrounds of both men are symbolized in the dotted rhythms of both themes, giving them something in common."

The Custer theme is also designed to work in harmony with the theme for his great love, Libby (de Havilland), "which musically and dramatically unites these two characters in a single bond," notes John Morgan:

> Max hated to analyze his music. I was saying to him how the love theme is interwoven from two other themes in the film. He said, 'Composers don't do that necessarily consciously. It's just part of their sound world.' He would write out his thematic plan ahead of time and refer to it. 'But I didn't sit down and try to intertwine themes the way Wagner would.' Still, a lot of times his themes are almost as subtle as Wagner, because you never would pick up their interconnection on a casual listen.
>
> Max said to me that good film music has to get across to people who are very bright and people who are not. And if there's a lot more in the music that you may find later in listening to it, well and good, but that's not the main purpose. Because it's not concert music. It belongs to the film.[11]

Pause for a moment to find Libby's theme in one of its various iterations on disc or the Internet; you will hear faster than you can read why it has been called the "Steiner love theme par excellence" by author Tony Thomas.[12] Its first three notes are major-key whole steps that reflect the warmth of de Havilland's smile and Libby's devotion. The theme then soars into a classic Steiner melody, one whose expansive shape has been compared to "Danny Boy" ("Londonderry Air"). Its romanticism is tinged with a sense of resignation, anticipating its use in *Boots'* finest scene: Custer and Libby's farewell before the battle, in which each knows—but cannot say—that they will never see each other again.

"I had this curious feeling," de Havilland said decades later, "as if this was actually a real farewell. Of course, that is exactly what it turned out to be."[13] Flynn and de Havilland had been in love, but the actress knew that a life with the self-destructive actor was impossible . . . adding extra poignance to the scene, which Steiner makes the movie's emotional climax.

An exquisite version of Libby's theme fills the pauses between the couple's forced-casual dialogue as Custer prepares to leave. Eventually an off-camera bugle call plays over the score in a different key. Custer and Libby gaze at each other, silent, until a thunderous, drumroll-like chord changes the mood in an instant from avoidance to heartbreaking honesty. "Goodbye," Custer says quietly. Like the characters, music drops all pretense. Libby's theme soars as they kiss for a wordless 21 seconds. A rare Steiner violin solo delicately accompanies Custer's parting words: "Walking through life with you, ma'am, has been a very gracious thing." As he leaves the room, Libby's theme turns harmonically dissonant as she slides into a faint.

The final battle rivals *Light Brigade* in its virtuosic action and in its musical build from guarded heroism ("Garry Owen"), and thoughts of Libby, to a wild, dissonance-filled collage of the score's many themes, evoking Charles Ives's avant-garde use of American folk tunes. *"FAST BUGLE— make separate . . . EVERYBODY x EVERYTHING . . . FERROCE."*[14] That "everything" included seven percussion, two harps, two pianos, six additional piccolos, two soprano saxes, six military snare drums, and other percussion supplements.

At the end of Hugo's orchestration score—nearly a thousand pages— Friedhofer drew the face of a stern Indian, proclaiming *"UGH! GREAT WHITE FATHER FROM COVE WAY GIVE ORCHESTRA GOOD SCREWING!"*[15] More than 50 years later, a member of the Moscow Symphony echoed those thoughts during a re-recording of the battle music: "Mahler easy. Steiner difficult."[16]

Achieving an integrity of musical line throughout the 6-1/2-minute sequence also wasn't easy. In the 1960s, when John Morgan mentioned to Max "how I loved *Light Brigade* and *Boots*' battle endings, he said, 'Yeah, but the difference is Curtiz. The editing of the battle was so much better' [in *Light Brigade*]. He said that with *Boots*, the editing went into close-ups more, and you couldn't maintain a musical idea as easily. It was a lot harder for him to write the music for it. So he was sensitive to the different styles of directors and editing."[17]

A week before the movie's successful release, Raoul Walsh sent his composer a note. "Dear Max: Many thanks for your very nice photograph. Had I known you would have made such a fine looking Indian chief, I would have had you in the picture. My sincere appreciation for your fine music you wrote for 'Boots' and I hope we will do many pictures together."[18]

THE UNITED STATES'S ENTRY INTO war that December had an immediate impact on Steiner's life. Although he was not at risk of internment, as he had been during World War I, Max's anxiety increased as the American West Coast prepared itself for possible attack.[19]

Politically, Warner Bros. was ahead of the curve. Two days before Pearl Harbor, Max finished work on *Captains of the Clouds*, starring James Cagney as an American who joins the Royal Canadian Air Force to fight Hitler. By the time of its release in February 1942, *Clouds* was a Technicolor recruitment poster.

The score's most haunting sequence is a quiet one. Not since *King Kong* had a Steiner film so featured the atmosphere of fog, with its shroud-like mystery and beauty. Fog is used to suggest danger as well, as an Air Force plane hovers lost in its misty veil. The resulting music for the scenes is hushed, Ravel-like impressionism.

Steiner's sketches detail his desired effect. *"Mysterioso—6 Divisi [Strings] an octave higher, or Harmonics . . .* [A vibration of a stringed instrument to create an overtone accompanying the principal note—usually an eerie effect.] *Gong, 2 flutes and vibraphone pianissimo . . . make this very 'foggy'—with two G's!"*[20]

BY THE TIME *CLOUDS* LANDED IN THEATERS, Steiner was racing to meet another deadline. He had three weeks to score what promised to be one of Warners' biggest hits of 1942.

Max and Louise had seen the Broadway smash *Arsenic and Old Lace* during their 1940 trip to New York.[21] Steiner was thrilled to be assigned Frank Capra's movie version; not only was it a comedy, a genre he rarely was given, but it starred Cary Grant, who'd progressed considerably since stilt-walking in Max's 1920 Broadway show *Good Times*.

On this, the only Steiner-scored Capra feature, there was little communication between composer and director. After finishing the shoot in mid-December 1941, Capra left to serve as a producer of war propaganda films.* But Max was fine on his own, finding a tonal balance that served the story's pitch-black comedy and frenetic slapstick.

He was helped by musical suggestions in the script. When Mortimer Brewster (Grant) discovers that his kindly aunts in Brooklyn have poisoned 12 bachelor boarders in their home (what better way to end their loneliness?), then buried them in the cellar, Mortimer tries to spirit his aunts away to Happy Dale Sanatorium. In moments of elation and panic, Mortimer sings a skipping nursery rhyme, "There Is a Happy Land Far, Far Away"— Happy Dale being that happy land. The tune is an actual children's song: the intrepid Warner research department traced it to the 19th-century volume *Sacred Songs for Church and Home*. Max gleefully uses it as his main theme, its bouncy tune a droll counterpoint to the macabre cavorting (*"a 'screwy' gavotte"*).[22] Pre-existing music is turned upside down, literally, when Max takes Wagner's Wedding March and inverts its familiar "bum-bum-ba-bum"

---

* In 1943, Steiner scored one of them, *The Battle of Britain*, without charge.

into a downward pattern, to reflect the impatience of Mortimer's fiancée. *"Appassionato—rather 'Horny!'"*

Just as Capra raced to complete the shoot before wartime service, Steiner faced a tight recording date imposed by a Warner tax deadline.[23] Naturally, he delivered—after which *Arsenic and Old Lace* sat on the shelf until September 1944. It could not be released until the play's Broadway run ended, which finally happened after 1,444 performances. Recalled a friend, "Max thought it was funny having to rush, and then take three years for the film to come out."[24]

A near-simultaneous project gave him more incendiary material to score. The melodrama *In This Our Life*, directed by John Huston, starred a near-hysterical Bette Davis as an heiress who drives her first husband to suicide; kills a child in a hit-and-run; frames a black law student for the crime; and seduces (at least verbally) her slimy rich uncle. Max scored the latter scenes with what he called *"Eine Kleine Incest Musik."*[25]

As in *Boots*, the composer contrasts diatonic melody with dissonant chromaticism to differentiate "good" sister Roy (Olivia de Havilland) from sociopathic Stanley (Davis). Stanley's motif is a descending syncopation, its slow

Josephine Hull, Jean Adair, and Cary Grant in a publicity still from *Arsenic and Old Lace*.

tempo and hiccupping rhythm suggesting her laziness—perhaps the ultimate sin for the industrious Steiner.

AN OCCASIONAL VISITOR TO RECORDING SESSIONS was 83-year-old Gabor. With his wife now treated by round-the-clock nurses, Max's father seemed a man without purpose. Recalled harpist Aida Mulieri Dagort, "The old man would be seated at a small table very close to and facing the orchestra. He seemed not at all interested in what was happening and would invariably remove his wallet from his pocket and start to clean it out. All the contents would be spread out on this little table . . . the musicians would follow every step in the cleaning out of the wallet, even to anticipating the next move. No one ever snickered or said a word. We just watched in silence."[26]

Even stranger were Max's late-night forays with Gabor to gambling clubs and parties. "I was out last night with my daddy at Heindorf's," he wrote Louise. "Got plastered—took Papa home at 5 a.m. after five cigars and four cognacs. He's sure had a hell of a time."[27]

Late-night drinking and nonstop work was distracting Steiner from more than just heartache. That June, he discovered that one of his servants had stolen "three new white coats, a pair of pants, all my Bourbon, the chamois to wipe off the car, and some of my shirts and ten dollars."[28] Around the same time, Steiner fired his cook, also for stealing.[29]

Among the few bright spots in his lonely life was his close friendship with a composer based at Paramount: 42-year-old Victor Young. Both men had a phenomenal gift for melody, and both pushed themselves to physical extremes. Recalled Steiner, "He loved to play cards and he never let his work interfere with this. He could record from nine in the morning until eight at night, then call the boys up and ask them to come over and play cards. They would play until four in the morning, then get up at 7:30, go to the studio and start recording. This was Victor's routine almost every day."[30] All this, despite a serious heart condition.

Young and Steiner also stood fast together in Max's endless, ongoing battle with ASCAP. In 1942 they adopted a new strategy: group action. Six composers—Young, Stothart, Webb, Deutsch, Leigh Harline and Arthur Lange—joined Steiner in writing ASCAP, on behalf of 65 film composers who demanded "proper recognition, classification and resulting performance participation."[31]

Little came of their plea, but it was an important first step toward a turning point, made possible by Steiner's persistence.

IN THE MEANTIME, the composer's financial worries escalated. Attorney Louis Minter urged Max and Louise to curb their spending, telling the separated pair, "If you do not generally carry out the above recommendations there can only be one result: poverty."[32] Minter was correct, but Max also believed that his lawyer's handling of his funds was making matters worse. In June 1942, a month after his 54th birthday, Steiner dismissed his longtime friend as manager of his money.[33]

Like other Warner staffers, much of Steiner's weekly check was being siphoned to war causes at the "request" of Jack Warner. By June 18, Max considered himself no less a charity case. In an act as humiliating as it was necessary, he asked his boss for a loan of $17,000 (about $270,000 today).[34] Below Max's letter was a P.S. from Leo Forbstein. "Knowing the splendid service that Mr. Steiner has always rendered this company, I would like to add my recommendation that this application for a loan be considered favorably." Warner agreed to the loan, although his motives likely were less due to largesse than with ensuring Max's indentured servitude.

In one way, fate was kind to Steiner in the summer of 1942. The calamity of his personal life put him in the perfect state of mind to write two classic scores, for films about social outcasts who find redemption through sacrifice and love.

IN 1925, NOVELIST OLIVE HIGGINS PROUTY suffered what was called at the time a breakdown. The best-selling author of *Stella Dallas* had struggled to balance duties as a wife and mother with a writing career; the death of her year-old daughter triggered a collapse. Seeking treatment in a sanitarium, she met a psychiatrist who put her onto a path of recovery, and inspired her to pen two novels related to her experience.[35]

The second, published in 1941, was *Now, Voyager*.

Spotting in it an Oscar-worthy role for an actress, Warners optioned the book before publication.[36] Its central character, Charlotte Vale, is a recluse crippled emotionally by her controlling mother. Thanks to a kind psychiatrist, Dr. Jaquith, she becomes confident and successful, and embarks on a complicated romance with a married man. The part was perfect for Bette Davis—but Hal Wallis approached 1940 Oscar winner Ginger Rogers, and then audience favorite Irene Dunne, before Davis demanded the role.[37]

There was no debate over who was going to score it.

Once again, a strong female character as embodied by Davis allowed Max to pour his emotions into a cohesive work of art. And although he had just over a month to score the film, *Now, Voyager* is among his most musically complex. Inspiration enabled him to create themes quickly, giving him time to develop them with a subtlety that proved worthy of a full book of study (Kate Daubney's excellent *Now, Voyager: A Film Score Guide*).

BURIED IN ITS MAESTOSO MAIN TITLE is a musical question. The theme begins on a G boldly played by brass and strings in three octaves; it ends its surging seven-note phrase on an irresolute C. This "voyager" motif recurs throughout the film's first third, as our heroine recalls early attempts to escape her mother's control, and later as she reinvents herself on an ocean voyage.

Cellist Eleanor Aller provided the musical voice of Charlotte's introversion; her playing of the "voyager" motif says what the patient cannot. Max accompanies Charlotte walking down the Vale staircase with a left-right rhythm that captures the monotony of her life and the servant-like way she is treated. Its rhythm expands into a plaintive but restrained melody that evokes the hopelessness of a person gripped by depression. The theme has "a major-minor duality," Daubney writes.[38] "The chords are dragging along behind the melody," seeming "not only to drag with her feet, but to slow her down with uncertainty as she approaches her mother."

As Charlotte begins to heal at Jaquith's Cascade Sanitarium, the two-note "walking" motif returns, now in a hopeful major key. The theme becomes a full dramatic statement with the reveal of Charlotte's physical transformation on ship. The camera is tight on her elegant white and black shoes; as it reveals the newly glamorous Charlotte, strings legato accompany her with an ascending, rhapsodic figure that helped make the moment iconic cinema: *"on her FACE—She is now BEOOTIFUL!"*[39] But the fact that her musical theme remains the same tells us that behind the makeover, Charlotte has not yet fully healed.

She soon meets the man who will be her lover, Jerry Durrance (Paul Henreid). As they dance and grow closer on the ship, Steiner shifts subliminally between source music and score; in his sketches he delineates the difference between diegetic music— *"we are in Nassau, we're in reality"*—and the music of Charlotte's mind— *"Add Vibraphone . . . Her Reflection."*

Steiner's score for Act One consists mostly of short, fragmentary themes. Then on ship, as Charlotte and Jerry's relationship deepens, magic happens.

After Charlotte reveals to Jerry her unhappy history, Steiner unspools what would become the most popular love theme he ever composed. *"RUBATO— [strings] DIVISI"* he notes, as we first hear the expansive melody that would become the song "It Can't Be Wrong."

Paul Henreid and Bette Davis in a publicity still from *Now, Voyager*.

Charlotte's romantic awakening—and Steiner's feelings for Louise—inspired a melody that helped lift *Now, Voyager* into cinematic myth, and would be associated with Bette Davis for the rest of her life. Steiner achieves this with help from images and dialogue that proved no less indelible: Jerry's lighting of two cigarettes, one of which he hands to Charlotte; and Charlotte's acceptance of their ultimate separation: "Don't let's ask for the moon. We have the stars."

Unlike the pinched "Charlotte walking" theme, "It Can't Be Wrong" is lush (*"Harp a la Ravel"*), and conveys immediately that Charlotte's life is changed. The authenticity of her love for Jerry is contrasted with the man to whom she briefly becomes engaged, at home in Boston. Their passionless amour is accompanied mostly by Tchaikovsky's Sixth Symphony, which the characters hear in a concert performance. Again, the use of pre-existing music for romantic scenes is a Steiner tip-off: this relationship is not the real thing.

In one of the score's most inspired choices, the theme for Jerry's troubled daughter Tina is related to Charlotte's depressed "walking" theme. But as Daubney observes, "Instead of the interminable descent"[40] of Charlotte's motto, Tina's theme "is begun a semitone higher, giving the melody a brighter context for its innate sadness" (*"INTENSE, not fast—a child pleading"*).

The themes' interconnection reinforces the idea that Charlotte sees herself in Tina, who also is unloved by her mother. And as Charlotte takes on the role of friend to the girl, Tina's theme blossoms into warmer contours, as Charlotte's has done.

In the final sequence, Charlotte is back at Cascade—now a member of its board, supervising Tina's progress. A reunion with Jerry beside a moonlit window allows a repetition of *Voyager*'s signature dialogue—the moon, the stars—and an encore of "It Can't Be Wrong." It ends with a hopeful key modulation and the sweeping emotion befitting Davis's most enduring melodrama. *"Slowly and mit Schmaltz . . . Hugo! Give your all—at the end only!"*

HAL WALLIS WAS AMONG THE FIRST to recognize the commercial potential of the love theme. "I think it is a good torchy song," he told the Warner-owned Music Publishers Holding Corp., "and I hope you will do whatever you can to have it plugged in connection with the picture."[41]

His instinct was vindicated when *Now, Voyager* opened to excellent reviews. "The music by Max Steiner is some of the most melodic ever heard in a movie theater," *Family Circle* wrote.[42] By year's end the movie was Warner's fourth highest-grossing title of 1942,[43] and "It Can't Be Wrong," with lyrics by James Kimball "Kim" Gannon, was poised to be a hit.

But due to disastrous timing, no orchestral record of the song could be made. That August, the American Federation of Musicians banned all commercial recordings by its members, in a bid for better royalties from record companies. The strike would last until 1944; however, the public still wanted music, and in 1943 "It Can't Be Wrong" managed to land on America's Hit Parade thanks to a workaround: vocal renditions by Frank Sinatra, Dick Haymes, and others were backed up by a capella vocalists taking the place of instrumentalists.

That March, the song tied for the number one spot for "popular music performances" on the nation's four radio networks.[44] A month later, it was ranked the fifth bestseller in sheet music.[45] Bing Crosby crooned it on radio, his phrasing suggesting less a heartfelt love affair than a spontaneous fling.[46] Billy Eckstine was more seductive in his version backed by Nelson Riddle's Orchestra.[47] Bugs Bunny warbled the tune in mermaid drag in the cartoon *Hare Ribbin'*. And *Now, Voyager*'s star even attempted a misbegotten cover on the 1976 album *Miss Bette Davis*.

During the score's recording, cellist Eleanor Aller bet Max $20 that he was about to win another Academy Award.[48] "I'll probably lose," Steiner wrote Louise shortly before the score was nominated, "but I don't care any longer! Nuts to them!"[49]

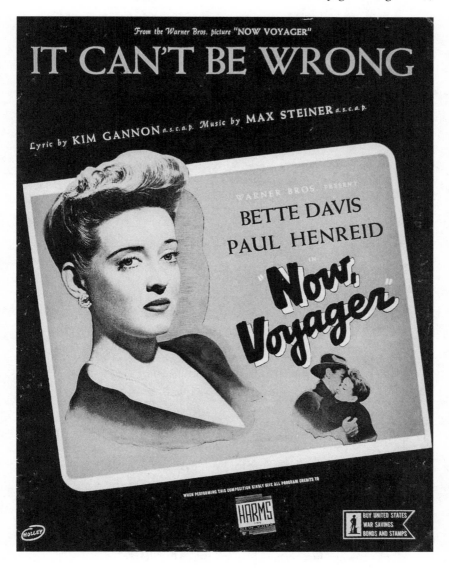

Of course, he cared very much. On March 4, 1943, a tuxedoed Steiner sat nervously at the Cocoanut Grove, awaiting Hollywood's verdict at the 15th Academy Awards. What happened that night is captured in the pages of *Variety*: "Best quip of the Academy dinner was that ad libbed by Max Steiner, who was Oscared for his scoring of *Now, Voyager*. When his name was called as a winner, there was no response. Again, he was called to come up front for his award. Still no answer. Over the hushed crowd a voice boomed, 'Is Max

Steiner here?' From a far corner of the Grove came a faintly audible speak, 'yeah, I'm out here on location.' The mob roared as he made the long voyage up to the speaker's table."[50]

THE FILM SCORES OF MAX STEINER

1941 Releases (continued)

One Foot in Heaven (8/41–9/41)
They Died with Their Boots On (10/41–11/41)

1942 Releases

Captains of the Clouds (11/41–12/41)
In This Our Life (1/42–2/42)
The Gay Sisters (3/42–4/42)
Desperate Journey (5/42–6/42)
Now, Voyager (6/42–7/42). AA.

During this period Steiner also recorded his score for *Arsenic and Old Lace* in February 1942. The film was not released until 1944.

Steiner was jubilant over his second Oscar, and by sheet music sales for "It Can't Be Wrong." After 300,000 copies sold, his ASCAP ranking was raised—a change that did nothing for his film music royalties but boosted his earnings for "Wrong." "We'll pay [for] the house out of this song," he wrote Louise hopefully.[51]

But his wife still was not ready to come home, and Max knew it. During the score's writing, his effusive updates to her about work were shadowed by explosions of rage. "Just received your 'interesting' letter," he wrote in one.[52] "You are absolutely right—I don't know either—Why should I miss you? I honestly never thought about us having grown apart and my being such a rotten husband—but it's O.K.—don't WORRY—I won't miss you anymore. As you say, Ronnie is the all-important issue—he must not suffer... He didn't ask to be brought into this lousy world."

HIS MOODS ALTERNATING BETWEEN ANGER, cynicism, and desperate romantic longing, Steiner was again in the ideal frame of mind for the project he was to begin days after completing *Voyager*.

"Monday I start on *Casablanca*," he wrote Louise on July 30, 1942.[53] "A beautiful picture . . . "

19

Yours, Herman Hupfeld

LA BELLE AURORE, AN OBSCURE NIGHTCLUB in southern France, would no doubt be forgotten today if not for a visit in 1938 by a traveling American.

Murray Burnett had just come from Vienna, where he witnessed first-hand the force of Nazism. Some of Hitler's soldiers patronized La Belle Aurore; there, ideologies were mostly put aside, as patrons listened to American jazz played by a black pianist.

Inside the club Burnett learned about Casablanca, a Moroccan city flooded with Europeans escaping Hitler. After returning to America, Burnett teamed with writer Joan Alison on a play that melded his impressions of the club with the latest news about war in Europe. The result, *Everybody Comes to Rick's*, incorporated Belle Aurore's pianist, who played a tune from Burnett's college days: "As Time Goes By."

Although backing for a Broadway production fell through, the play caught the eye of a Warner Bros. story editor, who shared it with Hal Wallis. Pearl Harbor brought extra relevance to the drama's themes of patriotism and sacrifice. Twenty-four hours after the attack, Wallis optioned the play.[1]

The producer remained *Casablanca*'s driving force. Wallis had signed a new deal with Warners, allowing him to personally produce four movies a year for the studio. As a result, no detail on *Casablanca* was too small for his eye. That process began with its script, synthesized from work by seven writers. The final draft produced characters both larger than life and vividly human, wartime propaganda that genuinely inspired, crackling dialogue, and irresistible romance.[2]

Executing Wallis's vision was director Michael Curtiz, whose genius for turning words into dynamic imagery was at its zenith.[3] But Wallis was the film's chief orchestrator. He recognized early on that music was a character in the film: it cemented the backstory of its lovers, Rick Blaine and Ilsa

Lund, and their favorite song reinflicts old wounds and rekindles their passion. In one scene, music even becomes a weapon, as free Europeans sing the French national anthem in defiance of the Nazis, on the battleground of Rick's Café.

The decision to retain "As Time Goes By" was Wallis's.[4] It was written in 1931 by Herman Hupfeld, a prolific but little-known composer, for the Broadway revue *Everybody's Welcome*. Despite the show's inviting title, it ran only 139 performances. A few recordings of the tune were made, but it was far from a standard at the time of *Casablanca* (Hupfeld did not receive screen credit in the film). The setting of Rick's Café also enabled Wallis to showcase many of his own favorite songs: "If I Could Be With You," "Shine," "It Had to Be You," "Sweet Georgia Brown," and "Love for Sale."[5] These melodies provide more than atmosphere: they are reminders of the American spirit that Rick embodies and the Nazis despise.

Wallis reflected more about the music of *Casablanca* than he had on any previous film. Four days before shooting began, he wrote a lengthy memo listing which songs he wanted, and details about score—noting, for example, that as Humphrey Bogart's Rick drunkenly recalls his romance with Ilsa, the playing by Sam of "As Time Goes By" would segue into an "orchestral treatment" of the theme.[6]

With the music of *Now, Voyager* fresh in his ears, Wallis assigned Steiner to the film on July 11, 1942, about three weeks before principal photography was complete. The likelihood that Max was not consulted during shooting is supported by one surprising fact.

Max Steiner hated "As Time Goes By."

"He absolutely detested the Hupfeld tune," Louise confirmed. "He said, 'They have the lousiest tune, they already have it recorded, and they want me to use it.' "[7]

Today, after more than eight decades of acclaim for the song, Max's judgment seems especially flawed. His hostility also seems curious, since he often incorporated other composers' melodies into scores without complaint. But his reasons were threefold. Weeks after writing the theme soon to be known as "It Can't Be Wrong," Steiner was confident he could give *Casablanca* a memorable song of its own. Secondly, he knew that such a song could yield him desperately needed royalties. He also believed that Hupfeld's syncopated tune was rhythmically unsuitable for adaptation into a short leitmotiv, which Wallis wanted used throughout the score.

In 1943, Max told a reporter that Wallis would have let him write his own theme—but unfortunately, "As Time Goes By" was referenced in dialogue and performed onscreen, and Ingrid Bergman, under contract to Selznick, had already had her hair cut for her next film, making reshoots impossible.[8]

That story was a cover for Steiner's wounded ego. Jack Warner always balked at retakes: if a movie's ending was in doubt, two versions were shot during production. Also, film stock had become more costly due to the war. Reshooting entire sequences of *Casablanca*, with Bergman reloaned from Selznick at additional cost, to please a staff composer? Calling that scenario unlikely is, to quote Claude Rains's Captain Renault, a gross understatement.

Wallis wrote in his autobiography that he "insisted" Max use the Hupfeld tune, after which "Steiner grudgingly began his work."[9] But Wallis conceded that "under great pressure, and with countless arguments, Max Steiner produced a rich, romantic score."

It is a testament to Max's professionalism that listening to *Casablanca*, one would assume that he not only loved "As Time Goes By" but had written it himself. Steiner set aside his disappointment to hear the Hupfeld melody from Rick and Ilsa's perspectives. He was aided by Hugo Friedhofer, who later said that Max "had a concept of it as being kind of a square tune, which requires translation from what's in the printed piano part to a more relaxed version. You can't play 'Ta-ta, ta-ta, ta-*ta*' . . . which is what it is in the original. So, I say this with all modesty, I said, 'Max, think of it this way.' [sings] With triplet phrasing. He kind of thought about it, and that's the way it came out."[10]

The theme's effectiveness is enhanced by the limited, specific use of it. Sam first plays "As Time Goes By" at Ilsa's request 33 minutes into the film. Rick storms over and orders him to stop. At this moment, the tune makes its first appearance in Steiner's score, mirroring Rick's shock at seeing Ilsa. Over a sustained, six-measure chord—a "swimmy" blend of *"vibraphone, harps, piano, celeste"*[11]—the tune is played by solo oboe, second vibraphone and second celesta, the musical equivalent of frozen water suddenly cracked.

Not until his flashback to prewar Paris do we hear the melody played ecstatically—in full octaves, with divisi strings (*Molto expressivo*), and in the waltz-like triplet form that Friedhofer recommended. During the flashback, variations on "As Time Goes By" are interrupted by romantic dance music and German menace borrowed from Steiner's *Confessions of a Nazi Spy* (*"Come Sopra . . . Reel 9 Part 2 Original Key"*). These give us needed pause to make the return of "As Time Goes By" more powerful, in the first of two usages that are all but guaranteed to quicken the collective heartbeat of audiences.

Inside Rick's apartment, during what will be their last happy moments together: *"APPASSIONATO KISS . . . 3/4 [time]."* Here, and later during Rick and Ilsa's final goodbye at the airport, Steiner lifts the Hupfeld melody into a near-delirious statement of romantic ecstasy. The composer had no difficulty seeing Ilsa as Rick did: Max was besotted by Bergman's beauty. She is the only cast member he mentions when discussing the film in correspondence. She "is masterful in it," he told Louise.[12]

In the apartment scene and the finale, Steiner's versions of "As Time Goes By" end with a dark, three-note chromatic pattern that descends ominously against the tune. This "fate" motif reminds us of the larger forces that prevent Rick and Ilsa from being together. Its appearance at the climax is a summation of the story's conflict: we hear it just after Rick's speech to Ilsa, as the plane propeller spins in close-up, and our three principals exchange silent looks. *"TRAGIC . . . The aeroplane effect is rather secondary . . ."*

THE SCORE FEATURES A SECOND pre-existing theme no less important than "As Time Goes By." The French national anthem "La Marseillaise" is a love theme of its own—the embodiment of the liberty our heroes fight for. Its performance still elicits cheers at screenings, as freedom fighters in Rick's Café sing it in defiant counterpoint to the Nazis' bellicose rendition of "Die Wacht am Rhein." Emotions ran deep during the scene's filming. Dan Seymour, playing the café doorman, was surprised to see many among the cast shedding actual tears. "I suddenly realized they were all real refugees."[13]

That scene's effectiveness is due not only to Curtiz's brilliant staging and its pivotal role in the story (it is the turning point for Rick rejoining "the fight"), but also due to the music's arrangement. On September 2, Wallis instructed Steiner: "On the 'Marseillaise,' when it is played in the café, don't do it as though it was played by this small orchestra. Do it with full scoring orchestra, and get some body to it."[14] Steiner did so with such effectiveness that few viewers ever notice that the instrumentation is larger than what we see onscreen.

Significantly, "La Marseillaise," not "As Time Goes By," is the theme that concludes the score, in an arrangement that starts with shimmering transluscence as Rick and Louis walk into the fog, then ends in a call-to-arms fortissimo. One film historian took Steiner to task for not ending with Hupfeld's tune.[15] To do so is to miss the point: Rick Blaine is no longer defined by lost love but by his patriotism and re-engagement with humanity. A major-key "Marseillaise" was exactly the right way to end the drama, as any viewing with an audience will confirm.

Steiner's contribution to *Casablanca* is incalculable. But the actual amount of underscore is surprisingly small; quality mattered more than quantity. Some of its music was borrowed. The propulsive main title is an adrenalized

Publicity stills from *Casablanca*.

rewrite of *The Lost Patrol*'s prelude (*"RHYTHMIC—lots of Tom Tom and Timpani"*). The "La Marseillaise" variation as Rick waits for Ilsa at the train station comes from *Emile Zola*. But such self-lifting was not done simply for expediency: the choices were dramatically right. Steiner took pains to rearrange the cues for their new context, and carefully notated their recording (regarding the main title: *"The woodwind could be miked to make it very strong"*).

Max had no way of knowing that *Casablanca* would be a defining work of his career—one destined to supersede even *Gone with the Wind* and *King Kong* in popularity. But from his first viewing, he was captivated by its romanticism; and as an Austrian directly affected by Hitler's barbarity, he was invested in its philosophy. By the end of his writing in early September, he could even joke about the most frustrating aspect of its creation.

"THE END . . . Fine," the final score page reads. *"Dear Hugo: Thanks for everything! I am very pleased with you! Yours, Herman Hupfeld."*

DURING *CASABLANCA'S* COMPOSITION, Max's son, Ronald, was staying with Louise in New York. Steiner's letters to his ex-wife mirror the emotion of Rick and Ilsa's stormy reunion, minus the poetry. A letter from Max to "Master Ronald Lawrence M. Steiner" includes a page of Xs, then concludes with "P.S. Give Mamma a couple of XXX although I <u>don't</u> think she cares for them any longer."[16]

Some of Louise's replies offered glimmers of hope. One note is signed "Your dutiful wife," with "a few XXX for you too."[17] Meanwhile, correspondence from Warner Bros. also lifted Steiner's spirits. "Dear Max: I ran with Colonel Warner last night 'CASABLANCA,'" wrote Steve Trilling, the boss' assistant.[18] "You can chalk up another success to your many fine endeavors on this unusually excellent scoring job. I know that the Colonel concurs with me on this as we both enjoyed it immensely."

Eight days later, Steiner received a telegram from Michael Curtiz. "DEAR MAX: WE PREVIEWED 'CASABLANCA' LAST NIGHT. MY CONGRATULATIONS TO YOU FOR MARVELOUS MUSIC. PERFECTLY CATCHING ALL MOODS AND DRAMA. THIS IS YOUR BEST AND MOST BRILLIANTLY CONCEIVED WORK."[19]

After a blockbuster gross of more than $3 million dollars by late 1943, *Casablanca* amassed a staggering $6.8 million by 1955.[20] But Max remained ambivalent about its success. He was proud of the film—"Be sure to see *Casablanca*," he wrote Louise—but he never mentions it in his autobiography, nor did he save any article about it in his scrapbooks. Stokowski "saw it <u>three times</u>," he told Louise, "and says the way I handled that lousy song was as important and clever as any of my own music."[21] *Casablanca* earned Steiner his 11th Academy Award nomination; but music was not among the three Oscars it received, for Best Writing, Screenplay; Best Director; and Best Picture.

Its music proved a winner elsewhere. "As Time Goes By" returned to the Hit Parade and became a fixture in popular music. Herman Hupfeld saw only some of that success; he died in 1951, age 57.

The song's ubiquity proved a double-edged sword for Warner composers. Months after praising Max's "excellent" score, Jack Warner wrote Leo Forbstein that in future, "I definitely want to use a theme song for our love motif.... Whenever Steiner, Waxman, or any of your other men try to write an original love theme it just doesn't come off. [Warner was forgetting "It Can't Be Wrong."] People remember the words and music of these old songs, and you can't expect Steiner, Waxman, or any one else to compete with 'As Time Goes By,' etc., and still write a complete score."[22]

Fortunately for lovers of original film themes, Warner's edict was not strictly enforced.

DAYS AFTER FINISHING *CASABLANCA*, Max tackled a project that the studio expected to be far more important. But *Watch on the Rhine* was a lifeless, verbose adaptation of Lillian Hellman's Broadway hit, about a wealthy family in 1940 America forced to confront Hitler's oppression abroad. Windy speeches left little room for music; no wonder Max found it "the most difficult job I have ever had."[23] Its best scene is silent except for score. As Sara Muller (Bette Davis) touches the furniture inside her childhood home, remembering the father she has lost, a gently ascending melody conveys more feeling than any of Hellman's ponderous monologues.

Rhine earned co-star Paul Lukas a Best Actor Oscar, then faded into obscurity—unlike a stranger slice of propaganda Steiner scored in 1943.

Mission to Moscow began as a directive straight from Washington. F.D.R. wanted Americans to embrace the United States's wartime alliance with the Soviet Union, despite Stalin's brutal rule, and the president encouraged the film's making.[24] Michael Curtiz did his best to bring zest to a deadly message picture, based on a book by Joseph E. Davies, former U.S. ambassador to Russia. Davies's self-serving account of his encounters with foreign leaders was adapted into what *Moscow*'s producer, Robert Buckner, called "an expedient lie for political purposes."[25]

The movie was among the most scrutinized of the war. The White House and Joseph Stalin himself would review the final result before its release—an added element of pressure that Steiner seemed to relish. "Tomorrow I start on *Mission to Moscow*," he wrote Louise on February 1.[26] "A wonderful picture which is in an awful rush to get out by request of the President." Excited to be involved in a film of national importance, Steiner also was energized by the task of using folk music and military songs from nearly every major European country. *"10 Reels are finished . . . Music by Vladimir Shostakovitch Styniya!"*[27]

But within weeks, Max had soured on the project. After a preview, he wrote that "the music is nil, as it is dubbed so low that you cannot hear a note, but [Harry] Warner whose personal production it is simply would not allow the music to be dubbed any louder, and even took some music out, which Jack Warner immediately put back . . . Jack wants nothing but music and Harry doesn't want any, and I am in the middle . . . I am very disappointed and very unhappy about it. I wish my name wasn't on it."[28]

Jack won the battle. In the final movie, score is prominent, although its two hours of militaristic anthems do nothing to humanize the drama.

The all-important screening for Stalin took place in Russia on May 23, 1943. According to U.S. ambassador William Stanley, "Stalin was heard to grunt once or twice."[29] The dictator approved *Mission*'s release in the Soviet Union, where it achieved its only real success.[30]

After the war, as Cold War tensions simmered, *Mission to Moscow* was cited by some U.S. politicians as proof of nefarious collusion between Russia and Hollywood.[31] Some of the movie's creators found work scarce as a result, but not Steiner. His ideology was simple: democracy was wonderful, dictators caused much of the world's misery, and law enforcement was necessary (he still collected guns and admired FBI chief J. Edgar Hoover). Max would face many troubles in the years ahead, but political clashes were not among them.

SANDWICHED BETWEEN BREAD-AND-BUTTER DRAMAS and propaganda pictures is a movie Steiner loved and ranks as his most heartfelt tribute to his adopted homeland.

The Adventures of Mark Twain was a late entry in Warners' series of 19th-century biopics. Producer Jesse L. Lasky saw the story of the iconoclastic author as a worthy successor to his previous flag-waver, *Sergeant York*.[32] Once in production, the studio's research department outdid itself in collecting data on Twain's changing physiognomy, the paddlewheelers he worked on, and the steamboat calls he used.[33]

In one of those calls, a crewmember melismatically shouted the words "Mark twain! Safe water!" The phrase began with a sustained first note, before sliding down in a comforting major-key resolution. In this four-note pattern, Steiner recognized a perfect main theme. Not only was it a musical statement of the hero's name (Samuel Clemens took his nom de plume from this riverboat call); Steiner's Maestoso version, in bright D major, heralds an epic film and a life lived large.

Heard under this theme like a steady engine is a square, four-note ostinato. Its upward/downward steps (B–C-sharp–E-sharp–C-sharp) suggest the turning of a paddlewheel, as well as the inexorable turning of time, in a story that spans from 1835 to 1910. A colleague of Steiner's called the theme "another 'Old Man River' "[34]—and while he was probably joking, there was an undertow of truth. In this "paddlewheel" pattern, Steiner conveys the same idea as Kern and Hammerstein's classic song: the lives of men are brief, but the river flows on, its twists and turns a mirror of our own journeys.

In the film, Twain's birth coincides with the appearance of Halley's Comet, a phenomenon that returns on the day of his death 74 years later. (Yes, this actually happened.) The comet's appearances are accompanied by a glimmering, Debussy-like motif that marks a rare Steiner foray into the otherworldly. Its slowly shifting chord clusters are dissonant and hypnotic, as vibraphone, harps, celesta, gong, and jingling triangle elicit a mood of fantastical mystery. (For the comet's return as Twain dies, Steiner adds a subtle, eerie effect: *"Voices . . . Stagger the breath! Half hum, half ooh."*)[35]

In a foreshadowing of Tom Sawyer and Huck Finn, Twain's childhood friends are evoked with a charmingly devious minor-key march. Its tune for bass clarinets and bassoons (woodwinds = rebels) ideally captures their piratical fantasies and other mischief.

Bassoons and bass clarinets also give growling voice to the jumping frogs of Calaveras County, here a contest between Twain and Bret Harte (John Carradine). Steiner's scoring is a gem of comic delicacy. *"Frog jumps into water—smallest cymbal with stick . . . [Harte] tickles frog! Brush on cymbal . . . Timpani with snare drum stick . . . THE FROG leaps. Orchestra as lightly as possible."* Admirers of this sequence included Leopold Stokowski, who considered it for performance at the Hollywood Bowl before choosing instead the finale of *Now, Voyager*.[36]

One standout scene has no precedent in Max's career. As young Twain is entrusted to steer a riverboat at night through treacherous waters and fog, Steiner uses the "paddlewheel" ostinato—just four notes of up-and-down pitches—as the musical foundation for more than *nine minutes*. What should turn monotonous becomes, through careful variation of the motif and its supporting lines, a classic of escalating suspense: *"From here on the DRAMA begins!!"*

The paddlewheel figure passes "through all manner of different harmonies and keys," observed musicologist Christopher Palmer. "Melodic details may be modified but its general shape and contour are always recognizable, always making us conscious of the waters surging beneath us. *["We'll never make it!' Add Harps and Piano."]* Finally, the peril is past, Twain is the hero of the hour and the Twain theme shares in the general rejoicing."[37]

The author's devotion to wife Olivia (Alexis Smith) allowed Steiner to write the grand love theme *Casablanca* denied him. Not that his expansive melody would have fit Ilsa Lund: the music for Mrs. Twain describes an individual. It blends tenderness, devotion, and sweeping passion, in a melody similar in mood to Dvořák's *Largo* theme from the *New World* Symphony, although it is pure Steiner in the breadth of its widely roaming intervals.

Louise's influence on the theme is likely. If Max's rambling letters could not persuade her to return to him, perhaps the poetry of his music could. Ronnie also feels present in the score. A visit to a toy shop elicits another tender *"Music Box"* blended with orchestra. Throughout 1942–43, Steiner constantly worried about Ronnie becoming ill—although, apart from frequent crying bouts, he was usually healthy.

Max's worst fears about his boy are reflected in the film's story, when Twain's son dies, aged 19 months. But this tragedy gives way to unexpected magic. As Twain sleeps in a chair at home, a double-exposure image of "pixies" climb on his body as they whisper encouragement to turn his life into stories. As Palmer notes, it "is the occasion for one of Steiner's most enchanting flights of fantasy: the Twain theme turned into a whistle . . . variations around a haunting bassoon theme that had earlier accompanied Twain's own Tom Sawyer–like boyish pranks . . . [It] shows at its best the vein of genuine folk poetry which Steiner tapped in a manner peculiarly his own."[38]

At this point, alas, the film deflates into a soggy, conventional biopic. Twain's acid critiques of gilded-age tycoons and racial inequality have no place in a movie made during wartime. Instead, Twain is depicted as an affable children's author and midwestern Baron Munchausen, fond of telling whoppers and giving amusing after-dinner speeches.

The result is a portrait of the social firebrand as whitewashed as Tom Sawyer's fence. But Steiner's music remains inventive to the end, from a glittering "gold rush" mini-symphony to a droll series of cultural variations on the Twain theme, as the aging author goes to Europe and Africa on a speaking tour to stave off bankruptcy. (Max probably could relate.)

As Steiner finished in January 1943, his mood was euphoric. "They previewed 'Mark Twain' day before yesterday (I didn't go). You never heard such raving. I've had letters from everyone. Every preview card mentioned the music. One soldier wrote: A nation who can produce a picture like this is worth fighting for! . . . Jack said, If this bastard asks me for a raise, I've got to give it to him."[39]

A note from studio vice president Charles Einfeld suggests a more plausible level of enthusiasm. "Your ears must be buzzing today after the preview of 'Mark Twain' last night, but I'd like to add my compliments for the wonderful score you provided. It is some of the most inspiring music I've ever heard, and in many ways, believe it to be your finest achievement."[40] Ditto Warner's telegram to his composer: "Saw Mark Twain—picture good—music simply wonderful—Jack."[41]

Twain's score received an Oscar nomination, and with hopes that the music would find its way into symphony concerts, Steiner arranged a nine-minute suite of its key themes. Conductors are advised to rescue this lovely piece of Americana from its undeserved obscurity.

SOON AFTER TWAIN'S COMPLETION, Max faced yet another family crisis. In May, Gabor's wife, Erna, seriously ill, left her home for a sanitarium. She never returned. Her son-in-law covered all costs for room, meal, nurses and more. "She is completely paralyzed now and her mind is half gone," Max wrote Louise.[42]

A depressed Gabor returned to Cove Way to live with his son. And while his presence dispelled some of Max's loneliness, it made him acutely aware that his father's health was failing as well.

BY 1943 STEINER'S DEBTS made his fantasy of radio work in New York an impossibility. And for a composer known for film music, a conducting career with a major symphony was out of the question. But decades before movie scores became concert hall mainstays, America's orchestras, ever on the search for money, looked at Hollywood with envy. And that spring, Steiner was approached with an offer as surprising as it was crackling with potential.

New York Sun writer William G. King was both a fan of the composer and a friend: in a letter to Max, he recalls "our screwball days together in Hollywood."[43] King's associates included Minnie Guggenheimer, philanthropist and founder of a popular series of summer concerts in New York. These were held at Lewisohn Stadium, a two-block-long athletic facility. Its Doric-columned amphitheater had room for twenty thousand attendees, who paid as little as 25 cents for a concert by members of the New York Philharmonic.

King knew that ticket sales were in a slump, and suggested to Guggenheimer a concert of film music, to be conducted by Hollywood's most acclaimed composer. The heiress was receptive, and King became an energetic go-between.[44] A concert date was set for August 3, and over the next three months, Steiner's feelings about guest conducting the New York Philharmonic, in a concert of his music, escalated from excitement to obsession. He wrote almost daily to Louise or King, debating which pieces of his and other composers to perform, and what popular vocalist should join him in a section of the concert featuring songs from Hollywood.

Charles Einfeld at Warner Bros. suggested Dinah Shore, but her failure to sign a contract with Warners nixed the deal.[45] Fredric March was considered "as a sort of Master of Ceremonies . . . he could explain some of the things that I am playing and also tell some anecdotes about them which I will, of course, supply."[46] This promising idea also was abandoned. In the meantime, Max drafted dozens of possible programs, and created concert suites for those he considered certainties, like *Gone with the Wind*.

"Henry Svedrofsky, who conducts the Standard Symphony Hour . . . says this will be my biggest success," he wrote Louise on June 4.[47] But "the more I work on my stuff, the less I can see how in God's name I can rehearse all of this music in two and a half hours . . . the Philharmonic plays only classical music. . . . They have never seen any music of mine and have never played under me."

Softening Max's anxiety was delight that his home studio was "highly interested and enthusiastic"[48] about the program. Jack Warner no doubt realized that if it proved a success, his movies would have a new outlet for promotion.

THE FILM SCORES OF MAX STEINER

1943 Releases

Casablanca (8/42–9/42). AAN.

Watch on the Rhine (9/42–10/42)

Mission to Moscow (3/43–4/43)

This Is the Army (6/43). Steiner pitched in to assist Ray Heindorf on this Irving Berlin extravaganza, which grossed nearly $10 million ($146 million today) for U.S. Army Emergency Relief. Max may have regretted not taking a screen credit: Heindorf won an Oscar for Best Music, Scoring of a Musical Picture.

During this period, Steiner recorded his score for *The Adventures of Mark Twain* (11/42–12/42). The film was not released until 1944. AAN.

He also scored the 54-minute propaganda film *The Battle of Britain*, part of producer Frank Capra's series *Why We Fight* (1/43).

By early summer, Max's letters to Louise had reached a manic pitch. "Hal Wallis sends love to Ronnie and you and says will postpone his picture to enable me to fulfill my N.Y. engagement. He thinks it's the most important thing that has <u>ever</u> happened to <u>Music</u> in <u>Pictures</u>! He thinks I <u>deserve</u> it and that I am the most outstanding composer of our decade (he means pictures of course)."[49] He reported that "Stoky" (Stokowski) would conduct highlights from the concert in Los Angeles. "So will Seattle, Frisco, Oklahoma & Cleveland—<u>so</u> far!! Not bad!! They are buying it—Blush!! . . . If I wrote it it <u>must</u> be good—'<u>It can't be wrong!</u>' "[50]

Preoccupied with music choices, Steiner left financial details to King. He even failed to sign a contract with the Guggenheimers, who proved evasive in discussions of cost. In the same letter gushing about Stokowski's support, Max angrily told Louise that he would pay for a second rehearsal himself if necessary, "Because, God damn it, I am <u>not</u> going to be a flop for anybody."[51]

By late June, Steiner's usual pleas for marital reconciliation were replaced by instructions to Louise as if she were an employee. "Find out what I am to wear. Soft shirt or stiff shirt—what kind of coat and pants." He made constant lists of possible scores to feature, offering a glimpse into what he considered his best work. "She / King Kong—either one of these only, as they are similar! / The Letter . . . Arsenic & Old Lace . . . to show I <u>can</u> write comedy . . . Jezebel? / Sergt YORK / Lost Patrol / Star is Born / They Died with their Boots on . . . "[52] His indecision, and fits of anger, continued throughout July. A *Little Women* suite? *Charge of the Light Brigade*? And still no signed contract? "AM EXTREMELY ANXIOUS AND NERVOUS AFTER ALL THE WORK AND EXPENSE I WENT TO GETTING MUSIC READY," he telegrammed King.[53]

Steiner also struggled over what other film composers to include. "If we played [Korngold's] 'Robinhood,' [*sic*] it would also be Warner Bros. and that is what you are trying to get away from, isn't it? . . . I am not familiar with it at all and would have to learn it." And in conclusion: "I have worked like a dog for eight weeks on all this music and spent about $300 of my own money [more than $4,000 today]."[54]

Ultimately, there would be no celebrity emcee, but by late July a vocalist had been engaged—one certain to grab headlines. The Guggenheimers chose the most popular male singer in America outside of Crosby: 27-year-old Frank Sinatra.

The crooner nicknamed "The Voice"—and, more derisively, "Swoonatra"—had created a near-riot nine months earlier, with his appearance at New York's Paramount Theater. But Steiner was suspicious of Sinatra, who in 1943 was as known for the screaming adulation of his female fans as he was for his silky phrasing. Max worried about being upstaged. "Sinatra, Steiner to Be at Stadium,"[55] noted the *New York Times*, in a talent pecking order matched by nearly every publication.

AFTER THREE MONTHS OF SLEEPLESS NIGHTS over what he now saw as a turning point in his life, Max Steiner arrived in New York via the deluxe Super Chief train.[56] The highpoint of his arrival was a reunion with Louise, who put aside their problems and supported him fully during the next week.

Nearly every local publication made note of the upcoming event or featured Max in a profile. The composer had done everything he could to ensure the concert's success. Now, its triumph or its failure was largely in the hands of others, and he could only hope that Sinatra and the Philharmonic musicians were sympathetic to his cause.

It didn't take long for him to get his answer.

20

Sucker

IT WAS A BROILING 90 DEGREES on the morning of Tuesday, August 3, 1943, as Max Steiner, fighting the flu, took the stage of Lewisohn Stadium for his one and only rehearsal with members of the New York Philharmonic. He had 90 minutes of music to rehearse for that night's concert, all of it new to the players.

Twenty years later, Steiner recalled what happened next.

The musicians "were completely uncooperative. The first cellist sat down, but never took his cello out of its cover. 'I don't have to rehearse this tripe. I'll just look at it. It will be alright tonight.' Like hell it was alright that night. These men knew their symphonic music, but apparently needed a lot of rehearsals to play any new works. I felt that my own orchestra in Hollywood could have played rings around them. I can only explain the behavior by their snobbish disdain for anything that came out of Hollywood."[1]

Adding to the tension was the presence of a *LIFE* magazine photographer, who was there to chronicle Frank Sinatra, not Steiner. But the crooner was nowhere to be found. Recalled Louise, "Mr. Sinatra was quite oblivious to the fact that one should be on time to a rehearsal. He kept Max and the orchestra waiting over an hour."[2]

That night, seven thousand audience members arrived at the Stadium.[3] Roughly a third of the venue's capacity, it was far from the sell-out crowd Steiner hoped for. Max had decided to begin the program with suites from *The Informer*, Newman's *The Blue Bird*, and Victor Young's *For Whom the Bell Tolls*, then end the first half with songs by Sinatra. After intermission, Steiner would conduct a 20-minute suite from *Gone with the Wind*. Two early non-film works of his would follow, "Petite Valse" and "Petite March"; then a *Now, Voyager* suite; and finally a closing set from Sinatra, including "It Can't Be Wrong."

A picture worth a thousand notes: rehearsing at Lewisohn Stadium. (Getty Images)

For an objective account of the night, let us begin as Max would have, with the *New York Times*:

> The 7,000 persons in the audience to hear Mr. Sinatra and Max Steiner, Hollywood "ace" film-music composer . . . were mostly young. They were Sinatra fans, and they were there to make a demonstration, and they succeeded, as their gleeful whoops, loud laughter, and handclaps frequently almost drowned out the sad, sweet music of the singer. . . . Mr. Steiner began the proceedings. . . . Then came the singer, and the demonstration began with hysterical giggles from the girls. . . . Mr. Sinatra's baritone had little real volume and little carrying power beyond what the amplifier gave it. . . . After the intermission Mr. Steiner gave three of his own film compositions, consisting of the

music for 'Gone with the Wind' and 'Now, Voyager,' for which he has just received the Academy Award again.' "[4]

No harsh dismissal. Just a shrug.

The *Daily News* noted the "disappointing figure" of attendees before turning to Steiner. "The technicolored music spread from the stage like a chemical fog, filling the mind with caressing sound and having a mild narcotic effect. . . . Taken from their film contexts, the works were amorphous and had little meaning."[5]

Musical Courier was in Max's camp. "The best orchestral numbers were two by Steiner, showing skill and imagination."[6] But the *New Yorker* yawned over an "unexciting evening," briefly mentioning Newman's *Blue Bird*. "There were other items . . . but why bother at all? Let's get to the really serious business of telling about Mr. Sinatra."[7]

Topping all in sarcasm was the *New York Post*. Steiner's "*Gone With the Wind* score reminded me of the producer who hired a composer and told him he was to have an absolutely free hand. 'You can write anything you like,' the producer said, 'as long as it sounds like Tchaikovsky.' "[8] That last sentence needled Max even 20 years later. "I defy him even now to point out to me how my Tara theme resembles Tchaikovsky."[9]

A rare voice of advocacy was Julian Seaman for *New York Cue*. "The Stadium advent of Max Steiner, conductor and cinematic composer par excellence, bestowed a tardy public recognition upon one of the most astute and scholarly musicians now practicing. Those who remember the . . . visual epics scored by Mr. Steiner will appreciate his adroit skill, sensitive artistry, and amazing competence."[10]

FROM THE MOMENT HE LEFT THE STAGE, Max was furious over what he considered the orchestra and Sinatra's betrayal. "It was a miserable evening. When I returned home, everybody on the Warner lot had read these unfair criticisms. It hurt me that a few of them seemed delighted to see me cut up by the critics. However, my orchestra boys were loyal. One thing which helped to pour a little balm on the wound was that my boss, Mr. Jack Warner, was so understanding. He called me to his office and told me: 'Max, I'm sorry this had to happen to you. I'm sure you did a good job and as far as I'm concerned you are and always have been a great success.' "[11]

The boss was probably grateful that the symphonic world had rejected Steiner, the composer Warner relied on more than any other.

Max was never reimbursed by Minnie Guggenheimer for $1,100 ($16,000 today) in out-of-pocket expenses for the concert. The publication of the *LIFE* photos, memorializing Max's misery, brought a fresh wave of embarrassment.

But King offered little sympathy. Claiming that the composer got "a million dollars worth of personal publicity," King advised him to "stop being a little sensitive plant."[12] When King wrote again, secretary Marie Teller made a note at the bottom of his letter: "Mr. Steiner said it wasn't necessary that he answer this."[13]

LEWISOHN STADIUM WAS A HUMILIATION the composer never forgot. It also pushed him closer to bankruptcy. As Marie wrote Beatrice that September, "Mr. Steiner . . . has to pay out half of his salary each week on his Federal taxes alone. . . . He will have to [sell] probably his home."[14] The restless energy that defined Max—now 55—was starting to diminish. One reporter described him as "plumpish, short, round-faced, bespectacled, and his black hair grows thinner each year."[15]

Of course, much work awaited him at Warners. Steiner had high hopes for *Saratoga Trunk*, a New Orleans–set romance based on the latest Edna Ferber doorstop of a novel. Stars Gary Cooper and Ingrid Bergman were eager to continue the affair they began months earlier on *For Whom the Bell Tolls* and "were often late or unavailable," author David Thomson wrote. "If only the film could have recorded what was delaying them."[16]

The bloated drama photographed instead is near-unwatchable. Delays in its release—Warner Bros. smelled a turkey—meant that Steiner had six months to work on his score. He was hopeful about two themes conceived to be song hits: the sweeping love theme "As Long as I Live," and a loping cowboy ballad for Cooper's character titled "Going Home." But like Lewisohn Stadium, the enterprise ended in failure. When *Trunk* finally opened in 1945, "As Long as I Live" proved only modestly popular. "Going Home" was ignored.

In the two years between *Trunk*'s making and its release, Max convinced Warners to publish three other songs of his. "Someday I'll Meet You Again" was a French ballad from *Passage to Marseilles*, a dour *Casablanca* wannabe starring Bogart. "Orchid Moon" was a tango from *The Conspirators*, another *Casablanca* knock-off starring Paul Henreid. And "When You're Away" was drawn from Max's score for the moving Barbara Stanwyck love story *My Reputation*. All three songs flopped.

Given the themes' attractiveness, why did all fail commercially as songs?

Most had weak lyrics. Some worked better as instrumental motifs in a score: "Someday I'll Meet You Again" loses its pop-song blandness when its first three notes are reworked as suspense music for a prison break. But "Orchid Moon" deserved a better fate; its sexy, foreboding tango was a natural for bands like Xavier Cugat's.

Max lifted its tune from an early RKO score for a film few saw: 1933's *Christopher Strong*. Steiner felt his theme deserved a second chance, but unfortunately *The Conspirators* fared no better. During its shooting, "the film became known as *The Constipators*, with 'Headache Lamarr' and 'Paul Hemorrhoid,'" its director Jean Negulesco recalled.[17] "The just valuation of the film was given by Max Steiner, who was called in to do the musical score. We saw the finished project together. After the show, the lights went on. Hopefully I waited for his comment. It was short, just one word: '*Ouch!*' Brief and to the point."

BY OCTOBER 1943, Max had more serious concerns than failed pop tunes. "Poor Erna . . . is on the way out," he told Louise.[18] "They just called me from the sanitarium and told me that she was raving all night last night."

Erna died a month later. "Papa was in a terrible state about it," Max wrote in 1964.[19] "She was wonderful to him, and he adored her. At Forest Lawn after the services were over, he stood outside the little chapel and banged his head against the masonry in agony. A funeral executive came over and said to me brusquely, 'Take the old man away from here. Another body is coming in.'"

DESPITE HIS STRESS AND OVERWORK, Max remained a soft touch for a friend. As a favor to Lou Forbes, he agreed to secretly score *Up in Arms*, the first starring film for Danny Kaye. Normally Warner Bros. would have loaned him out at a mark-up, but Max was already fully booked, so he quietly took producer Samuel Goldwyn's payment under the table and tripled his workload. "It probably will be a killing job," he wrote Louise, "but I'll do it . . . to make a few dollars on the side. How I can write [three scores simultaneously] I do not know."[20]

It helped that one of those projects was a nostalgic celebration of his own Broadway past.

Purportedly a biography of George Gershwin, *Rhapsody in Blue* had been in the works since shortly after the composer's death in 1937.[21] The complexity of Gershwin's personality was reduced to the tale of a genial Horatio Alger–type (Robert Alda) torn between girls good and bad (Joan Leslie, Alexis Smith) and music high and low (to write a symphony or a song?).

But the movie recreates some of Gershwin's career milestones with surprising fidelity, including the failed performance of his first attempt at opera, *135th Street*. In real life, Steiner conducted the latter during its brief inclusion in *George White's Scandals*. In the movie, Paul Whiteman leads *135th Street*, but the substitution isn't surprising: Whiteman co-conducted the *Scandals* with Max, and he figured more importantly in Gershwin's life as the man who commissioned *Rhapsody in Blue*. Max was consigned to writing underscore for the movie; if he was disappointed not to be shown in its story, he never expressed it.

But he was hardly silent when Oscar Levant arrived to portray himself onscreen. Although "George just loved him and I always have too," Max smarted over Levant's caustic depiction of him in the book *A Smattering of Ignorance*. "When Oscar came on the lot, I faced him with it: 'What's the idea of giving me the business? I thought you were supposed to be my pal. You devoted twelve pages to panning the hell out of me.' Oscar just smiled and put his arm around me. 'I always malign the people I love best,' he explained. 'Just remember, I used twelve pages to say how lousy you are and I only used two pages to say how good Newman is.' Now, how can you fight that kind of logic?"[22]

At home, Max faced only worsening calamity. He now owed more than $28,000 in back taxes ($400,000 today). In a gesture of support, Hal Wallis and his wife came to Cove Way and offered to buy most of the Steiners' antiques and furniture.

His household staff was a disaster. After an argument with his latest cook, "Ten minutes later . . . she was packed and out of the house," he told Louise. "She said that she had another job and hated everybody's guts in the house, including Ronnie."[23]

Most heartbreaking was the declining health of his 85-year-old father. By March 1944 Gabor was in the hospital. "Last night he was so irrational that they had to move him out of the ward," Max wrote Louise. "I will have to make up my mind that he won't last very long."[24]

On May 2, doctors amputated half of one of Gabor's feet. "He knows what's up and is afraid to die," Max wrote.[25] "He won't turn out the light at night because he is frightened to be alone. . . . He wants me to be with him constantly and wants to see the baby as much as possible; almost as if he wanted to crowd us being together as much as possible in the short time he has left on this earth."

Days later, doctors removed one of Gabor's legs.

On March 22, Max went to his own doctor and received a troubling diagnosis: a tumor was found on his back. Surgery was scheduled for June.[26] At home, a letter waited in Beatrice's shaky hand. She was paralyzed by arthritis and desperately needed money.

Only in such Job-like circumstances could the other event that spring seem like a gift from the gods. David O. Selznick was calling... and he needed Max urgently.

SINCE GWTW'S RELEASE, the 42-year-old producer had won accolades for another Best Picture winner, *Rebecca*. But Selznick struggled to find a project to top his most famous film; and in 1942, he settled on another epic rooted in war. *Since You Went Away* was based on Margaret Buell Wilder's novel, in which a mother of two shares her struggles on the home front in letters to her husband, who serves in World War II. Like *Little Women*, it depicted American democracy through the sacrifices of a single, mostly female family.

Selznick's mania for control surpassed even his micromanagement of *GWTW*. After rejecting a screenplay by Wilder, he wrote his own. Before director John Cromwell called action, he insisted on watching each rehearsal. Married co-stars Jennifer Jones and Robert Walker separated when Jones

Jennifer Jones, Claudette Colbert, and Shirley Temple in a publicity still from *Since You Went Away*.

became Selznick's lover, and later his wife. And after five months and 132 shoot days, Selznick refused to trim the film's 172-minute run time.[27]

Initially, Selznick favored Herbert Stothart to write the music. "I am anxious to have the score written during production [to avoid] a poor job that has to be rushed."[28] No sooner was a deal with Stothart in place than Selznick forsook him for a new candidate, Bernard Herrmann—who turned the producer down.[29]

David then checked the availability of Waxman, Copland, and Korngold . . . but not Steiner.[30] Apparently, Selznick's dislike of Max's methods—waiting for a finished film before starting, any "mickey-mousing"—still ran deep.

As shooting wrapped, David made what appeared to be his final choice. Alexandre Tansman was a Polish-born composer whose friends included Ravel and Stravinsky. Selznick was starstruck by his concert hall credentials, but Tansman had little experience in Hollywood; and after hearing some generic music Tansman wrote as a test, Selznick flew into a panic and released him.[31]

Now, the producer had barely a month before more than two hours of music needed to be completed—and even he knew there was only one option.

PERHAPS THE ONLY HAPPY INDIVIDUAL that May was Jack Warner. He demanded top dollar to loan Steiner to Selznick: $3,300 a week. David agreed, adding in a memo, "I consider myself very lucky indeed to get him."[32]

Max still considered Selznick one of the world's great filmmakers—but he foresaw the misery ahead. The movie was "simply wonderful," he wrote Louise, "but you know what it means to work for Selznick. I have four weeks in which to finish the picture. . . . I don't really mind this time because I like this picture better than 'Gone with the Wind,' if that is possible; but, with all my troubles, of course it is hard work to hack out new tunes."[33]

Yet within a week he had created most of the score's key themes. Selznick listened and sighed with relief. "I spent a couple of hours with Max this morning," he wrote on May 12, "and before I left him we had come to an agreement on every single theme. . . . He has done magnificent work in so short a time. I am wildly enthusiastic about how the score is going to shape up. Thank heavens for Maxie."[34]

But even Steiner could not create enough material for so long a score in so short a time. Instead, he and Selznick agreed to supplement original themes with music from their past collaborations. For once, Max was grateful to draw on existing pieces: he knew that Selznick already liked them, and Steiner would reshape them to fit the new narrative. *Little Lord Fauntleroy's*

"Dearest" theme was rearranged for muted brass to represent absent father Tim, as seen through the adoring eyes of daughter Jane (Jones). A sprightly comic "honeymoon" theme from *A Star Is Born* now described the friendship between younger daughter Brig (Shirley Temple) and the Hiltons's crusty boarder, Col. Smollett (Monty Woolley).

"Janet's Waltz," from *A Star Is Born*, became the motif for ladies' man Tony Willett (Joseph Cotten). Its use here is droll. In *A Star Is Born*, the waltz represented the love between the story's leads. In *SYWA*, it reflects Willett's smooth-operator act. In Tony's first scene, the waltz accompanies him as he flirts with the married Anne. Like her, we're charmed. But the waltz stops abruptly when another woman calls to Tony from across the room, asking him to call her. Anne smiles knowingly before the waltz resumes; her reaction, and the music's pause, tell us that Tony is a player, albeit an endearing one.

Steiner's original motifs are first-rate. His exultant main theme corresponds to the meter of the title, "Since . . . You . . . Went . . . A-way," its opening five notes a deceptively simple descent of major-key intervals (E-flat–D-flat–C–B-flat–A-flat). As arranged for full orchestra with divisi strings and chimes, it establishes in seconds the story's scope and straight-for-the-heart emotion. Two lighter themes show Max's skill at humor: Colonel Smollett's cantankerous motto, and a waddling melody for bass clarinet for family dog Soda (Max's love for his own dog, Prince, may have influenced this motif).

Another Steiner original is as attractive as it is problematic. It accompanies Fidelia, the Hiltons's maid; she is played by Hattie McDaniel, *GWTW*'s Mammy. As written by Selznick, Fidelia has none of Mammy's insight or energy. She is loved by the Hiltons, but her role conforms to the stereotypes of 1940s servant parts. Correspondingly, Steiner's Fidelia theme is bluesy and, unlike music for the rhythmically vital Hiltons, slow. *"Lazily,"* Max writes in his sketch.[35]

"Her theme emphasizes racial difference," author Nathan Platte observed.[36] "Fidelia is not musically linked to anyone, and her theme's blue notes and swung rhythms set it apart from the rest of the diatonic, straight-note themes." Countering the implicit racism is the warmth and beauty of Max's melody: despite imbedded societal prejudices, it was not in his nature to see characters as less than human.

Unusually, most new themes are not for individuals but for pairings: Anne/Tim, Jane/Bill (Walker), Brig/Colonel Smollett. "Steiner's score emphasizes the latticework of social connections . . . through themes that pair characters together," observed Platte.[37] Tellingly, the only major character to have *no* musical theme is Agnes Moorehead's Emily Hawkins, a gossipy socialite whose selfishness is the antithesis of the Hiltons' generosity.

SELZNICK MAY HAVE BEEN "WILDLY ENTHUSIASTIC" over Max's work, but fissures between producer and composer soon arose.

For a birthday party lasting less than three minutes, Selznick mapped out a laborious plan for how each beat should be scored. When he heard the result, he complained that "there are two or three times too many bits and pieces," forgetting his own edict.[38] Steiner created a seamless new version, which probably resembled what he would have done if left alone.

For a scene in which Brig prays for her absent father, Steiner wrote a piece of simple, affecting music. Selznick replaced it with Bach's *Ave Maria*. Max's reaction on paper was a silent scream: *"Alteration #64!!!! MUSIC BY DAVID O. SELZNICK."*

But even Selznick could not fault the music that comes minutes later. Jane is saying goodbye to Bill Smollett, the soldier she loves. As she walks, then runs alongside his moving train, Steiner's tender version of the main title theme is interrupted by a powerful fate chord (*"All Aboard!"*). The main theme takes on the chugging rhythm of the locomotive: *"Strings [play] near the bridge . . . Anvil, Harp."* The train accelerates, as music assumes a brutish force: *"Accelerando—Add Snare Drum (Brush) . . . full BRASS."* The string section expands like a final cry—then fades on an unresolved chord as the train disappears, leaving Jane alone. Music could have made the scene hopefully romantic. Instead, it tells us that Jane will never see Bill again.

NATURALLY, MAX REQUIRED A BATTALION of orchestrators, some of whom wrote brief cues based on his themes.[39] The shortage of time probably explains the lack of jokes in Max's sketches, with a few exceptions. Reel 16, mourning Bill's death: *"Everybody is crying—including the budget!"* And on the final page: *"TUTTA SFORZA—and SFORBSTEIN! And SFORBES!"*

The joys and sorrows of the Hilton family allowed Max to find fleeting escape from his own problems. It required not only quick decision-making but intense focus, a scenario that often brought out his best. Additional time probably would have produced an even better score: in the film's second half, themes are often simply restated and lack the subtle development Steiner gave his motifs in scores like *Now, Voyager*. But given the limitations, his accomplishment was considerable.

IN JUNE 1944, LOUISE STEINER AGREED to play first harp for the recording. Like *GWTW*, it took place on the acoustically superb stages of United Artists. Days often began on a cheerful note, recalled second harpist Aida

Dagort: "In the morning when the doors were opened for the first time, a bunch of pigeons would fly out."[40]

But soon, the tension between Max and Louise was clear to all among the 90-piece orchestra. "I was playing second harp," Dagort recalled.[41]

> There was a scene in the picture where . . . Monty Woolley runs to catch a train. Max had written an arpeggio for us to show the character's hurry and anxiety. . . . We did the take many times, and Max was never satisfied, but he said nothing in the way of instructions.
>
> I realized he wanted us to follow the action more closely so I whispered to Louise, "He just wants us to drag the beginning of the arpeggio, and rush the end."
>
> All was very quiet on stage as we were all so tired. Louise turned to me and said in a very loud voice for all to hear, *"I know what he wants."*
>
> I got up and walked off the stage. Let her play it and screw it up by herself, I thought.
>
> Meanwhile Max just stood there and chewed on his cigar, saying nothing. I went out in the fresh air thinking my career was over. [But] Max was a generous, darling man. I was challenging his wife's competency, but the incident was never referred to again.

Fifty years later, Louise recalled the session more tersely: "That was the very last one that I recorded with Max."[42]

UPON HEARING THE RECORDING, Selznick sent a note of congratulations—qualified as usual. "On the whole, I'm happy about and grateful for your characteristically outstanding labor . . . and even if there are certain things about the score that are not to your satisfaction . . . I deeply appreciate how hard you worked, and what a Herculean task it was to get the score done, under the circumstances, in the limited time that you had. I am particularly mindful of the personal problems that you had during the period, and also of the fact that you were not feeling too well physically. . . . I do hope that somehow you'll manage to get a little rest."[43]

Selznick followed his note days later with demands for additional changes.[44]

At least he shielded his composer from one critic. John Cromwell disliked Steiner's work, and on June 26 the director sent David a note. "I have always felt that Max had the wrong conception of music's function for a picture, and he will continually try to dramatize the scene, either a bit preceding it or simultaneously. In an ordinary picture that's bad enough, but certainly in one where we are making every effort to capture every-day reality it is to me a definite detriment. . . . Max has seen himself in the light of 'David Selznick presents Max Steiner in SINCE YOU WENT AWAY.'"[45]

Cromwell probably didn't know the degree to which Selznick directed Steiner's approach, and David made none of Cromwell's recommended changes. If anything, his enthusiasm for the score grew as the film's July 20 release date neared. Five years after CBS passed on releasing music from *GWTW*, Selznick had Lou Forbes record a suite of *SYWA* themes, and had the music sent to two hundred radio stations.[46]

Hours before the film opened, Selznick sent another note to his beleaguered composer. "Dear Max: I am really extremely happy with the score now, and hope you feel the same way about it. There are parts of it that I think are magnificent, including especially the Jane-Bill theme, but this is not to say that I don't like all of it. I know no one in the business that could have done as fine a job on so much film in so short a time. I still love you and hope you are the same."[47]

Released one month after D-Day, which added more than two hundred thousand names to the list of Allied casualties, *Since You Went Away* resonated powerfully with moviegoers and earned a massive $7 million.[48] The following year, it earned nine Academy Award nominations, including Best Picture and Best Scoring of a Dramatic or Comedy Picture.

But when the envelopes were opened at Grauman's Chinese on March 15, 1945, *Going My Way* was named Best Picture. And so it went, through each of the nominated categories.

With one exception.

The announcement of Max Steiner's name was more than just another victory for the composer. Five years earlier, Max was among the few *GWTW* nominees to leave without an Oscar. On March 15, "This time I was the only one to win an Academy Award for my work. So I guess there is retribution."[49]

The recorded *SYWA* suite received considerable airplay in the months before the Oscars; familiarity with the score may have been a deciding factor in its win. Whatever the cause, the honoring of the music had a poetic justice. *Since You Went Away* is a synthesis of Steiner's work with Selznick, and its writing typified their stormy, superb history of collaboration. Just as Max had won a single Oscar for his RKO work, and one Oscar for Warner Bros., he now had a third trophy that honored his Selznick years.

If Max was jubilant, David was anything but. Fiercely competitive, he left the Oscars bitter after losing every major category. And although a few successful projects lay ahead for him, his future, as he had feared, was one of diminishing returns.

He and Steiner never worked together again.

THE FILM SCORES OF MAX STEINER

1944 Releases

Passage to Marseilles (11/43–12/43)
Up in Arms (11/43–12/43) Goldwyn/RKO
Since You Went Away (5/44–6/44). Selznick International. AA.
The Conspirators (7/44–8/44)

1945 Releases (continued in Chapter 21)

Roughly Speaking (11/44–12/44)
Rhapsody in Blue. Steiner began work in fall 1943, but rescoring and re-editing continued until shortly before the film's release in 1945. AAN.
Saratoga Trunk (fall 1943). Unreleased until 1945.
One More Tomorrow (12/43 to 1/44). Unreleased until 1946.
My Reputation (3/44–4/44), released in 1946.

The nine months between the release of *Since You Went Away* and Max's trip to the Academy podium had been a time of unremitting bleakness. Just before the score's recording, Steiner underwent surgery to have the tumor on his spine removed. The operation was a success, but he had no time to rest.

Gabor was dying.

In Charles Dickens's *Little Dorrit* the family patriarch, after a life haunted by debt, spends his final hours hallucinating that he is once again requesting money from strangers. Gabor's final hours were an aching reversal of that scene. "Towards the end, he lost his mind," Max recalled.[50] "He kept Kleenex in bed with him and thought it was money. He gave it away to everyone who came into the room and would say: 'Here's $10,000 for you, but don't tell anybody about it.' He loved my little boy dearly, so Ronnie got more Kleenex than anybody else."

On September 9, 1944, Gabor Steiner died at the age of 86. Overwhelmed by grief, Max honored his father in the only way he could. At Gabor's funeral, Louis Kaufman played *On the Beautiful Blue Danube* by Johann Strauss, the composer who had launched the Steiner dynasty in the 1870s.

But even in death, Gabor seemed determined to cause chaos. Before the service, Kaufman stepped into the cubbyhole from which he would be playing, and asked his wife Annette to assess the audio balance from the chapel. "She quickly walked into the chapel," Louis remembered, "mounted the small podium, and turned to discover she was imprisoned behind Papa Steiner's coffin, which had shot out silently behind her! The coffin filled the width of the podium, so she had to squeeze down underneath it to crawl out on her hands and knees. She had been startled to see Gabor's beautiful features so unexpectedly, but reported that the violin and organ balance was excellent. The dignified service proceeded to the strains of muted violin and organ performing the beloved Viennese waltz, so close to Gabor Steiner's heart."[51]

THAT SAME MONTH, ON SEPTEMBER 16, a letter arrived from an attorney representing Louise. It vaguely referenced the "difficulties that have disturbed her relationship with you."[52]

Days later, divorce papers arrived.

"I was tired of living with nerves and never knowing when Max would get upset over nothing," Louise later said of her decision.[53] "I did so want to be fair to Max and Ron and myself. But Max and I seemed to grow apart, even though our common bond was our son and, of course, music."

Steiner made no attempt to hide his pain from coworkers. He "told all of us how heartbroken he was," Aida Dagort recalled.[54] "He treated the musicians as old friends, which they were. Max was loved by everyone who worked for him."

The year 1944 had been the most debilitating of Steiner's 56 years. Despite a lifetime of work, he felt he had nothing. Nothing except a son whom he seldom saw—Ronnie was shuttled between coasts and nannies—and whom Max feared he was about to lose, as his third divorce began.

Fortunately, a temporary balm arrived in the usual fashion. *Roughly Speaking*, directed by Michael Curtiz, starred Rosalind Russell in the true story of Louise Randall, a career woman we follow from the collapse of an early marriage that leaves her with three children, to her happy, nomadic life with a second husband (Jack Carson) and a fourth child. Together, the family constantly reinvents itself with grit and good humor.

The film's message of carrying on in the face of hardship was a perfect tonic for Max. He responded with a nostalgic score that blended original themes with well-chosen period songs that signaled the passage of time, from "It Had to Be You" to Warner Bros.' own "We're in the Money (The Gold Diggers' Song)."

It could hardly have been accidental that *On the Beautiful Blue Danube* was played in a scene featuring Randall's beloved father, shortly before his death.

Max's sketches are filled with charming drawings and his usual low humor (when a character asks "Can you see the Big Dipper?" Max scribbles, *"Nobody can even find my Big Dipper"*).[55] Some jokes are more acid than usual, especially since Russell's character was named Louise. *"Louise in Bed—Mine is in DRED." "[He] kisses Louise—what a sucker! She walks out. (I wish I could!)"*

For neither the first nor the last time, music had given Steiner's life renewed purpose. And just ahead lay another pair of soon-to-be-iconic titles, both of them prime examples of a genre he had yet to tackle:

Film noir.

21

Au Revoir and Bonjour

ON NEW YEAR'S EVE 1944, Max and Louise reunited for a last night of celebration. The occasion was an "au revoir" party for friends at Cove Way; their former dream home had been sold for $57,000.[1] Most of that money was used to pay tax liens, and Max still owed thousands to the government, his attorneys, and others.

Eager to move on, Louise agreed to alimony of $350 for 15 weeks, then $175 until January 1950.[2] Custody of Ronald would be shared. "It was a ridiculous settlement," she later said. "That was one tenth of Max's salary. But I was tired of squabbling, so—fool that I was—I said I would accept the terms. Being still young [38] and able to earn my own living, I felt too independent."[3]

While the divorce was finalized, Max found distraction in a project that reveled in an ideal of romantic chemistry. *The Big Sleep* was Hollywood's second major attempt to bring Raymond Chandler's L.A. crime fiction to the screen, after the success of RKO's *Murder My Sweet*. Warner Bros. upped the ante, hiring Howard Hawks to direct and produce, Humphrey Bogart to star as private dick Philip Marlowe, and Lauren Bacall—Mrs. Bogart by May 21—as its femme fatale. Hawks emphasized his stars' crackling sexual tension, turning "a film noir mystery into a screwball love story," David Thomson observed.[4] In choosing Steiner to score, Hawks further ensured that the focus would be on romance versus who-killed-who.

Max made sure to balance heavy dramatic cues with romance and whimsy. His scherzo-like theme for Marlowe is another variant on Richard Strauss's *Till Eulenspiegel's Merry Pranks*—music for an outsider and trickster. Max literally takes his cues from the detective's reactions: *"EAR BUSINESS,"*[5] he notes of Bogart's frequent ear-tugs, signifying thought or bemusement.

Lauren Bacall and Humphrey Bogart in a publicity still from *The Big Sleep*.

Steiner's main title is a maestoso prelude of dense, stepping chords. *"Hand Cymbal, Big Gong, Chime"* clang its melodramatic theme, which reflects Chandler's title—a metaphor for death. But most of the score is fleet-footed and insinuating. A pizzicato suspense rhythm follows Marlowe from clue to clue, its hopping staccato suggesting his fast-working mind. A swooning figure for strings and celeste evokes the opioid haze in which vixen Carmen Sternwood lives.

The classic sequence of Marlowe's tryst with a sexy book store clerk (Dorothy Malone) is scored with a suggestively upward-spiraling waltz. The supple melody implies that under other circumstances, this bespectacled bad girl would be a worthy partner for Marlowe.

Steiner withholds his Bogart–Bacall love theme until halfway through the picture. Although written in $\frac{3}{4}$, its tempo is slow, its melodic line distinguished by dramatically held notes at the end of its phrases. Max knew he was composing for a larger-than-life duo, and gives their music gravitas.*

---

* *The Big Sleep* was subject to many reshoots after Steiner's score was completed in February 1945, but his music was hardly affected.

HIS NEXT MAJOR FILM—a tale of marital discord and financial struggle—hit closer to the bone. *Mildred Pierce* was based on a novel by Raymond Chandler's rival in crime, James M. Cain. But *Mildred* wasn't about murder: it focused on the tribulations of a single mother fighting to build a restaurant business in 1930s Los Angeles. Warner Bros. knew that audiences seeing Cain's name would expect a dash of homicide. The job of adding it fell to Jerry Wald.[6]

Wald was now the studio's top producer after the exit of Hal Wallis, who left after years of escalating battles with Jack Warner. Wald was determined to make *Mildred Pierce* a smash that would ensure his primacy on the lot. He hired Michael Curtiz to direct and, in a risky move, Joan Crawford—recently let go from MGM—to star. Wald also got his murder, by having Mildred's sociopathic daughter, Veda (Ann Blyth), shoot Mildred's two-timing lover, Monte (Zachary Scott).

Steiner's score is acutely psychological, often revealing extra information about characters' motives. Mildred's theme is the most sonorous: during the main title, it is timed to crashing waves that reveal with each incoming tide a new set of credits. The theme's first three notes (D-flat, C-natural, A-flat) match the name "Mildred Pierce," before the theme soars upward, into a heraldic declaration of Mildred's determination.

In the film's first scene, Monte is shot by an off-camera assailant. His last word—"Mildred"—is accompanied by a deliberate Steiner misdirect, as Mildred's theme is softly played. Only at film's end will we learn that Monte was *remembering* her, not accusing her. Moments later, we see Mildred contemplating suicide at the edge of a pier. Steiner's sketches make it clear that he is taking note of Crawford's performance: *"RISOLUTO—Jaw set."*[7]

Music for Veda is a conscious contrast in style (jazz versus symphonic) and length (a short motif versus Mildred's expansive melody). As Kate Daubney notes, "Veda has aspirations to wealth and society far beyond her mother's means, as does Mildred's lover, Monte. Steiner consistently represents the 'otherness' of this existence with jazz and woodwind instrumentation and constructs an instrumental connection between Veda and Monte long before their relationship begins."[8] The lazy syncopation of Veda's music links her to other Steiner anti-heroines. Her theme "vacillates without any firm tonality," author Eva Rieger observed, "thus communicating that despite her strong will (her theme climbs upward), she is deficient as a person."[9] (*"Hugo! As NASTY as possible." "ACID—The 'BITCH' AGAIN!"*)

Steiner again uses pre-existing music to signal a character's insincerity. Playboy Monte doesn't get an original theme: instead, he seduces Mildred while playing a record of Steiner's "It Can't Be Wrong" from *Now, Voyager*.

Ann Blyth and Joan Crawford in a publicity still from *Mildred Pierce*.

Some critics have misread this as a lazy self-repeat. While self-promotion may have been a motive, the song's use is a calculated comment on Monte's womanizing—just as the re-use of "Janet's Waltz" in *Since You Went Away* reflected Tony's insincerity with the opposite sex.

For the famous moment when Mildred slaps Veda, only to be slapped in return, Steiner creates a sound increasingly prominent in his postwar music. *"PIANO—let it ring . . . "* The reverberant color of one or two pianos, pedal down to create an echo, and often doubled with timpani or harp, would bring a fresh dramatic effect to Steiner's postwar scores.

Originally, dialogue in the film's last scene made explicit that Mildred and ex-husband Bert would reunite.[10] Wald excised it for a more effective wordless conclusion. Steiner adds *"Chimes, Vibraphone, Bells"* to a final statement of Mildred's theme, economically telling us what lies in the pair's future.

As Max finished the score on June 14, a letter arrived from Jack Warner. "Dear Max: I want to pay you praise for your intelligent scoring of *Mildred Pierce*. In my opinion it was the best you have done because most of the music was not over done. Keep up the good work."[11] Welcome as the note must have been, Warner's "over done" comment probably rankled, given how often Max's boss ordered him to write *more* music than Steiner thought necessary.

One of the year's top grossers, *Mildred Pierce* received six Oscar nominations. And although score was not among them, 1945 Best Actress winner Joan Crawford would describe her musical collaborator (with typical theatricality) as "a great, great artist."[12]

In 1945, Max was also investing time in a project that would have more far-reaching results. After 12 years of feuding with ASCAP, he turned the group of composers he assembled in 1942 into something more official. The Screen Composers Association, or SCA, announced its formation in July 1945.[13] Its members included every top composer in Hollywood. Its goal was collective bargaining; and although its creation was just a first step, it was a significant one.

Having severed business ties with Louis Minter, Steiner now took counsel from a more effective attorney, Leonard Zissu. In exchange for a percentage of royalties distributed to film composers, Zissu greatly assisted the SCA, which on July 20 elected Max its president. Recalled Steiner's friend David Raksin, "He gave his time, his energy, his money, his wit, and his great heart to the cause of film composers. He was the name around which we could rally. He refused to be intimidated."[14]

An even more significant event occurred one month after the group's formation. The day was August 14, 1945. On a Warner Bros. set, as cameras rolled on a now-forgotten film, the stage door flew open and in strode Jack Warner, entourage in tow. "We will all stop shooting now today," he told his employees. "We have won. The war is over!"

According to one observer, actor Richard Erdman, "We hugged one another . . . and we moved out onto the streets on the lot. It was chaos and growing. Horns were honking. People were screaming, and laughing and crying. . . . Cowboys and Indians . . . janitors and producers all from their own little kingdoms, out they came. . . . Mike Curtiz, ever the filmmaker, mounted a crane with a camera and operated it himself, capturing the spectacle on high, and then, most breathtaking of all, out from the music stage emerged that great studio orchestra . . . led by Erich Wolfgang Korngold, pumping his baton, conducting and marching them onto the streets . . . playing 'America the Beautiful.' What a day. Glorious! Glorious!"[15]

The end of World War II signaled the start of a new era in Hollywood. At last, studios could drop propaganda titles from their slates. And as the industry recalibrated, so did Steiner.

His changing style is evident in his last major film of 1945. *A Stolen Life* was a tour-de-force for its co-producer and star Bette Davis, who portrays twin sisters: Kate, an introverted artist, and Pat, her self-centered doppelganger. What reads as absurdity plays as engaging melodrama. The selfish Pat marries Kate's love, a lighthouse keeper played by Glenn Ford, but Pat dies in a boating accident that kindly Kate survives. When rescuers mistake Kate for Pat, our heroine assumes her dead sibling's identity, allowing her to be "married" to the man she loves.

The film benefited from its melancholy, fog-shrouded depiction of coastal life in Maine. That setting dictated Davis's original idea for its score: music based on Debussy's sea portrait *La Mer*.[16] When that work's publishers dictated a use "without any cuts," the subject was dropped.[17]

Instead, Steiner wrote a score capturing the flavor of Debussy-style impressionism with tailor-made music. Max relished creating sequences that suggested the soft, obscuring textures of weather—here, the lonely call of a foghorn and the mist that pervades a story of mistaken identity. Brass is used sparingly, with woodwinds emphasized to evoke the sea, along with two harps, pianos, and celeste.

The resulting score "reflected a subtle change in both film and musical styles" from his previous work, as John Morgan noted when restoring the score decades later. "Steiner's music was leaner and less prone to follow the dialogue in operatic terms. The thematic and harmonic material were somewhat simpler and the various themes were more clearly defined."[18] The "schmaltz" common in Max's scores for Selznick was replaced by a less emotive approach.

By giving distinct themes to each twin sister, Steiner engages in his own dialogue with the viewer, wryly commenting on the dangerous games of deception we see. "Bad" sister Pat is defined with languorous syncopation; skipping grace notes on the melody suggest her flippancy. Steiner will use Pat's theme to alert the viewer which sister is which when Bill (Ford) mistakes Pat for Kate.

After Pat is killed and Kate is misidentified as her sister, music tells us what will happen next. As Kate silently ponders the situation, it is Pat's insinuating theme we hear. We now know that our heroine is about to assume her sister's identity.

In the past, Steiner had sometimes borrowed short passages from earlier works, often due to deadline. *A Stolen Life* marks a change in this practice, with the lifting of a full sequence from an earlier film. As Kate wakes up from the accident, we hear in its entirety "A Boat in the Fog" from *King Kong*. Today, when most of Steiner's movies are a computer click away, such self-borrowing may seem like laziness. But in an era when he believed that his past work was "dead," this reuse was not only an act of expediency, but an effort to keep his music alive.

The year 1946, when *A Stolen Life* was successfully released, would be Hollywood's most profitable to date. Eighty million patrons, many of them returning servicemen, attended movie theaters at least once a week, amid a new age of American prosperity.[19]

The year 1946 also happened to be when Steiner's current studio contract was coming to an end. Ever on Max's side, Leo Forbstein wrote a memo that February to Warner executive Steve Trilling.

> I think we should start a new contract with him for five years beginning March 1st, at $2250.00 per week and also an option for five years at $2500.00 [about $34,000 today]. I think for a man of his caliber this is not asking too much, as you know we have been receiving as high as $3500 a week for his services on loan-out and I am getting many calls every day for his services at other studios with price no object . . .

In his Warner Bros. office, 1946. (MS Papers; L. Tom Perry Special Collections, Brigham Young University)

I assure you that I will always try to sneak in an extra picture or two for Steiner to do during each year which would compensate not having to bring in someone else to do them. He also has been here for the past eight years with us and in those eight years he has scored over eighty pictures, which is a pretty good record for any man to do.[20]

Max would never have a better contract.

But composer and studio didn't always agree on the best use of his talents. His first title of 1946, *The Beast with Five Fingers*, was a rare Warners foray into horror. The grisly little shocker starred Peter Lorre as a seemingly mild-mannered secretary who murders his employer, a one-handed concert pianist, only to be haunted by visions of his victim's disembodied digits. According to screenwriter Curt Siodmak, Paul Henreid was initially cast as the hero, but the former onscreen lover of Davis and Bergman rejected his latest co-star: "You want me to play against a goddamned hand? You think I'm crazy?"[21]

Max had a similar reaction. But the studio's thinking isn't hard to explain: a lesser film like *Beast* needed Steiner's dramatic oomph in a way that a stronger movie did not. And typically, he delivered an outstanding score, for his only fantasy-horror tale post-*Kong*.

It was Siodmak who suggested using Bach's D Minor Chaconne as the piece played throughout the story by doomed pianist Francis Ingram.[22] Its grave majesty gives chills, with emphatic chords that convey inescapable doom. After Ingram's death, ghostly reprises of the melody haunt the house, and Steiner incorporates the theme in his score. Its most effective use is a "swimmy," distorted rendition as the wheelchair-bound Ingram experiences hallucinations and falls to his death down a staircase. A rare moment of contrast in the score is a sunny, Bizet-like Tarantella that describes the Italian village that provides the story's setting.

Reviews for *Beast* were surprisingly positive. But to the end of his life, Max hated the movie, forbidding conductor Charles Gerhardt from including its score on a 1970s disc of Steiner suites.[23]

ALTHOUGH *BEAST*'S CREDITS LISTED Hugo Friedhofer as orchestrator, the attribution was an error. By 1946, Hugo had moved on to focus on his own composing career. A year later, he would receive a richly deserved Oscar for *The Best Years of Our Lives*. Replacing him as Max's aide was a 43-year-old French-born composer of concert music named Murray Cutter, whose Hollywood orchestration work included *The Wizard of Oz*.

The Steiner-Cutter partnership would be as close as the one that preceded it. "Cutter told me he was delighted to work for Max," recalled historian James D'Arc, "as Steiner's sketches were very complete and practically orchestrated themselves."[24] But Cutter's true musical passion lay elsewhere. "To him it was just a job," added John Morgan.[25] "He respected Max, but to him film music was a secondary art. Murray had an enormous room of symphonic scores; Stravinsky was a favorite. But he was great at orchestrating film music."

HOWEVER LOATH STEINER WAS TO ADMIT IT, assignments like *The Beast with Five Fingers* and his next film, director Raoul Walsh's *Cheyenne*, gave him freedom to experiment without input from producers anxiously circling an A-project. Superficially, *Cheyenne* was a western about a mysterious bandit robbing stagecoaches; but it was buoyed by a witty, twist-filled script and screwball chemistry between Dennis Morgan and Jane Wyman. Added for good measure was sexy saloon girl Janis Paige singing the title tune, one of Max's catchiest melodies.

Left to his own devices, Steiner latched onto the film's comic-romantic impulses. "I pulled a new trick on them by writing it like musical comedy and sort of kidding the picture," he wrote Louise.[26] "I took an awful chance because Leo was away and had never heard a note of it until the preview. Result—Warner went absolutely crazy over the music.... Hundreds of people asked the theater manager and the ushers where the music or records could be bought." Hyperbole to be sure, but *Variety* did note that "Steiner's rousing score is likewise no small factor in a film loaded with exciting b.o. [box office] potentials."[27]

A poignant legacy of *Cheyenne* is a recording Max made at home with Ronnie, age six. As 58-year-old Steiner plays the movie's title song on piano, he tries to convince his son to sing along. Ronnie resists. What the boy craved wasn't more of his father's music: it was his attention and love.

Over the last six years, neither Max nor Louise had spent much time with their son. Ronald's increasing tantrums and crying spells should have alerted his parents that their boy needed help. Instead, they attributed his outbursts only to the stress of their divorce.

As Louise struggled to start a new life on the east coast, Ronnie would spend most of the next decade with his father. But Max, now living in a rented Westwood home, left his lonely boy mostly in the hands of servants while he worked in his music room. In an attempt to compensate, he showered him with expensive gifts. "There was no discipline," Louise recalled, "and even

Ronald admires Papa's acetate collection, mid-1940s.
(Louise Steiner Elian Papers; L. Tom Perry Special
Collections, Brigham Young University)

friends of ours would tell Max how much he was actually harming Ron in
giving him too much."[28]

In fall 1946, Steiner enrolled his son in Urban Military School in Los
Angeles, where he hoped Ronnie's temperament would be tamed by discipli-
nary supervision. Max's decision was made partly out of necessity: the house
was too small for them both. Steiner confided to Louise that he was "leading a
horrible life. My eyes are not getting better [and] do not stand night work very
well any longer. Therefore I commonly awaken about 3:30 a.m., cannot sleep
any more, am too nervous to stay in bed, therefore I am up for the day, don't
know what to do, conduct or write at about 9 a.m. and spend the rest of the nite
looking at Ronnie's picture. . . . I eat alone and badly, because there is no room
in this small house for a cook. . . . To sum up, nothing is right with me or for me,
neither my health, my financial situation, my house, my living conditions."[29]

Deepening Max's pain was his sense of betrayal by his ex-wife. For eight years,
the pair exchanged bitter letters over their son and their divorce settlement.

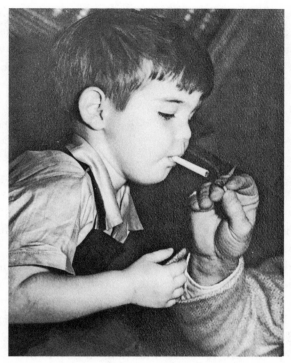

Parenting, Steiner-style. (Louise Steiner Elian Papers; L. Tom
Perry Special Collections, Brigham Young University)

By now, Louise realized that her alimony was insufficient. Max refused to
pay more. "I didn't divorce you, <u>YOU DIVORCED ME</u> . . . fought with me
constantly because I wasn't enthusiastic about your singing career. So far there
have been no results except our divorce and Ronnie being split up between
his parents . . . my entire existence revolves around Ronnie, without Ronnie
I have no longer any interest in ANYTHING, neither in you, anyone else or
myself. Remove Ronnie and everything stops."[30]

HIS SPIRITS IMPROVED SLIGHTLY with a move to a larger home, also on the west
side. Max relied on a chauffeur and friends for transportation, which led to
one amusing incident.

> I had been settled in [the house] only a couple of days when I went to
> a poker game one night in the valley. We played until about three in
> the morning, then Ray Heindorf drove me home. My new residence
> was still so unfamiliar to me that I wasn't sure of the address. We finally

found the street, but it was so foggy that I couldn't pick out the house. I picked out one that looked something like mine with stone steps in front, but I wasn't sure. Ray insisted upon staying with me, so we sat on the steps and reminisced. At dawn's early light we discovered that we had been sitting on the steps of my home all night long.[31]

THERE WAS ONE GLIMMER OF HOPE in Max's life that summer: a new companion.

Leonette Blair was a petite, 5-foot 2-inch redhead of Irish descent, born Leonette Ball in Illinois in 1899.[32] Like Max's earliest loves, she was an ex-performer. In the 1920s she had traveled the country as a chorus girl, an "exhibition hoofer," and a blues singer. "I was not a great one, but I managed to plough through life," she later recalled with characteristic diffidence.[33] By 1946, she was selling real estate.

In Steiner's autobiography, Max paints a meet-cute scenario for their first encounter, describing Lee as a real estate agent who helped him find his home, then nursed him through a cold with delicious dinners. Reviewing this account years later, Louise Klos called it "completely untrue. Max and I had met Lee and her husband, Bob Blair, in 1938. Bob was a manager of a theater circuit in New Orleans. Years later they came to L.A. to live. Bob divorced her for a younger woman, and Lee was very upset, naturally. And Max was a person who couldn't be alone."[34] Steiner echoed that account in a private letter. "Her husband, who was also a friend of mine, divorced her the same time that Louise divorced me, and I suppose that is what threw us together."[35]

The elegant, even-tempered Lee was a perfect partner for Max. "She is probably the kindest person I have ever met," he acknowledged. "Never have I known her to let anyone down who has ever come to her in need. She has a great sense of theater and a terrific memory for music."[36]

Still, Steiner could not forget Louise. Near summer's end in 1946, he visited his ex-wife's rental home in Connecticut to escort Ronald back to Los Angeles. "He told me about Lee," Louise recalled. "I thought that was fine. I liked Lee. At that same time, he asked me if I would reconsider and come back. I told him I would think about it, and I still loved him, but [I said] 'Give me time.'"[37]

Decades later, Louise scribbled stacks of notes about her life. Of this moment in 1946 she wrote hesitatingly, "The decisions one makes at the time most certainly I felt sincerely. Can so easily be critical when the realization of the development of one's life has missed. And yet, I know that I sincerely thought that ..."[38]

Max steps out with Lee at the premiere of *Night and Day*, 1946. (MS Papers; L. Tom Perry Special Collections, Brigham Young University)

Here she stops, and draws a line through the sentences.

STEINER'S STATE OF UNCERTAINTY may explain his surprising hostility toward a prestigious assignment. "I am stuck with this Horrible picture,"[39] he wrote of *Cloak and Dagger*, a Gary Cooper thriller directed by Fritz Lang. It was based on operations of the OSS, forerunner of the CIA, in postwar Europe. The brutal drama anticipated decades of James Bond spy adventures. It also marked the first independent production of Milton Sperling, Harry Warner's son-in-law, whose "United States Pictures" would release its titles under the Warner banner.

Perhaps Max was depressed by the movie's depiction of a devastated Europe, menaced by ex-Nazis.* But as usual, he checked his disdain at the

---

* Steiner felt more in his element writing expansive melodies for another war-themed drama of this era, *Tomorrow Is Forever*. It focused on the toll of war on a single family, allowing Max to write the kind of lyrical score he preferred.

door and crafted a score that heightened the film's air of nightmarish oppression. Much of the music is derived from his main title march, its jack-booted rhythm suggestive of the Fascist powers that drive the story.

For scenes depicting German agents, Steiner featured an obscure wind instrument: the sarrusophone, best known as the sound of walking brooms in Disney's version of *The Sorcerer's Apprentice*. Its frog-like, almost flatulent color was to be used *"only for the Nazis."*[40] And although Max now kept mickey-mousing to a minimum, he felt the technique was right for a scene in which Cooper's laconic spy repeatedly flips a coin in the air, as he awaits a decision from a frightened Nazi agent he's cornered. It's a welcome moment of humor in a score that, like the film, is a grim harbinger of Cold War decades to come.

"You have done a magnificent job," producer Sperling wrote Max on August 15.[41] "All I hope is that we are fortunate enough to get you on all of our pictures." Sperling would request Steiner for five of his future releases.

Max's happiest assignment in 1946 was *Life with Father*, the movie of Broadway's longest running non-musical. Its shoot had been a prickly affair, despite an ideal cast led by William Powell as Clarence Day, the severe but loving patriarch of a New York family circa 1890. Playwrights Howard Lindsay and Russel Crouse exerted veto rights over any changes suggested by Michael Curtiz, and production was also closely monitored by Clarence Day's widow, Lavinia ("Vinnie"), played onscreen by Irene Dunne.[42]

Max could focus entirely on the story's musical pleasures. He saw the Broadway production three times, and met with Lindsay and Crouse to discuss period songs.[43] Much source music was chosen before filming, including "Sweet Marie," used as Vinnie's theme as it had been on Broadway. For a café scene, Max insisted on a tune from Johann Strauss's operetta *The Gypsy Baron*—commissioned for the Theater an der Wien in 1885.

Max wrote only one major original theme, but like Clarence Day it dominates the film. His tune for the arrogant, endearing paterfamilias is one of Steiner's catchiest comic melodies: a cheerfully cocksure promenade that describes Clarence's self-satisfaction. The tune's downward sloping rhythm echoes the emphatic statements Day loves to make: "Da-da-DUM dum-da-dum-dum dum-dummmm . . . " Its certainty is tempered only at the film's climax, when Vinnie experiences a health crisis, and Clarence's theme— usually played by forceful trombones—is heard delicately on *"Oboe solo d'amore . . . dolce."*[44]

Jack Warner was elated by the warmth and wit Steiner brought to the often static film. "DEAR MAX. JUST RECEIVED THE LIFE FATHER REVIEWS

WHICH TREMENDOUS. CONGRATULATIONS AND THANKS TO YOU FOR YOUR PART IN MAKING THIS GREAT PICTURE POSSIBLE."[45] *Life with Father* became one of the highest-grossing films in Warner Bros. history. And although Steiner's Oscar-nominated music lost to Miklós Rózsa's *A Double Life*, Max was thrilled to receive the Golden Globe Award for Best Score.

Life with Father was a rare bright spot in a year dominated by yet more financial anxiety. Declining another request for money from Beatrice, Marie Teller wrote her, "It takes half of Mr. Steiner's salary to pay his federal, state and personal property taxes, and then by the time he pays alimonies, his agent, his chauffeur's salary, my salary, payments on the house, car expenditures, Ronnie's schooling, insurances, and other incidentals, he hasn't anything left of the balance at all."[46]

Based on Max's private letters, she was not exaggerating.

Steiner's dark mood found a perfect outlet in a project that remains unjustly overlooked. Count Martin Scorsese among the champions of *Pursued*, a western noir directed with muscular intensity by Raoul Walsh.[47] Robert Mitchum starred as Jeb Rand, an orphaned loner at odds with his adopted family, who may have been involved in his parents' deaths.

Max admires his *Life with Father* Golden Globe, 1948. (MS Papers; L. Tom Perry Special Collections, Brigham Young University)

As Walsh biographer Marilyn Ann Moss noted, the drama was "rife with Freudian themes: notions of forbidden sexuality, repressed memories, the longing for an idealized family, childhood trauma, and more than a hint of in-cest"[48]—Jeb is in love with his adoptive sister (Theresa Wright). Even daytime scenes have a feeling of perpetual night, thanks to the chiaroscuro camerawork of James Wong Howe. The movie is filled with hallucinatory images: one-armed men. sparkling spurs at a murder scene. Its waking-nightmare feel is mirrored in Steiner's score, as obsessive and intense as the work of Bernard Herrmann.

So why did Max always claim he hated the movie?

The answer may lie in the gulf between his early vision of the story and the final film. Convinced to break his usual policy of waiting to see the edited movie, "I read the script and thought it was the finest I had ever seen [*sic*]. I started writing themes, and I did the entire score. Then I saw the picture. It was terrible. What I had seen in the script was completely changed. I've never been so disappointed in a picture in my life."[49]

Like many Steiner anecdotes, this one collapses under scrutiny. Screenwriter Niven Busch was involved in the production to its completion, and one can hardly imagine a better realization of the script. What's more, Steiner's music—supposedly composed before the movie was "completely changed"—fits the characterizations and atmosphere perfectly. One suspects that Max confused *Pursued* with another film. If not, we can only wonder how his early vision differed from the movie that he scored with such conviction.

His main title theme announces the story's turmoil. The motif is dominated by two notes: a falling half-note pattern that is repeated obses-sively, its thick orchestration for brass suggestive of a hunting call. A churning ostinato below the theme evokes the troubled psyche of Jeb, as he tries to find his parents' killers.

Jeb's flashbacks to the night of his parents' death, which he witnessed as a child, inspire one of the most startling passages in a Steiner score. As twisted images of glistening spurs, torn floorboards, and a frightened boy burst onscreen, strings play a stabbing phrase an octave above their usual range, punc-tuated by brutal fortissimo chords for piano, harps, muted brass, bass drum, triangle, and cymbal. Not until the work of Alex North and Jerry Goldsmith in the 1960s would any Hollywood score use such dissonant, percussive effects.

Even the familiar "Londonderry Air," better known as "Danny Boy," takes on a sinister flavor, as the theme for the Cain-and-Abel relationship of Jeb and adoptive brother Adam. Heard first on a music box, it transitions into the minor key for funereal variations, as the men's conflict becomes a fight to the death.

THE FILM SCORES OF MAX STEINER

1945 Releases (continued)

The Corn Is Green (11/44–12/44). Max's interpolation of Welsh folk songs for this Bette Davis drama was his most extensive collaboration with chorus master Dudley Chambers.

The Big Sleep (2/45). U.S. servicemen saw an early cut of the film in 1945, but the film widely shown today—re-edited and partially re-shot—was not released to the general public until 1946.

San Antonio (3/45–4/45)

Mildred Pierce (5/45–6/45)

1946 releases

Tomorrow Is Forever (7/45–8/45). International Pictures/RKO.

A Stolen Life (9/45)

The Man I Love (10/45–11/45)

Night and Day (12/45–1/46). Max wrote underscore for this legendarily ludicrous (but profitable) biopic of Cole Porter, starring Cary Grant. AAN.

Her Kind of Man (1/46). Additional music.

The Beast with Five Fingers (3/46–4/46)

Cloak and Dagger (7/46–8/46)

1947 releases (continued in Chapter 22)

Cheyenne (6/46–7/46)

Life with Father (9/46–10/46). AAN.

Pursued (12/46)

Solo pianos are another dominant color. In *Pursued*'s quietest yet most chilling scene, Jeb rides his horse across the desert in a wide shot. On a ridge above him, a small, silhouetted figure silently follows on horseback. Steiner takes the two-note, falling semitone pattern of the main title and turns it into a two-note ostinato for pianos, supported by low strings—"BUM-bum, BUM-bum . . . " Few viewers today fail to recognize this as an inversion of the two-note pattern made famous as the shark theme in *Jaws*.

Of course, John Williams's *Jaws* music is not a plagiarism of Steiner. Countless composers have used the same half-note interval in scores—but Max's early use of the device shows how keenly he understood the power of minimalism.

Writer Niven Busch loved the score. "Every time I see *Pursued* I am struck with an increasing admiration for the marvelous sensitivity and beauty of the score which you composed. I hate to think of this beautiful score becoming lost after the picture has played its engagements. Couldn't you round it out in concerto form?"[50] Steiner's old friend Roy Webb also took time to write. "Saw your picture 'Pursued' and thought the score was wonderful. You are still batting 100%."[51]

Steiner was indeed at the peak of his game. And the next two years would give him ample chance to show that, even as he approached his sixtieth year, his gift for creating psychologically incisive music and indelible character themes was undiminished.

This period would also mark the final days of Hollywood's golden age, before upheavals social and technological rewrote the future of cinema—and the life of the medium's most prolific composer.

22

Indian Summer

"I ALWAYS REMIND PEOPLE culture is like a tree," screenwriter Curt Siodmak once observed.[1] "It always blooms one last time before it dies."

For the Hollywood studio system, that final bloom came in the late 1940s. For Max Steiner, it marked the highest point of a long professional crescendo, and inspired a rush of sustained creative brilliance.

By 1947 America was hungry for more adult storytelling, after confronting the brutal realities of World War II. Hollywood responded with more realistic dramas, and a heavy supply of what we now call film noir. Its shadow hovers over most of Steiner's best titles of the time, including one forgotten gem.

Deep Valley starred Ida Lupino as a rural loner who aids an abused convict on the run (Dane Clark) with whom she falls in love. Director Jean Negulesco infused the film with poetry and danger; Steiner heightened both, with a musical character study of a woman who finds courage through tragedy. The score's Ravel-infused harmonies, and a Debussy-like habanera theme, may explain Steiner's many pencil-sketch jokes in French: *"Comprez voos?" "MOIS L'AMOUR TOJOUR."* (Even his crudities are continental. Re. Lupino climbing a ladder: *"She goes up . . . What a girl!! She doesn't know about SOISANT NEUF [69]."*)[2]

Eleanor Aller's solo cello becomes the voice of the emotionally battered girl, who is almost mute due to a stammer. Steiner captures Libby's repression in a scene of unforgettable tension. As she listens helplessly to a torrent of abuse from her father, a storm grows outside, which finally explodes in a rock landslide. The dialogue's slow crescendo is mirrored by a building orchestral rumble that finally erupts in terrifying dissonance.

Steiner was facing his own share of tumult. While scoring *Deep Valley*, "Steve Trilling, Jack Warner's assistant, called me. 'Max, we've got another picture called *The Woman in White*. Fix it up for us. It doesn't need much music, a few bars here and there."[3] (*Woman* and *Deep Valley* had to be finished before a March tax deadline.)

The Woman in White was based on Wilkie Collins's 1859 mystery novel that helped invent the genre—and its screen version needed more aid than "a few bars here and there," since its script turned Collins's thriller into a dialogue-heavy slog. Mitigating the tedium was a literally towering performance by Sydney Greenstreet: his Count Fosco is a gluttonous Napoleon of crime, whose latest scheme involves forced marriage and murder. Max evokes Fosco's money obsession, and Greenstreet's Brando-like girth, in a four-note pattern that climbs with ferocity—pure malevolence, unshatterable force. For much of the score, Max emulated British folk music, flavored with harpsichord. "The most charming English music was produced during the second half of the eighteenth century," Steiner wrote a colleague in 1960.[4] In "*Woman in White* . . . I used the style of contemporary English music, and while the picture was not a big success, the score got wonderful comments." (True.)

Jack Warner loved both scores; but the story of this composing marathon ends on a sour note. Believing that *Deep Valley*'s wistful love theme had the makings of a pop hit, Max persuaded Warners to publish it with lyrics. The song proved "a colossal flop," he wrote Louise, "on account of the picture also having taken such a nose dive."[5]

It did not deter him from trying again, and again.

FAR WISER WAS THE DECISION MAX MADE in spring 1947. "Lee and I have decided to get married," he wrote Louise.[6] "We are both very, very fond of each other and seem to have lots in common. Lee is a very wonderful person, likes music, is a wonderful cook, has a great sense of humor and above all is intensely fond of children. She loves Ronnie and he seems to like her too. That of course is almost the most important consideration."

Read between the lines and one can see the letter as a seeking of permission from the woman he still loved. But if Steiner's relationship with Lee lacked the passion he felt for Louise, Lee's calm presence, intelligence, and patience were exactly what the composer needed.

On April 1, 1947, Max and Lee married in Las Vegas's Little Church of the West.[7] Only Max would choose to be married on April Fools' Day, after a previous wedding on Halloween.

STEINER HAD BARELY RETURNED FROM VEGAS when he started on another compelling noir. *The Unfaithful* was a loose remake of 1940's *The Letter*.

At Warner Bros. Note images of Maximilian and Ronald behind Max. (MS Papers; L. Tom Perry Special Collections, Brigham Young University)

Steiner's approach on the earlier film had been to stand outside the character of Bette Davis's murdering adulteress, using score as a voice of condemnation. *The Unfaithful*, reset in postwar L.A., gave Max a rare chance to revisit a story from an opposite point of view.

This time, protagonist Chris Hunter (Ann Sheridan) is a sympathetic victim who kills her ex-lover, now stalking her, in self-defense. Chris's brief affair took place years earlier during the war, after her marriage to a G.I. she barely knew. Instead of wagging a finger at her infidelity, the film encourages us to understand it.

Unlike *The Letter*, Steiner's music gives compassionate voice to Chris and her growing terror of being caught. That *agitas* is literalized in a syncopated timpani rhythm, which beats throughout the score like a pounding heart (with the same rhythmic pattern as Chopin's "Funeral March"). Only in the movie's last seconds, as Chris and her husband decide to put the past behind them, does the theme change from its oppressive minor key to a celebratory major. The addition of chimes suggests that the marriage will endure.

Steiner's own domestic life was less harmonious. On the eve of his 59th birthday, he was informed by the military school Ronald attended that the seven-year-old was ignoring his studies and acting out. Against the school's recommendation, Max brought his son home for a break.[8] There, the boy was both overindulged and ignored.

Lee did her best to walk the line between winning Ronald's trust and imposing much-needed discipline. She "was a wonderful stepmother," Steiner later wrote, but "she did not sanction my overindulgence of the boy."

Not long after we were married, Ronnie had his heart set on a model airplane that flew by means of a little gasoline motor. The one he chose cost $75 [about $850 today]. It was about six feet long.

I couldn't refuse him, so we bought the plane and showed it to Mommy. "What are you thinking of to spend that much money for a toy for a seven-year-old?" she said. "You're going to spoil him for life!" She was so annoyed with me that she left the house and stayed away all afternoon.

Ronnie and I went down in the garden to fly the plane. It was attached to a long wire. I had been holding the wire. Now Ronnie begged: "Please Daddy, let me hold it." I should have known better, but it was his plane. Of course, he let go and the plane disappeared into the blue.

We searched the entire neighborhood, but we never saw the plane again.[9]

Money was better spent on a new home. On June 23, Steiner made his first payment on a house at 3961 Alcove Avenue in North Hollywood, not far from Warner Bros.[10] Max loved having a back yard again, in which he gardened roses and camellias, and stole brief naps under a shady oak tree.

THAT JULY, THE COMPOSER BEGAN WORK on his fourth film that year. "I think it is excellent," Steiner wrote a friend of the new project, "a combination of *Lost Patrol* and *The Informer*. Not a woman in the cast."[11]

That last sentence illuminates his approach to *The Treasure of the Sierra Madre*, John Huston's searing adaptation of B. Traven's 1927 novel. Male bonding, and division, is at its heart; and as Max observed, the story fused *The Lost Patrol*'s isolation with *The Informer*'s dark view of the power of money to destroy friendship.

Producer Henry Blanke was Steiner's main creative partner: "I never saw Huston."[12] (Huston viewed music "as a sort of necessary evil," according to another collaborator.[13]) Max had a generous five weeks to score the movie, which Jack Warner pegged as a commercial risk. Yes, Humphrey Bogart was a draw—but this was no *Casablanca*. Bogart's treasure hunter, Fred C. Dobbs, is an unshaven bum whose likeability turns to malevolence, as the finding of gold warps his mind against his only two friends. Warner implored Huston to change the story's end, in which Dobbs is beheaded by bandits. Huston refused. The director also insisted that he shoot on location in Mexico with a $3 million budget.[14] It was a staggering sum for a film with no love story, little hope, and a hero who dies headless in a ditch.

Today, the movie is widely considered Huston's masterpiece; but there is no such consensus on the score. Musicologist Christopher Palmer dismissed its main title as "a piece of routine Spanishry" and rebuked Steiner for not writing separate character motifs but rather a "collective theme for the trio and their enterprise, a well-rounded melody admirable enough in its own right, but incongruous and consistently intrusive."[15]

One can imagine a different type of score, as spare as the sunbeaten landscape that dominates the film. But for Max, the purpose of *Treasure*'s music was to illuminate psychology, and to imbue the story with grandeur. For viewers willing to accept his approach, the result offers multiple tutorials in the creation of tension and pathos.

Is *Treasure*'s main title more "Spanish" than "Mexican"? Yes—but geographical precision is no guarantee of good film music. (For *North by Northwest*, which opens in bustling Manhattan, Bernard Herrmann wrote a Spanish-tinged fandango.) *Treasure*'s main title plunges us into a brutal, militaristic soundscape. First comes a thunderous two-note motif representing the mountain that dominates the story. Then Steiner introduces a strident, Stravinskian theme for Gold Hat, the bandit who haunts Dobbs's journey. Before we've seen this killer we feel his menace, with a shrieking piccolo pattern and two-note rhythm ("Ba-*DUM*, Ba-*DUM*"). This pattern evokes the pounding of Gold Hat's horse's hooves; the chug of a locomotive (Gold Hat later attacks the train carrying our heroes); and the pounding hearts of viewers whenever he appears.

The main title ends with the score's central theme: a four-note motto evoking the hypnotic allure of gold. Yes, it is a variation on *The Informer*'s "coin" motif; but the new version surpasses its predecessor with a lustrous beauty and menace. Bernard Herrmann, a master colorist, loved the theme and asked orchestrator Murray Cutter how its sound was achieved.[16] The answer: two celestas, two pianos, harps, two vibraphones, glockenspiel, violins tremolo, and shimmering percussion that included bells and triangle.

Max chose not to score the film's first 21 minutes, as we watch Dobbs join forces with Bob Curtin (Tim Holt) and garrulous, seasoned prospector Howard (Walter Huston, John's father). As in *King Kong*, only when the troupe begins its journey into the unknown—here, the eponymous mountains—does music begin.

Steiner's choice of a single "friendship" theme for the trio, titled "Pardners," is deliberate: initially, Dobbs, Bob, and Howard are united in their mission. Max's upbeat melody, alternately jaunty and stoic, signifies that bond. The theme is crucial in reminding us of the bond's fragility during a scene suggested to Huston by author B. Traven: what if kindly Bob Curtin hesitated before saving Dobbs from a mine cave-in, after gold is discovered? The result shows that even a good man like Bob is not immune to temptation. The fact that he chooses to rescue Dobbs defines the difference between them.

For Steiner, this scene was a perfect chance for music to enhance narrative. After the cave-in trapping Dobbs, the camera holds on Curtin, motionless. On the soundtrack, the gold theme insinuates itself, played in eerie tritones. After several beats, Bob finally runs toward the mine, as Steiner's "Pardners" theme takes over with determination. The onscreen action would be understandable without music. But thanks to the score, we *feel* Curtin's struggle, and celebrate the reawakening of his humanity.

At times, music transports us away from the bleak terrain. As the men reflect on future plans, Curtin shares his happiest memory, of a California peach harvest he joined as a child. "Whole families workin' together. At night, after a day's work, we used to build big bonfires and sit around and sing to guitar music." Softly, as if in a dream, that memory manifests itself in a Mexican folk-style melody, whispered by guitars and mandolins. "It is marvelously tender and evocative," Christopher Palmer acknowledged.[17] "No consciously-composed 'emotive' or 'nostalgic' music would have worked half so well."

Score also represents unseen forces of evil. As Gold Hat and his killers approach the trapped prospectors from a distance, soft percussion makes us feel the threat. Over a ceaseless rhythm, brass and a shrill piccolo evoke our heroes' panic. *"This whole sequence . . . will be played piano [softly] . . . I THINK it will work, in fact be very effective, the THICK TUBA and Trombones, Drums, etc. held down. Should sound very ominous!"*[18]

In *Treasure*'s final third, story and score acquire an almost supernatural overtone. Howard, a healer, leaves Dobbs and Curtin in order to help a sick Indian child. Steiner suggests a ghostly omniscience during the shadow-filled medicine ceremony, augmenting the hushed ensemble with a wordless mixed chorus.

Back at camp, Dobbs's paranoia over their fortune grows. Steiner evokes his mania in a buzzing figure for violins—the furies in Dobbs's mind. Dobbs shoots Curtin and leaves him for dead (a shocking act left unscored). When he returns to find Curtin gone, Steiner's whirling, demonic strings climb higher and higher, the "gold" theme screaming in counterpoint. Finally, all come to a sudden stop, replaced by a violent piccolo trill. *"One tone higher / One tone higher / One tone higher / Crescendo ... "* Then: *"Woodwind—make it shrill!"*

Dobbs's beheading happens offscreen, but stabbing chords make the action clear, with the most violent mickey-mousing in Max's oeuvre. *"MURRAY: HEAD CHOPPING BUSINESS!"* The movie's coda allows Max to blend darkness and light: the prospectors' gold is lost to blowing wind, which Steiner captures with his "gold" theme joined softly by six voices. But Howard and Curtin escape with their lives and can laugh over this final trick of fate. Max accompanies their shared farewell with a chorale-like statement of the "Pardners" theme, *"quasi-Maennerchor"* (like a German male singing club). In a bookend to the start of their quest, Steiner emphasizes fraternity— the opposite of Dobbs's selfishness that ends in his destruction.

After viewing the film with score, Jack Warner wrote his studio's sales manager, "This is definitely the greatest motion picture we have ever made."[19] Many critics agreed, and fourteen months later, *Treasure* won three Oscars, for Best Director, Writing, and Supporting Actor (Walter Huston). With typical magnanimity Max sent the director a telegram. "DEAR JOHN. CONGRATULATIONS. I AM VERY PROUD OF YOU AND YOUR FATHER. BE-LIEVE ME YOU BOTH DESERVED IT."[20] By then, Steiner had been honored by the Venice Film Festival, which named his work for *Treasure* the Best Musical Score of 1948.

TWO MONTHS AFTER *TREASURE'S RELEASE*, Max was assigned a new Huston project: *Key Largo*, a crime-thriller riff on *Treasure*'s themes of greed and en-trapment. Again, it juxtaposes nature—a hurricane in the Florida Keys—with

Humphrey Bogart, Tim Holt, and Walter Huston in publicity stills from *The Treasure of the Sierra Madre*.

conflict among the principals: a World War II vet (Humphrey Bogart); the widow of his fallen friend (Lauren Bacall); her hotel-owner father (Lionel Barrymore); and a crime boss (Edward G. Robinson) holding them hostage in the property.

Max's score is exciting, but at its best in its quietest passage, as Frank McCloud (Bogart) recounts the heroism of his friend George to his widow, Nora. Steiner creates a moving elegy for the dead man, whom we never see; its melody is rooted in the perfect-fourth interval familiar from the opening of "Taps." (Max makes the connection explicit by using "Taps" as counterpoint.) Later, as McCloud struggles to outmaneuver Rocco, this theme transcends its original meaning to symbolize McCloud's heroism and sacrifice.

The film's most famous use of music was not by Steiner. In an act of petty cruelty, Rocco forces his alcoholic moll Gaye (Claire Trevor) to sing for a drink. Producer Jerry Wald wanted to use the standard "Mean to Me"; when rights issues arose, Warners' clearance department suggested an even better choice: the 1929 torch song "Moanin' Low."[21] Trevor's superbly faltering rendition cemented her win of a 1948 Oscar. Her singing is a cappella, emphasizing the frailty of her voice. But after Rocco denies Gaye her promised drink, Steiner provides subtle, empathic commentary, weaving "Moanin' Low" into later cues to remind us of her humiliation.

ELEVEN MOVIE ASSIGNMENTS IN 1947 left Max with little time for seeing anyone—including his own son. Ronald was still out of school and restless at home. "About a week ago he got mad because I wouldn't let him out of the house after dark and he stomped his foot at me and said, 'I wish you weren't my daddy,'" Steiner wrote Louise.[22]

Guilt-ridden, Max bought Ron a television set.

The composer suffered another blow with the death of his beloved aunt Ida, his last relative in Austria. It "was a terrific shock," he wrote, "and only God knows how much of our belongings, antiques, jewelry, books, etc. will have been stolen."[23] He vowed never to return to Vienna.

To bolster his bank account, Steiner wrote every major book publisher, proposing a part autobiography, part "technique of scoring for pictures."[24] He found no takers. Like it or not, Warner Bros. remained Max's best patron—and his assignments in the new year of 1948 inspired two of the best scores of his career.

IT WAS JERRY WALD who convinced a dubious Jack Warner to option *Johnny Belinda*, a modest Broadway hit for playwright Elmer Harris. Wald was drawn to stories that others considered unfilmable; *Belinda* qualified, with its plot of a deaf-mute country girl who is raped, then pressured to give up her child.[25]

After 12 years of forgettable roles, 30-year-old contract player Jane Wyman gave the performance of her life as Belinda McDonald, who escapes her silent isolation thanks to her love for her son and support from a kindly doctor. It was, as director Jean Negulesco observed, a "story of tolerance, the story of a girl child . . . becoming aware of life around her and of her own feelings, the rebirth of consciousness."[26]

Max ensured that its heroine's emotions, conveyed without dialogue, would come through with clarity and poignance. The score's childlike perspective on adult brutality foreshadows Elmer Bernstein's music for *To Kill a Mockingbird*. Its melodic material is varied: a tune with a gentle Scottish hitch for Lew Ayres's Dr. Richardson, cat-like mews played by strings and woodwinds for town gossips.

Belinda's rape gives the score its most intense and unusual sequence. Her attacker is Locky McCormick, a sexually frustrated villager who stalks his target at a dance. When Locky corners Belinda in her home, the dance's fiddle music returns, now as echoing, nondiegetic score. The fiddle's earlier jollity has become a demonic scratching, juxtaposed against a dissonant, sustained chord for low strings and piano (held pedal). *"MURRAY: This 'Violin' sequence never gets loud."*[27]

Low woodwinds and brass are added to the swirling orchestral cauldron below the fiddle. As McCormick attacks, violins and piccolo create the cries that Belinda cannot. For anyone who thinks Steiner was stuck in the past, this sequence is essential listening: it anticipates the solo-violin and dissonant orchestral harmonics used by Jerry Goldsmith in the 1960s and '70s. Steiner also offers a moving coda. After the rape, we hear a minor-key version of the doctor's theme, played on solo cello. Steiner tells us who Belinda is thinking of in her most desperate moment.

Not until the film's 61-minute point—when Belinda is told "You're going to be a mother"—does Steiner play his ace. As the camera holds on her face, showing shock, then happiness, solo violin and celesta play for the first time the score's main theme. It is a lullaby, simple in construction: mostly three-note cells of ascending full steps (B-flat–C-flat–D-flat held for three beats, then an answering G-flat–A-flat–B-flat). It is the kind of melody that hides in plain sight, elemental but beautiful in its flowing lyricism.

Steiner recognized the tune as a standout, which was why a practical joke played on him struck him with terror. Max was conscientious in his efforts not to borrow from other composers, but he knew that the risk of

Stephen McNally and Jane Wyman in a publicity still from *Johnny Belinda*.

accidental plagiarism was ever-present. "Sometimes when I am working on my music at home, Lee will say, 'Papa, you can't do that, it's a steal on such-and-such tune.' This is invaluable help to a composer, because we hear so many tunes that we don't know ourselves whether a tune is wholly ours or another's."[28]

While working on *Belinda*, Steiner shared his melody with Victor Young. "Victor had a sound-proof recording room in his house," Max recalled.

> There was a tape recorder on the wall. He left me for a moment while I was playing, saying, "I'll be right back, I want to straighten some records out. But play *Belinda* again for me, I can hear you from here."
>
> Two nights later we had a poker game at Victor's. When we were assembled, [Victor's wife] turned on the radio and music came on. It was the tune from *Belinda*, beautifully orchestrated and played by a large orchestra. My jaw dropped.
>
> "My God," I asked him, "How did you make a record?" Victor turned to me disdainfully. "What do you mean a record?" he asked. "I wrote that piece. Where do you come off to say that this is your tune?" I was so upset I could not play cards anymore. "My God," I fumed, "I've got to go home and write a new tune."

Victor had, of course, taken down my tune on his tapes as I played, and had spent half the night orchestrating this thing and then had it copied. He had a recording date two days later. He had thrown this piece in and made a record of it. Then he played it back to me as if it was his own. I was frantic until everybody collapsed with laughter and I realized it was a joke. It must have cost Victor $200 to $300 [$3,000 today], but the gag was worth it to him. He thought the whole thing was hilarious.[29]

AFTER SCREENING *JOHNNY BELINDA* WITHOUT SCORE, Jack Warner declared it a bomb, and suggested adding voice-over to convey Belinda's thoughts. But once Steiner's music was added, anxiety turned to excitement. Wald was flooded with letters of praise after an industry preview, including one from Billy Wilder. "What a beautiful, moving job," Hollywood's best-known cynic wrote.[30]

Max in turn wrote Wyman "to tell you how much I enjoyed your performance . . . and what pleasure it was to write the music for the picture. I am sure you will win the Academy Award for your performance."[31] Steiner's prediction came true the following March. But for the composer, Oscar night 1949 was another source of bitterness. *Belinda*'s score was nominated, and Max expected victory—but composer Brian Easdale won for *The Red Shoes*. It was another case of apples and oranges: Easdale clearly was being honored for *Shoes*'s ballet score, mostly used as diegetic stage music. To the end of his life, Steiner remained incensed;[32] but in 1949 he was circumspect. "DEAR JANE," he telegrammed Wyman, "CONGRATULATIONS I AM VERY HAPPY FOR YOU AND YOU DEFINITELY DESERVED IT."[33]

IT'S ONE OF THE MOST-QUOTED STORIES in film music lore. During the 1940s, Max was crossing the Warner lot when he passed Erich Wolfgang Korngold. They paused to speak.

STEINER: Erich, we've both been working at Warners for about ten years now. During that time, it seems to me that your music has gotten worse, whereas mine has gotten better. Why do you suppose that is?
KORNGOLD: That's easy, Steiner. It's because you have been stealing from me and I have been stealing from you![34]

Another version of the exchange was recalled by Erich's son George. In this telling, Steiner ran into Korngold and remarked, "You know, Erich, when you first came to Warners your music was full of energy. But I notice lately it doesn't have the same snap." Korngold replied, "Yes, Max. When I got here I didn't understand the language very well. Now I do."[35]

Each version speaks to a truth: Korngold was tired of Hollywood. In 1947, the 50-year-old abandoned film scoring to write concert music. Warner Bros. was sanguine over his departure, since it was making fewer of the lavish period dramas that were Korngold's forté. But they had hoped he would score a last swashbuckler—one finally in production after eight years of development.

Adventures of Don Juan was planned as a saucier follow-up to Errol Flynn's 1938 *The Adventures of Robin Hood*. Script problems delayed its making, and by the time cameras rolled in October 1947, Flynn had lost his passion for acting and for life.[36] While Max was conducting his *Johnny Belinda* score in January 1948, the actor, looking a decade older than his 38 years, was tottering drunk on a nearby soundstage.

On January 14 production halted for two weeks.[37] Its budget soared past $3 million, as Jerry Wald faced the fact that the old Flynn was gone forever. Fortunately, the producer had steered the script away from drama toward boudoir comedy, with winks at Flynn's image as a hedonist. Wrote Wald in a memo, "The picture should start on a glamorous, high comedy basis and should only touch a sincere note when Don Juan meets the one woman whom he respects."[38]

It was a savvy call, infusing the film with wit and making it even more appealing to its eventual composer, Steiner. In his youth, Max's charm and confidence had won him many female conquests. As he began *Don Juan* in April 1948, his 60th birthday neared. But unlike Flynn, Max's internal flame still burned bright, and *Don Juan* gave Steiner full rein to musicalize his romantic passion.

A common misconception is that Max wrote a "Korngold" score. *Don Juan* is pure Steiner, from its harmonic language to its orchestration, which is more transparent than Korngold's "Christmas tree" of ornamentation. Its satiric humor is Steiner's, as is its famous main title theme—one so catchy that it's reappeared in everything from the George Hamilton parody *Zorro the Gay Blade* (1981) to producer Steven Spielberg's *The Goonies* (1985).

Initially, Max struggled to find the theme. To clear his mind, he and Lee set off for a weekend of gambling in Las Vegas. Author James D'Arc recalls what happened next, as told to him by Lee: "It was during their drive back to Los Angeles that the six-note motif (*da-daaaa-da-dada-daaaa*) came to her husband. [But] they were not accustomed to keeping a cache of manuscript paper in the car. Max was desperate . . . 'He had me singing those notes all during the trip back to Los Angeles so he wouldn't forget them!' Lee recalled."[39] (Writer Curt Hardaway has pointed out that the theme's six notes "perfectly match the full name of the title character, Don Juan de Marana.")[40]

As Don Juan jumps from escapade to escapade, the motif cements a kaleidoscopic score that may be Steiner's most bravura since *Kong*. Latin folk music was a key source of inspiration. "I love to write Spanish music," he wrote a journalist in 1954.[41] "Did you ever see *Don Juan*? . . . I enjoyed doing this picture more than any other I ever wrote."

Amid its whimsy and purring melodies, the score also guides our understanding of Don Juan. We meet our hero as he woos a regal beauty in her castle. Steiner's Serenade uses a Spanish Phrygian scale; its de Falla–like melody for solo violin is decorated with elegant grace notes and birdlike trills (with a meter that hints of Viennese waltz). Welcome to Don Juan Seduction 101: he will use the same love speech, accompanied by the same Serenade, with each of his rote attempts at seduction. Steiner is telling us that the Don can't resist an attractive woman—and also that he chooses not to differentiate among them.

Like Lady Catherine, we swoon at the music's beauty . . . until her off-hand reference to "my husband" stops the Don cold. Steiner underlines this comic halt and Juan's reaction ("Your husband?") with a wobbly clarinet and (phallic?) trombone slide, its cartoonish sound the perfect button to the poetry preceding it.

Juan escapes to the packed streets of London, where a royal procession is taking place. Its pageantry inspires a Technicolor *marcia* for brass, guitars, mandolin, and ten percussion players. Steiner wittily incorporates a fragment of Maurice Greene's 18th-century song "Trust Not the Treason of Those Smiling Lookes"—excellent advice as the Don spots his next would-be amour.

Throughout, Max juxtaposes classicism with playfulness. An exception is his exquisite theme for Queen Margaret of Spain; its haunting, sarabande-like exoticism identifies her as that "one woman [Don Juan] respects." Steiner also was transfixed by the beauty of actress Viveca Lindfors: *"She exits, [Don Juan] stands. Mine would stand too with that girl!"*[42] Later, Max follows the model of Richard Strauss's tone poem *Don Juan*, giving his hero and the queen an achingly beautiful love melody that conveys such genuine regret (the pair must part), one wonders what memories Max summoned for its writing.

Space prevents a full description of the score's treasures—its jagged, clawing motto for ruthless Duke de Lorca or the *accelerando* thrill of the duel scenes (*"I don't want to 'Mickey Mouse' this fight at all"*). Each cue finds the composer at the top of his game, as buoyant as the hero evoked in Steiner's rousing main theme.

THE FILM SCORES OF MAX STEINER

1947 Releases (continued)

Love and Learn (1/47)
Deep Valley (1/47–2/47)
My Wild Irish Rose (3/47). AAN.
The Unfaithful (4/47)
The Voice of the Turtle (5/47–6/47)

1948 Releases

The Woman in White (2/47)
The Treasure of the Sierra Madre (8/47–9/47)
Silver River (10/47)
My Girl Tisa (late 1947)
April Showers (12/47)
The Decision of Christopher Blake (12/47). Max loved scoring this
    dramatic fantasy based on a Moss Hart play. Its music blends
    Mozartean classicism with Carl Stalling burlesque, as we see
    a boy's daydreams inspired by his parents' imminent divorce.
    Ultimately the couple reconcile—an ending that Steiner's own
    parallel drama could not achieve.
Winter Meeting (1/48)
Johnny Belinda (1/48). AAN.
Key Largo (4/48)
Adventures of Don Juan (5/48–6/48)
Fighter Squadron (8/48–9/48)

Adventures of Don Juan was previewed on May 26, 1948, and after seeing the movie with an audience, Jack Warner had just one note about music: *More*.

Warner marveled at the energy Steiner gave to Errol Flynn, who during the filming of some scenes couldn't even stand. At Jack's behest, Max added score for the final duel, which Steiner felt worked better with sound effects alone.[43] Warner was delighted—Jerry Wald and director Vincent Sherman far less so, as they made clear in a letter to the boss. "In the first four reels we do not believe there is five minutes of silence. So please, let's fix it now and not wait for the critics to point out how over-scored the picture is."[44]

The pair detailed a list of proposed music cuts and reductions. Warner disregarded them all, and six decades later Sherman had only raves for Steiner's music. The score, he said in 2008, "was excellent and perfectly fitted the material. Max had a sense of the *bigness* of the film. . . . And he was very cooperative. He knew how to give it the feeling of importance that it needed."[45]

Reviews were enthusiastic, but *Don Juan* was not the box office smash Warner Bros. had banked on. (A re-release of *The Adventures of Robin Hood* that year probably sowed confusion.) For Steiner and his studio, its relative failure that December marked the end of an era: the last, costs-be-damned extravaganza from a factory whose golden days were coming to a close.

TWO MONTHS EARLIER, ON OCTOBER 1, the studio system had been a dealt a mortal blow, with a government ruling demanding "divorce [of] production and distribution from exhibition."[46] Studios had to sell the chains of movie theaters they owned around the world. The ruling eliminated the need to make as many films, and cut off a major source of studio revenue.

Industry news was already sour. By 1948, movie attendance had plummeted from 80 million a year in 1946 to 60 million.[47] It kept falling, as audiences forsook the local Bijou for free entertainment from a new medium: television.

Amid studio tumult and continuous work, Max felt every one of his 60 years. "Thanks for the birthday card and the picture," he wrote Beatrice.[48] "I didn't recognize myself . . . I am fat and old now . . . I am beginning to get very, very tired. . . . It is rather discouraging to have worked as hard as I have to have achieved a measure of success, and then have the income tax people take everything away so that one is not able to save a dollar a week for one's old age."

Steiner had no choice but to soldier on—even as a personal loss reminded him of life's unpredictability, and the toll of Hollywood labor.

23

Falling Star

LEO F. FORBSTEIN WAS IN A JOCULAR MOOD in February 1946 as he reminded Jack Warner's assistant, Steve Trilling, that Max's contract was up for renewal. To convince Warner to approve a raise for their top composer, Forbstein played to Trilling's cynical side, joking that "with the Warner spirit, if [Max] lives for ten years, it will be a miracle."[1]

Two years later, on March 16, 1948, Forbstein died of a massive heart attack. He was 55.

"Yesterday afternoon, Leo Forbstein passed away," a stunned Max wrote his son, who had just turned eight. "What is going to happen to the studio, no one knows."[2] (Nor can we know how an emotionally troubled eight-year-old processed this information.)

Five days later, Steiner was a pallbearer at Forbstein's funeral. More than a thousand mourners listened as themes from Warner film scores echoed through Wilshire Temple, played by a 96-piece orchestra.[3] It was led by the man chosen to be Forbstein's successor: 39-year-old Ray Heindorf, Warners' most versatile music employee since the early 1930s.

Heindorf and Max worked well together. During recording sessions for movie musicals, including those for Warners' newest star, Doris Day, Heindorf took the lead, with Max a more subdued presence. Recalled actress Janis Paige, who worked with them on *Cheyenne* and *Love and Learn*, "The great thing about it was, there was a lack of ego. They helped each other."[4]

For the Day films, Heindorf provided song arrangements, Max the mostly light-comic underscore. The musicals were not the prestige titles Steiner preferred, but he enjoyed these low-pressure reminders of his youthful days on Broadway.

IN EARLY 1949, AS STEINER FACED another year of financial struggle and flagging health, Louise Klos was in a state of bliss. She had saved up earnings from playing harp in two Broadway shows and was ready to realize a lifelong dream: vocal studies in Europe. That April, she sailed for France with voice teacher Richard Hageman and his wife. For six weeks they enjoyed the sights of Paris.[5]

Meanwhile, Steiner's tax woes had climbed to a debt of $50,000, more than half a million dollars today. Max planned to plead with the IRS for a compromise settlement;[6] in the meantime, one constant cause of stress—the demands of film scoring—also proved his salvation.

It is no small irony that novelist Ayn Rand's paean to individualism, *The Fountainhead*, was optioned by Jack Warner. The studio head personified the dictatorial businessman that Rand's hero, Howard Roark, defies in the novel. But Warner himself had a defiant streak; and to his credit, the 1949 film of Rand's bestseller was faithful to its source. (Rand insisted on writing the script.)[7]

The Fountainhead dramatized her philosophy of objectivism, "the concept of man as a heroic being, with his own happiness as the moral purpose of life, with productive achievement as his noblest activity."[8] Its ode to self-interest over teamwork may have been extreme, but it reflected the Cold War tenor of the time. And some of its themes have aged surprisingly well. As critic David Thomson observed, "It's easier now than it was then to see how accurately Ms. Rand had identified a modern subject: the need for dramatic vision in great public buildings, and the way in which that vision must stay private, inspired and uncompromised by urban maneuvering. . . . *The Fountainhead* was and remains a powerful film."[9]

Amid growing emphasis at Warners on cost savings over quality, Steiner connected with the tale of an artist clinging to ideals in a world of mediocrity. His score has the thematic richness of a symphony; indeed, it has an antecedent in one. Richard Strauss's 1898 tone poem *Ein Heldenleben* (*A Hero's Life*) depicts "The Hero," "The Hero's Adversaries," "The Hero's Companion," and "The Hero at Battle"—ideas that correspond exactly to *The Fountainhead*.

Befitting the story of a maker of skyscrapers, director King Vidor stresses verticality in his imagery. Steiner followed suit: his questioning, idealistic theme for Roark (Gary Cooper) spirals upward with vertiginous energy in the score's opening bars. Conversely, Max's theme for Dominique, Roark's emotionally elusive mistress (Patricia Neal), "wends downwards in curves of typically feminine shapeliness," observed Christopher Palmer.[10] The Roark and Dominique themes may move in opposite directions, but Steiner ingeniously links them harmonically, foreshadowing their coming together. And yes, a double meaning is intended here; *The Fountainhead* is all about power and sex.

Gary Cooper in a publicity still from *The Fountainhead*.

Roark's chief adversary is critic Ellsworth M. Toohey, champion of the second-rate. His reptilian, chromatically plunging motif (*"Critic theme...acid color"*)[11] won Rand's approval. "She despised most modern music," wrote Glen Alexander Magee, "and grouped its composers with the creators of modern art as 'envious mediocrities'... The Toohey theme has a kind of slithering malevolence. This perfectly conveys Rand's intentions."[12]

The Fountainhead's most famous scene is also its most imaginatively scored. Early in the film, Dominique gazes down at Roark from afar as he operates a drill in a quarry. He returns her stare. No dialogue—just the grind of Roark's symbolic drill. (The scene's in-your-face eroticism still elicits gasps and appreciative whoops from audiences.) Steiner uses the throbbing low sound of the machine as an instrument: his orchestra consists only of high, ethereal violins, supported by vibraphone, xylophone, and marimba. No rhythm... virtually no harmonic support to the violins... just a pure, dreamy melody line that floats high above the drill's reverberation, evoking desire and imagined consummation.

The Fountainhead was received with hostility by most critics, and its profit was slim. But Max came out a winner, with *Variety* praising his "thrilling accompaniment."[13] Even Ayn Rand was pleased. She shared her thoughts in a now-lost gift sent to Max; he replied, "My dear Mrs. Rand: Thanks for the book and your inscription which I shall always treasure. I'm glad that you liked the music."[14]

Inhabiting the defiant persona of Howard Roark also gave Max a respite from his own losing battles. "I have just worked my entire life for nothing," he wrote Louise of his tax crisis.[15] "The only bright thing in my life is Ronnie." A temporary lifeline came from the usual source. Jack Warner agreed to another loan, and as of March 1949, hundreds of dollars were subtracted each week from Steiner's salary.[16]

STEINER FINISHED HIS STRESSFUL YEAR with three major scores. Two of them closed important chapters in Warner history; the other looked ahead to the sound of a new decade.

Raoul Walsh's *White Heat* gave James Cagney a career-crowning role as gangster Cody Jarrett, whose casual savagery was unmatched onscreen until the Mafioso operas of Martin Scorsese. Max had a scant two weeks for scoring, but delivered the aural equivalent of lit gasoline.

Cody's bloody crime spree ends on the roof of a chemical plant, which he turns into a Hiroshima-like ball of flame. "Made it, Ma!" he screams, a moment before immolation. "Top of the world!" Steiner bases much of his score on this metaphor of ascent and explosion. His main title crystallizes both ideas in a shrieking, octave-leaping theme heard as we see steam from a train. Amazingly, Steiner lifted this theme from his 1938 score for *Angels with Dirty Faces*, also a Cagney vehicle. But in its hypercharged re-orchestration, it is even more perfect for *White Heat*'s protagonist and its apocalyptic despair.

For Cody's bursts of panic, Steiner reimagines the downward-spiraling "buzzing" effect for strings that defined Fred C. Dobbs's mania in *Sierra Madre*. (*White Heat* is filled with fast chromatic runs up and down, evoking a maze that neither Cody nor the viewer can escape.) But in Jarrett's rare moments of calm reflection, Max also shows us the damaged man behind the monster with a forlorn theme for strings and low woodwinds.

James Cagney in a publicity still from *White Heat*.

Steiner crafted an equally incendiary farewell for Cagney's female counterpart at Warners, Bette Davis. The actress would spend decades trashing *Beyond the Forest*, her rancor reflecting anger at the studio after three years of weak scripts and slumping box office. But this "*Madame Bovary* played as pulp fiction,"[17] to quote one critic, is a garish jewel. Davis's adulteress-turned-murderer, Rosa Moline, is a blowsy hot mess. Bored with life in coal-polluted Wisconsin, Rosa pours her toxic energy into affairs. She dreams of escape to Chicago, on a train that—shades of Anna Karenina—will play a part in her demise.

Forty-one-year-old Davis's performance is fearless in its repulsiveness. Steiner stirred the pot with a score that gives hysterical voice to Rosa's sense of entrapment and lust. His main title, one reviewer wrote, "sent lightning-flashes . . . flaring across the screen."[18] A fortissimo two-note pattern leaps up a perfect fourth (*Ba-DUMMM*), then repeats, its second note a half-step down (*Ba-DUMMM*), then repeats, another half-step down. Its hammering syncopation puts Rosa in Steiner's musically congruent world as a "bad" woman, indolent and selfish. The half-step fall with each repetition of the phrase also foreshadows the plot: Rosa's dreams will slip further away with each disastrous decision she makes.

Thick percussion—pianos, celesta, harp in its low register, vibraphone—serves the score's cleverest idea. As Rosa obsesses about a lover in Chicago, she sings a fragment of Fred Fisher's 1922 song of the same name. Steiner weaves the first six notes of its familiar chorus—*Chi-CAH-go, Chi-CAH, go*—throughout his score with increasing frenzy, as the city becomes Rosa's idée fixe. He also links the phrase to the smoky belches and chugging rhythm of the train that symbolizes her dream of escape. By film's end, the theme is a pounding, deliberately assaultive earworm that follows Rosa to her death beside the train she never stopped chasing.

Steiner's score was Oscar-nominated, and received praise from Jack Warner that was as enthusiastic as it was inscrutable. "J. L. is very, very happy," Max wrote a friend.[19] "He said the job reminded him of *Now, Voyager*."

"PILE OUT, YOU TRAMPS, it's the end of the line," snarls a jail matron as we meet nineteen-year-old Marie (Eleanor Parker), a pregnant innocent arrested for a crime committed by her boyfriend, now dead. It's the opening scene of *Caged*, which launched a postwar movie mainstay: the women's prison film.

Realistic for its day with its implied lesbianism and acts of institutional cruelty, it required a different kind of score. Steiner's solution was a gradual transition, from his traditional orchestral ensemble to a looser, jazz-inflected style. *"Quasi Blues—open Trumpet (Hot), Alto Sax (Hot), Brass (open) Hot,"* Max notes for a scene in which Marie's transformation into hardened prison veteran is almost complete.[20] The next year, Alex North received deserved acclaim for his jazz-based score for *A Streetcar Named Desire*. Months earlier, Steiner showed that he was also attuned to the music of his time.

But other cultural changes were more painful to accept. By the time of *Caged*'s release in 1950, movie attendance had dropped 50 percent from its postwar high.[21] Studio staff grew smaller, as actors and directors abandoned seven-year contacts to go independent—or to forge fresh paths after getting a pink slip. Warner Bros.' once-magnificent music department became a ghost town. "I am the only composer under contract," Steiner wrote a colleague.[22] "Last year I only did six pictures at Warners in comparison to twelve the year before."

A month after his 62nd birthday, Steiner was thrilled to learn that he would be loaned to Paramount, to score George Stevens's *A Place in the Sun*. Excitement turned to anger when Paramount refused to meet Jack Warner's price.[23] Franz Waxman got the job, as well as 1951's Academy Award. Months later, Warner Bros. announced that Steiner would score Alfred Hitchcock's *Strangers on a Train*—but the director opted instead for a previous collaborator, Dimitri Tiomkin.[24]

Losing two of the era's most prestigious films was bad enough. Scoring low-budget dreck at Warners felt to Max like punishment for a crime he didn't commit. Most galling was *Sugarfoot*, a Randolph Scott B-western. Steiner's pencil sketches drip with vitriol: *"With STINKING Dialogue."*[25] He closes his score with the oversized penmanship that signaled deepest disapproval. *"EPILOGUE. The only thing I don't understand is why they shot these poor three lousy actors [onscreen] instead of the producer, the DIRECTOR and the scriptwriters! Max."*

AS INSPIRATION FLAGGED, Steiner turned more to reusing old score themes. *Crime School*'s bluesy main title became Joan Crawford's world-weary motto in *Flamingo Road. In This Our Life*'s prelude opened the muddled mystery *Lightning Strikes Twice. Dallas*, one of Gary Cooper's dullest films, reworked Max's score for *The Oklahoma Kid. Operation Pacific*, starring John Wayne, derived action music from *Submarine D-1* and romance from *That Certain Woman*.

Steve Trilling's atta-boy memos to Steiner had turned into admonishments over spending. While scoring *Operation Pacific* in just two weeks, Steiner swallowed his pride and wrote Jack Warner's enforcer, "Dear Steve: After our conversation this morning, I have revised my orchestration and will only use the men whom we had under contract."[26]

One anecdote catches the spirit of the time. "There was a wonderful little guy named Sylvester Singer," Max recalled.[27] "He was a fiddle player, not too great but adequate. Leo Forbstein had given him a contract. I kept him on, and he also chauffeured for me. But when Forbstein passed away, the studio let Sylvester go. He died in the 1950s. Sylvester asked to be buried across from Warner Bros. where there was a second sort of subsidiary Forest Lawn. I asked one of the boys in my orchestra, 'Why didn't Syl want to be buried in the main Forest Lawn?' 'Well,' said my boy thoughtfully, 'I guess he wanted to be close to the place where they fired him.' "

OCCASIONALLY, QUALITY TITLES reignited Steiner's imagination.

By 1950, two young playwrights—Arthur Miller and Tennessee Williams—were reshaping theater, with searing explorations of cracks in the American dream. Jack Warner smelled box office in Williams's Southern-gothic poetry and carnality—a formula that yielded paydirt in 1951, with *A Streetcar Named Desire*. But before it came a film of Williams's first Broadway success, *The Glass Menagerie*. Williams co-wrote the script, and Steiner was invigorated by this "very big picture and a terrific amount of work."[28]

Alas, the movie overinflated the intimate, stifled world of Laura Wingfield (Jane Wyman, game but too mature); her restless brother (Arthur Kennedy); and the family's delusional matriarch (stage legend Gertrude Lawrence, miscast). Max came closest to the play's pianissimo heartbreak. Adopting Laura's point of view, he puts the viewer inside her terror of the outside world and her fragility. He also proved that at 62, he was not too old to innovate.

Steiner carefully crafted "a glass effect in music"[29] to match Laura's collection of tiny animal figurines that give the story its title. *"ETHEREAL—TRANSPARENT,"*[30] he wrote of the ensemble that included small bells, two celestas, two harps, vibraphone, and four muted violins. This delicate ensemble plays one of two themes Steiner gives Laura: a dancing trip up and down the C-major scale (the brightest of musical keys) to evoke her childlike relationship with her glass figures. Its optimism heightens the sadness of Laura's second theme: a two-chord pattern that rises and falls with hypnotic listlessness, as a high, sustained note for violins floats far above in the ether. No Steiner theme captures more hauntingly the paralyzing fog of depression.

Tennessee Williams rightly protested Jack Warner's tacked-on happy ending, which failed to make the film a hit—but the playwright did regard one aspect of the movie a triumph. "Max Steiner has written a beautiful score,"

Williams wrote Warner, "one that I think is really notable, which blends perfectly with the moods of the play."[31]

IT WAS NOT *THE GLASS MENAGERIE* but the composer's next movie—a deliciously old-fashioned swashbuckler—that earned Steiner his sole Oscar nod of 1950. *The Flame and the Arrow* was the brainchild of its star and producer, Burt Lancaster. Eager to escape typecasting as a film noir fall guy in movies like *The Killers*, Lancaster saw *Arrow* as a way to showcase the athleticism he mastered pre-Hollywood as a circus acrobat.[32]

For the first time, the actor's toothy smile invited audiences to enjoy his performance, as Robin Hood–style outlaw Dardo Bartoli. *Arrow* also encouraged Steiner to concoct a score blending balletic energy and bouncy comedy. Its rollicking main theme will stay in your ears for days: ornamented with mandolin, guitar, and harp, its Italianate $\frac{12}{8}$ tune beckons us into a world of carnival celebration, while its ascending intervals reflect Lancaster's lighter-than-air leaps and rope swings that make *Arrow* such a delight. Max was clearly having a ball, even if his sketches grouse over the number of musical notes required. *"Grazioso STINKOSO . . . They run. (THAT'S ALL THESE BASTARDS DO—RUN!!!)"*[33]

THAT SAME YEAR OF 1950, Steiner was elated to conduct his first album of film music, after signing a contract with Capitol Records.[34] With the introduction of long-playing albums months earlier, record companies were finally recognizing the commercial potential in movie scores.

Music by Max Steiner offered suites from his trio of Oscar winners: *The Informer, Now, Voyager, Since You Went Away*. But the composer's spirits were crushed by indifferent reviews, mostly from classical critics with no time for movie scores. Worse, the album didn't sell. "It is very close to a complete flop," he told Louise. "The reason is probably due to the fact that the pictures are too old."[35]

Steiner had hoped its sales would soften another blow: his tax compromise offer to the government had been rejected. "I was asked to pay $42,000 [$415,000 today] plus interest," he wrote Louise. Warner Bros., he added, "asked me to take a 35% cut . . . I am the only one they are cutting so evidently my 'star' is going down."[36]

STEINER SEEMED UNABLE TO ESCAPE into the joy of composing as he had in the past. Remarks in his sketches show an anger often diametrically at odds with the compassion he displays musically on the same page. Case in point: 1951's *Jim*

Thorpe, All-American. Burt Lancaster starred as the real-life athlete considered by many to be the United States's finest, but whose spirit was crushed by an onslaught of problems—the rescinding of his Olympic medals, racism (he was part-Indian), alcoholism, divorce, and the death of a son.

Sensitively directed by Michael Curtiz, *Thorpe* inspired a score that was alternately heartbreaking and galvanizing. In a surprising prelude, Max hijacks his own Warner fanfare with college-style vocal whoops and Indian music inflections. Later, Thorpe's heritage is evoked with more delicacy, as Steiner augments traditional percussion with indigenous instruments.

Then, as Thorpe is exploited and succumbs to self-pity, a change occurs in Steiner's pencil sketches. Musically he writes cues of great empathy—but his comments sour into the most vulgar and bitter on record. *"Happy Indians! (FUCK 'EM!!)" "[Segue] Into highly educational remarks by several verstunkene INDIANER!"*[37] There's much more, and worse.

It is likely that *Jim Thorpe*'s story tapped into Steiner's own fear of growing irrelevancy. The film's protagonist and his race weren't the source of Steiner's anger. Max's penny-pinching employers were.

AS MAX STEWED OVER HEALTH, work, and money, a continent away his former wife was preparing to enjoy the most thrilling week of her musical career. On May 24, 1951, a month before her 45th birthday, Louise took the stage of Paris's *Salle Chopin-Pleyel* to give her first singing recital in Europe. She followed it four days later with a solo recital in London.

Her exhilaration was short-lived.

"Miss Louise Steiner attempted too much," the *Times of London* demurred.[38] "Her voice, whose quality is that of a high mezzo-soprano, has the inherent dignity for *Dido's Lament*, but not the staying power nor the steady line." Britain's *The Stage* took issue with a voice of "unvarying brightness, and although she sang in five languages, an American accent pervaded most of them."[39]

The reviews confirmed Louise's fear that she had begun her new career too late. After a decade of living alone, she was broke and forced to sell belongings to pay rent. No concert engagements lay ahead. Instead, she spent her days writing long letters to the person she loved and resented most, venting mixed emotions of nostalgia, recrimination, and regret.

LOUISE: *No word from Ronnie, not even a card for my birthday. No lines wishing me success for my concerts—no __nothing__! . . . I remember when you were a very thoughtful person.*

Aspiring diva Louise Steiner, ca. 1951. (Louise Steiner Elian Papers; L. Tom Perry Special Collections, Brigham Young University)

MAX: *As usual, you are all wrong. You did not send either Ronnie or me your address in London, so we did not know where to write or wire you.*

LOUISE: *Try to understand my loneliness . . . I spend what little I have to eat and sleep . . . I've become [Schubert's] Wanderer.*

MAX: *I asked Ronnie to write to you but he is so full of play when he comes home after school and what with his piano lessons and the television, he really hasn't much time left; and, therefore, he writes half a letter one night and the other half the next night when, and if, he gets around to it.*[40]

In 1952 Louise returned from Europe to New York, where she sought work as a harpist. She would never sing publicly again.

With resignation came an increasingly conciliatory tone toward Max. "I can't begin to tell you how much I enjoyed seeing you and Lee," Louise wrote after a visit to Los Angeles.[41] "I feel so happy that we have such a lovely understanding and friendship. She is a truly lovely person whom I sincerely admire."

She even came close to the admission Steiner once longed to hear. "My dearest Max, what silly things we do in our lives, and as we look back—begin to appreciate what we really had—in each other. I hope that perhaps you feel as I do? . . . how I wish I could have understood you then as I do now—continued on together . . . I am humbly sorry for any hurt I have caused you, and hope you will try to understand and forgive me. I have played your music very often, and get a real thrill and joy out of it. . . . I'm still in love with your music, and always will be, Max, and after all, that is your expression, so—well—I'll say no more now, but please know my profound admiration of you as a person, as well as a great musician."[42]

AMID A SEA OF CINEMATIC DROSS, one literally gigantic assignment came Steiner's way in the summer of 1952. It became the most influential motion picture of the year—and few would ever know Max was part of it.

This Is Cinerama was the game-changing answer to Hollywood's toughest problem: how to get TV-addicted audiences back into movie theaters. The solution was spectacle. The new format of Cinerama more than doubled the traditional motion picture in size and width. The process used three side-by-side cameras to film a single image; three projectors then screened that image, creating a panoramic effect.

The result, projected on a curved screen, was startlingly immersive—especially when viewers found themselves "riding" a plunging rollercoaster, at the start of the process's debut feature, *This Is Cinerama*. Adding to its sense of realism was six-track stereophonic sound. Stereo was a technology studios had tinkered with for years, but chosen not to utilize; why install expensive sound systems if business was booming? But by 1952, wrap-around stereo was another draw that TV's tinny speaker couldn't match.[43]

Cinerama's backers included Merian C. Cooper, still thinking big two decades after *King Kong*. For him, music would be a key ingredient in the film. He and his team shot a sequence at La Scala opera house, and ended the movie with patriotic U.S. anthems sung by the Mormon Tabernacle

Publicity still for *This Is Cinerama*.

Choir. For everything else, he had one composer in mind. "Max," Cooper told his old friend, "I want you to write the best music you've ever written in your life."[44]

Steiner was eager to oblige. But as Warner Bros. began the paperwork, and Max prepped for a trip to New York to see the giant film format, everything fell apart.

> I had a call from Steve Trilling. "Mr. Warner has changed his mind," he told me. "He doesn't want you to do Cinerama. We have just finished a picture with Gary Cooper called *Springfield Rifle*. It needs a helluva score and he thinks you're the only one who can do it."
>
> My bosom pal, Lou Forbes, was available and this gave me a great idea. Why not put Lou on salary, send him to New York to find out all the details [on Cinerama] and pass them on to me. He could get everything set up and conduct the orchestra. As he sent me back cue sheets, I could write the music here, supervise the operation and the orchestrations. A new system would have to be worked out for our click tracks because all of our ordinary measurements were off for this new medium.[45]

Steiner's role shifted mostly from composing to supervising—while keeping the entire operation secret from Jack Warner. Max put out S.O.S. calls to Roy Webb ("He writes almost exactly like I do," Steiner told Forbes[46]), and to Warner B-composers Paul Sawtell and Howard Jackson. Murray Cutter led an army of orchestrators. Max scored *Cinerama*'s epic climax: a flyover of America, designed by Cooper to show "the beauty and power and glory of these United States and its people."[47] (The arch-conservative intended his movie to be a weapon against communism.)

During a miserably hot summer, Steiner phoned and wrote daily to Forbes. Each week brought new challenges—logistical, technical—and Steiner's fuse grew shorter. "I do not want to appear ridiculous and inefficient in front of these people," he wrote Forbes. "If you will mind me and do exactly as I tell you, you will come off very well . . . This is a big job, Lou, and I am getting killed with it."[48]

Max relied just as heavily on music editor Hal Findlay, who handled the task of turning Cinerama's unique frame rate—26 per second, versus the usual 24—into a new click-track system for composing and recording. As they worked, a deadline closed in: *Cinerama*'s gala premiere was set for September 30 in New York. By August Cooper was tightening the screws on Steiner, even though the movie was still being shot. Coop "told me that the only thing that is holding him up now is the music," Max wrote Forbes.[49] "I explained to him that without cue sheets I was helpless . . . the [prologue], he informed me, is going to be shot the end of the week. How on earth can anybody have music written for a picture that hasn't been shot as yet?"

Steiner's own contribution, for the film's thrilling overview of America's natural wonders, would be the score's highlight. His achievement is all the greater since Max was working from written descriptions of the scenes. If he was able to see any of the footage being edited in New York, history has no mention of it.

Recording sessions under Forbes's baton went smoothly, and the score was delivered just in time. By then, Max also had recorded his music for *Springfield Rifle*—a film forgotten by Christmas. "I have lost my voice completely due to fatigue and worry," he wrote Louise.[50] "My larynx is so swollen that [my doctor] cannot see what is the matter with it." It took weeks of bed rest to fully recover.

It is a testament to Max's generosity—and his woeful lack of self-interest—that he supervised and scored one of the most technically difficult films of the 1950s, as well as one of the most profitable, without charging a penny.[51]

THE FILM SCORES OF MAX STEINER

1949 Releases

A Kiss in the Dark (7/48)

South of St. Louis (10/48–11/48)

The Fountainhead (12/48)

Flamingo Road (1/49–2/49)

Without Honor (early 1949). United Artists.

The Lady Takes a Sailor (6/49)

White Heat (7/49)

Beyond the Forest (9/49). AAN.

Mrs. Mike (9/49) United Artists. Music supervision/additional music. Steiner's contribution included the song "Kathy" (lyrics by Ned Washington), written for co-star Dick Powell. Despite Max's aggressive attempts at promotion, the song was ignored.

1950 Releases

Backfire (circa 1/49). Additional music.

Caged (10/49–11/49)

Young Man with a Horn (11/49–12/49)

The Glass Menagerie (1/50–2/50)

The Flame and the Arrow (circa 3/50). AAN.

The Breaking Point (7/50)

Dallas (8/50)

Rocky Mountain (8/50–9/50)

1951 releases

Lightning Strikes Twice (5/50)

Sugarfoot (6/50–7/50)

Raton Pass (10/50–11/50)

Operation Pacific (12/50)

Jim Thorpe—All-American (1/51–2/51)

I Was a Communist for the F.B.I. (3/51)

On Moonlight Bay (4/51–5/51)

Force of Arms (6/51)

Come Fill the Cup (7/51). Additional music.

Close to My Heart (7/51)

Distant Drums (12/51)

1952 releases

Room for One More (11/51)

The Lion and the Horse (12/51–1/52)

This Woman Is Dangerous (1/52). Additional music.

Mara Maru (2/52)

The Miracle of Our Lady of Fatima (5/52–6/52). AAN.

The Iron Mistress (6/52–7/52)

This Is Cinerama (7/52–9/52). Cinerama Productions Corp.

Springfield Rifle (8/52–9/52)

Taking a back seat in his life was Max's 12-year-old son. Steiner had enrolled Ronald in an expensive private school near home, but the boy remained a poor student. More frustratingly for Max, he was indifferent to music.

> I gave him piano lessons until he was twelve. But he wouldn't keep at it, so we gave up. But one time I took him to the home of a friend who had two young daughters. One of them, Genevieve, was twelve. Her father had bought her a Hammond organ and she played a difficult piece for us called "Pizzicato." Ronnie listened to her very quietly.
>
> When we got home he said: "Papa, buy me an organ." I answered, "You've got to learn piano properly before you go to organ." This is not quite true, but I wanted to get out of buying a $1,500 organ, which I knew would hold his interest for about two days. "Okay," Ronnie agreed, "then buy me the sheet music for the Pizzicato. I want to learn it."
>
> The boy worked on this piece with his teacher for about three days. When we paid a visit to Genevieve's home, Ronnie sat down and played the Pizzicato so well that we were amazed. I reported to Lee, "Now we're in. He'll study now that he sees that he can do it, too."
>
> He never went near the piano after that. He had simply wanted to show this girl that he could do as well as she did.[52]

The year 1953 began with good news: Steiner's 21st Oscar nomination. It came for a rare quality film among his Warners *oeuvre*, *The Miracle of Our Lady of Fatima*, based on the true story of three children in 1917 Portugal who claimed to see the Virgin Mary. Max had been agitated throughout its

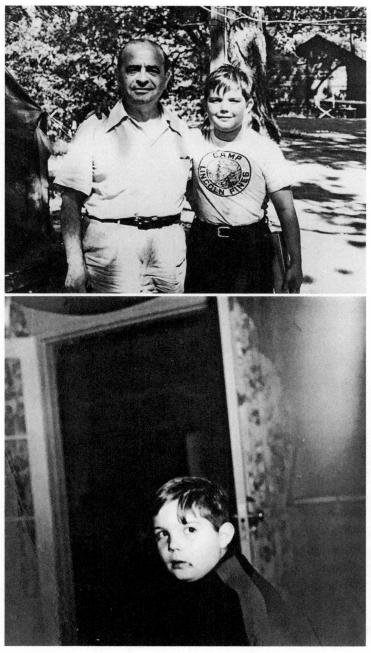

In sunshine and darkness: Ronald Steiner, the little boy lost. (Louise Steiner Elian Papers; L. Tom Perry Special Collections, Brigham Young University)

scoring: "I have to be very careful with the music in order not to get criticized by the church."[53] (In the privacy of his pencil sketches, he was less reverent. *"Harps and Pianos are going 'mad' on account of the picture being just 'so-so.'"*)

Steiner found some of his inspiration from Richard Strauss: *Fatima*'s main theme evokes the awe of *Also Sprach Zarathustra*'s famous opening in its octave-leaping majesty. From its stirring chorales for brass and organ, to its pastoral writing for the children, *Fatima* achieves spirituality without sanctimony. Never mind that Steiner was not religious: he could imagine the conviction of those who were.

Once again, the Academy Award was denied him, and this loss would be particularly symbolic. On March 19, Max's former protégé Dimitri Tiomkin claimed two Oscars for his work on *High Noon*, for score and song ("The Ballad of *High Noon* [Do Not Forsake Me, O My Darlin'])." Tiomkin had not only won dual Oscars on a single night—he accomplished what Max had failed to do for decades: write a score that contained a giant hit song.

Tiomkin's achievement would change movie music—just as it would add to the growing shadow over Max Steiner's future.

PART FIVE

Twilight of the Gods

24

A Jewish Aloha

THE WORLDWIDE SUCCESS of *This Is Cinerama* gave Hollywood a new map for profit-making. And by April 1953, studios had more reason to hope, after the launch of another format that could be experienced only in theaters: 3-D.

To promote *House of Wax*, his studio's first release in three dimensions, Jack Warner enlisted Steiner to score a special advance trailer for the chiller.[1] The movie went on to gross $23 million (more than $200 million today), although its score was assigned to second-tier composer David Buttolph. Max was given a mediocre 3-D western, *The Charge at Feather River*, which had greater need of his dramatic punch.

But 3-D, Cinerama, and Cinemascope—the widescreen format that remains an industry staple—were not enough to halt the studio system's slow fade to black. "There simply weren't enough films being made," Steiner's friend John Morgan observed. "Max was making well over $100,000 a year, and Jack Warner was trying to save money. Also, by 1953 you had producers and directors who brought in their own directors of photography, their own composers."[2]

By summer, as his seven-year contract from 1946 neared expiration, Steiner foresaw what once seemed unimaginable. After 17 years and more than 125 films at the studio, Warner Bros. was about to cast the 65-year-old adrift.

AT LEAST HIS LAST ASSIGNMENTS under contract had quality. *So Big* starred Jane Wyman, in the third film of Edna Ferber's 1925 Pulitzer winner. The usual Ferber formula—a self-sacrificing woman, a multi-generational narrative— was given specificity and warmth by director Robert Wise. Wise had first met Steiner in 1934, when Wise, then a 19-year-old new hire in RKO's editorial department, schlepped film cans to the scoring stage of *Of Human Bondage*.[3]

Nearly two decades later, Wise was delighted to work with "such a fine musician and composer and conductor."[4]

The score's highlight is "Selina's Waltz," a joyous, dancing melody that proved Max's lyrical gifts were as strong as ever when the material engaged him. But the month of its recording was bittersweet. "Steiner to Leave Post at Warners," the *New York Times* announced on July 15, 1953.[5] The article, and others, mercifully characterized his departure as a move versus a push. According to *Hollywood Reporter*, the composer "will devote his time to the music publishing business and to the scoring of a limited number of major films a year."[6] Indeed, Max did have ideas about publishing, prompted by 20 years of watching others profit from his work while he saw next to nothing in royalties.

Fittingly, his last movie under contract teamed him once more with his favorite director, Michael Curtiz. The 66-year-old Hungarian was also being shown the door by Warners, the company Curtiz had joined in 1926. Their parting effort was *The Boy from Oklahoma*, starring Will Rogers Jr. It was no classic, but no disgrace.

"My dear Mike," Max wrote on July 20, "I just saw 'Boy from Oklahoma' and I think it is a very cute picture and you did a swell job as usual. Although you do not need much music in it, I will try my best to help whenever it is possible."[7]

He closed with two sentences that said much between their lines.

Isn't it curious that "Boy from Oklahoma" was your last picture for Warners and it will also be my last picture at this studio?

Do you know that my first picture with Warners was 'Charge of the Light Brigade'—so I started with Mike Curtiz and I will finish with Mike Curtiz.

Curtiz replied with a note equally brief but also full of feeling.

Dear Max,
I sincerely appreciate your wonderful letter and hope we will be able to work together again.

I think of you always as a fine man and a great artist.
Wish you all happiness and the best of health.[8]

As one would expect, Max's sketches for *Boy* are filled with asides about his soon-to-be-ex-employer. *"Diminuendo . . . Coach out of sight! Going away from Warner Bros. too!"*[9] As cowboys musicalize: *"I want them to sound rather happy. They don't know what Warner has in store for 'em!"* And on the final page, a comical cartoon of an Indian in profile: *"Fine! Aloha! Oy!! A Jewish Aloha! See you again . . . Chief Thundercock."*

By August 21, Max had cleaned out his office and left the lot, in a departure that haunted him to the end of his life. "I have had many disappointments," Steiner said in 1970.[10] "I feel bad about Jack Warner, who did not even say goodbye after all those years with him."

FOR DECADES, MAX HAD THREATENED to quit Hollywood for new pursuits. Now, that path had been forced on him—and he knew he had only a short window of time to spin his dismissal as an upward career move.

Steiner reached out in every direction he could think of. A telegram to old friend Alfred Newman, music director at Fox. (Result: an invitation to "get together," but no work.)[11] A bid to score the next Cinerama release. (New producers chose other composers.)[12] A letter to David Sarnoff, asking if "you might have a niche for me in your network." (Sarnoff's office replied, praising Max's "wonderful work," and Steiner began talks with RCA Records.)[13] A letter to David O. Selznick, now barely working after years of worsening neuroses and amphetamine use.

"According to the papers you are going to be active again," Max wrote, "and I would be very grateful if you would talk with me about your publishing tie-up, as I am going into the publishing business myself."*[14] Significantly, Steiner offered himself not as a composer but as a publisher. Max's first work in America had been as a copyist at the publishing house Harms. Now, Harms's manager Max Dreyfus led an even larger company, Chappell; and in 1953, 79-year-old Dreyfus was receptive when Steiner proposed "Max Steiner Music," a subdivision of Chappell that the composer would run from Los Angeles.[15]

The two Maxes signed a three-year agreement, and on September 17, Steiner moved into his first L.A. office not on a studio lot. "I cannot tell you how happy I am to move back into 'My Old Home,'" he wrote Dreyfus.[16]

Even better, Steiner had secured a major motion picture score, for which he would retain the publishing. Columbia's *The Caine Mutiny* was among the most anticipated dramas in Hollywood. Based on Herman Wouk's bestseller, it told the (fictional) story of a venerated naval captain

---

* Steiner and Selznick discussed reteaming for a stage musical of *Gone with the Wind*. Neither was alive by the time two poorly received adaptations limped on the boards in 1972 and 2008.

whose breakdown prompts the mutiny of its title. Humphrey Bogart played the unstable Captain Queeg, in his 12th and last collaboration with Steiner.

Producer Stanley Kramer convinced Max to take $10,000—below Steiner's asking price.[17] But Kramer sweetened the deal by giving Max publishing rights and, according to Lee Steiner, by promising future collaborations.[18] "Columbia undoubtedly will be after me for albums, etc., as soon as they hear something recorded," Steiner wrote that October.[19] But soon, elation became anxiety. Kramer's previous production was *High Noon*, which spawned the song hit "Do Not Forsake Me O' My Darlin.'" Kramer's expectations were every bit as high on *Caine*.

"Steiner is having sleepless nights and tasteless meals these days," noted the *San Francisco Chronicle*.[20] "He's trying to compose a theme for *The Caine Mutiny* that will end up on the hit parade. According to Steiner, his problem . . . is to develop a theme which is dramatic, naval, happy, and exploitable—all in eight bars . . . 'So far I haven't written a note. Just writing a theme is not difficult. What's hard is writing a composition that can be exploited. . . . The range you can use is lessened because a human voice does not have the range of the orchestra. . . . Although I'd like to make everyone happy with a hit, I may end up with a simple composition. If so, I hope they'll all forgive me.'"

He knew they wouldn't.

The result was a catchy anthem titled "Full Speed Ahead." Similar in spirit to "Anchors Aweigh," Steiner's rousing march tune ticked all the boxes Kramer demanded—dramatic, naval, upbeat, exploitable. But unlike Tiomkin's ballad for *High Noon*, which evoked the western's main conflict of a showdown between a sheriff and a band of outlaws, the jaunty "Full Speed Ahead" had nothing to do with *Caine*'s real story: the battle between an erratic captain and his crew. Instead, Max's tune largely existed to placate the U.S. Navy's concerns about a negative depiction of their branch. As such, it was more an addendum than an encapsulation of the film.

The movie itself offered little room for music. "Just between you and me, 'The Caine Mutiny' score is not so great," Steiner wrote a friend, "because the picture does not provide an opportunity to show up the score."[21] He also bemoaned the pecuniary tyranny of studio head Harry Cohn: "We had 46 musicians or thereabouts. . . . This whole Columbia outfit is an awful cheap bunch."[22]

By February 1954, Steiner held out hope for just one aspect of the project. A long-in-the-works album would combine Max's score with dialogue from

Score paper becomes larger as Max's vision worsens, ca. 1954.
(MS Papers; L. Tom Perry Special Collections, Brigham Young
University)

the film. The first of three records he signed to make for RCA—a result of
his note to David Sarnoff—the *Caine* disc was widely expected to be a smash.

But a month before the film's release, Herman Wouk refused to allow dialogue from the movie to be included on the album. After a few test discs were
made, the record was killed.*[23]

The Caine Mutiny became 1954's second highest-grossing film, earning
seven Academy Award nominations, including Best Score. But the Oscar
went to *The High and the Mighty*—scored by Dimitri Tiomkin.

Kramer never asked Steiner to work with him again.

BY SUMMER 1954, MAX'S PUSH for new work was giving way to weary disappointment. Major pictures came tantalizingly close—Billy Wilder's *Sabrina,*

---

* In 2017, Steiner's score was released on CD. One wonders if Wouk, still alive at age 102,
picked up a copy.

Douglas Sirk's *Magnificent Obsession, Strategic Air Command* starring James Stewart—but each deal fell through.[24] The reasons varied: salary demands, Steiner's desire for publishing rights, industry ageism, and rivals' gossip about his sight. Rumors about the latter were all too true. "I can no longer see lines on the music paper without a magnifying glass," Max confided to Louise.[25]

"It seems that nothing I touch comes off," he wrote attorney Leonard Zissu.[26] "I have cut my living expenses in less than half and we have put our house on the market . . . I am very depressed and worried."[27] Then, the most defeated sentence in all of Max's letters:

"I never thought that that could happen to Steiner."

INCREASED TIME AT HOME forced him to confront a crisis he'd long overlooked. Ronald, now 14, was increasingly unstable. Max prided himself on keeping acetate recordings of his scores; Ronald often gave them to friends, or shattered the discs in fits of anger.[28] Unsupervised, the boy roamed Los Angeles using the Steiner name to charge expenses.

Louise was now living in L.A. doing occasional studio work. At last she could share custody of her son—but Ronald felt little connection to the mother he barely knew. "I am very sorry to hear about the trouble you had with Ronnie," Max wrote her.[29] "I don't know what to do or what to say. He acted up with me when he was here once or twice, but I slapped him down. You see he is now at the worst age. He is not a boy anymore and he isn't a man as yet either . . . you will have to just try and overlook these little outbreaks."

When Louise returned to New York to play harp in the Broadway hit *Kismet*, Ronald traveled with her for a month. There, he was left to wander the city alone and incur more debts. He had developed an obsession with fast, expensive cars, just as his father had as a teen. But although his parents were nearly broke, Ronald asked Louise to "find out the exact prices" of a Maserati ("my favorite car under $10,000"), urging her not to tell dealers "that I am only 14 years old. Be sure that they think you are interested in it."[30]

By July, even Max recognized that his son was out of control. The result was an extraordinary six-page letter in which Steiner tried to be firm, but acknowledged his own weaknesses.

My darling boy . . .
There will have to be a complete change of attitude and habits as far as you are concerned if you want to stay at 3961 Alcove Ave. . . . Mind you, I am not blaming you entirely. This is partly due to my great love for you and that I spoil you continually, due to the fact that I was trying

to make a broken home up to you, etc., all of which is incidentally not my fault, but someone else's. However ... you have become very arrogant and unmanageable.

When Al [a servant] read that you were coming home he said, "Oh Lord, the good times are over." [Cook] Alma also expressed the belief that if you ever talked to her again like you did on the day you left for New York, she would quit and never come here again ...

I no longer will wait for you to come home late at night from downtown when you have been to a show. ... There is a curfew on here now on account of these youth gang boys and unless you are home by 9:00 you will be picked up by the police ...

You will never again be allowed to talk to me either the way you did before you left because the next time you do, I am going to slap you, but good, and believe me, I can do it even if you are bigger than I am. I never spoke to my father in the tone that you speak to me, and it is the beginning of a very bad omen for your future ...

Why do I write all of this today? Because of the following: I am not well. My eyes have taken a sudden turn for the worse and I have decided to take the A.T.C.H. treatment which is a very dangerous drug. ... I cannot have any excitement or nervousness because this drug can bring on a heart attack and I could drop dead at any moment ...

I am sure that my boy is a good boy at heart. ... Try and fit in with us. I haven't had a drink in two weeks nor will I ever again be able to have a drink so that is one phase out of my life that will have stopped. One of the reasons that I sometimes did drink is because of my great concern and worry over you ...

One more thing ... When I hear how you talked to [Lee] the day she packed your things to go to New York, I was so disgusted that I couldn't even talk. She was not feeling well and you were lying there on the bed watching TV and letting her pick up your clothes, shoes, and bend over and pack for you. You didn't even deem it necessary to help her lift the bag on the bed after the awful operation she had. ... Then in the afternoon you went out with that homosexual, Stanley ... when I had told you NOT to go out with this man.

... Of course, my darling boy, this doesn't mean that we don't love you and are looking forward to your homecoming. I miss you so much that I have been sleeping in your room all the time you are gone.[31]

That fall, Max and Lee enrolled Ronald in Blair Military Academy in New Jersey. There, his grades remained poor, and a Thanksgiving visit to Louise in New York was a disaster.

"[He is] arrogant, demanding, and defiant," she wrote Max.[32] "I have explained to him time and again about the financial situation . . . he says it bores him to talk about it . . . you have <u>spoiled</u> him, but instead of stopping it, you continue to give him anything and everything he wants. . . . Max, how I would love to just talk with you someday about our son. He is such a fundamentally good kid, but it has to be brought out."

Max promised to have a talk with Ronald, but nothing changed.

PROFESSIONALLY AT LEAST, Steiner caught a break. Seven months after leaving Warner Bros., he learned that his ex-boss didn't wish to end their association: Jack just wouldn't pay him an annual six figures. Instead, Warner hired Max on a per-picture basis, starting with *King Richard and the Crusaders*, the studio's first Cinemascope, stereo feature. Jack "told everyone that he has come to the realization that you have to make bigger and better pictures in order to survive," Steiner wrote Louise. "I hope he meant it."[33]

The composer asked for $12,000 and publishing rights. Warner countered with $10,000 and no publishing. Max accepted.[34] "I am working like a weasel," he wrote Leonard Zissu.[35] "Nothing but battles [in the movie]."[36] Like most early Cinemascope titles, *Richard* prioritized action over characterization (Rex Harrison's sly sultan is the sole acting treat). Much of *Richard*'s music is in the fanfarial vein of Miklós Rózsa scores like *Ivanhoe*, but Max's voice is distinct in the propulsive fight scenes, which take full advantage of the spatial separation stereo allowed.

Jack Warner fell in love again with the scope and sweeping romance of Max's music and hired him for an even bigger feature. *Battle Cry* was the studio's expensive entry into the war-is-hell genre launched by Columbia's *From Here to Eternity*. Raoul Walsh directed what was conceived as a three-hour film of Leon Uris's bestseller about U.S. Marines who put aside their ethnic differences to wallop the Japanese at Guadalcanal and Tarawa.

Steiner was ecstatic to be working on what he considered "one of the greatest pictures I have ever seen."[37] His spirits were also buoyed by a pay bump to $12,500. But Warner Bros. decided to shorten *Battle Cry* to 149 minutes, allowing one more theater showing a day.[38] Max was writing to a three-hour, 15-minute cut, and many of his best cues were discarded, with just one standout theme remaining. That melody was inspired by the usual marketing imperative: "If Steiner can write a good hit tune . . . it would be a great help," Raoul Walsh wrote Jack Warner.[39] "Give him a bottle of Manischewitz wine and maybe he will come through with that one."

The result was "Honey Babe," a lusty march based on an Appalachian folk tune, and sung throughout the film by its heroes. With lyrics by three-time Oscar winner Paul Francis Webster, "Honey Babe" sold decently as sheet music and helped Max earn a surprise Academy Award nomination.

Just as satisfying was the decision of RCA to allow him after 15 years to record *Gone with the Wind*. Spurred by a theatrical re-release of the film, Max arranged the score as a 38-minute suite, conducted in London by the respected Muir Mathieson. Finally, Max had a successful album—one that remains in print more than 60 years later. There was also a new pop adaptation of the Tara theme titled "My Own True Love," with lyrics by Mack David (of Disney's *Cinderella* and *Alice in Wonderland*).

Sheet music sales earned Max $2,000 within months of the song's release;[40] and further financial assist came from *Helen of Troy*, a Warner Cinemascope epic which paid Max a stellar $17,500.[41] *Helen* was motivated by the hot movie trend of sword and sandal spectacles. In an inspired choice, Robert Wise was hired to see if a new ingredient—intelligence—could be added to the toga-filled formula. He largely succeeded.

Helen gave Max another beautiful heroine to be inspired by in Italian actress Rossana Podesta, cast as the eponymous "face that launched a thousand ships." The score would be Steiner at his coloristic best; his only work set in mythic pre-history, it revels in sensuous themes, including a riotous use of harp to suggest pagan splendor.

Max achieves the difficult task of evoking Helen's godlike status, as well as Podesta's warm accessibility, with a melody both soaring and tender. His musical research is clear from his use of Aeolian (early Greek) scales, but his climactic battle cues are thrillingly modern, with much use of his favorite two-note, semi-tone rhythm (i.e., the future *Jaws* motif), played with percussive, harshly accented ferocity.

BUT DESPITE STEINER'S SIZABLE PAYDAY for *Helen*, the composer remained in dire financial straits. And as usual, there was trouble with Ronald. Blair Academy informed Max of the 15-year-old's close friendship with a man in his late 50s. Steiner poured out his frustration in a letter to Blair's headmaster: "Ronnie does not easily make friends and even when he does, he has a terrific crush on a boy one day and the next day they don't talk any more."[42]

It would be Max's last letter to Blair. That month, he failed to make a necessary payment. By summer, Ronald had left the Academy and was living again at home.

"Max Steiner Music" had also proved a bust. Max Dreyfus, Steiner wrote his lawyer, "has no interest in anything but show tunes."[43] No wonder: Dreyfus's clients included Lerner and Loewe, whose *My Fair Lady* was about to open on Broadway.

In fall 1955, Steiner made a last bid for success as publisher, with a radical action that would have been unthinkable to him three years earlier.

Republic Pictures was a studio synonymous with low-budget programmers and Saturday morning serials. But president Herbert J. Yates was not averse to the occasional quality title; and by 1955, television was gutting Republic's profits by offering similar second-tier entertainment. Yates was ready to gamble again on prestige. When the studio head offered Steiner a pair of well-mounted films, plus half of the music publishing, Max agreed—leading to one of Steiner's finest movies of the 1950s.[44]

FIRST CAME THE ALSO-RAN. *The Last Command*, directed by Frank Lloyd (*Mutiny on the Bounty*), chronicled events leading up to the battle of the Alamo. Republic's streamlined telling focused on frontiersman Jim Bowie (Sterling Hayden) and reduced the climactic siege to just seven minutes of screen time. Max's best music in the film is for the Alamo itself. He gives the abandoned mission a quasi-religioso theme of beauty and sadness, conjuring the ghosts of sacrifices past and soon to come. His red-blooded song for the main title, performed by Gordon MacRae, captures Bowie's spirit with catchy syncopations ("What a maaaan was 6-foot 6 Jim *Bow*-ie"). Max was clearly hoping for a *High Noon*–style hit—the tune becomes the motif for Bowie, and for courage itself—but Steiner's ambitions were dashed by the movie's obscurity.

It was Max's second film for Republic that deserves a much higher place in movie lovers' affections. *Come Next Spring* marked a happy reunion with two other Warner Bros. refugees: stars Ann Sheridan and Steve Cochran. Cochran optioned *Spring*'s script and produced the drama, in a bid to move beyond his typecasting in gangster roles. The bucolic *Spring* was set in 1920s Arkansas, where reformed alcoholic Matt Ballot (Cochran) returns to make amends with the wife and two children he abandoned 12 years earlier. Its story of family bonds slowly rebuilt, amid quiet joys and near-tragedy, is a forerunner of 1985's Oscar winner *Places in the Heart*, and no less moving.

Much of Steiner's score is based on a heartfelt main title theme, sung over credits by Tony Bennett. Although the Bennett single made Britain's Top 30 chart, Americans ignored it, preferring another movie-inspired song: Bill Haley's "Rock Around the Clock" from *The Blackboard Jungle*. The latter marked the first appearance on Billboard charts of rock 'n' roll, a genre soon to leave songwriters like Max in the dust.

Despite disappointing record sales, hopes remained high for *Come Next Spring*. "Given a careful exploitation and selling campaign," *Hollywood Reporter* noted, "this little film might acquire the prestige and literary dignity of a rural *Marty*"[45]—1955's Best Picture winner.

But Republic dumped the movie amid mounting business woes.

Today, the timeless story of *Come Next Spring* and its touching score await rediscovery. Along with *We Are Not Alone*, it is the most unfairly neglected title in Steiner's filmography.

THE FILM SCORES OF MAX STEINER

1953 Releases

The Desert Song (9/52–10/52)

The Jazz Singer (10/52–11/52). Underscoring for Warners' remake starring Danny Thomas and Peggy Lee. AAN.

By the Light of the Silvery Moon (12/52)

Trouble Along the Way (1/53)

House of Wax. Advance trailer only. (4/53)

So This Is Love (4/53). Steiner's last movie musical.

The Charge at Feather River (5/53–6/53)

So Big (7/53)

1954 Releases

The Boy from Oklahoma (8/53)

The Caine Mutiny (11/53). Columbia. AAN.

King Richard and the Crusaders (4/54)

1955 Releases

Battle Cry (6/54–8/54). AAN.

The Violent Men (8/54). Columbia.

The McConnell Story (spring 1955)
Illegal (spring 1955)
Helen of Troy (2/55–6/55)
The Last Command (5/55). Republic.

1956 Releases (continued in Chapter 25)

Hell on Frisco Bay (summer 1955)
Come Next Spring (fall 1955). Republic.
The Searchers (10/55–11/55)

By October 1955, 67-year-old Max quietly let his dreams of a publishing empire die. He had little fight left. "I had a slight heart attack," he wrote Louise.[46] "My eyes are getting gradually worse and I am just not sharp any-more . . . If the studios ever found out . . . I would never get another picture."

But fate was kind in bestowing one last gift in 1955: Steiner's final screen masterpiece.

THE SEARCHERS CAME TO MAX not via its director, John Ford, but its producer. Merian C. Cooper envisioned a reunion of the creative trio behind two of his most acclaimed projects, *The Lost Patrol* and *The Informer*. But the renewed partnership proved a rocky one. Ford eschewed a big-orchestra approach in his films, preferring spare folk song accompaniments. When Cooper proposed hiring Steiner, a compromise was struck: country vocalist Stan Jones would write and perform a title song with his group, the Sons of the Pioneers (a Ford favorite). Max would incorporate Jones's melody throughout his score.

The blend fit the film magnificently. Jones's ballad delineates anti-hero Ethan Edwards (John Wayne), a loner who spends years roaming post–Civil War America, hunting for the niece who was taken as a child by Indians. *What makes a man to wander? / What makes a man to roam? / What makes a man leave bed and board / And turn his back on home?*

The Searchers forces us to answer these questions for ourselves. First-time viewers wonder if Ethan will embrace—or execute—the girl he seeks, Debbie (Natalie Wood), after Ethan learns she has become a Comanche chief's bride. Edwards's search for missing family probably struck a chord with Max, who anguished over the disconnect he faced with his own son.

The mystery at Ethan's core is brilliantly explored in Steiner's music. It transforms Stan Jones's plaintive tune into a complex orchestral character portrait: heroic, isolationist, tragic. Typical is an early exchange between Ethan and his brother Aaron. Aaron is Debbie's father, and husband of Martha, the woman Ethan secretly loves. As the brothers speak, cellos play a wordless quote from the title song: *What makes a man to wander?* By playing this phrase at this moment, Steiner answers part of the song's question.

By the early 1950s, Steiner's use of American folk songs had become standardized to the point of reflex. For *The Searchers*, Max reached deeper. The list of folk themes he used, some at Ford's instruction, is a long one—but never before did Steiner use this music with such psychological acuity.

Ethan's service in the Confederacy is mentioned only in passing, but this key element of his makeup is accentuated with the Southern anthem "Bonnie Blue Flag." And if *The Searchers'* title ballad defines Ethan's obsessive quest, a second song defines his heartache, and the tie that binds him to Debbie. The 1857 ballad "Lorena" is a song of lost, forbidden love. Its lyrics—not sung in the film—suggest the depth of Ethan's love for Martha, and allow the viewer to wonder if his feeling was reciprocated. "We loved each other, then, Lorena, more than we ever dared to tell . . . A duty, stern and pressing, broke the tie which linked my soul with thee."[47]

It is "Lorena" that we hear, played by yearning violins over solo guitar, in *The Searchers's* legendary first shot, as Martha opens the door of her dark home to frame herself in the light of the expansive prairie beyond, and Ethan approaches. The tune returns in a variety of guises: a minor-key dirge as Ethan finds Martha's ravaged body; the breaking up of the search posse as Ethan, Martin Pawley, and Brad Jorgensen begin their quest alone; and Ethan's first sight of the adult Debbie, now a hated Comanche—but also Martha's daughter.

The "Searchers" and "Lorena" themes are united at the film's climax, as Steiner crafts one of the great dramatic sequences of his career. As Edwards confronts the terrified Debbie, after killing her Comanche husband Scar, Ethan's "Searchers" theme churns with psychotic fury. We are in Debbie's mind, seeing her uncle as a monster fueled by hate and vengeance.

Music crescendos as Edwards steps forward and scoops Debbie into his arms—an act that mirrors his picking her up as a child in the film's first scene. Then, as if transformed by this contact, Ethan silently changes. On the soundtrack, a rhapsodic statement of "Lorena" signals this psychological shift. Without the need of words, strings convey the hopefulness of the ballad's final lyrics: *We'll sing those songs again, Lorena, you'll be in my arms again.*

As Ethan carries his niece away—"Let's go home, Debbie"—Steiner's music tells us that a third person walks alongside them, unseen but not forgotten.

Natalie Wood, John Wayne, and Jeffrey Hunter in a publicity still from *The Searchers*.

Steiner is no less inspired in his original themes. *The Searchers* opens and concludes with a violent statement of Scar's theme, the finest "Indian" music in Steiner's oeuvre. The Comanches' shadow, it seems, will always hover over Ethan.*

While Merian C. Cooper was pleased with Steiner's work, Ford was not. The director "felt there was too much music in the picture," historian/director Peter Bogdanovich recalled.[48] "[Ford said,] You've got a guy alone in the desert, and the London Philharmonic's playin'!'" Although most of Steiner's score remained in the film, enough cuts and changes were made to cause co-producer C. V. Whitney to send Max a conciliatory letter that December.

"It looks as if the picture is a smash hit," he wrote.[49] "I am sorry you are not altogether satisfied with the musical score as cut, but I can assure you that the end result is typically American. This, I am sure, is what Mr. Ford wanted to achieve."

---

* Kathryn Kalinak observed that just as Puccini's *Tosca* opens with a statement of the murderer Scarpia's theme, the pun-loving Max begins *The Searchers* with the theme of its killer, Scar, and even labels the cue "an Indian *Tosca*." See Steiner's original pencil sketch, MSS 1547, 136.

FOR MAX, COMPLETION OF *The Searchers* inspired both relief (he was exhausted) and depression (he was unemployed). The future had never been more uncertain.

It is fortunate that the 67-year-old could not see what lay ahead; for although he was soon to achieve one of the greatest ambitions of his lifetime, it would come at an unimaginable cost.

25

Götterdämmerung

AN AMERICAN MASTERPIECE. A film ranked among the ten greatest by *Sight & Sound*. Accolades for *The Searchers* have been near-continuous—at least, they have been since the 1970s. In 1956, it was just another well-reviewed money-maker; and instead of giving Max Steiner's career a relaunch, its release that May marked the start of a long, agonizing stretch of unemployment for the 68-year-old.

Talks with George Stevens to score the epic *Giant* collapsed, after Dimitri Tiomkin swooped in.[1] Max's secretary of 25 years, Marie Teller, suffered a heart attack and was forced to retire.[2] With her departure, Steiner lost the most important organizing force in his life.

Ronald was now a danger to himself and others. For his 16th birthday, Max bought his son a Volkswagen, with predictable results. "I don't see him from morning til night," Steiner wrote Louise in April.[3] "His birthday was March 2nd and to date he has 6,000 miles on his car. The repairs to date total $400. [A] trip to Las Vegas almost wrecked the car forever. . . . He forgets everything you tell him, such as locking the house up when he goes out. . . . The other day [we] asked him to get some tomatoes from the store; he made three trips and forgot them every time."

Ronald stayed home long enough that spring to write his New York–based mother a letter. Its spelling and unsteady scrawl suggest the writing of a boy half his age. "Things at home are not very good at all. Daddy . . . told me he never has been this worried all the time he has been in America. . . . We may have to move into a small apartment soon."[4] And months later: "I am getting a 1947 car for $80 and if I take car [*sic*] of it daddy will help me buy a better car around Christmas. . . . Daddy doesn't have any money right know [*sic*]. . . . He owes the government $22,000."[5]

"Today I am out of work exactly <u>one year</u>," Max wrote Louise.[6] "I have no money at all and do not know where to get any. . . . Sorry this is such a sad letter. I am almost crazy with worry."

BY NOW, STEINER'S MUSIC WAS HEARD more often on television screens than in movie theaters. RKO's film library had been licensed for TV showings in December 1955.[7] *King Kong* became inescapable on American sets, and never left pop culture again. Other studio libraries followed—and the explosion of old movies on television offered a fresh round of ammunition to Max, as his two-decade fight for ASCAP residuals entered a new phase.

The composers group he co-founded was 360 members strong. Now called the Composers and Lyricists Guild of America, it re-approached ASCAP and proposed royalties for film scoring on a per-minute basis.[8] It was the start of a concentrated four-year battle.

A rare bright spot of the time was a celebration of the group's ten-year anniversary. It was "a real humdinger of a party," David Raksin recalled.[9] Max, "the guest of honor, was presented with a plaque engraved with flamboyant though quite sincere prose. . . . He was, [he said,] touched, but a plaque? It would have seemed, he continued, more appropriate for the Association to have given him, say, a new Cadillac or maybe even Marilyn Monroe. He paused for reflection and said quietly: 'On the other hand, I'm not sure what I would do with either of them; I haven't driven in years.' What a man!"

ALTHOUGH STEINER RETAINED MANY FRIENDSHIPS in the industry, his closest one was on the rocks. By 1956, Victor Young's continued success in film, TV, and records sparked gnawing jealousy in Max. A tipping point came when Victor was named music director of a TV special produced by David O. Selznick, which earned Young an Emmy.[10]

But on November 10, 1956, envy gave way to grief. Victor Young was dead, the victim of a cerebral hemorrhage at age 56.

"When my buddy died, I gave up cards and have never touched them since," Steiner wrote in 1964.[11] "Without him, it just doesn't seem right to play anymore."

Hollywood gave Max a way to say goodbye. Young had just started work on *China Gate*, a Vietnam-set thriller written and directed by firebrand Sam Fuller. Years ahead of most Americans, Fuller knew of the pact between the United States and France to combat communist takeover of Vietnam. Fuller turned fact into pulpy fiction, with the tale of an undercover mission to kill

Commies sent "directly from Moscow." Leading our heroes is a Eurasian chanteuse-turned-spy named "Lucky Legs" (Angie Dickinson).

Young had written a title song to be performed in the movie by Nat King Cole. Young also sketched a few preliminary motifs—just enough to get Steiner started. "I offered to finish my dear friend Victor's score for almost nothing."[12] Fuller, an admirer of both composers, agreed.[13]

Pencil sketches confirm that the final score was written by Max and Howard Jackson, who had assisted on *This Is Cinerama*.[14] Steiner emulated Young's style with a sexy, sax-wailed theme for Lucky Legs. He also used his late friend's rough sketches when possible. The result was seamless, but nothing in the music was as affecting as the card that appears in the film's opening credits:

"Music: VICTOR YOUNG. Extended by his old friend: MAX STEINER."

It is easy to imagine who suggested the card's wording.

MAX'S SOLE OFFER after *The Searchers* came from RKO—a studio now crumbling after years of mismanagement by Howard Hughes.

Death of a Scoundrel was a juicy melodrama, starring George Sanders as a rake and fraudster who is found murdered in the opening scene. The story then flashes back to chart his affairs and betrayals. Steiner counterpoints the movie's cynicism with a deliciously lyrical score. For anti-hero Clementi Sabourin, Max concocts a Hungarian-style folk tune for cimbalom, a zither-like instrument that hints at Sabourin's peasant origins. He also delivers a thunderous, brass-heavy "doom" motto for the film's open and close. It reminds us that while Sabourin may enjoy a life of decadent delight, his ultimate fate is harsh. Max rarely joked in his sketches anymore—he could barely see the paper—but *Scoundrel*'s main theme inspired a droll annotation: *"Gone with the Wind at Tehachapi."*[15]

Max scored two more RKO titles in 1957. *All Mine to Give* was a poignant, fact-based tale of an immigrant family in 19th-century America whose children must find new homes after their parents' deaths. Its score was Steiner at his emotional best; his wistful main theme nods at the family's lineage with a lilting Scottish hitch, while subtly suggesting the tragedy ahead. But like his other RKO title, the family film *Escapade in Japan*, *All Mine to Give* was little seen, and by 1958 the studio had finally gone bust.

IN LATE 1957, JACK WARNER CALLED AGAIN. The reason was obvious: who better than Max to score a Civil War–era drama starring Clark Gable?

Max summed up *Band of Angels'* shortcomings when he called it *"Gone with the Wind—Junior."*[16] Although based on a novel by Robert Penn Warren (*All the King's Men*), *Band* was an inert love story masquerading as social drama. Its hero is Gable's Hamish Bond, who falls in love with a mixed-race servant while grappling with the ghosts of his slave-trading past.

The film played "like a creaking D. W. Griffith tale of the South, injected with anachronistic allusions to the 1950s Civil Rights movement," critic Glenn Erickson observed.[17] But Steiner's score is first-rate. His jaunty theme for Hamish plays at a slow gallop tempo, suggesting an older and wiser Rhett Butler. The minor chords that end its melody suggest a man who has seen too much to retain his early romantic illusions.

Steiner's last project of 1957 was more promising. *Marjorie Morningstar* was Warners' lavish adaptation of Herman Wouk's latest novel, about a wide-eyed Jewish girl (Natalie Wood) who Learns About Life after being seduced by a self-centered theater director (Gene Kelly). Producer Milton Sperling had considered Alex North for the score, but at the 11th hour he opted for his old good luck charm Steiner.[18]

Like the movie, Max's score is attractive and superficial. His rapturous main theme for Marjorie suggests the wide-eyed gaze of every male in her orbit but little of the character's inner life. More empathic is his music for her Uncle Samson, played by Ed Wynn, an old friend of Max's.[19] Samson is an entertainer facing the last act of his life—another Steiner surrogate. Max defines him with a warmly comic theme for woodwinds that reflects his loping walk, his humor, and his unfailing support of his niece. In the film's closing minutes, Marjorie returns to the summer camp where Samson last performed, and died. As she reflects on the scene, Samson's theme quietly returns. All too briefly, music illuminates a character's thoughts, as Marjorie recalls the one person who loved her unconditionally.

STEINER WAS GLAD TO BE WORKING AGAIN, but all of his earnings were siphoned to creditors. Another loan from Warner Bros. for $5,000 barely helped.[20] And his 70th birthday on May 10, 1958, was a time of gloom: a strike by the American Federation of Musicians had shut down all recording in Hollywood. Instead, scores were recorded on the cheap in England, Europe, or Mexico. The practice continued even after the strike, as Max discovered when after an eight-month hiatus he received a call from Warner Bros.

John Paul Jones, starring Robert Stack, had been in the planning since Errol Flynn's heyday.[21] But not until the late 1950s did producer Samuel Bronston clinch financing for a biopic about the American Revolution's best-known naval hero ("I have not yet begun to fight!"). It was shot mostly in Spain due to European financing, and production dictated that it be scored in London. As a result, that October Steiner returned to Britain for the first time in 44 years. He also braved a lifelong fear of flying, making his only trips by plane.[22]

It proved an unhappy visit, due to "miserable damp and cold weather." And the movie, Max knew, was "not so hot."[23] But he pumped its episodic narrative with patriotic fervor. The first three notes of his clarion main theme match John Paul Jones's name; in a simple, incisive choice, Max uses a perfect fourth interval (F, down to C, back to F) to capture in a mere trio of notes the iron will of Jones's character, before his theme unspools into a rousing march melody. Had this tune been used for *The Caine Mutiny*, Stanley Kramer might have had the song hit he desired.

The score's tuneful majesty was further proof to Jack Warner that there was still creativity to mine from Max. No sooner had Steiner returned from Britain than he was assigned a new film. It would put him on a fresh career trajectory.

Max had briefly crossed paths with director Delmer Daves in 1949, when Steiner scored the forgettable comedy *A Kiss in the Dark*. Since then, Daves had distinguished himself with provocative westerns like *Broken Arrow* and *3:10 to Yuma*. In 1958, Daves continued his winning streak with *The Hanging Tree*, a western that allowed Gary Cooper to add darker shades to his persona—a trend begun in Cooper's previous film, *Man of the West*.

In Daves, Steiner gained a sympathetic director and a loyal friend. Both men were unafraid of showing emotion, and both were noted for their warm sense of collaboration. "Delmer had a perpetual smile on his face," actress Janis Paige recalled.[24] "He was a tall, handsome man with wonderfully piercing eyes. I was doing something in my first film, *Hollywood Canteen* [directed by Daves]. I looked at Delmer and he had big tears in his eyes. It was so impressive to me that he could get moved by his actors. He was a happy, hard-working man who loved what he did."

The Hanging Tree would be the finest of Steiner and Daves's eight collaborations. Dramatically, it lives in the same hellish prairie-verse as *The Searchers*: Cooper plays Joseph Frail, a mysterious drifter new to the fractious mining town of Skull Creek, Montana. Frail takes in the sole survivor of a stagecoach attack (Maria Schell) and tries to protect her from a lecherous miner (Karl Malden). Attempted rape, murder, and Frail's near-hanging by a mob create an almost unremitting tone of brutality and sadness.

De rigueur for the time, its score would be built around a title song, with music by Jerry Livingston and lyrics by Mack David. The song was a good fit for the drama, and Steiner easily adapted its tune into a foreboding leitmotiv; it defines Cooper's haunted hero and the mystery of "the hanging tree." Only in the film's last, briefly hopeful moments does the tune seem intrusive. A faux-Elvis vocal and electric guitar undercut the poetry of the closing shot, as Frail slowly leans down to kiss the woman who saved his life. His silent act of submission was made for a Steiner musical coda, but commerce dictated otherwise.

BY SPRING 1959, MAX AND LEE HAD SOLD their North Hollywood home and resettled in the area that for Steiner symbolized success: Beverly Hills. For a deposit, he may have used his payment for the film that, on paper at least, was among Warners' most important that year.

Hovering over *The FBI Story* was its unofficial producer, J. Edgar Hoover.[25] The widely feared FBI chief signed off on each element of the 149-minute docudrama, and not surprisingly, the movie became a hagiographic slog. Even Jimmy Stewart as a fictional agent recounting the bureau's big wins—killing Dillinger, capturing Soviet moles—couldn't give the film a human heart. But Steiner's score is written in the tense, crackling vein of *The Hanging Tree* and imbues the movie with what excitement it possesses.

Intriguingly, his main title march, the FBI theme, is a major-key variant of the fascistic march he wrote for 1946's *Cloak and Dagger*, which chronicled the OSS's hunt for Nazis. Max was probably drawing a line between the FBI's focus on anti-communism and the OSS's pursuit of Hitler's cohorts. The theme is a gift to *The FBI Story*: in a film that jumps from vignette to vignette, music suggests a throughline of injustice being fought through the decades. When Hoover heard the stirring march as the movie screened at Radio City Music Hall, he reportedly wept.[26]

By now, Warner budgets had crept back up to A-picture level. Max was being paid a healthy $1,250 a week (more than $10,000 today) for near-continuous work.[27] He was also being hired for more than one picture at a time; and concurrent with *The FBI Story* was a new teaming with Delmer Daves.

That project, *A Summer Place*, would change Max Steiner's life.

BY THE MID-1950S, HOLLYWOOD WAS AIMING much of its product at teenage baby boomers. It was an audience that preferred dark drive-ins to plush movie palaces, and pop-rock ballads to the orchestral sounds of Steiner. But with 1957's *Peyton Place*, 20th Century Fox unlocked the key to luring both generations into theaters. *Peyton Place* was a steamy tale of lost virginity, rape, and other sexual scandals in a "respectable" New England town. When Sloan

Wilson's 1958 novel, *A Summer Place,* created another bestseller about libidi-
nous teens and their hypocritical parents, Warner Bros. snapped up the rights.

Delmer Daves cast Dorothy McGuire and Richard Egan as ex-sweethearts
now trapped in loveless marriages to others. Sandra Dee and Troy Donahue
played their children, whose biological pull toward each other is thwarted
(for a time) by their disapproving parents.

The soapy drama benefited greatly from Daves's humanism. "I have two
kids who are just about the same age of these two in *A Summer Place*," he said,
"and I know how difficult communication between generations can be."[28] For
music, a young composer like Leonard Rosenman (*Rebel Without a Cause*)
was the logical choice. But Daves believed that Steiner could capture the
struggles of both generations in the story.

On May 13, 1959, three days after his 71st birthday, Steiner signed a contract to score the film for $15,000.[29] He was thrilled to tackle material that
demanded a strongly emotional approach and chose to emphasize the gener-
ational divide between adults Sylvia and Ken, and their children, Molly and
Johnny.

For Sylvia, he rescued a theme written two years earlier. It was intended for
David O. Selznick, who in 1957 was auditioning composers for what became
his last production, *A Farewell to Arms*.[30] Selznick passed on Steiner, but it

Troy Donahue and Sandra Dee in a publicity still from *A Summer Place.*

was just as well: Max's soaring theme would find far more listeners as the voice of Sylvia's suppressed desire.

To evoke location, the composer also self-borrowed, using his autumnal main theme from *A Stolen Life*, which was set like *A Summer Place* on coastal Maine. So far, so familiar.

It was in Steiner's approach to Molly and Johnny that he accidently stumbled onto the musical Madame Curie moment he had sought for decades.

Logically enough, Max decided that a theme for the kids' immature but intense relationship should sound as young as possible. He wasn't a fan of the "Blueberry Hill"–style pop that was replacing Crosby on the charts, but he was certainly aware of it. And he decided that a theme with a similar, simple style would suit the characters.

It is impossible now to hear "Molly and Johnny's Theme"—better known as "Theme from *A Summer Place*"—without thinking of what it has come to represent. It takes only a second to recognize the tune: just play its opening piano-triplet figure, which introduces high, unison violins playing a dreamy, in-the-clouds melody. The emotion it elicits may be pure camp: *Ah, the 1950s, in all their polyester glory. Does anyone still write Muzak?* But for listeners introduced to it in the early '60s, it also connotes a time of lost innocence—nights in a back room or beach house, before Dealey Plaza, Vietnam, and all the rest destroyed the American Dream.

"The melody and harmonic structure is very straightforward, bright and breezy," John Morgan observed, "and has none of the Wagnerian-Straussian chromatic harmonic complexities Steiner employed in so many scores in the past. His chordal progressions for the Molly and Johnny Theme is reminiscent of that four-hand piano ditty 'Heart and Soul,' which every kid who had a piano played, and which conjured up 'young.'"[31]

According to Max, it was Warner music publisher Victor Blau who first spotted the tune's commercial potential: "Nobody thought it was worth a damn but Victor."[32] Steiner saw the tune with a dismissive eye. "He told me that he was actually making fun of rock 'n' roll," Morgan recalled.[33] "He said, 'The cliché is the piano: [sings triplet rhythm] da-da-da, da-da-da . . . ' Once he came up with those chords, he couldn't help but write a nice melody to it."

By July 1959, with the film in post-production, Blau was encouraging music industry colleagues to give a listen. Lyrics were commissioned; but their female point of view (*"I . . . grew up last niiiiight"*) were deemed a mistake by the studio: "We'll have a pretty tough time of getting a male vocalist to do this."[34] A new set of lyrics, by Mack Discant, were accepted.

But a recording destined to make pop music history convinced everyone that words were unnecessary. On September 11, 1959, one of America's most popular "easy listening" arrangers, Percy Faith, entered New York's Columbia 30th Street Studio.[35] There, he led the Percy Faith Orchestra in an instrumental recording of "Theme from *A Summer Place*." The arrangement was almost identical to the version heard in the film, as orchestrated by Steiner and Murray Cutter. Faith's recording was released as a single just ten days after its recording, one month ahead of the movie.[36]

In stores across the nation, it sat collecting dust.

A Summer Place the film attracted more attention when it premiered on October 22, 1959—but not always the kind Warner Bros. hoped for. Critics mostly panned it, with the *New York Times* blasting "one of the most laboriously and garishly sex-scented movies in years."[37] That same critic derided "Max Steiner's music hammering away at each sexual nuance like a pile driver."

The winsome "Theme from *A Summer Place*" hardly hammered away— but it did get under listeners' skins. Audiences flocked to the movie, and exited theaters humming Steiner's theme. In January 1960, Percy Faith's single began climbing up the charts. And on February 22, "Theme from *A Summer Place*" became the Number One record in America. It remained there the following week . . . and the next . . . holding the top spot for an unprecedented nine weeks.

That record was unbroken until 1977. Astonishingly, 71-year-old Max Steiner had written what *The Billboard Book of Number One Hits* calls "the most successful instrumental single of the rock era."[38] Recorded by more than thirty artists, "Theme" sold 7 million copies (3 million were of the Percy Faith recording).[39] Its success ricocheted around the globe: in the UK the Faith single charted at Number Two. In Italy the tune reached Number One, as "Scandalo Al Sole."

"I have just had the biggest hit in twenty years in the music business," an ecstatic Steiner wrote a colleague in July 1960.[40] "It is number one in Italy, Japan, Hong Kong, etc."

The phenomenon led to another milestone. On April 13, the 3rd Annual Grammy Awards were held in Los Angeles and New York. Nominated for Record of the Year were "Are You Lonesome Tonight?" (Elvis Presley), "Georgia On My Mind" (Ray Charles), "Mack the Knife" (Ella Fitzgerald), "Nice 'n' Easy" (Frank Sinatra), and "Theme from *A Summer Place*" (Percy Faith).

Elvis, Ray, Ella, and Frank all lost, to music by a man who four years earlier couldn't find a job.

Few pop tunes have resurfaced in as many movies, invariably for laughs. Max himself started the trend, using the theme jokingly for a make-out party in 1961's *Susan Slade*. In 1971, Charlton Heston roamed an empty Earth in *The Omega Man* listening to the tune on 8-track tape. Since then, its soothing strings have cued a satiric-narcotic mood in *National Lampoon's Animal House, Diner*, Tim Burton's *Batman, Ocean's Eight, Mad Men, The Simpsons, The Shape of Water*, and too many others to mention. There's even a disco version.[41]

MAX HAD COMPOSED ONE OF THE BEST-SELLING SONGS in the history of recorded music. In a plot twist worthy of Hollywood, he had succeeded by not really trying. It "was amazing," John Morgan recalled.[42] "He said it wasn't his intent. It was a happy surprise."

That surprise fulfilled two of Steiner's greatest ambitions. Not only did it give him a record-breaking hit; within three years of the song's Grammy win, 50 years of financial struggle were finally behind him. The Percy Faith disc and sheet music sales alone brought Steiner more than a quarter of a million dollars within months—more than $2.2 million today.

THE YEAR 1960 BROUGHT MORE GOOD NEWS. Four years after the Composers and Lyricists Guild of America renewed its battle with ASCAP over residuals, a decision was finally reached—in the composers' favor. ASCAP agreed to pay film composers for past works aired on television (and later, for releases on video and other formats).[43] The verdict would earn Steiner and his estate millions in the years ahead, making it doubly certain that Max would never be hungry again.*

A Summer Place guaranteed Max a spot on the Warner Bros. composing roster. Most of his titles during the next two years would be for Delmer Daves, who sometimes referenced Steiner's anticipated contribution when writing a new script.[44] Max was deeply grateful.

Those collaborations—*Parrish, Youngblood Hawke*, and others—doubled down on the sudsy slush of *A Summer Place*, with diminishing creative results. All offered illicit sex among photogenic youth and treacly scoring far below Steiner's best. One factor trumped their flaws: the movies made money.

---

* ASCAP royalty statements are available only to their recipients. But at least 150 Steiner films were shown during his lifetime on television; and since ASCAP royalties generally equal or exceed record sale royalties, TV showings of *A Summer Place*—plus the many films that reused its theme—likely generated millions by itself.

Warner Bros. also rewarded Max with two big-budget films of Broadway hits. *The Dark at the Top of the Stairs* was a haunting adaption of William Inge's drama, about a traveling salesman (Robert Preston) losing his magic touch on the road and in his marriage. *A Majority of One* offered one more chance to score romantic comedy, as Rosalind Russell's Jewish widow finds love with a Japanese bachelor (Alec Guinness, in typical casting for 1961 Hollywood).

Steiner even dabbled in television, writing cues for the Warner-produced series *Hawaiian Eye*. But despite TV's lucrative potential—royalties could be enormous—Max quickly lost interest. He griped to a reporter, "They have fitted [music] into four categories: 'Hurry,' 'Fight,' 'Love Scene' and 'Mysterious.'" He also summed up the beats of TV drama, which he said ranged "from 'Oh, you S.O.B.' to 'I Love You.'"[45] After royalties for *A Summer Place*, he could conveniently forget that most of his film projects could be similarly described.

THE FILM SCORES OF MAX STEINER

1956 Releases (continued)

Death of a Scoundrel (mid-1956). RKO.

1957 Releases

China Gate (late 1956–early 1957). 20th Century Fox.
Band of Angels (7/57)
All Mine to Give (summer 1957). RKO.
Escapade in Japan (12/57) . RKO.

1958 Releases

Fort Dobbs (circa 10/57–11/57)
Marjorie Morningstar (circa 12/57–1/58)

1959 Releases

John Paul Jones (circa 12/58–1/59)
The Hanging Tree (circa 9/58–10/58)
The FBI Story (circa 3/59–4/59)
A Summer Place (7/59–8/59)

1960 Releases

Cash McCall (circa 9/59–11/59)
Ice Palace (3/60–4/60)
The Dark at the Top of the Stairs (circa 5/60–6/60)

1961 Releases

The Sins of Rachel Cade (8/59–1/60)
Parrish (fall–winter 1960)
Susan Slade (circa 3/61–4/61)
A Majority of One (8/61–9/61)

1962 Releases

Rome Adventure (1/62–2/62)

In interviews of the time, Max depicted his life as one of domestic tranquility, interrupted only by the latest scoring request from Mr. Jack L. Warner. And if Steiner's life were a Warner Bros. biopic, his story would end here.

But one subplot in the drama, long overlooked, was about to explode.

RONALD STEINER'S 18TH BIRTHDAY IN 1958 had brought Steiner fresh alarm. Now legally an adult, the boy continued to rack up debts, leading Max to write two dozen L.A. businesses, to "notify you that my son . . . is not authorized to charge any purchases or bills to my account or on my credit."[46]

Louise grew concerned enough about Ron's behavior to take music jobs in Los Angeles to be near him. One day she received a call from Max, urging her to come to his home.

> Max said to our son, "What do you want from me, Ron? I give you everything, I give you money, I give you carte blanche to do whatever you want, what do you want?" Ronnie said, "Daddy, I just want to be able to talk with you. To ask you different things. But you never have time."
> And there, I'm afraid, was the answer.
> Ronnie drove to New York by himself several times to see me. He'd pick up people to give them a ride; he'd feel sorry for them. One time he picked up a sailor. I said, "Ronnie, you're taking chances. Be careful."[47]

Ronald Steiner, ca. 1961. (Louise Steiner Elian Papers; L. Tom
Perry Special Collections, Brigham Young University)

By 1961, 21-year-old Ronald was still living with Max, with vague dreams
of becoming an actor. Steiner used his influence to enroll him at USC, one of
the West Coast's most expensive colleges. When Ronald failed to show up for
classes, his father finally had had enough.

November 14, 1961
My dear boy . . .
    To come in to me after I had been recording for eight hours and
say to me, "Dad, I am going to New York"; I said "When?"; you said
"Now", was quite a shock.
    You left a path of bills. Apart from this I have given you $100 a
week for months, sometimes $50 extra. I paid for two years tuition at
USC and you never went.
    Now we see an application for a three channel telephone [in your
car]. What do you need a phone in your car for . . . and who do you
think is going to pay for it? I want you to stop such nonsense. I think

you are a little bit out of your mind, thinking you need a three channel telephone in your car like I need Khrushchev's hat.

I suggest to you that you try and get a job in New York, in a gas station or wherever it is possible, and also go and see all the theatrical agencies and see whether you can finally cash in on all the money that we have spent for you on your dramatic education . . . all of which fell into the toilet . . .

I also think it would be best for you to stay away a while until things have cooled down. I have told you over the phone that we have received threatening phone calls. One of them suggested that he would like to beat you up because you charged something at his place . . . now he wants to knock every tooth out of your head when he sees you . . .

I am 73 years old, I do not wish to move, especially with my eyesight failing and my so very necessary exercise in the pool each morning, without which as Dr. Beigelman tells me, I would have been blind long ago. I had very great trouble writing "Majority of One." My eyesight has so deteriorated that I am almost helpless . . .

How about the army? This might do it. I hate to see you go, but it is better than just lying around doing nothing.

I am sorry to have to write you a letter like this, but I am half out of my mind. I have to have an operation for prostate trouble . . . and you want a three channel telephone in your car. How long do you think I can keep on loving you like I did for 21 years?[48]

In March 1962, Ronald Steiner enlisted as a private in the U.S. Army.[49] On April 27, while based in Fort Ord, California, he disappeared.[50]

The note's stationery was elegant. In the top-right corner, the words "Royal Hawaiian Hotel" were embossed in a handwritten font. Did Ronald know that his parents had stayed at that hotel for two idyllic weeks in 1938?

His note was a single page.[51] Its opening words echoed most of the letters he had written his mother: formal and apologetic.

Saturday 9:00 pm
Dear Mom,
Thanks for the Easter Card. I was very thoughtful [*sic*] not to have sent you one and I'm sorry. I couldn't adjust to army life and life in general so the only thing left to do is to take my own life. Please don't be to

upset because it way [*sic*] bound to happen sooner or later. I love you
very much and am sorry for the way that I've treated you at times. Give
grandma my love and know my spirit will always be with you. All my
love for ever and ever your son
     Ronnie

On April 29, Max was finishing work on his latest Delmer Daves picture,
Rome Adventure. At 7 a.m., the telephone rang.

"The Associated Press called and told me that my son was dead," Steiner
would recall.[52] "He had committed suicide at the Royal Hawaiian Hotel in
Honolulu. He had gone AWOL from Fort Ord, driven to San Francisco,
wrecked his car trying to kill himself and then took a plane to Hawaii. I was
absolutely devastated at the news. I loved my child very dearly. He was a wonderful boy, twenty-two years old, 6′2″ tall, very handsome and a fine gentleman . . . I don't think I shall ever fully recover from the grief and shock."

"Max said, 'Your son is dead!'" Thirty years later, the exchange remained
seared in Louise's mind.

"Just like that. I said, 'You're kidding. My God—no!' He said, 'He's *dead!*
Your son is *dead!*' Like that. It was the most cruel way that anybody could tell
another person."[53]

Having failed in his first attempt at suicide, Ronald had checked into the
Royal Hawaiian Hotel and taken a fatal overdose of pills.[54]

Sometime after hearing the news, Steiner went into his music library. He
removed his private disc of his score for *The Miracle of Our Lady of Fatima*—
the story of a group of children rewarded by the Virgin Mary for their faith
in God.

Max dragged his record needle across the disc, etching into it a permanent
scratch.[55]

He then returned the disc to its folder.

26
Coda

FOR FIVE MONTHS AFTER RONALD'S DEATH, Max Steiner seldom left home.

The 74-year-old composer did not work. His son's suicide was the primary reason, but not the only one.

Steiner was now legally blind.

Cataracts had reduced him to a helpless state. For nearly half a year, he simply sat, trapped in a world of darkness and guilt.

THE STORY OF STEINER'S LIFE would likely end here if not for one person. By October 1962, director Delmer Daves's latest film, *Spencer's Mountain*, was ready for scoring, and Daves held firm in his choice of composer. Max was touched by his friend's loyalty and began to pull himself together.

He relied more than ever on his orchestrator, Murray Cutter, and on Lee, who was now used to holding a giant magnifying glass in front of oversized music paper for her husband. Besides his usual cue sheets that broke down the action of each scene, Max relied heavily on the film's dialogue track.

As for the movie, "he couldn't see it," Daves recalled.[1]

Spencer's Mountain drew its story from the source that later inspired TV's *The Waltons*: Earl Hamner Jr.'s novel about a family's struggles during the Depression in rural Wyoming. The cast was first-rate, from Henry Fonda and Maureen O'Hara as the sparring, loving heads of the family, to octogenarian Donald Crisp in his final screen role.

But despite magnificent photography around Wyoming's Grand Tetons, *Spencer's Mountain* is depressingly synthetic—overwritten and full of leering references to animal husbandry and the locals' lusty sex lives. Fonda claimed that it "set the movie business back twenty years."[2] An exaggeration; but *Spencer's Mountain* was a creative misfire—with one exception.

Nothing rallied Steiner like the need to prove himself. Although forced to work without seeing a shot of the film, Max drew on his love for his adopted country to produce the truest expression of Hamner's story that *Spencer's Mountain* offered.

"The main theme is imbued with that sense of childlike wonder, which is the trademark of the perennially youthful creative imagination," Christopher Palmer observed.[3] "Prefaced by a quotation on horns from 'America the Beautiful,' [his main theme] reflects both the tranquility and beauty of lake, wood, and mountain." Some cues have the bland simplicity that reflect the influence of *A Summer Place*. But overall, the score is prime Steiner—melodic, life-affirming, essential to the film it accompanies.

Many movie critics agreed with Fonda's harsh review, but audiences made *Spencer's Mountain* a hit. Max was back in the game, especially after two cataract surgeries that restored much of his vision.[4] Much, but not all—he would have difficulty seeing for the rest of his life.

DURING HIS RECUPERATION, Max put time to good use, dictating an autobiography. He titled the manuscript *Notes to You*, an anachronistic pun on the '30s slang insult "Nuts to you." Much of the book, a rough first draft, focuses on his youth in Vienna, with lengthy reminiscences of London and Broadway. When the narrative reaches Hollywood, the text becomes a jumble of stream-of-consciousness anecdotes.

There is little discussion of his creative process. And in spite of the book's attempts at jollity, sadness hovers over its pages. "I have one or two hobbies left," he concludes.[5] "I like to swim every morning before I go to work and again when I return before my dinner. Photography has been a life-long hobby of mine, but bourbon is my greatest hobby now." He acknowledges that sex, once a driving force, was in the past. "I once had another hobby which I didn't give up, but, alas, it gave me up. There are some good things in life which do not improve with age."

Recalling the death of his father, he wrote, "I may buy a plot near where he is buried and have a sign placed over it: 'Coming attraction: Max Steiner.'"

Notes to You was never published.

A sense of melancholy also hangs over one of Steiner's last projects: *A Distant Trumpet*, a drab western marking director Raoul Walsh's swan song. Max's flagging energy is apparent in the constant repetition of *Trumpet's* main theme, an exciting one until it outstays its welcome. Its recording in November 1963 assumed a funereal air after John F. Kennedy's assassination.

A Distant Trumpet is a forgettable film; but its title is a perfect, poetic description of the mood surrounding it.

IN MAY 1964, STEINER WAS SURPRISED to receive an offer from a studio he had never worked with before. It proved an unexpected delight, and the last fulfilling experience of his career.

The Americana sound of *Spencer's Mountain* is probably the reason Walt Disney Studios approached Max for *Those Calloways*, a live-action drama set in 1920s New England. Steiner was treated like visiting royalty. He had ten weeks to write and conduct the score, with a larger orchestra than Warner Bros. was usually willing to hire.[6]

Brian Keith and Vera Miles starred in the picaresque story of a family's adventures, from the discovery of first love (*Shane's* Brandon de Wilde and Linda Evans were the juveniles) to the rescue of an endangered flock of Canadian geese. Max was "highly enthusiastic about the picture, and apparently deeply touched by it," producer Winston Hibler wrote Walt Disney.[7]

It showed. At 76, Steiner could still write music that overflowed with melody and a joy for life. His main title is like an overture, played over different scenes introducing characters, locale, and the geese that will unite a fractured family. From the first bar, Max pulls us into the story, as a theatrical *ba-DUM* from full orchestra leads to a series of upward key modulations: musically, we are soaring into the sky. This climbing progression leads us into Steiner's theme for the geese: a fast, ecstatic waltz, supported by fluttering woodwind trills that create a thrilling feel of flight. In its flowing beauty, one can hear a composer fully connected to his creativity after months of struggle and depression.

For the long-suffering Liddy (Miles), Max writes a tune of quiet introspection, akin to the feel of *Johnny Belinda*. A hushed Indian theme is among Steiner's most subtle, while a growling jug-band tune for a mischievous bear is a comic delight. Inevitably Steiner "catches" some of the bear's movement; how fitting that here, Max was mickey-mousing for the very man who created Mickey Mouse.

"We have finished re-recording the picture and wedding the music to the visual," Hibler wrote Disney in September 1964.[8] "It was a happy marriage. Max Steiner created a melodic and sensitive score for us. I can truthfully say that of all the pictures I have produced, *Those Calloways* has proved the most gratifying in every way."

BY NOW, STEINER WAS FINANCIALLY SECURE ENOUGH to stop working, and his eyesight made composing a chore. But Max simply couldn't give up the profession that had been his life for 35 years.

His search for work led to one last film. It would be an unworthy coda.

Warner Bros.' *Two on a Guillotine* was a low-budget horror-comedy that paired Cesar Romero with newcomers Connie Stevens and Dean Jones. The plot was older than the talkies: young heiress must spend the night in a "haunted" house to collect an inheritance. It is a sign of Max's desperation that he agreed to score a movie that made *The Beast with Five Fingers* look like *Casablanca*. "It wasn't a picture," Max recalled, "it was an abortion."[9] Producer-director William Conrad considered Steiner wrong for the project and put his hopes for a pop hit on a gratuitous discotheque scene, featuring the Merseybeat band The Condors. The shaggy quartet filmed their song "Go, Baby!" in a single day, while buxom extras shook their stuff for over-head, handheld cameras.

Max's sweepingly anachronistic score tries to find a balance between punching up the movie's shock effects and kidding them. For a running gag involving a magician's rabbit, he crafted a jokey tune played on ocarina, a 12,000-year-old wind instrument associated with the supernatural. Conrad hated it.[10]

Hopeful to the last that Max would produce another hit, Warner Bros. distributed a disc of the score's main theme. "The enclosed Steiner melody from *Two on a Guillotine* is our *Summer Place* for 1965," Victor Blau wrote dutifully.[11]

FRIDAY, OCTOBER 2, 1964, WAS A DAY of "moderate to heavy smog," the *Los Angeles Times* reported. The weather was a warm 82 degrees.

On that sunny, uncomfortable day, Max Steiner bid farewell to his career.

Around noon, the 76-year-old was driven to Warner Bros., where he joined many old friends among the 47 musicians. They included Eleanor Aller and Norma Drury, who first played for Max in 1931. From 1:00 to 6:15 p.m., *Guillotine*'s last cues were recorded under the baton of Murray Cutter. "Max tried to conduct the final recorded take," a friend recalled.[12]

Guillotine opened in early January 1965 and died at the box office. When William Conrad blamed Steiner, a furious Max shot back. "There was a big mistake in the thing," he told an interviewer.[13] "The guillotine was in the wrong place. They should have cut off William Conrad's head for producing the thing. They said I killed the picture. That I wouldn't take after all the years."

He would never compose again.

It is a small mercy that although *Two on a Guillotine* was Max's final score, it was not the final movie of his to be released. The opening of *Those Calloways* had been delayed by Disney's media push for *Mary Poppins*. Unveiled in late January 1965, *Calloways* was not a commercial success, but those who saw it were likely to agree with Disney publicity director Dick McKay. "Not least of its assets is the Max Steiner score," McKay wrote a colleague. "It is truly magnificent."[14]

THE FILM SCORES OF MAX STEINER

1963 Releases

Spencer's Mountain (12/62)

1964 Releases

Youngblood Hawke (8/63–9/63)
A Distant Trumpet (11/63–12/63)

1965 Releases

Those Calloways (7/64) Walt Disney Productions/Buena Vista Distribution Company
Two on a Guillotine (9/64–10/64)

On May 10, 1965, Steiner turned 77. A few screen projects hovered as possibilities—most intriguingly Warners' *Who's Afraid of Virginia Woolf?*[15]—but none materialized. When a junior executive at Fox asked, "Mr. Steiner, have you ever scored a western?" Max was speechless.[16]

He still received fan letters and photo requests—from Britain, Europe, Australia, Japan, even Vietnam. Only one nation seemingly ignored him. "The only country from which, to my knowledge, I have never received even one fan letter is Austria, my own country where I was born and bred."[17]

In his adopted homeland, things were brighter. A fan named Albert K. Bender founded the Max Steiner Music Society, created "to bring together all persons interested in the music of the Dean of Film Music."[18] The Society enlisted as members many of Steiner's collaborators: Fred Astaire, Vivien Leigh, John Huston, John Wayne, Hal Wallis, and others. Bette

Davis accepted the ceremonial title of First Honorary Director. "I am truly honored," she wrote. "All of us who benefited owe him our everlasting thanks. He often improved our acting."[19]

Wrote Jack Warner, who outlasted Max at his studio by a year, stepping down in 1966, "I am proud and happy to count Max Steiner as an old and valued friend. Max was an important member of that small band of creative men who were always ready to do their utmost for our studio and our films . . . we could always depend on him to deliver an outstanding score."[20]

The most authentic-sounding, and melancholy, tribute came from a director whose dismissive opinion of Max had seemingly mellowed. "I would esteem it a great honor to be an honorary member of your association," wrote John Ford.[21] "I love and esteem Max Steiner. . . . You forgot to mention among his credits the magnificent job he did for 'The Informer.' You're right, we don't have music like that anymore. SAD."

MAX STILL WENT TO THE MOVIES. Some entertained him, including director Roger Corman's Edgar Allan Poe series, which featured old friends like Peter Lorre.[22] But most new films sparked anger. Typical was his reaction to *Doctor Zhivago*: "He hated the score," a friend recalled.[23] "He said, 'Unlearned harmonies,' because in Lara's Theme, Maurice Jarre didn't use the best chords for the melody."

"Composition is a highly developed art that's now dominated by young men who can only hum a tune," he told a reporter.[24]

If most interviewers failed to glean fresh insights from Steiner, that wasn't true of a new acquaintance made in the mid-1960s. An aspiring film composer, 21-year-old John Morgan would repay Max's friendship in surprising ways.

In 1958, Morgan—then in the fifth grade—had traveled to Warner Bros. on a school field trip. He had learned "Tara's Theme" on piano, in case his class saw Steiner during a visit to the music department. They did. "He was short," Morgan recalled, "but you still felt that presence, a giant in the room. Max asked, 'Do any of you play an instrument?' I raised my hand and said, 'Piano.' I went up and played 'Tara's Theme' from memory. Max was kind of aghast. The orchestra clapped, and Max made a comment like, 'This kid wants my job!' But he was honored, and it was a great memory. I went home excited, and I looked out for his films after that."[25]

Shortly after Steiner's retirement, Morgan decided to formally meet his idol. A friend provided his phone number, "but I found out it was in the

Last official portrait, mid-1960s. (MS Papers; L. Tom Perry
Special Collections, Brigham Young University)

book. He didn't mind people calling. So I went up to visit him, and Max liked
me because I knew his music so well."[26]

Over the next six years, Morgan collected more specific information about
Steiner's work than any other individual.

Max's favorite restaurant was Chasen's in West Hollywood. From 8
o'clock to midnight, we'd have conversation and dinner. And I would
go to his house on Laurel Way. He was very friendly, although he always
crumpled his brow in a kidding way. We would go into his little studio
and he said, "What do you want to do?" I wanted to work through all
his [music] sketches. The first one was *King Kong*. We put it on the
piano and he played through it and I would grill him mercilessly: Why
did he do this? Why did he do that? He would feign annoyance, but he
was still up on the music and it was a lot of fun.

Lee was helping him write things down. Max couldn't have had a
better wife to keep his legacy going. I remember when Max and I were

talking, she would come in and out, almost like a ghost. I would almost spend the night there, because I would talk to Max to the wee hours.[27]

A rare professional pleasure came in 1967, with another re-release of *Gone with the Wind*. Two years after David O. Selznick's death at age 63, *GWTW* remained one of the few 1930s titles so prestigious that it could only be seen in theaters.* Max was delighted by fresh attention to his score, and by the first album to feature selections from the original 1939 soundtrack recording. Sales were substantial.

Discussing the album in 1967, Steiner "had a twinkle in his eye," recalled interviewer Myrl A. Schreibman.[28] "And when he spoke . . . his European Jewish accent and his warmth made me feel right at home." That recorded interview has echoes of the whimsical Max of old:

> *Max: You want a cigar?*
> *Myrl: No, thank you.*
> *Max: You want two cigars?*
> *Myrl [laughs] No, thank you.*
> *Max: Would you like three cigars?*
> *Myrl: No, thank you. [laughing] Would you like a cigar?*
> *Max: I'll have one, thanks.*

But flashes of humor were outnumbered by vitriol for the current state of the industry. "I saw four pictures lately—I have been quite ill and I haven't gone much—and I never heard anything worse. All four of them have been nominated [for Oscars], and I think they just smell to high heaven . . . annoying, repetitious. . . . They must be thinking of Boris Karloff all the time."[29]

What happiness Max found usually came from the calm, ever-supportive Lee. "She is without a doubt the best thing that ever happened to me in my life," he wrote in his autobiography.[30] "Despite the light touch and, I hope, humor of this book, I had not always been a happy man until I found Lee. Speaking of humor, this is another endearing quality of hers. She gives me a laugh many a time."

---

* The film's TV premiere came in 1976.

Steiner was also buoyed by news that several of his scores were about to receive their first modern recordings. In 1966, Arkansas-born, London-based conductor Charles Gerhardt began meeting with Max, to plan RCA albums featuring suites of his music.[31] Steiner was flattered by Gerhardt's knowledge and his suggestions, which included *The Big Sleep* and *The Fountainhead*. They discussed a new recording of *Gone with the Wind*; the ultimate 44-minute disc, released in 1974, proved a sensitive re-recording of Steiner's masterpiece.

STEINER HAD NOT RECEIVED AN OSCAR NOMINATION SINCE 1955. But in 1968, the Motion Picture Academy would honor him a final time.

The 40th Academy Awards were conducted by fellow Oscar winner Elmer Bernstein. Much had changed since Bernstein's first days in Hollywood in the 1950s, when he was "greylisted" due to his liberal politics. Elmer joined the Screen Composers Association formed by Steiner, and "from time to time, I began to get little notes from Max. Although we had no personal relationship at the time, they were notes which congratulated me on something he had seen or heard."[32]

Bernstein never forgot that kindness. When assigned to conduct the 1968 Oscars, "I was very happy to be able to choose the music of Max Steiner on that occasion to use as the overture of the Academy Awards show. This was done without Max's knowledge, and it was done because if I had to pick one person whose work represented everything that we had attained since, it was Max Steiner."[33]

On April 10, 1968, millions around the world watched as Bernstein kicked off the Oscars with a medley of four Steiner themes. The swoony romanticism of *Now, Voyager*'s love theme segued into the lusty soldier's march from *Battle Cry*; then came *A Summer Place*, leading to a triumphant coda based on "Tara's Theme."

A month later, on May 10, 1968, Maximilian Raoul Steiner turned 80. That night, a birthday party was held at his home attended by many friends, including Roy Webb, Lou Forbes, and Murray Cutter. Members of ASCAP sang a medley of birthday wishes based on Steiner themes, arranged by his old Broadway pal Harry Ruby. It was a joyous night.[34]

Two years later, in 1970, Max celebrated his birthday with similar cheer, despite declining health. Guests were greeted by a jovial Max "in a Beethoven wig and impressively bedecked with sash and many medals," his fan club reported. After dinner, "Mr. Steiner made his way to the piano in the family room and played a few themes while brightly lit candles cast their flickering fingers of light upon the keys. A momentous hush befell the guests."[35]

Recalled Elmer Bernstein, "I was able to see and understand fully at close range the warmth, the wit, and even at that point some of the sadness that made him great as a person. . . . It was at the end of the evening that Max, quite suddenly and without urging, went to the piano. He sat down for one more time, just improvising, and that is the last memory I have of Max."[36]

BY 1971, STEINER'S BODY WAS FAILING. "His stamina was pretty good until the end," said John Morgan.[37] "The last time I saw him he was starting to be sick, and he was sad. He was in his robe and pajamas, tired, and couldn't move around well. When I left, he hugged me. He always did."

By then, Max had received a diagnosis of cancer. But he retained his sense of humor even as the end approached.

"Nurses had been attending him in his home," recalled Al Bender.[38] "So many types of medicine were in the room that Max said to Lee one day, in a very weak voice, 'Mommy!' (He always called Lee this affectionately.) 'They should call this place Medicine Square Garden!'"

ON TUESDAY, DECEMBER 28, 1971, MAXIMILIAN RAOUL STEINER died at Mt. Sinai Hospital. He was 83 years old.

Two days later, 75 colleagues, including Jack Warner, assembled at Forest Lawn, where Max was buried and a memorial was held. David Raksin, Elmer Bernstein, and 78-year-old Merian C. Cooper gave eulogies. "Do you think Maxie is dead?" Cooper boomed. "No. Maxie, never! His music will live on like those men of Vienna whom he followed—Mozart, Beethoven, the Strausses, all of them. Maxie's music has a true drama, screen drama, music as immortal as anything will ever be."

Steiner had foreseen the day with humor. In 1943, a cemetery attendant had brusquely ordered him to remove "the old man"—Max's grieving father—from Erna Steiner's grave. "I will never go to Forest Lawn again," he wrote in 1964.[39] "But if I should die and be forced to go there, my last request would be that they change the name to Old Forester Lawn, in memory of all the bourbon I have consumed. I have made my dear wife, my little mama, promise me that she would put a couple of packs of pinochle cards, two gin rummy decks, two bottles of bourbon and a box of cigars in my coffin, in case I meet Victor Young where I'm going."

Max finished the game of life resoundingly in the black. His estate contained a balance of $100,508.73. Among his beneficiaries was the Braille Institute.[40]

IN 1973, RCA BEGAN ISSUING Charles Gerhardt's recordings of golden age film scores. Many of the discs, including those featuring Steiner, became bestsellers. And on December 30, 1975, friends and admirers—among them Miklós Rózsa, Ray Bradbury, and Ray Harryhausen—assembled for the unveiling of Max's star on the Hollywood Walk of Fame. It was placed on the southwest corner of Vine and Selma, near the Brown Derby, where Steiner had his first meal upon arriving in Hollywood in 1929.

In 1981, Lee donated Max's pencil sketches, acetate recordings, and papers to Brigham Young University. Her husband had no link to the college, but he could not have found a more passionate or meticulous curator than BYU's James D'Arc. On March 6, 1981, the university honored Lee in what would be her last public appearance. She died of heart failure, age 82, on October 9, 1981.

Max's homeland of Austria offered a belated tribute on his centennial. In 1988, a plaque was unveiled outside Max's birthplace, now the Hotel Wien. By then, a walkway to the nearby Prater, leading to the ever-popular Riesenrad, had been renamed the Gabor Steiner Path.

Starting in the 1990s, John Morgan expertly reconstructed the scores of *King Kong*, *She*, *The Charge of the Light Brigade*, *The Adventures of Mark Twain*, *The Treasure of the Sierra Madre*, and others for new recordings. They were superbly conducted by William T. Stromberg and are essential listening for any student of film music.

While restoring the scores, Morgan reflected on Steiner's dimming prominence in film music discussion, despite his enduring influence.

There's little doubt that Max opened the door on film music. He did more of putting it all together than any composer. And one of the problems we have today is that so many composers imitated Steiner, some of the freshness of Max may have been lost because of that. But he was, in more ways than not, the first. Those years at RKO pretty well demonstrated almost everything that film scores can do. He experimented with soft endings, loud endings, with dialogue, with sound effects. All the techniques that composers still use today were there.

For many years, up to the late '40s, he was considered the very top. And I don't think anyone up through the 1940s is better than Steiner at his best. But today, Steiner often doesn't get his due—when they look at Steiner-era composers, Korngold comes out on top. I think it's because Korngold came in with such an international reputation. But I'm always gratified when contemporary composers, like Elliot Goldenthal who writes very avant garde music, say that Max Steiner is their number one. And Spielberg named his son Max after Steiner.*

I think Max suffered in reputation the same way Michael Curtiz does as a director. He never got credit for being an artist. They didn't buck the studio system, they embraced it.

With Herrmann, there's always a sinister undertone, even on a light film. With Max, even with heavy films, I sense a joy of composing. Even on a *Dark Victory* that isn't happy, you just feel this joy . . . I think because Max was a joyful person who just loved writing.[41]

In the years after Ronald Steiner's death, Louise Klos started over, creating for herself a rewarding third act. She played harp for the Royal Ballet and the Bolshoi. With second husband Fred Elian, she traveled the world until Fred's death in 1983, three weeks before their 20th anniversary. Louise continued to make music, touring across Europe and Asia.[42] She retired in 1996, age 90, and died six years later.

During Louise's last decade, music and Max Steiner were almost daily topics of conversation. She connected with admirers around the world, and shared memories of her life with Max in an essay for the CD release of *King Kong*.

AS FOR THE GIANT APE HIMSELF, the King of Skull Island was alive and well as the world entered the 21st century. Kong's exploits were seen and heard on an ever-expanding list of media, from home video to digital streaming, along with those of other cinema icons: Rick and Ilsa, Scarlett and Rhett, and countless more whose inner passions achieved their fullest realization thanks to Steiner's dramatic insight.

---

* In a nod to Steiner, Spielberg nicknamed his favorite composer, John Williams, "Max"—the name Spielberg later gave his first child.

To the general public, he is a forgotten figure. To cineastes, he is a historical footnote.

But to any viewer watching a movie scored by Max Steiner, he remains a living presence. Every day, somewhere on the planet, his work transports audiences into worlds larger than life in their heightened emotion, yet instantly relatable in their expressions of joy, pain, and romantic fulfillment.

Just listen.

Acknowledgments

WHEN MAX STEINER arrived in America in 1914, he found his path eased by the many friends he had already made in Europe and Britain. It's a scenario to which this author can relate. Writing a biography of Bernard Herrmann in the 1980s gave me a running start on Max, thanks to friendships formed on that earlier project.

One name towers above the rest. James V. D'Arc, former curator of the L. Tom Perry Collection at Brigham Young University, ensured that Steiner's pencil sketch scores, acetate recordings, correspondence, and thousands of other documents were saved after Max's death. Jim convinced Lee Steiner to donate this material to BYU, and he subsequently released many Steiner acetates in CD editions, beautifully remastered by Ray Faiola. Jim also acquired for BYU the papers of Louise Klos, which included some of Max's most revealing correspondence.

This book is unimaginable in its current form without James D'Arc's dedication to the preservation of Steiner's life work. Every lover of film music is in his debt.

In the 1960s, composer John W. Morgan elicited from Max a candor missing from most of his "official" interviews. In addition to preserving these memories, John reconstructed dozens of Steiner scores for their first stereo commercial recordings. Most were conducted by William T. Stromberg and produced by Stromberg's wife, Anna. All were indispensable throughout my writing. I am especially indebted to John, who always made time to answer my questions, to dissect the process behind Steiner's creative choices, and to bring Max back to life with examples of his humor, erudition, and vulnerability.

When I began this book, the list of living Steiner colleagues was all too short. I'm grateful for three exceptions: Olivia de Havilland (and her associates Suzelle Smith and Alice Gilbert), Richard Sherman, and, especially, Janis Paige. Thirty-five years ago, my Herrmann research included interviews with several Steiner friends and admirers, whom I thank and miss in equal measure: Louis and Annette Kaufman, David Raksin, Elmer Bernstein, Miklós Rózsa, Robert Wise, Ray Harryhausen, Ray Bradbury, Charles Gerhardt, Eleanor Aller Slatkin, Don Christlieb, Ronald Haver, Robert Osborne, and Tony Thomas.

Two contemporary researchers shared rare Steiner documents with unconditional generosity. N. William Snedden specializes in Steiner family history circa 1830–1930; the articles he unearthed do much to illuminate the mysteries of Max's youth. Stephen Butler, in tandem with his wife, Jane, has collected thousands of pages of Steiner data. Blessed with a deadpan wit and a giant heart, Stephen assembled a 327-page Steiner filmography—an invaluable reference while creating my own list of Max's screen work.

No less essential were Leonard Maltin, who guided this project by example and with friendship; the late Rudy Behlmer, whose motto of "Never assume" inspired many fresh searches; Jon Burlingame and Richard B. Jewell, both impeccable scholars; and Nathan Platte, Selznick expert par excellence.

For biographers, libraries are like churches, and on this project three were especially close to heaven. The RKO Radio Pictures records at UCLA's Library Special Collections, Performing Arts, contain perhaps the largest repository of Steiner-penned documents outside of BYU. The Warner Bros. Archives, USC School of Cinematic Arts, were scrupulously overseen during my work by Brett Service, who ensured that countless files were ready for this author's perusal. And Vienna's Theater Museum houses everything from an original *Die Fledermaus* program to an 1897 ticket for the Riesenrad. Its staff, led by Gertrud Fischer, Claudia Mayerhofer, and Daniela Franke, made a visitor from America feel like an honored guest.

Elisabeth Gruber, dramaturg of Vienna's Ronacher Theater, provided an extensive, delightful tour of that institution. Peter Petritsch, owner of the Riesenrad, shared his thoughts on the Steiner legacy. And kudos to London's Victoria & Albert Museum, Theatre & Performance collection; Steve L. Wilson and Michael L. Gilmore of Harry Ransom Center, University of Texas at Austin; John Calhoun, New York Public Library, Billy Rose Theatre Division; Mike Pepin and Robert Vaughn, Louis B. Mayer Library, American Film Institute; Mark Quigley, UCLA Film & Television Archive; Helmut Reichenauer, Museum der Johann Strauss Dynastie; Doris Vater-Dannhäuser and Dr. Hannelore Köhler of Lutherische Stadtkirche, Vienna; Sabine Koller and Irma Wulz, Archive of the Jewish Community of Vienna; David A. Olson, Columbia Center for Oral History; and Anne Rhodes, Yale University Library.

The antiquated typefaces of 19th-century Austria, and the florid handwriting of Gabor Steiner, were inscrutable until I met a miraculous translator named Claudia Taake. Her determination to find meaning within the most faded of letters led to many of the most striking details in the early chapters of this book. (Thanks also to Lena Strothe for additional translating.)

For other assistance, I am indebted to Warren Sherk, Head of Special Collections at Margaret Herrick Library, Academy of Motion Picture Arts and Sciences; his colleagues Louise Hilton and Stacey Behlmer; the indefatigable Edward Comstock of the USC Film and Television Archive; Ben Harry, curator of the L. Tom Perry Collection at BYU; his colleagues Brent Yorgason, Jeff Lyon, and Cindy Brightenburg; and documentarian Diana Friedberg, who shared precious audio interviews with Lee Steiner and others. Thanks also to Julie Kirgo, Richard L. Procter, Alan K. Rode, Scott MacQueen, Charles Chabot, Leslie Megahey, William Rosar, Peter Wegele, Marilee Bradford, Leslie T. Zador, William Wellman Jr., David Robinson, Ted Abenheim, James Curtis, Teresa Barnett, John Bowab, Mary Ellin Barrett, Aaron Fruchtman, Aaron Gandy, George J. Ferencz, Glen Aitken West, Snorre Smári Mathiesen, Peter Filichia, Theodore S. Chapin, Merrill McCord, Vince Giordano, Peter Mintun, Jim Knuttel, Rusty Frank, Thomas Yotka, and Nick Redman.

I have long admired Gary Giddins's brilliant writing on jazz and film, and his definitive biography of Bing Crosby. Twelve years of friendship have only increased that respect; and when Gary suggested in 2015 that I undertake this book, my life was set on a transformative course.

I also have Gary to thank for introducing me to literary agent Georges Borchardt, one of the most accomplished and gracious individuals I have the pleasure to know. My deepest thanks to this lion of 20th-century literature for representing me.

No author could have more collaborative or experienced editors than Norman Hirschy and Joellyn Ausanka of Oxford University Press. Norm and Joellyn made what can be the most stressful period on a project—its completion—an absolute joy. My thanks also to Elizabeth Bortka for her judicious editorial input.

Decades ago, as a 19-year-old journalism student with the vaguest of career goals, I mentioned to my brother, Wayne Bryan, that no biography of Bernard Herrmann existed. Wayne replied matter-of-factly, "Why don't you write one?" I have Wayne to thank for much of what followed in my professional life, along with my parents, Elwayne and Carolyn Smith.

Last but far from least, my extraordinary wife, Michelle Guy, provided emotional support, research assistance, and unfailing encouragement throughout this grand adventure.

Here's looking at you, kid.

Steven C. Smith
November 2019

Notes

FRONTMATTER

1. Details about Selznick's discussions with Stothart about *GWTW* come from DOS memo to Whitney and Lowell Calvert, November 17, 1939, HRC 1237:3.
2. Hitler obtained a print of *GWTW*, which became one of his favorite films. He and other Nazis saw a parallel between Germany's defeat in WWI and Margaret Mitchell's depiction of the fallen American South. Nina Silber, "Worshiping the Confederacy Is about White Supremacy—Even the Nazis Thought So," *Washington Post*, August 17, 2017.
3. DOS memo to Whitney and Lowell Calvert, November 17, 1939, HRC 1237:3.
4. Steiner also worked uncredited on several film scores that earned Oscar nominations (e.g., *Intermezzo*) and wins (*This Is the Army*).
5. *Star Wars*' 1977 soundtrack album sold more than 4 million copies. See Jeffrey Paul Smith, *The Sounds of Commerce: Marketing Popular Film Music* (New York: Columbia University Press, 1998). *Titanic*'s 1997 soundtrack album sold an estimated 30 million copies, making it the largest selling instrumental score album in history. See Daniel Bukszpan, "Remembering James Horner," *Fortune*, June 23, 2015.
6. Although an authorized figure for Williams's net worth has not been made public, the amount of $100 million has been widely reported. The sum is highly plausible when one considers salary, soundtrack albums, live performances, and home video residuals related to his music for *Jaws, E.T.*, nine *Star Wars* films, four Indiana Jones films, entries in the *Harry Potter* and *Jurassic Park* series, plus more than 80 other motion pictures. See Patrick Gleeson, "How Much Money Does the Average Film Scorer Make?" *Houston Chronicle*, June 29, 2018.

CHAPTER I

1. Norbert Rubey and Peter Schoenwald, *Venedig in Wien* (Vienna: Ueberreuter, 1996), 73 (hereafter abbreviated as *VIW*).

2. Helmut Jahn and Peter Petritsch, *The Vienna Giant Ferris Wheel* (Vienna, 1989), 10–11.

3. *VIW*, 104. Also see "The Last Screw," *Illustrated Vienna*, June 25, 1897.

4. For details of the planning of "Venice in Vienna," see *VIW*, 39–45.

5. For details of the park's geography and attractions, see *VIW*, 46–62.

6. Frederic Morton, *A Nervous Splendor: Vienna 1888–1889* (New York: Penguin, 1979), 4.

7. *VIW*, 44.

8. "In the Realm of Restaurants," *Venedig-Zeitung*, June 1903, MSS 1547, Box 7, Folder 1.

9. *VIW*, 65–72. Also see Gabor Steiner article, *Illustrated Wochenpost*, November 29, 1930.

10. Morton, *A Nervous Splendor*, 18.

11. Journalist Berta Zuckerkandl's account of this exchange between Klimt and Rodin is quoted by Tag Gronberg, *Vienna: City of Modernity, 1890–1914* (Bern: Peter Lang, 2007), 81.

12. Gabor Steiner, "My Encounters with Emperor Franz Joseph," *Neues Wiener Journal*, January 12, 1930.

13. For details of Maximilian's administration of the Theater an der Wien, see *VIW*, 9–19.

14. For a history of the theater, see W. E. Yates, *Theatre in Vienna: A Critical History, 1776–1995* (New York: Cambridge University Press), 1996.

15. "*Feuilleton*," *Der Zwischen-Akt*, no. 169, July 17, 1869. See also N. William Snedden, "Max Steiner: A Chronicle of Published Sources," billsnedden.wordpress.com/2018/07/24/max-steiner-a-chronicle-of-published-sources/

16. H. E. Jacob, *Johann Strauss, Father and Son: A Century of Light Music* (New York: Crown, 1939), 164.

17. Egon Gartenberg, *Johann Strauss: The End of an Era* (State College: Pennsylvania State University Press, 1990), 301–306.

18. *Wiener Sonn-und Montags-Zeitung*, May 30, 1880; *Neue Illustrirte Zeitung* 37, June 6, 1880.

19. *VIW*, 10–11.

20. Ibid., 24–26.

21. Max Steiner, *Notes to You*, Chapter VI.

22. For a history of Franz Steiner's administration of the Theater, see *VIW*, 20–23, and Gartenberg, *Johann Strauss: The End of an Era*, 253–57.

23. Gabor Steiner, "Sixty Years Working in Theater." *Neues Wiener Journal*, November 17, 1929.

24. *Trauungsbuch fur die Israelisilche Kultusgemeinde in Wien* (marriage book for the Israeli religious community in Vienna), www.familysearch.org

25. *Die Neuzeit*, March 23, 1883; *Morgen-Post*, March 27, 1883; and *Die Presse*, March 30, 1883. Copy of wedding entry obtained from Archiv der Israelitischen Kultusgemeinde Wien.

26. Birth certificate obtained from Archiv der Israelitischen Kultusgemeinde Wien.
27. Steiner, *Notes to You*, Chapter I.
28. Morton, *A Nervous Splendor*, 315.
29. Ibid., 241.
30. *Taufbuche der evangel. Kirchengemeinde Augsb. Bekennsn.* www.familysearch.org.
31. *VIW*, 42–43.
32. Ibid., 75.
33. David Sokol, "Little Monarch of Sound Discusses Music: Max Steiner Is Erudite," *Illustrated Daily News*, July 23, 1935.
34. Steiner, *Notes to You*, Chapter IV.
35. *VIW*, 77. As of 2019, artifacts from Gabor's early cinema exhibitions can be seen in the museum devoted to the park's history, located in the Prater.
36. Ibid., 77.

CHAPTER 2

1. "In the Realm of Restaurants," *Venedig-Zeitung*, June 1903, MSS 1547, Box 7, Folder 1.
2. Steiner, *Notes to You*, Chapter II.
3. Ibid., Chapter III.
4. Ibid., Chapter V. See also *VIW*, 85–86.
5. Steiner, *Notes to You*, Chapter II.
6. Ibid., Chapter II. Rudolf Hollman died at age 63 in 1908; see *Salzburger Volksblatt*, July 2, 1908.
7. Ibid., Chapter VI. Steiner erroneously credits this event as occurring during the lifetime of Maximilian Steiner, but Maximilian died 15 years before von Suppé.
8. Steiner, *Notes to You*, Chapter VI.
9. Richard Traubner, *Operetta: A Theatrical History* (New York: Doubleday, 1983), 112.
10. Steiner, *Notes to You*, Chapter IV.
11. Ibid., Chapter IV.
12. Copies of this and other early Steiner pieces can be found in MSS 1547, Boxes 15 and 16.
13. Schreibman, Myrl. "On *Gone with the Wind*, Selznick, and the Art of 'Mickey Mousing': An Interview with Max Steiner," *Journal of Film and Video* 56, no. 1 (2004).
14. Quoted by Tony Thomas, "The Max Steiner Factor," notes for *The Lost Patrol/ Virginia City/The Beast with Five Fingers* (Tribute Classics, 1995). Compact disc.
15. Quoted by Tony Palmer, *Wagner and Cinema*, ed. Joe Jeongwon and Sander L. Gilman (Bloomington: Indiana University Press, 2010), 11.
16. Steiner, *Notes to You*, Chapter IV.
17. MS letter to Frederick Day, July 24, 1936, MSS 1547, Box 2 Folder 13.
18. Steiner, *Notes to You*, Chapter IV.
19. Tony Thomas interview with MS, CBC, 1961.

20. *Der Humorist*, October 10, 1900; *Deutsches Volksbatt*, October 31, 1900. For more about Gabor's operation of Danzers, see *VIW*, 27–28.

21. The late researcher Edward Leaney made note of Max conducting at London's People's Palace. Attribution for this apparently does not survive.

22. Max Steiner, "Music Hath Charms," *Boxoffice*, August 22, 1936.

23. *Wiener Morgen-Zeitung* 272, October 3, 1902.

24. Steiner, *Notes to You*, Chapter XII.

25. Ibid.

26. Neil Harris, "John Philip Sousa and the Culture of Reassurance," *Perspectives on John Philip Sousa* (Washington DC: Library of Congress, Music Division), 20–32.

27. Steiner, *Notes to You*, Chapter IV.

28. Ibid., Chapter IV.

29. For more about Strauss's concerts at "Venice in Vienna" and the involvement of Mahler, see *VIW*, 93–94.

30. In a 1945 ABC radio interview, Steiner remarked that Mahler "taught me composition and orchestration." Audio from the collection of John W. Morgan (hereafter abbreviated as JWM).

31. Steiner, *Notes to You*, Chapter VI.

32. Ibid., Chapter VI.

33. Gabor Steiner, "My Encounters with Emperor Franz Joseph," *Neues Wiener Journal*, January 12, 1930. See also *Neues Wiener Tagblatt*, November 2, 1904.

34. Steiner, *Notes to You*, Chapter III.

35. *Statistical Report about the Conservatory for Music and the Performing Arts*, 1904–1906 school records.

36. Steiner, *Notes to You*, Chapter IV.

37. Ibid., Chapter V.

38. Ibid.

39. Ibid.

40. MS letter to Louise Klos (hereafter abbreviated as LK), April 17, 1956, Louise Steiner Elian Papers, BYU (hereafter abbreviated as LSE), Box 7.

41. Steiner, *Notes to You*, Chapter V.

42. Ibid., Chapter V.

43. A near-complete set of Danzers Orpheum theater programs can be found in Vienna's Theater Museum (hereafter abbreviated as THAUS).

CHAPTER 3

1. *VIW*, 137.

2. *Neues Wiener Journal*, November 30, 1907.

3. Ibid.

4. Steiner, *Notes to You*, Chapter VII.

5. *VIW*, 32–33, 75.

6. Steiner, *Notes to You*, Chapter VIII.

7. Ibid., Chapter VII.

8. Ibid.

9. Steiner, *Notes to You*, Chapter VIII. Steiner erroneously lists his age as 19.

10. Ibid., Chapter VIII.

11. Several Steiner drawings from this period can be found in LSE, Box 1.

12. Steiner, *Notes to You*, Chapter VIII.

13. Ibid.

14. Ibid.

15. Max Steiner Music Society journal, Spring 1972, 8. The article quotes Max as claiming that Charlie Chaplin, then a "junior comedian" in the troupe, was responsible for losing the orchestra parts. Chaplin scholar David Robinson persuasively refutes this. Chaplin may have been present as a member of the Fred Karno troupe, but he was by then a star of the company who would not have been responsible for musicians' parts. (Robinson to author, November 28, 2017.)

16. Steiner, *Notes to You*, Chapter VIII.

17. Ibid.

18. Ibid.

19. For contemporary accounts of Steiner's work during this period, see MS letter to Ivy Wilson, November 30, 1948 (MSS 1547, Box 4, Folder 1), Steiner, *Notes to You*, Chapter VIII, and Edward Leaney, "A Max Steiner Chronology," *The Max Steiner Collection* (Provo, UT: Brigham Young University Press), 1996.

20. Leaney, "A Max Steiner Chronology."

21. Copy of wedding certificate obtained by author.

22. Steiner, *Notes to You*, Chapter X.

23. *Neues Wiener Tagblatt*, May 30, 1909. See also Rubey/Schoenwald, *VIW*, 29–30.

24. For more about the Ronacher, see Luz Eberhardt Seeling, *Ronacher: The History of a House* (Vienna: Graz, 1986).

25. *VIW*, 29–32. See also original Ronacher Theater Programs, THAUS.

26. Steiner, *Notes to You*, Chapter IX.

27. *VIW*, 32. See also original Ronacher Theater Programs, THAUS. In *Notes to You*, Steiner incorrectly lists W. C. Fields among the performers he brought to the Ronacher. In fact, Fields spent 1912 performing in America.

28. Steiner, *Notes to You*, Chapter IX.

29. Ibid., Chapter VII.

30. Accounts of Steiner's arrest and failed directorship of the Ronacher can be found in *Illustrierte Kronen Zeitung*, December 22, 1912, *Hull* (England) *Daily Mail* (Yorkshire, England), December 23, 1912, *Neues Wiener Tagblatt*, December 24, 1912, and *New York Clipper*, January 18, 1913. Steiner's own account appears in *Notes to You*, Chapter IX.

31. Steiner, *Notes to You*, Chapter IX.

32. Ibid.

33. LK letter to Edward Leaney, August 16, 1995, MSS 1547, Leaney Collection.

34. *Railway Official Gazette* (London), August 1913.

35. Original theater programs for *Come Over Here* can be found in the Theatre & Performing Arts Collection, Victoria & Albert Museum, London.

36. Steiner, *Notes to You*, Chapter X.

37. *New York Clipper*, July 26, 1913. Also see *Chicago Tribune*, August 3, 1913.

38. Herbert G. Goldman, *Fanny Brice: The Original Funny Girl* (New York: Oxford University Press, 1992), 66.

39. "Come Over Here Selections, Parts 1 & 2," HMV (C290), 1913. 78 rpm disc.

40. Leaney, "A Max Steiner Chronology."

41. Steiner, *Notes to You*, Chapter X.

42. Ibid.

43. Leaney, "A Max Steiner Chronology."

44. Steiner, *Notes to You*, Chapter X.

45. Ibid.

46. Ibid.

47. Ellis Island records, https://www.libertyellisfoundation.org/

CHAPTER 4

1. Ellis Island records, https://www.libertyellisfoundation.org/

2. Max Steiner, "The Music Director." In *The Real Tinsel* (New York: Macmillan, 1970), 388.

3. Steiner, *Notes to You*, Chapter I.

4. Ibid., Chapter XI.

5. Ibid.

6. Ibid.

7. Ibid.

8. *Variety*, April 1915. See Also Steiner, *Notes to You*, Chapter XI.

9. Steiner, *Notes to You*, Chapter XII.

10. Ibid., Chapter XI.

11. Ibid.

12. "History of the Motion Picture: The Silent Years, 1910–1927," *Encyclopaedia Britannica*   https://www.britannica.com/art/history-of-the-motion-picture/ The-silent-years-1910-27

13. Steiner, *Notes to You*, Chapter XI.

14. Steiner, *The Real Tinsel*, 388.

15. Ibid., 388–89.

16. For concise accounts of film music during the silent era, see William Darby and Jack Du Bois, *American Film Music: Major Composers, Techniques, Trends, 1915–1990* (Jefferson, NC: McFarland, 1999), 1–10; Michael Slowik,

After the Silents: Hollywood Film Music in the Early Sound Era, 1926–1934 (New York: Columbia University Press, 2014), 33–38; and Kathryn Kalinak, *Settling the Score: Music and the Classical Hollywood Film* (Madison: University of Wisconsin Press, 1992), 53–65.

17. "Music by the Reel," *Cue*, August 14, 1943.

18. Steiner, *Notes to You*, Chapter XI.

19. Ibid.

20. MS letter to Beatrice Tilt, October 7, 1941, MSS 1547, Box 1, Folder 7.

21. Steiner, *Notes to You*, Chapter XIII.

22. Ibid., Chapter XII.

23. Ibid.

24. Ibid.

25. Ethan Mordden, *Ziegfeld: The Man Who Invented Show Business.* (New York: St. Martin's Press, 2008), 4.

26. Steiner, *Notes to You*, Chapter XII.

27. Production credits on Steiner's Broadway shows can be found at the Internet Broadway Database: https://www.ibdb.com/

28. Steiner, *Notes to You*, Chapter XII.

29. Ibid.

30. Steiner, *The Real Tinsel*, 397.

31. Oscar Levant, *A Smattering of Ignorance* (Garden City, NY: Doubleday, 1940), 96–97.

32. Martin Rubin, *Showstoppers: Busby Berkeley and the Tradition of Spectacle* (New York: Columbia University Press, 1993) 66–68.

33. "Variations," *Music Magazine/Musical Courier*, August 12, 1920.

34. Steiner, *Notes to You*, Chapter XII.

35. Mordden, *Ziegfeld*, 189.

36. Alan Kendall, *George Gershwin: A Biography* (Milford, CT: Universe, 1987), 39–41.

37. William G. Hyland, *George Gershwin: A New Biography* (Santa Barbara, CA: Praeger, 2003), 48.

38. Thomas S. Hischak, *The Jerome Kern Encyclopedia* (Lanham, MD: Scarecrow Press, 2013), 195. Also see "Harry Bache Smith: An Inventory of His Papers," Harry Ransom Center, University of Texas, Austin.

39. "*Peaches* at Garrick," *Philadelphia Inquirer*, January 23, 1923.

40. JWM interview with James V. D'Arc (hereafter abbreviated as JVD), February 7, 2011.

41. MS letter to J. Huntington Hartford, July 6, 1960, MSS 1547, Box 3, Folder 2.

CHAPTER 5

1. In 1937, Steiner discouraged David O. Selznick from hiring Russell Bennett for a project, despite his impeccable qualifications—a reflection of Max's discomfort around the orchestrator. (DOS letter to Marcella Rabin, September 9, 1937, collection of JWM.) Nevertheless, Steiner and Russell Bennett did work together on

at least three screen projects: *I Dream Too Much* (1935), *Lost Horizon* (1936), and *Intermezzo* (1939).

2. Robert Russell Bennett, ed. George J. Ferencz. *The Broadway Sound: The Autobiography and Selected Essays of Robert Russell Bennett* (Rochester, NY: University of Rochester, 1999).

3. John McGlinn, "Finding the Bliss," *Sitting Pretty*, New World Records, 1990.

4. Eliscu interview transcript, ca. 1985, for *The RKO Story* (BBC TV documentary, 1987).

5. Steiner, *Notes to You*, Chapter XII.

6. Philip Furia, "Ira Gershwin: The Art of the Lyricist," *The George Gershwin Reader* (New York: Oxford University Press, 1996), 65.

7. *Lady, Be Good!* 1925 program, Billy Rose Theater Division, New York Library for the Performing Arts, New York, New York.

8. Hyland, *George Gershwin: A New Biography*, 25–26.

9. Ancestry.com. *New York, Passenger and Crew Lists 1820–1957*, Ancestry.com Operations, Inc., 2010.

10. New York, NY, Marriage License Indexes, 1907-2018.

11. Steiner, *Notes to You*, Chapter XII.

12. MSC, Scrapbook 1.

13. Elliott Arnold, *Deep in My Heart* (New York: Duell, Sloan and Pearce, 1949), 167.

14. *Hit the Deck*, 1927 theater program, Billy Rose Theater Division.

15. Hugh Fordin, *Getting to Know Him: A Biography of Oscar Hammerstein II* (New York: Random House, 1977), 90–96.

16. Steiner, *Notes to You*, Chapter XII.

17. John S. Wilson, "Benny Goodman, King of Swing, Is Dead," *New York Times*, June 14, 1986.

18. Richard B. Jewell, *RKO Radio Pictures: A Titan Is Born* (Berkeley: University of California Press, 2012), 25–26.

19. For the definitive account of RKO's formation, see Jewell, *RKO: Radio Pictures: A Titan Is Born*, 1–32.

20. Ibid., 1.

21. Murray Spivack interview transcript, ca. 1985, for *The RKO Story* (BBC, 1987).

22. Jewell, *A Titan Is Born*, 22.

23. Sam Kashner and Nancy Schoenberger, *A Talent for Genius: The Life and Times of Oscar Levant* (New York: Villard, 1994), 86–90.

24. Thomas interview with MS, CBC, 1961.

25. Ibid.

26. Steiner, *Notes to You*, Chapter XII.

27. *Variety*, December 25, 1929, 55.

28. The details of Steiner's original RKO contract are re-stated in a four-page letter from the studio to MS, January 18, 1939 (MSS 1547, Box 5, Folder 4).

CHAPTER 6

1. *Variety*, December 25, 1929.
2. Steiner's address, phone number, and job title appear in Los Angeles telephone directories of the early 1930s. (Los Angeles Public Library Collection)
3. *Film Daily*, November 1929.
4. Eliscu interview transcript, ca. 1985, for *The RKO Story* (BBC, 1987).
5. For a comprehensive account of Spivack's career, see *An Oral History with Murray Spivack* (Beverly Hills, CA: Academy of Motion Picture Arts and Sciences, Oral History Program, 1995).
6. Spivack interview transcript, ca. 1985, for *The RKO Story* (1987).
7. Ibid.
8. Max Steiner Music Society journal, 1970.
9. Spivack oral history, AMPAS, MHL, 25.
10. Steiner, *The Real Tinsel*, 390.
11. Ibid., 390.
12. For a rich account of this period, see Slowik, *After the Silents*.
13. Ibid., 76.
14. Spivack interview, *The RKO Story* (1987).
15. Levant, *A Smattering of Ignorance*, 97–98.
16. Accounts of Steiner scoring silent versions of RKO talkies are anecdotal. See Clifford McCarty, "A Max Steiner Filmography," *The Max Steiner Collection* (Provo, UT: BYU, 1996).
17. Max Steiner, *The Case of Sgt. Grischa*, pencil sketch, RKOSR Box 490M.
18. Edward Watz, *Wheeler & Woolsey: The Vaudeville Comic Duo and Their Films, 1929–1937* (Jefferson, NC: McFarland Classics, 1994), 86.
19. Jewell, *A Titan Is Born*, 28.
20. Max Steiner, "Scoring the Film," *We Make the Movies*, ed. Nancy Naumburg (New York: Norton, 1937), 219.
21. Steiner, *Notes to You*, Chapter XIII.
22. Spivack oral history AMPAS, MHL, 33–34.
23. Grace Kingsley, "Hobnobbing in Hollywood," unidentified newspaper, 1933, MSS 1547, Scrapbook 1.
24. JWM interview with JVC, February 7, 2011.
25. Spivack interview, *The RKO Story* (1987).
26. Details of this contract were restated in a letter from the studio to Steiner, January 18, 1939. MSS 1547, Box 5, Folder 4.
27. Levant, *A Smattering of Ignorance*, 91.
28. Peter Wegele, *Max Steiner: Composing, Casablanca, and the Golden Age of Film Music* (Lanham, MD: Rowman & Littlefield, 2014), 10–11.
29. Steiner, *Notes to You*, Chapter XIII.
30. David Thomson, *Showman: The Life of David O. Selznick* (New York: Alfred A. Knopf, 1992), 130.

31. Jewell, *A Titan Is Born*, 33.

32. *Cimarron* files, RKOSR, Box 111SS.

33. Ibid.

34. Steiner, *Notes to You*, Chapter XIII.

35. "News and Reviews: Remarks on 'Cimarron,' " *Hollywood Daily News*, February 1931.

36. "Over a 'Wow' of a 'Cimarron,' " *Hollywood Filmograph*, February 14, 1931.

37. Jewell, *A Titan Is Born*, 33.

38. "Daily Musicians Report," February 20, 1931. *Traveling Husbands* music and production files, RKOSR, Boxes 205M and 12P.

39. "AFI Catalog of Feature Films," https://catalog.afi.com/Film/4117-ARE-THESE-OUR-CHILDREN?sid=29bc126f-071b-46a6-82fa-ccd59685d7a6&sr=5.5264587&cp=1&pos=0

40. *Los Angeles Times*, October 11, 1931.

41. Born on April 5, 1899, Kaun died in Baden-Baden, West Germany, on January 3, 1980. His father, Hugo, was a Berlin-born composer of symphonic works and operas. See "Hugo Kaun Papers," New York Public Library Manuscripts, call number JPB 04-5.

42. Steiner, *Notes to You*, Chapter XIII.

43. MSS 1547, Box 5, Folder 4.

44. Spivack interview, *The RKO Story*.

45. Jewell, *A Titan Is Born*, 35.

CHAPTER 7

1. See Thomson, *Showman: The Life of David O. Selznick* (New York: Knopf, 1992). Also see Ronald Haver, *David O. Selznick's Hollywood* (New York: Knopf, 1980).

2. Robert Belcher interview transcript, ca. 1985, *The RKO Story* (1987).

3. William Dozier interview transcript, ca. 1985, *The RKO Story* (1987).

4. Kevin Brownlow, *The Parade's Gone By* (New York: Knopf, 1968), 431.

5. Watz, *Wheeler & Woolsey*, 160.

6. Script files, RKOSR, Box 164S.

7. Production files, RKOSR, Box 16P.

8. Thomas interview with MS, CBC, 1961.

9. Robert Reid, "Music and Songs: Max Steiner," *Author and Composer*, October 1933. Steiner is quoted as saying "In *Symphony of Six Million* . . . I tried out an idea in musical underscoring never used before. The suggestion was made by David O. Selznick." MSS 1547, Scrapbook 1.

10. Quoted by Wegele, *Max Steiner*, 26–27.

11. Reid, "Music and Songs: Max Steiner," *Author and Composer*, MSS 1547, Scrapbook 1.

12. Wegele, *Max Steiner*, 28–29.

13. All comments on Steiner's notations for this score, and all Steiner remarks written on the score and quoted in this chapter, are found in *Symphony*'s original pencil sketch. MSS 1547, Vol. 8.

14. Marie Teller to John Simons, August 24, 1937, MSS 1547, Box 4, Folder 1.

15. Ronald Haver, "The Selznick Style," program notes for screening of *Symphony of Six Million*, undated. (Author's collection.) The information likely comes from Haver's communication with Steiner for the book *David O. Selznick's Hollywood*.

16. Production files, RKOSR, Box 16P.

17. Quoted by Haver, "The Selznick Style."

18. *Symphony of Six Million* press book, Margaret Herrick Library, Academy of Motion Pictures Arts and Sciences. Beverly Hills, CA. Hereafter abbreviated as MHL.

19. "Movieditorial," *Herald-Express*, March 26, 1932, MSS 1547, Scrapbook 1.

20. "'Symphony' Rated As Classic," *Hollywood Herald*, March 23, 1932, MSS 1547, Scrapbook 1.

21. JWM interview with author, 2016.

22. Undated newspaper ad, 1932. MHL.

23. Thomson, *Showman*, 131–32.

24. Ibid., 131–32.

25. See Preliminary Budget, RKOSR, Box 16P.

26. Steiner, *Notes to You*, Chapter XIII.

27. Steiner quotations about this score (in italics) are from his original pencil sketch. MSS 1547, Vol. 16.

28. RKOSR, Box 16P.

29. Ibid.

30. "New Pictures," *Hollywood Herald*, July 30, 1932, MSS 1547, Scrapbook 1.

31. Fay Wray, *On the Other Hand: A Life Story* (New York: St. Martin's Press, 1989), 103.

32. Merian C. Cooper, eulogy for Max Steiner, memorial service, Forest Lawn, Glendale, California, December 30, 1971. (Audio courtesy of Jim Knuttel.)

33. MS memo to Daniel O'Shea, July 28, 1932. From the collection of JWM.

34. "Lost Worlds and Forgotten Music: Max Steiner's Legendary RKO Scores," Bill Whitaker, liner notes, *The Son of Kong/The Most Dangerous Game* (Marco Polo, 2000).

35. The pencil sketch of Harling's complete score survives. RKOSR, Boxes 481M, 482M.

36. Vaz, *Living Dangerously*, frontispiece.

37. Steiner quotations about this score (in italics) are from his original pencil sketch. MSS 1547, Vol. 82.

38. Max Steiner, "Setting Emotions to Music," *Variety*, July 31, 1940.

39. Whitaker, "Lost Worlds and Forgotten Music," 23.

40. RKOSR, Box 18P.

41. Ibid.

42. Ibid.

43. Elizabeth Yeaman, *Hollywood Daily Citizen*, Fall 1932, MSS 1547, Scrapbook 1.

44. Overage report, August 13, 1932. RKOSR, Boxes 19P and 104P.

45. Ibid.

46. "Max Steiner Acting," unidentified publication, October 10, 1932, MSS 1547, Scrapbook 1.

47. "Radio," unidentified publication, July 26, 1932, MSS 1547, Scrapbook 1.

48. Quoted by Behlmer, "All This and a Stolen Life, Too: Bette Davis in Stride at Warner Bros.," liner notes, *All This, and Heaven Too/A Stolen Life* (Naxos, 2003), 4.

CHAPTER 8

1. Alan K. Rode, *Michael Curtiz: A Life in Film* (Lexington: University Press of Kentucky, 2017), 130.

2. Thomson, *Showman*, 140–50, and Jewell, *A Titan Is Born*, 62–64.

3. Behlmer, "*King Kong*: The Eighth Wonder of the World." *King Kong: Original Motion Picture Soundtrack* (Rhino Records, 1999). 6.

4. Ibid., 6.

5. Ronald L. Haver, quoted by Behlmer, ibid., 7.

6. For accounts of *Kong*'s making, see the documentary "RKO Production 601: The Making of Kong, Eighth Wonder of the World," *King Kong Collector's Edition* (Warner Home Video, 2005), and Vaz, *Living Dangerously*.

7. Behlmer, "*King Kong*: The Eighth Wonder of the World," 8.

8. Ibid., 13.

9. Steiner, *Notes to You*, Chapter XIII.

10. Ibid.

11. Ibid.

12. Jewell, *A Titan Is Born*, 63.

13. MS to Tony Thomas. Thomas, "Max Steiner: Vienna, London, New York and Finally Hollywood," *The Max Steiner Collection* (Provo, UT: BYU), 1996.

14. MS to John L. Bach, March 11, 1940, MSS 1547, Box 2, Folder 12.

15. JWM to author, August 30, 2016.

16. Steiner quotations about the score in this chapter, unless otherwise noted, are from his original pencil sketch. MSS 1547, Vol. 91.

17. "Ray Bradbury on Max Steiner," liner notes, *King Kong: The Complete 1933 Film Score*. Naxos, 1999, 7.

18. JWM to author, August 30, 2016.

19. In the 1960s, Steiner told John W. Morgan that the scene was not in the film by the time he was scoring it. JWM to author, August 30, 2016.

20. Spivack, oral history, AMPAS, MHL, 54–60.

21. Ibid., 57–58.

22. Nathan Platte, *Musical Collaboration in the Films of David O. Selznick 1932–1957*, dissertation, University of Michigan, 2010.

23. "Reconstruction Notes by John Morgan," liner notes, *King Kong: The Complete 1933 Film Score*, 20.

24. Ibid., 20.

25. JWM to author, August 30, 2016.

26. Figures taken from a letter from E. L. Scanlon to Merian C. Cooper, September 14, 1938, Merian C. Cooper Collection, L. Tom Perry Special Collections Library, Harold B. Lee Library, Brigham Young University, Provo, Utah, Box 9, Folder 15.

27. Jewell, *A Titan Is Born*, 63.

28. Cooper eulogy for Max Steiner, memorial service, December 30, 1971.

29. Rudy Behlmer, "*King Kong*: The Eighth Wonder of the World," 5.

30. Rudy Behlmer, *Inside Warner Bros. (1935–1951)* (New York: Viking, 1985), 10–11. See also Jewell, *A Titan Is Born*, 68.

31. Steiner, *Notes to You*, Chapter XIII.

32. MS to Sam Fox, February 15, 1933. MSS 1547, Box 5, Folder 12.

33. Vaz, *Living Dangerously*, 236.

34. Ibid., 237.

35. "Ray Harryhausen on Max Steiner," liner notes, *King Kong: The Complete 1933 Film Score*, 5.

36. Vaz, *Living Dangerously*, 237.

37. Ray Bradbury on Max Steiner, 7.

38. Bradbury, "The Film, The Music, and the Man," Max Steiner Music Society journal, Winter 1974.

39. Jewell, *A Titan Is Born*, 63.

40. Ibid.

41. Quoted by JVD, "Curiously Appropriate," liner notes, *King Kong: The Complete 1933 Film Score*, 17.

42. Ibid., 17.

43. Quoted in *King Kong*, original souvenir program, March 1933. LSE, Oversized Boxes, 1.

44. "Music on the Screen," *Variety*, February 27, 1934.

45. Cooper eulogy for Max Steiner, memorial service, December 30, 1971.

46. Quoted by JVD, "The Ear Must Hear What the Eye Sees," Max Steiner at RKO (BYU Music Archive, 2002).

47. Danny Elfman, *King Kong, Original Motion Picture Soundtrack* (Rhino, 1999), 3.

48. Christopher Palmer, *The Composer in Hollywood* (London: Marion Boyars, 1990), 29.

49. Vaz, *Living Dangerously*, 248–49.

50. Whitaker, "Lost Worlds and Forgotten Music," 14, and JWM, "Arranger's Notes," *The Son of Kong*, 30.

51. Recalled session harpist Louise Klos, "He really thought it was a cute idea." Ibid., 20.

52. Steiner quotations about the score are from his original pencil sketch. MSS 1547, Vol. 104.

53. Whitaker, "Lost Worlds and Forgotten Music," 27.

CHAPTER 9

1. "Agreement Between RKO Studios, Inc. and Max Steiner," June 22, 1933, MSS 1547, Box 5, Folder 4.
2. "Max Steiner Resigns from Radio Music Post," *Hollywood Reporter*, June 7, 1933.
3. MS to Hubbell, April 19, 1933, MSS 1547, Box 5, Folder 5.
4. Hubbell to MS, June 16, 1933, MSS 1547, Box 5, Folder 5.
5. Hubbell to MS, October 27, 1933, MSS 1547, Box 5, Folder 5.
6. *Sweepings* pencil sketch, MSS 1547, Vol. 117.
7. Anne Edwards, *A Remarkable Woman: A Biography of Katharine Hepburn* (New York: William Morrow, 1985), 106–7.
8. Hepburn interview transcript, ca. 1985, *The RKO Story* (1987).
9. Steiner, *Notes to You*, Chapter XIII.
10. Ibid.
11. "Beethoven in Hollywood," *Progressive Weekly*, September 2, 1939, MSS 1547, Scrapbook 1.
12. Steiner, "How to Appreciate Music in Motion Pictures," *Motion Picture Studio Insider*, May 1936.
13. Steiner, *Notes to You*, Chapter XV.
14. Steiner, "Scoring the Film," *We Make the Movies*, 221.
15. Steiner, *Notes to You*, Chapter XV.
16. Steiner, *We Make the Movies*, 223–24.
17. "Motion Picture Music," *Overture*, November 1947. MSS 1547, Scrapbook 3.
18. Quoted by Wegele, *Max Steiner*, 36.
19. "Music Hath Charms," *Boxoffice*, August 22, 1936.
20. *Melody Cruise* production files, RKOSR, Box 28P.
21. Spivack interview transcript, *The RKO Story* (BBC 1987).
22. Steiner, *We Make the Movies*, 232.
23. Ibid.
24. Jewell, *A Titan Is Born*, 75.
25. Arlene Croce, *The Fred Astaire and Ginger Rogers Book* (Boston: Dutton, 1972), 27.
26. Eliscu interview transcript, The RKO Story (1987).
27. Todd Decker, *Music Makes Me: Fred Astaire and Jazz* (Berkeley: University of California Press, 2011), 1–5.
28. Ibid., 4–5.
29. JWM to author, August 30, 2016.
30. Hal Borne interview transcript, 1986, *The RKO Story* (1987).
31. Data in this paragraph comes from *Flying Down to Rio* production files, RKOSR, Box 37P.
32. Spivack interview transcript, *The RKO Story* (1987).
33. *Hollywood Citizen News*, November 30, 1933. MSS 1547, Scrapbook 1.
34. Tim Page, "The Pleasures of Richard Strauss," *New York Review of Books*, January 31, 2015.

35. Gene Raymond interview transcript, ca. 1985, *The RKO Story* (1987).

36. Hermes Pan interview transcript, ca. 1985, *The RKO Story* (1987).

37. Raymond interview transcript, ca. 1985, *The RKO Story* (1987).

38. MS to Jules Levy, November 20, 1934, MSS 1547, Box 3, Folder 6.

39. Jewell, *A Titan Is Born*, 81.

40. LK, Autobiographical Notes. After retiring in the 1990s, LK made copious hand-written notes about her life. These can be found at LSE and have been assembled by the author into a single document hereafter called "Autobiographical Notes."

41. "Studio Director Sued for Divorce," *Daily News*, November 15, 1933. MHL.

42. Ibid.

43. "Mrs. Max Steiner Obtains Divorce," *Examiner*, December 14, 1933. MHL.

44. See "Audree van Lieu alimony payments," MSS 1547, Box 1, Folder 9.

45. Autobiographical Notes, LSE.

46. Aida Mulieri Dagort, *Harps Are Not for Angels* (Bloomington, IN: Xlibris, 1999), 132–33.

47. Quotations and biographical information about Louise in this chapter are from Autobiographical Notes, unless otherwise noted.

48. "A lot of composers" through "play for him"—Scott Eyman, "A Hollywood Melody," *Palm Beach Post*, July 31, 1996.

49. LK interview with JVD, May 7, 1996.

50. Dorothy Cooper Jordan interview transcript, ca. 1985, *The RKO Story* (1987).

51. *Little Women* production files, RKOSR, Box 35P.

52. MS to John L. Bach, March 11, 1940, MSS 1547, Box 2, Folder 12.

53. When MGM remade *Little Women* 15 years later, Steiner's "Jo" theme was licensed from RKO and used throughout Adolph Deutsch's score.

54. Ibid., 76.

55. Emanuel Levy, *George Cukor: Master of Elegance* (New York: William Morrow, 1994), 78.

56. Hepburn interview transcript, *The RKO Story* (1987).

CHAPTER 10

1. Jewell, *A Titan Is Born*, 73–85.

2. Dorothy Jordan Cooper interview transcript, *The RKO Story* (1987). Also see Vaz, *Living Dangerously*, 250.

3. Tom Donnelly, "It's All Ghost Music," *Washington D.C. Daily News*, April 17, 1947. See also "Music in the Cinema," *New York Times*, September 29, 1935.

4. RKOSR, *The Lost Patrol* production files, Box 38P.

5. Ibid.

6. Steiner, *Notes to You*, Chapter XIII.

7. "Music in the Cinema," *New York Times*, September 29, 1935.

8. RKOSR, Box 38P.

9. Steiner quotations about this score are from his original pencil sketch. MSS 1547, Vol. 104.

10. This alternate ending can be found in Steiner's original pencil sketch. Ibid.

11. RKOSR, Box 38P.

12. "Outstanding Stunts: Film Soundtrack Program," *Variety*, January 20, 1934.

13. "John Ford Scores," *Hollywood Spectator*, February 10, 1934.

14. "*The Lost Patrol* Ranks with the Best of the Season," unidentified publication, 1934, MSS 1547, Scrapbook 1.

15. LK interview with JVD, May 7, 1996.

16. Jeremy Arnold, "Of Human Bondage," TCM website, http://www.tcm.com/tcmdb/title/3911/Of-Human-Bondage/articles.html

17. Jewell, *A Titan Is Born*, 86.

18. Pandro S. Berman Oral History, American Film Institute, 1972, 260–61.

19. *Of Human Bondage* production files, RKOSR, Box 43P.

20. Steiner quotations about this score are from his original pencil sketch. MSS 1547, Vol. 117.

21. Steiner, "The Inside on Music."

22. Copland, *Our New Music: Leading Composers in Europe and America* (New York: McGraw-Hill, 1941), 260–75.

23. "Concert and Opera," unidentified publication, July 1943, MSS 1547, Scrapbook 2.

24. Steiner, *Notes to You*, Chapter XIII.

25. In 1934 the film lost $45,000. Jewell, *A Titan Is Born*, 86–69.

26. Louis Kaufman and Annette Kaufman, *A Fiddler's Tale: How Hollywood and Vivaldi Discovered Me* (Madison: University of Wisconsin Press, 2003), 116.

27. Annette Kaufman to Edward Leaney, February 16, 1990, MSS 1547, Leaney Collection.

28. Annette Kaufman to Leaney, August 11, 1993, MSS 1547, Leaney Collection.

29. Annette Kaufman to Leaney, February 16, 1990, MSS 1547, Leaney Collection.

30. See ASCAP papers, MSS 1547, Box 5, Folder 5.

31. Lillian K. Braun to MS, November 7, 1934, MSS 1547, Box 5, Folder 5.

32. *Stingaree* music files, RKOSR, Boxes 632M and 633M.

33. Ibid.

34. Pandro S. Berman interview transcript, *The RKO Story* (1987).

35. Memorandum, July 23, 1934, Production Code Administration Files, MHL.

36. Borne interview transcript, *The RKO Story* (1987).

37. Arlene Croce, *The Fred Astaire and Ginger Rogers Book*, 126.

38. LSE, Autobiographical notes.

39. Steiner, We Make the Movies, 232.

40. *The Gay Divorcee* production files, RKOSR, Box 50P.

41. Music files, RKOSR, Boxes 544M, 562M, 563M, 564M, 565M.

42. Ibid.

43. RKOSR, Box 50P.

44. O'Heron to Kahane, July 2, 1934. From the collection of JWM.

45. Contract dated June 12, 1934, MSS 1547, Box 5, Folder 4.

46. MS to Kahane and six other RKO executives, September 29, 1934. From the collection of JWM.

47. Spivack oral history, AMPAS, MHL, 65.

48. MS to Kahane, October 4, 1934.

49. Spivack oral history, MHL, 65–66.

50. Ibid., 67.

51. Ibid., 67–68.

52. Jewell, *A Titan Is Born*, 96.

53. "*The Gay Divorcee* a Hit," *Hollywood Reporter*, October 1, 1934, MSS 1547, Scrapbook 1.

CHAPTER 11

1. David Sokol, "Little Monarch of Sound Discusses Music," *Illustrated Daily News*, July 23, 1935.

2. Robert Reid, "Max Steiner," *Author and Composer*, October 1933, MSS 1547, Scrapbook 1.

3. *Hollywood Citizen-News*, August 22, 1935, MSS 1547, Scrapbook 1.

4. MS to Ruby Laffoon, July 19, 1934. MSS 1547, Scrapbook 1. See also "Col. Max Steiner," *Hollywood Reporter*, January 24, 1934.

5. Harry Mines, "Raves and Raps," *Los Angeles Daily News*, February 26, 1938.

6. Most of Steiner's acetate collection survives and can be found at MSS 1547.

7. Jewell, *A Titan Is Born*, 106. Also see Kathryn Kalinak, *Settling the Score*, 114.

8. Ibid., 106.

9. Scott McGee, "The Informer," TCM website, http://www.tcm.com/this-month/article/147130%7Co/The-Informer.html

10. Steiner quotations about this score, unless otherwise noted, are from his original pencil sketch. MSS 1547, Vol. 82.

11. Kalinak, *Settling the Score*, 115–16.

12. Steiner, *Notes to You*, Chapter XIII.

13. Steiner, "How to Appreciate Music in Motion Pictures."

14. Palmer, *The Composer in Hollywood*, 32.

15. Steiner, *Notes to You*, Chapter XIII.

16. Ralph Holmes, "*The Informer* Is Feature at Fox," *Detroit Evening Times*, May 11, 1935.

17. "The Musical Background," *Hollywood Citizen-News*, April 30, 1935.

18. Richard Watts, Jr., "Sight and Sound," *Herald-Tribune*, September 1, 1935.

19. Gus Kahn to MS, July 16, 1935, MSS 1547, Box 3, Folder 3.

20. Frank Capra to MS, July 11, 1935, MSS 1547, Box 2, Folder 13.

21. Jewell, *A Titan Is Born*, 106.

22. Teller on behalf of MS to Donald Gledhill, August 8, 1939, MSS 1547, Box 6, Folder 11.

23. George Zachary to MS, January 15, 1948, Box 2, Folder 16.

24. Linda Danly, ed. *Hugo Friedhofer: The Best Years of His Life: A Hollywood Master of Music for the Movies* (Lanham, MD: Scarecrow, 1999), 88.

25. MS to Kern, December 17, 1934, MSS 1547, Box 3, Folder 3.

26. Kern to MS, December 18, 1934, MSS 1547, Box 3. Folder 3.

27. *Top Hat* script files, RKOSR, Box 382S and Box 383S.

28. Steiner, *Notes to You*, Chapter XIII.

29. LK letter to MS, July 2, 1951, MSS 1547, Box 2, Folder 1.

30. LK interview with JVD, May 7, 1996.

31. LSE, Oversized Boxes, 1.

32. Steiner, *Notes to You*, Chapter XIII.

33. Jewell, *A Titan Is Born*, 113.

34. Edward Martin, "Cinemania" column, *Hollywood Citizen-News*, September 6, 1935.

35. Steiner quotations about this score are from his original pencil sketch. MSS 1547, Vol. 138.

36. "Music by Max Steiner from the Following Pictures," typed list of composition highlights, 1944, MSS 1547, Box 2, Folder 13.

37. MS to Paul Wesson, September 28, 1955, MSS 1547, Box 2, Folder 13.

38. JWM interview with JVD, February 7, 2011.

39. Nan Blake to "Mr. Benedict," RKO Studios, July 26, 1935, MSS 1547, Scrapbook 1.

40. Richard D. Saunders, "Better Quality Discovered in Movie Music," *Hollywood Citizen*, July 27, 1935.

41. Edward Martin, "Cinemania" column, *Hollywood Citizen-News*, September 6, 1935.

42. Steiner quotations about this score are from his original pencil sketch. MSS 1547, Vol. 158.

43. JWM interview with JVD, February 7, 2011.

44. "*The Three Musketeers*: The Film/The Music." In *The Three Musketeers: Original Motion Picture Score* (Provo: BYU Film Music Archives), 2007.

45. Ibid.

46. "Music in the Cinema," *New York Times*, September 9, 1935.

47. "The Three Musketeers," *Hollywood Filmograph*, October 5, 1935.

CHAPTER 12

1. Haver, *David O. Selznick's Hollywood*, 11. This book is the ultimate source on Selznick's work.

2. Unnamed memo author to DOS, August 22, 1935. From the collection of JWM.

3. Autobiographical Notes, LSE.

4. "Steiner Requests Release at Radio," *Hollywood Reporter*, November 15, 1935.

5. DOS to John Hay Whitney, December 5, 1935. From the collection of JWM.

6. "M.B." to DOS, December 19, 1935. From the collection of JWM.

7. Ibid.

8. Decker, *Music Makes Me*, 66.

9. As of 2019, Steiner's pencil sketch for this sequence is misfiled at RKOSR in *Carefree* (1938) music papers, 665M.

10. Thomson, *Showman*, 200–201.

11. B. B. Kahane to "Mr. Woit," January 2, 1936. Courtesy of Richard Jewell.

12. J. J. Nolan to Daniel O'Shea, December 11, 1935, RKO records. Courtesy of Richard Jewell.

13. MS to Frederick Day, March 24, 1936, MSS 1547, Box 2, Folder 13.

14. DOS to Phil Ryan, January 24, 1936, HRC 642:15.

15. Charles Goldberg, "Lowdown on High-ups," *Jewish Voice*, February 28, 1936.

16. DOS, "LLF, Musical Scoring to Be Made For," January 8, 1936; DOS "LLF, Music Notes," January 23, 1936; DOS, "LLF, Music Notes," January 31, 1936, HRC 463:6.

17. DOS to Phil Ryan, November 19, 1935, HRC 642:15.

18. Steiner, "How to Appreciate Music in Motion Pictures."

19. Steiner quotations about this score, unless otherwise noted, are from his original pencil sketch. MSS 1547, Vol. 101.

20. Platte, *Making Music*, 103.

21. Steiner, "How to Appreciate Music in Motion Pictures," May 1936.

22. Platte, *Making Music*, 101.

23. Ibid.

24. MS to DOS, MSS 1547, Box 4, Folder 13.

25. DOS to MS, MSS 1547, Box 4, Folder 13.

26. "Film Preview," *Variety*, February 21, 1936.

27. "Steiner Musical Director 'Little Lord Fauntleroy,'" *Hollywood Screen World*, March 10, 1936.

28. "M.B." to Loyd [*sic*] Wright, February 17, 1936. From the collection of JWM.

29. "Steiner to Selznick," *Hollywood Reporter*, April 16, 1936.

30. "M.B." to Loyd [*sic*] Wright, February 17, 1936. From the collection of JWM.

31. Jules Levy to MS, May 13, 1936, MSS 1547, Box 3, Folder 6.

32. Homer Canfield, "Camel Caravan, Amos 'n' Andy Plan Changes," unidentified 1936 article, MSS 1547, Scrapbook 1. Nathaniel Shilkret left RKO the following year.

33. Kaufman, "*The Three Musketeers*: The Film/The Music."

34. Marie Teller to William G. van Schmus, March 1, 1940, MSS 1547.

35. Ibid.

36. Stanley Bigelow, "Federal Orchestra Concert Offers New Music," *Los Angeles Evening News*, May 16, 1936, Scrapbook, Book 1.

37. Donald Spoto, *Blue Angel: The Life of Marlene Dietrich* (New York: Doubleday, 1992), 130.

38. For accounts of *Allah*'s troubled making, see Thomson, *Showman*, 206–22, and Maria Riva, *Marlene Dietrich by Her Daughter* (New York: Random House, 1992), 383–99.
39. Steiner, *Notes to You*, Chapter XIII.
40. Typed invitation, MSS 1547, Box 2, Folder 12.
41. Thomson, *Showman*, 221.
42. Barbara Keon to MS, July 18, 1936, HRC 407:4.
43. Steiner quotations about this score are from his original pencil sketch. MSS 1547, Vol. 66.
44. Russell Birdwell, undated press release, 1936, MSS 1547, Box 2, Folder 12.
45. "GOA, Music Notes," September 7, 1936, and October 9, 1936, HRC 407:4.
46. Don Christlieb, *Recollections of a First Chair Bassoonist: 52 Years in the Hollywood Studio Orchestras* (Sherman Oaks, CA: Christlieb Products, 1996).
47. Platte, *Making Music*, 105.
48. DOS to MS, October 26, 1936, MSS 1547, Box 4, Folder 13.
49. MS to DOS, October 30, 1936, Box 4, Folder 13.
50. JWM interview by JVD, February 7, 2011. For more on push-pull and early sound recording, see Robert Gitt's documentary *A Century of Sound: The History of Sound in Motion Pictures: The Sound of Movies, 1933–1975*. It is available via the UCLA Film & Television Archive.
51. "New Film Triumphs in Use of Color," *Literary Digest*, November 6, 1936.
52. "Selznick's 'Allah' Prod'n of Beauty, Artistry, Charm," *Hollywood Reporter*, October 31, 1936.
53. MS to Sol Bernstein, November 3, 1936. From the collection of JWM.
54. "Garden of Allah," *Variety London*, 1936, MSS 1547, Scrapbook 1.
55. Thomson, *Showman*, 222.
56. Pascal Bonetti to MS, November 1, 1936, MSS 1547, Box 7, Folder 3.
57. Lloyd Pantages, "French Government Honors Max Steiner," *Los Angeles Examiner*, November 26, 1936.
58. Steiner, *Notes to You*, Chapter XIII.

CHAPTER 13

1. Ronald L. Davis, *The Glamour Factory* (Dallas, TX: Southern Methodist University Press, 1993), 22–24.
2. Ibid.
3. Charles Foster, *Once Upon a Time in Paradise: Canadians in the Golden Age of Hollywood*, Toronto: Dundurn Press, 2003), 997.
4. Tony Thomas, album notes, *The Classic Film Scores for Bette Davis* (RCA Victor, 1973).
5. Carroll, *The Last Prodigy: A Biography of Erich Wolfgang Korngold* (Lanham, MD: Amadeus Press, 1997), 238–39.

6. MS to Forbstein, February 21, 1936, MSS 1547, Box 6, Folder 11.

7. LK interview with JVD, May 7, 1996.

8. "Hal Wallis Papers: Biography/History," MHL. https://collections.oscars.org/link/bio/404

9. Aljean Harmetz, *The Making of* Casablanca: *Bogart, Bergman, and World War II* (New York: Hachette, 2002), 267.

10. Ronald L. Davis, *Just Making Movies: Company Directors on the Studio System* (Jackson: University Press of Mississippi, 2005), 35.

11. For a blow-by-blow account of *Charge*'s filming, see Rode, *Michael Curtiz*, 187–200.

12. Wallis and Charles Higham, *Starmaker: The Autobiography of Hal Wallis* (New York: Macmillan, 1980), 36.

13. Carroll, *The Last Prodigy*, 261.

14. Roy Obringer to Mr. Wilder, August 20, 1936, MSS 1547, Leaney Collection.

15. JWM interview with JVD, February 7, 2011.

16. Wallis to Forbstein, September 19, 1936, WARC, TCOTLB Production Box.

17. Linda Danly, ed., *Hugo Friedhofer*, 5–10.

18. JWM interview with JVD, February 7, 2011. Hugo and Max briefly crossed paths at RKO in 1934, but did not collaborate until 1936. HF interview with Diana Friedberg, December 11, 1975.

19. Thomas introduction to Danly, *Hugo Friedhofer*, 1–2.

20. Danly, *Hugo Friedhofer*, 3–4.

21. Ibid., 41–44.

22. Steiner quotations about this score, unless otherwise noted, are from his original pencil sketch. MSS 1547, Vol. 27.

23. Quoted by JWM, album notes, *The Charge of the Light Brigade: The Complete Max Steiner Score* (Tribute Film Classics, 2009).

24. Ibid.

25. MS pencil sketch, *The Amazing Dr. Clitterhouse*, MSS 1547, Vol. 5.

26. Wallis to Forbstein, September 19, 1936, WARC, TCOTLB Production Box.

27. Quoted in album notes, *Band of Angels: Original Motion Picture Soundtracks and Scores* (Label X/LXCD 3, 1987).

28. JWM interview with author, 2016.

29. Reproduced in the booklet for *The Charge of the Light Brigade: The Complete Max Steiner Score* to the 1936 film.

30. Original Steiner pencil sketch, *The Charge of the Light Brigade*.

31. "List of Pictures for which Max Steiner Composed and Conducted the Music: Warner Bros. Pictures," document probably compiled by Marie Teller, ca. 1955, MSS 1547, Box 4, Folder 7.

32. Memos by Wallis, dated October 15 and October 19, include direction regarding editing and sound mixing, indicating postponement of final delivery. WARC, TCOTLB Production Box.

33. JWM interview with JVD, February 7, 2011.
34. Steiner, *Notes to You*, Chapter XIII.
35. Appendix 1, Historical Journal of Film, Radio and Television (1995).
36. "The Charge of the Light Brigade," *Variety*, October 17, 1936.
37. Joseph McBride, *Frank Capra: The Catastrophe of Success* (Jackson: University Press of Mississippi, 1992), 363.
38. Frank Capra, *The Name Above the Title: An Autobiography* (New York: Macmillan, 1971), 198.
39. Tiomkin and Prosper Buranelli, *Please Don't Hate Me* (New York: Doubleday, 1959), 204.
40. Behlmer, *America's Favorite Movies: Behind the Scenes* (New York: F. Ungar, 1982), 32.
41. LK interview with JVD, May 7, 1996.
42. Behlmer, *America's Favorite Movies*, 33.
43. Steiner, *Notes to You*, Chapter XIII.
44. Tiomkin, *Please Don't Hate Me*, 204.
45. LK Oral History with Janet Bishoff, October 24, 1990.
46. Autobiographical notes, LSE.
47. LK to MS, October 30, 943, MSS 1547, Box 1, Folder 10.
48. Dagort, *Harps Are Not for Angels*, 117–19.
49. Extensive photographs of the home can be found in LSE, Box 1.
50. *Hollywood Reporter*, January 29, 1937.
51. Ussher, "Music in the Films," *Daily News*, 1940, MSS 1547, Scrapbook 2.
52. E. W. Biscailuz letter to MS, September 10, 1937, MSS 1547, Box 3, Folder 4.
53. Promissory note signed by MS, December 18, 1936, MSS 1547, Box 3, Folder 13.
54. DOS to Henry Ginsberg, March 24, 1937. From the collection of JWM.
55. DOS to Ginsberg, March 26, 1937, HRC 227:2.
56. "*A Star is Born*, Notes," March 29, 1937, HRC 513:7.
57. MS to DOS, April 8, 1937. From the collection of JWM.
58. HRC 640:14. For more on this, see Platte, *Making Music in Selznick's Hollywood*, 126–29.
59. MS to Jack L. Warner, April 5, 1939, MSS 1547, Box 4, Folder 14.

CHAPTER 14

1. "Max Steiner and Selznick Part; He's at WB," *Variety*, April 14, 1937.
2. MS to Minter, December 31, 1938, MSS 1547, Box 4, Folder 20.
3. MS to Frederick Day, May 13, 1937, MSS 1547, Box 2, Folder 13.
4. *Fortune*, December 1937, quoted by Behlmer, *Inside Warner Bros. (1935–1951)* (New York: Viking, 1985), 56.
5. Ibid.
6. Davis, *The Glamour Factory*, 8.

7. Wallis and Higham, *Starmaker*, 14.

8. Davis, *Just Making Movies*, 30.

9. Gordon Casson, "Beethoven in Hollywood," *Progressive Weekly*, September 2, 1939.

10. Henry Blanke oral history, UCLA, 1969, 104.

11. LK interview with Kate Daubney, June 18, 1999, MSS 1547, Oversized Boxes, 1.

12. JWM to author, August 30, 2016.

13. Ray Faiola, "The Score," liner notes, *The Glass Menagerie: Complete Original Motion Picture Soundtrack*. BYU Music Archive, 2001.

14. Dagort, *Harps Are Not for Angels*, 122–23.

15. Vincent LoBrutto, *Sound-on-Film: Interviews with Creators of Film Sound* (Westport, CT: Praeger, 1994), 12–13.

16. Dagort, *Harps Are Not for Angels*, 129.

17. Ibid., 118.

18. Scott Eyman, "A Hollywood Melody," *Palm Beach Post*, July 31, 1996.

19. Steiner, *Notes to You*, Chapter XIII.

20. Ibid.

21. Wallis and Higham, *Starmaker*, 36–37.

22. JWM interview with JVD, February 7, 2011.

23. Ibid. See also LK interview with JVD, May 17, 1996.

24. Steiner quotations about this score are from his original pencil sketch. MSS 1547, Vol. 144.

25. Steiner quotations about this score are from his original pencil sketch. MSS 1547, Vol. 152.

26. Wallis and Higham, *Starmaker*, 36–37.

27. Steiner quotations about this score are from his original pencil sketch. MSS 1547, Vol. 97.

28. Frank Miller, "The Life of Emile Zola," TCM website, http://www.tcm.com/this-month/article/66967%7C0/The-Life-of-Emile-Zola.html

29. Steiner, *Notes to You*, Chapter XIII.

30. Sherree Owens Zalampas, *Adolf Hitler: A Psychological Interpretation of His Views on Architecture, Art and Music* (Bowling Green, OH: Bowling Green State University Popular Press, 1990), 113.

31. Marie Teller to John Simons, August 24, 1937, MSS 1547, Box 4, Folder 2.

32. Simons to MS, September 9, 1937, MSS 1547, Box 4, Folder 2.

33. Dr. Felix Zipser to MS, October 11, 1937, MSS 1547, Box 4, Folder 1.

34. MS to Zipser, October 27, 1937, MSS 1547, Box 4, Folder 1.

35. MSS 1547, Box 1, Folder 5.

36. Behlmer, album notes, *Now, Voyager: The Classic Film Scores of Max Steiner* (RCA, 1973).

37. JWM interview with author, 2016.

38. DOS to Marcella Rabwin, September 9, 1937. From the collection of JWM.

39. AFI Catalog of Feature Films: "The Adventures of Tom Sawyer." https://catalog. afi.com/Catalog/moviedetails/913

40. Platte, *Making Music in Selznick's Hollywood*, 132.

41. Steiner quotations about this score are from his original pencil sketch. MSS 1547, Vol. 158.

42. Joseph D'Onofrio, "The Adventures of Tom Sawyer," TCM website, http://www. tcm.com/this-month/article/538%7C0/The-Adventures-of-Tom-Sawyer.html

43. When the son of a film composer mentioned his father's work on a Davis movie to the actress, Davis smiled and replied, "Max Steiner was *my* composer." JWM to author, August 30, 2016.

44. Steiner quotations about this score are from his original pencil sketch. MSS 1547, Vol. 86.

45. *Jezebel* final script, 61–63, WBARC, *Jezebel* Production Box.

46. Hammond, "Max Steiner's Music for the Bette Davis Films," Max Steiner Music Society journal, 1972.

47. William Darby and Jack Du Bois, *American Film Music*, 39–42.

48. Korngold to Wallis, February 11, 1938, quoted by Behlmer, *Inside Warner Bros.*, 52–53.

49. Levant, *A Smattering of Ignorance*, 106.

50. MS to Hal Wallis, April 5, 1939, MSS 1547, Box 4, Folder 2.

51. Steiner quotations about this score are from his original pencil sketch. MSS 1547, Vol. 55.

52. R. Vernon Steele, "Making Good Pictures Better," *Pacific Coast Musician*, December 17, 1938, MSS 1547, Scrapbook, Book 1.

53. LK interview with JVD, May 7, 1996.

54. MS to Arthur Faltin, May 27, 1938, MSS 1547, Box 2, Folder 16.

55. Ibid.

56. LK to Mrs. M.F. Strong, June 10, 1938, LSE, Oversized Boxes, 1.

57. *Hollywood Reporter*, September 14, 1938.

58. Faltin to MS, September 15, 1938, MSS 1547, Box 2, Folder 16.

59. MS to Faltin, September 21, 1938, MSS 1547, Box 2, Folder 16.

60. Autobiographical notes, LSE.

61. Ibid.

CHAPTER 15

1. R. Vernon Steele, "Making Good Pictures Better," Scrapbook, Book 1.

2. Ibid.

3. Tony Thomas, "Max Steiner: Vienna, London, New York, and Finally Hollywood," *The Max Steiner Collection* (Provo, UT: Brigham Young University, 1996).

4. Max Steiner, "Setting Emotions to Music," *Variety*, July 31, 1940.

5. Mary Ellen Ryan to MS, November 19, 1940, MSS 1547, Box 4, Folder 16.

6. MS to Sol Bornstein, December 1936. From the collection of JWM.

7. MS to Minter, December 31, 1938, MSS 1547, Box 4, Folder 20.

8. G. Y. Loveridge, " 'I'm Half Nuts,' Says Screen Master," MSS 1547, Scrapbook 2.

9. Ibid.

10. Behlmer, "Film Notes," *Dark Victory: Original Motion Picture Score* (BYU, 2006).

11. JWM, "Music Notes," *Music for the Bette Davis Films All This, and Heaven Too/A Stolen Life* (Naxos, 2007), 9.

12. Steiner quotations about this score are from his original pencil sketch. MSS 1547, Vol. 40.

13. Ed Sikov, *Dark Victory: The Life of Bette Davis* (New York: Henry Holt, 2007), 143.

14. Warner Bros. press release, WBARC, Dark Victory Production Box.

15. Sikov, *Dark Victory*, 143.

16. Bette Davis to David Frost, *The David Frost Show* (TV), May 8, 1971.

17. Charlotte Chandler, *The Girl Who Walked Home Alone: Bette Davis, A Personal Biography* (Simon & Schuster, 2006), 240.

18. Scott Allen Nollen, *Warners Wiseguys* (Jefferson, NC: McFarland, 2007), 147.

19. Steiner quotations about this score are from his original pencil sketch. MSS 1547, Vol. 118.

20. Kate Daubney, *Now, Voyager: A Film Score Guide* (Santa Barbara, CA: Greenwood Press, 2000), 17.

21. Steiner quotations about this score are from his original pencil sketch. MSS 1547, Vol. 53.

22. G. Y. Loveridge, " 'I'm Half Nuts,' Says Screen Master," MSS 1547, Scrapbook 2.

23. JWM to author, December 23, 2016.

24. Autobiographical notes, LSE.

25. Ibid.

26. MS to LK, undated card ca. 1939, LSE, Oversized Boxes, 1.

27. Steiner's financial problems comprise hundreds of pages of the collection found at MSS 1547.

28. MS to Mrs. Philip Baker, November 11, 1938, MSS 1547, Box 3, Folder 1.

29. Aljean Harmetz, *The Making of Casablanca*, 245–46. See also Thomas Doherty, *Hollywood and Hitler: 1933–1939* (New York: Columbia University Press, 2013).

30. Harmetz, *The Making of Casablanca*, 66–67.

31. Wallis and Higham, *Starmaker*, 70–71.

32. MS to Charles Einfeld, March 29, 1939, MSS 1547, Box 2, Folder 15.

33. MS to William G. King, September 14, 1938, MSS 1547, Box 3, Folder 4.

34. Ibid.

35. Behlmer, "The Saga of *Gone with the Wind*," liner notes, *Gone with the Wind: Original Motion Picture Soundtrack*, 27.

36. MS to Wallis, March 29, 1939, MSS 1547, Box 4, Folder 1.

37. MS to Warner, April 5, 1939. From the collection of JWM.

38. Warner to MS, April 6, 1939. From the collection of JWM.

39. Quoted by Behlmer, *Dodge City and The Oklahoma Kid: Original Motion Picture Scores.*

40. Goulding to MS, June 30, 1939, MSS 1547, Box 3, Folder 1.

CHAPTER 16

1. Louis Kaufman and Annette Kaufman, *A Fiddler's Tale*, 117.

2. Behlmer, "The Saga of *Gone with the Wind*," 15–16. Also see Haver, *David O. Selznick's Hollywood*; Michael Sragow, *Victor Fleming: An American Movie Master* (New York: Pantheon Books, 2008); Thomson, *Showman*; and James Curtis, *William Cameron Menzies: The Shape of Films to Come* (New York: Pantheon, 2015).

3. Thomson, *Showman*, 299.

4. DOS to MS and Forbes, October 9, 1939, reprinted in Rudy Behlmer, *Memo from David O. Selznick* (New York: Macmillan, 1973), 225–26.

5. MS to Kern, August 29, 1939, MSS 1547, Box 3, Folder 4.

6. Myrl Schreibman, "On *Gone with the Wind*, Selznick, and the Art of 'Mickey Mousing.'"

7. The thematic fragment can be heard in the final films, and found in Steiner's pencil sketches for each. MSS 1547, Vols. 5 and 42.

8. Bruno David Ussher, "Max Steiner Establishes Another Film Music Record," 1940 pamphlet, MSS 1547, Scrapbook 2.

9. Steiner quotations about this score, unless otherwise noted, are from his original pencil sketch. MSS 1547, Vol. 71ab.

10. Myrl Schreibman, "On *Gone with the Wind*, Selznick, and the Art of 'Mickey Mousing.'"

11. Ibid.

12. Ibid.

13. WBARC, *Four Wives* Production Box.

14. DOS to Henry Ginsberg, July 28, 1939, HRC 175:13.

15. Steiner quotations about this score are from his original pencil sketch. MSS 1547, Vol. 83.

16. Steiner, *The Real Tinsel*, 396.

17. James R. Silke, *Here's Looking at You, Kid: 50 Years of Fighting, Working, and Dreaming at Warner Bros.* (Boston: Little, Brown and Company, 1976), 97.

18. DOS to MS and Forbes, October 9, 1939, in Behlmer, *Memo from David O. Selznick*, 225–26.

19. Frank S. Nugent, "The Screen: Reviews and News," *New York Times*, December 1, 1939.

20. Jack Sullivan to T. C. Wright, July 5, 1939, WBARC, *We Are Not Alone*, Production Box.

21. MS to John L. Bach, March 11, 1940, Box 2, Folder 12.

22. Wallis to MS, October 25, 1939, MSS 1547, Box 4, Folder 1.
23. Danly, *Hugo Friedhofer*, 46.
24. LSE, Oversized Boxes, 1.
25. Behlmer, "The Saga of *Gone with the Wind*," 15–16.
26. DOS to Hal Kern and Lou Forbes, October 10, 1939, HRC 1237:3.
27. DOS, November 15, 1939, quoted by Behlmer, "The Saga of *Gone with the Wind*," 27.
28. "*Gone with the Wind* Music Notes Corrected by DOS," November 7, 1939, HRC 413:5.
29. Ibid.
30. Platte, *Making Music in Selznick's Hollywood*, 164.
31. LK interview with JVD, May 7, 1996.
32. Platte, *Making Music in Selznick's Hollywood*, 160.
33. Quoted in Behlmer, *Memo from David O. Selznick*, 230.
34. Ibid., 230.
35. All quotations by Steiner and *GWTW*'s orchestrators/co-composers, unless otherwise noted, are from the score's original pencil sketch, MSS 1547, Vol. 71ab.
36. Danly, *Hugo Friedhofer*, 60–64.
37. See Chapter 13, page [TBD].
38. JWM to author, August 30, 2016.
39. Behlmer, "The Saga of *Gone with the Wind*," 27.
40. Platte, *Making Music in Selznick's Hollywood*, 192.
41. LK interview with JVD, May 7, 1996.
42. Behlmer, *Memo from David O. Selznick*, 230.
43. Platte, *Making Music in Selznick's Hollywood*, 160.
44. "*GWTW* Music Notes," HRC 413:5.
45. Behlmer, "The Saga of *Gone with the Wind*," 29.
46. Ibid., 28.
47. Danly, *Hugo Friedhofer*, 63–64.
48. For more on the recording, see Platte, *Making Music in Selznick's Hollywood*, 167–69.
49. Platte, *Making Music in Selznick's Hollywood*, 169.
50. MSS 1547, Vol. 71ab.
51. Schreibman, "On *Gone with the Wind*, Selznick, and the Art of 'Mickey Mousing.'"
52. Behlmer, "The Saga of *Gone with the Wind*," 32.
53. Sragow, *Victor Fleming*, 352.

CHAPTER 17

1. Nugent, "The Screen in Review," *New York Times*, December 20, 1939.
2. "Gone with the Wind," *Variety*, December 20, 1939.

3. Karl Krug, "*Gone with the Wind* Thrilling and Magnificent," *Pittsburgh Sun Telegraph*, January 27, 1940.

4. *Gazette*, Schenectady, February 10, 1940.

5. Warner to MS, December 29, 1939, MSS 1547, Box 4, Folder 14.

6. Petula Dvorak, "The Wrong Oscars Envelope Wasn't the First Academy Awards Fiasco. This Was," *Washington Post*, March 4, 2018.

7. LK interview with JVD, May 7, 1996.

8. Steiner, *Notes to You*, Chapter XIII, offers one example of this.

9. MS to Don Yena, March 11, 1940, MSS 1547, Box 2, Folder 2.

10. Guinness World Records, http://www.guinnessworldrecords.com/world-records/highest-box-office-film-gross-inflation-adjusted/

11. Memo from Wallis to Will Hays, August 24, 1939, in Behlmer, *Inside Warner Bros.*, 105.

12. Steiner quotations about this score are from his original pencil sketch. MSS 1547, Vol. 52.

13. Davis, *The Glamour Factory*, 269. Also see Rode, *Michael Curtiz*, 262–68.

14. Steiner quotations about this score are from his original pencil sketch. MSS 1547, Vol. 166ab.

15. Autobiographical notes, LSE.

16. Ronald Steiner baby book, LSE, Box 6.

17. Autobiographical notes, LSE.

18. Ibid.

19. Michelangelo Capua, *Anatole Litvak: The Life and Films* (Jefferson, NC: McFarland, 2015), 48–50.

20. Steiner quotations about this score are from his original pencil sketch. MSS 1547, Vol. 4.

21. Hammond, "Max Steiner's Music for the Bette Davis Films," Max Steiner Music Society journal, 1972, 8.

22. Steiner mentioned the link between this theme and Ronald to JWM. JWM to author, August 30, 2016.

23. Steiner, *Notes to You*, Chapter XIII.

24. Ibid.

25. Warner to MS, May 23, 1940, MSS 1547, Box 4, Folder 14.

26. Goldwyn to MS, June 14, 1940, Box 3, Folder 1.

27. Friedhofer shared this with JWM. JWM to author, August 30, 2016.

28. Russell A. Barker, "Composer's Life Story Presented Tomorrow Night in New Radio Program," unidentified publication, June 20, 1940, Scrapbook 2.

29. Minter to MS, February 29, 1940, MSS 1547, Box 4, Folder 20.

30. This arrangement is referenced in a document citing "a new agreement dated July 30, 1940," stating that Minter is "to act as Mr. Steiner's business manager." MSS 1547, Box 4, Folder 20.

31. Minter to MS, October 10, 1940, MSS 1547, Box 4, Folder 20.

32. Steiner, *Notes to You*, Chapter XIII.

33. Friedhofer AFI Oral History, interview by Irene Kahn Atkins, 1974, 184.

34. MS to Blau, July 5, 1940, Box 5, Folder 3.

35. Jan Herman, *A Talent for Trouble: The Life of Hollywood's Most Acclaimed Director, William Wyler* (Boston: Da Capo Press, 1997), 211.

36. Steiner quotations about this score are from his original pencil sketch. MSS 1547, Vol. 96.

37. Friedhofer AFI Oral History, 183–84.

38. Ibid.

39. JWM to author, August 30, 2016.

40. MS to Blau, July 5, 1940, MSS 1547, Box 5, Folder 3.

41. Steiner, *Notes to You*, Chapter XIII.

42. "Stars of Opera Requested for Movie Musical," *Seattle Times*, January 26, 1941.

43. Steiner quotations about this score are from his original pencil sketch. MSS 1547, Vol. 48.

44. David Neumeyer, "The Resonances of Wagnerian Opera and Nineteenth-Century Melodrama in the Film Scores of Max Steiner," *Wagner & Cinema* (Bloomington: Indiana University Press, 2010), 118–22.

45. "Max Steiner Renewed," *Hollywood Reporter*, May 12, 1941.

46. Dagort, *Harps Are Not for Angels*, 132–133.

47. David Thomson, *Gary Cooper* (New York: Faber and Faber, 2009), 78.

48. Leo F. Forbstein to Victor Blau, January 29, 1941, WBARC, Sergeant York Production Box.

49. Steiner quotations about this score, unless otherwise noted, are from his original pencil sketch. MSS 1547, Vol. 137.

50. "Concert and Opera," *New York Times*, July 1943, Scrapbook 2.

51. Autobiographical notes, LSE.

52. Steiner, *Notes to You*, Chapter XIII.

53. Quoted by Bill Whitaker, "Lost World and Forgotten Music," 20.

54. Friedhofer to JWM; JWM to author, July 14, 2016.

55. MS to Beatrice Steiner, October 7, 1941, MSS 1547, Box 1, Folder 7.

56. Mark Schubart, "Max Steiner Makes a Case for Hollywood Composers," unidentified New York publication, August 2, 1943, MSS 1547, Scrapbook 2.

57. Autobiographical Notes, LSE. Louise also shared this story in several interviews. Max is apologetic in letters after Louise's departure but never specifically references this event in surviving correspondence.

58. Ibid.

CHAPTER 18

1. MS to LK, September 13, 1941, LSE, Oversized Boxes, 1.
2. MS to LK, October 16, 1942, LSE, Oversized Boxes, 1.
3. Steiner quotations about this score are from his original pencil sketch. MSS 1547, Vol. 121.
4. Peale made these remarks in a sermon, a copy of which he sent to Jack L. Warner on January 3, 1942. WBARC, *One Foot in Heaven* Production Box.
5. "*One Foot in Heaven* Great," *Hollywood Reporter*, September 30, 1941.
6. Davis, *Just Making Movies*, 35.
7. MS to Louise, September 28, 1941, LSE, Oversized Boxes, 1.
8. Ibid.
9. Kathryn Kalinak, *How the West Was Sung: Music in the Westerns of John Ford* (Berkeley: University of California Press, 2007), 134.
10. Daubney, *Max Steiner's Now, Voyager: A Film Score Guide*, 19–20.
11. JWM to author, August 30, 2016.
12. Tony Thomas, "Max Steiner: Vienna, London, New York, and Finally Hollywood."
13. John C. Tibbetts, James M. Walsh, editors, *American Classic Screen Interviews* (Lanham, MD: Scarecrow Press, 2010), 27.
14. Steiner quotations about this score are from his original pencil sketch. MSS 1547, Vol. 157.
15. This drawing is reprinted in the notes accompanying *They Died with Their Boots On: Digital World Premiere Recording*. Marco Polo, 1999, 22.
16. JWM, "Arranger Notes," *They Died with Their Boots On: Digital World Premiere Recording*, 28.
17. JWM interview with JVD, February 7, 2011.
18. Walsh to MS, November 14, 1941, MSS 1547, Box 4, Folder 2.
19. Marie Teller on behalf of MS to Beatrice Steiner, March 12, 1942, MSS 1547, Box 1, Folder 8.
20. Steiner quotations about this score are from his original pencil sketch. MSS 1547, Vol. 23.
21. LK interview with JVD, May 7, 1996.
22. Steiner quotations about this score are from his original pencil sketch. MSS 1547, Vol. 9.
23. Jack L. Warner to MS, March 3, 1942, MSS 1547, Box 4, Folder 14.
24. JWM, quoted by Ryan Brennan, "Capra, Cary, and a Clan of Crazy Brewsters," *Arsenic and Old Lace: The Complete Max Steiner Score to the 1944 Film* (Tribute Film Classics, 2011), 14.
25. Steiner quotations about this score are from his original pencil sketch. MSS 1547, Vol. 81.
26. Dagort, *Harps Are Not for Angels*, 126.
27. MS to LK, January 12, 1943, LSE, Oversized Boxes, 1.

28. MS to LK, January 16, 1942, MSS 1547, Box 1, Folder 10.

29. MS to LK, December 6, 1942, LSE, Oversized Boxes, 1.

30. Steiner, *Notes to You*, Chapter XIII.

31. MS and others to ASCAP, November 6, 1942, MSS 1547, Box 6, Folder 1.

32. Minter to MS and LK, April 17, 1942, MSS 1547, Box 4, Folder 20.

33. MS to Minter, June 16, 1942, MSS 1547, Box 4, Folder 20.

34. MS to Jack L. Warner, June 18, 1942, MSS 1547, Box 4, Folder 14.

35. Jeanne Allen, editor, *Now, Voyager: Wisconsin/Warner Bros.* Screenplay Series, 14–15.

36. Ibid., 18.

37. Sikov, *Dark Victory: The Life of Bette Davis*, 199.

38. Daubney, *Max Steiner's Now, Voyager: A Film Score Guide*, 59.

39. Steiner quotations about this score are from his original pencil sketch. MSS 1547, Vol. 116.

40. Daubney, *Now, Voyager: A Film Score Guide*, 60.

41. Wallis to Hermann Starr, October 2, 1942, WBARC, *Now, Voyager* Production Box.

42. "The Reel Dope," *Family Circle*, October 9, 1942, MSS 1547, Scrapbook 2.

43. Jeanne Allen, *Now, Voyager*, 27.

44. "NBC, CBS, Blue, Mutual Plugs," unidentified publication, March 10, 1943, MSS 1547, Scrapbook 2.

45. "Ten Best Sheet Music Sellers," *Variety*, April 5, 1943.

46. "Command Performance" radio broadcast, June 19, 1943.

47. Recorded 1953, MGM Records.

48. Aller interview with Diana Friedberg, 1975. Courtesy of DF.

49. MS to LK, January 12, 1943, LSE, Oversized Boxes, 1.

50. "The Long Voyage," *Variety*, March 10, 1943.

51. MS to LK, July 5, 1943, LSE, Box 1.

52. MS to LK, July 8, 1942, LSE, Oversized Boxes, 1.

53. MS to LK, July 30, 1942, LSE, Oversized Boxes, 1.

CHAPTER 19

1. Many sources chronicle the origins of the play. This author recommends Aljean Harmetz's *The Making of Casablanca: Bogart, Bergman, and World War II*.

2. Ibid.

3. For more on the Curtiz-Wallis partnership, see Rode, *Michael Curtiz: A Life in Film*, 309–37.

4. On April 21, 1942, Wallis wrote a detailed outline about music for the film, addressing both source music and score. See WBARC, *Casablanca* Production Box.

5. For more about Wallis's musical choices, see Leonard Maltin's essay "As Songs Go By: All the Music of *Casablanca*," *Hooked on Hollywood: Discoveries from a Lifetime of Film Fandom* (Pittsburgh: GoodKnight Books, 2018).

6. Wallis to Michael Curtiz, April 21, 1942, WBARC.

7. Whitaker, "Lost Worlds and Forgotten Music," 24.

8. Mark Schubart, "Max Steiner Makes a Case for Hollywood Composers," Scrapbook 2.

9. Wallis and Higham, *Starmaker*, 90–91.

10. Friedhofer, American Film Institute oral history, 159–60.

11. Steiner quotations about this score, unless otherwise cited, are from his original pencil sketch. MSS 1547, Vol. 24.

12. MS to LK, July 30, 1942, LSE, Oversized Boxes, 1.

13. Harmetz, *Making of Casablanca*, 213.

14. Quoted by Wegele, *Max Steiner*, 148.

15. Frank Miller, *Casablanca: As Time Goes By* (UK: Virgin, 1992), 199–200.

16. MS to LK, July 24, 1942, MSS 1547, LSE, Oversized Boxes, 1.

17. LK to MS, July 30, 1942, MSS 1547, Box 1, Folder 10.

18. Trilling to MS, September 15, 1942, MSS 1547, Box 3, Folder 13.

19. Curtiz to MS, September 23, 1942, MSS 1547, Box 2, Folder 13.

20. Harmetz, *Making of Casablanca*, 283.

21. MS to LK, June 25, 1943, LSE, Box 1.

22. Warner to Forbstein, April 16, 1943, quoted by Behlmer, *Inside Warner Bros.*, 221.

23. MS to LK, October 2, 1942, LSE, Oversized Boxes, 1.

24. Rode, *Michael Curtiz*, 341.

25. Clayton R. Koppes, Gregory D. Black, *Hollywood Goes to War* (New York: Tauris Parke, 2000), 191.

26. MS to LK, February 1, 1943, LSE, Oversized Boxes, 1.

27. MS to LK, January 12, 1943, LSE, Oversized Boxes, 1.

28. MS to LK, April 23, 1943, MSS 1547, Box 1, Folder 10.

29. Culbert, *Mission to Moscow*, 37.

30. Ibid.

31. Rode, *Michael Curtiz*, 352–53.

32. Frank Miller, "The Adventures of Mark Twain," TCM website, http://www.tcm.com/this-month/article/60075%7C0/The-Adventures-of-Mark-Twain.html

33. The main source used for steamboat calls was *Pageant of the Packets: A Book of American Steamboating* by Garnett Laidlaw Eskew (New York: Henry Holt, 1929). See WBARC, *The Adventures of Mark Twain*, Production Box.

34. MS to LK, May 27. 1943, LSE, Box 1.

35. Steiner quotations about this score, unless otherwise cited, are from his original pencil sketch. MSS 1547, Vol. 2.

36. Margaret Gledhill to MS, July 12, 1945, MSS 1547, Box 6, Folder 11.

37. Palmer, *The Composer in Hollywood*, 40–41.

38. Ibid.

39. MS to LK, January 21, 1943, LSE, Oversized Boxes, 1.

40. Charles Einfeld to MS, January 20, 1943, MSS 1547, Box 2, Folder 15.

41. Quoted by MS to LK, January 12, 1943, LSE, Oversized Boxes, 1.

42. MS to LK, April 23, 1943, MSS 1547, Box 1, Folder 10.

43. William G. King to MS, November 3, 1943, MSS 1547, Box 3, Folder 4.

44. LK interview with JVD, May 7, 1996.

45. MS to LK, May 27, 1943, LSE, Box 1.

46. MS to King, June 17, 1943, Box 3, Folder 4.

47. MS to LK, June 4, 1943, LSE, Box 1.

48. Ibid.

49. MS to LK, June 12, 1943, LSE, Box 1.

50. MS to LK, June 21, 1943, LSE, Box 1.

51. Ibid.

52. MS to LK, June 25, 1943, LSE, Box 1.

53. MS to King, July 1, 1943, MSS 1547, Box 3, Folder 4.

54. MS to King, July 14, 1943, MSS 1547, Box 3, Folder 4.

55. "Sinatra, Steiner to Be at Stadium," *New York Times*, July 28, 1943.

56. MS to LK, July 5, 1943, LSE, Box 1.

CHAPTER 20

1. Steiner, *Notes to You*, Chapter XIII.

2. LK interview with JVD, February 7, 1996.

3. "Frank Sinatra Sings to 7,000 at Stadium," *New York Times*, August 4, 1943.

4. Ibid.

5. Douglas Watt, "7,000 Hear Sinatra Sing at Stadium," *Daily News*, August 4, 1943.

6. *Musical Courier*, August 1943, MSS 1547, Scrapbook 3.

7. Robert Bagar, "Sinatra So-So at Stadium," *New Yorker*, August 4, 1943.

8. John Briggs, "Sinatra's Secret Revealed," *New York Post*, August 4, 1943.

9. Steiner, *Notes to You*, Chapter XIII.

10. Julian Seaman, "Film Symphonies," *New York Cue*, August 7, 1943.

11. Steiner, *Notes to You*, Chapter XIII.

12. King to MS, October 7, 1943, MSS 1547, Box 3, Folder 4.

13. Teller notation on letter from King to MS, November 3, 1943, MSS 1547, Box 3, Folder 4.

14. Marie Teller to Beatrice Steiner, MSS 1547, September 17, 1943, MSS 1547, Folder 1, Box 8.

15. Delos Lovelace, "Who's News Today," *New York Sun*, August 2, 1943.

16. Thomson, *Gary Cooper*, 92–93.

17. Jean Negulesco, *Things I Did . . . and Things I Think I Did* (New York: Simon & Schuster, 1984), 122.

18. MS to LK, October 25, 1943, MSS 1547, Box 1, Folder 10.

19. Steiner, *Notes to You*, Chapter XIII.

20. MS to LK, October 4, 1943, MSS 1547, Box 1, Folder 10.

21. WBARC, Rhapsody in Blue Production Box.

22. Steiner, *Notes to You*, Chapter XIII.

23. Ibid.

24. Ibid.

25. MS to LK, May 8, 1944, MSS 1547, Box 1, Folder 10.

26. Marie Teller to LK, MSS 1547, May 23, 1944, Box 1, Folder 10.

27. For more about the film's production, see Thomson, *Showman*, 394–403.

28. DOS to Daniel O'Shea, May 26, 1943, HRC, 600:7.

29. Platte, *Making Music*, 217–18.

30. Ibid., 218.

31. Ibid., 218–23.

32. DOS to Daniel O'Shea, April 29, 1944, HRC 600:7.

33. MS to LK, May 8, 1944, MSS 1547, Box 1, Folder 10.

34. DOS to O'Shea, May 12, 1944, HRC 600:7.

35. Steiner quotations about this score, unless otherwise cited, are from his original pencil sketch. MSS 1547, Vol. 141.

36. Platte, Making *Music in Selznick's Hollywood*, 225.

37. Platte, *Musical Collaboration in the Films of David O. Selznick, 1932–1957*, 450–51.

38. Platte, *Making Music in Selznick's Hollywood*, 227–29.

39. His orchestrators were Eugene Zador, Frank Perkins, Jerome Moross, Frank Skinner, and Leonid Raab. William Lava, Adolph Deutsch, and David Buttolph wrote short passages based on Steiner themes. See Platte, *Making Music in Selznick's Hollywood*, 329.

40. Dagort, *Harps Are Not for Angels*, 131–32.

41. Ibid.

42. LK interview with JVD, May 7, 1996.

43. DOS to MS, June 21, 1944, HRC 199:5.

44. Platte, *Making Music in Selznick's Hollywood*, 231.

45. John Cromwell to DOS, June 26, 1944, HRC 509:4.

46. Platte, *Making Music in Selznick's Hollywood*, 231–32.

47. DOS to MS, June 21, 1944, HRC 199:5.

48. Thomson, *Showman*, 401.

49. Steiner, *Notes to You*, Chapter XIII.

50. Ibid.

51. Louis Kaufman and Annette Kaufman, *A Fiddler's Tale*, 117–88.

52. Irving H. Walker to MS, September 16, 1944, MSS 1547, Box 1, Folder 10.

53. Autobiographical notes, LSE.

54. Dagort, *Harps Are Not for Angels*, 133.

55. Steiner quotations about this score are from his original pencil sketch. MSS 1547, Vol. 132.

CHAPTER 21

1. Earl C. Adams to Louis B. Minter, January 18, 1945, LSE, Oversized Boxes, 1.

2. Divorce Judgment, May 4, 1945, LSE, Oversized Boxes, 1.

3. Autobiographical notes, LSE.

4. David Thomson, *Humphrey Bogart* (New York: Faber and Faber, 2009), 78–85.

5. Steiner quotations about this score are from his original pencil sketch. MSS 1547, Vol. 15.

6. *Mildred*'s journey from novel to film is told by Albert J. LaValley in his introduction to *Mildred Pierce*, Wisconsin/Warner Bros. Screenplay Series, 1980.

7. Steiner quotations about this score are from his original pencil sketch. MSS 1547, Vol. 110.

8. Daubney, *Now, Voyager*, 25–26.

9. Eva Rieger, "Wagner's Influence on Gender Roles in Early Hollywood Film," *Wagner & Cinema*, 145–46.

10. See *Mildred Pierce*, Wisconsin/Warner Bros. Screenplay Series, 1980.

11. Warner to MS, June 14, 1945, Box 4, Folder 14.

12. Crawford to Albert K. Bender, "Just for Max: A Publication of the Max Steiner Music Society," early 1970s, LSE, Oversized Boxes, 1.

13. "Max Steiner Heads Screen Composers," *Variety*, July 24, 1945.

14. David Raksin, Max Steiner memorial eulogy, December 30, 1971.

15. Quoted by Alan K. Rode to author, March 17, 2019.

16. Rudy Behlmer, "A Stolen Life," *Music for the Bette Davis Films All This, and Heaven Too/A Stolen Life* (Naxos, 2003), 7–8.

17. Ibid., 7–8.

18. "Music Notes," JWM; Ibid., 9.

19. Wegele, *Max Steiner*, 78.

20. Forbstein to Steve Trilling, February 20, 1946. From the collection of JWM.

21. Siodmak, quoted in Moving Pictures Berlinale #9 (London/Berlin, 1998).

22. Siodmak's script references a Bach piano transcription made for one hand. Tony Thomas attributes the choice of the Chaconne to Siodmak in his notes for *Beast*'s re-recording (*The Lost Patrol/Virginia City/The Beast with Five Fingers* [Marco Polo, 1996]). According to Warner Bros. publicity notes, the one-hand arrangement was made by Victor Aller, a noted pianist and brother of cellist Eleanor Aller.

23. JWM to author, 2016.

24. JVD, album notes, *The Treasure of the Sierra Madre* (Marco Polo, 1996).

25. JWM interview with JVD, February 7, 2011.

26. MS to LK, July 14, 1946, LSE, Box 7.

27. "Cheyenne," *Variety*, April 22, 1947.

28. Autobiographical Notes, LSE.

29. MS to LK, July 14, 1946, LSE, Box 7.

30. Ibid.

31. Steiner, *Notes to You*, Chapter XIII.

32. Some sources, including a 1940 census, list her birth year as 1900.

33. Lee Steiner interview with Diana Friedberg, 1970s. Courtesy of DF.

34. LK to JVD, "Corrections to *Notes to You*" and interview, May 7, 1996.

35. MS to Frederick Day, March 10, 1948, MSS 1547, Box 2, Folder 13.

36. Steiner, *Notes to You*, Chapter XIII.

37. LK interview with JVD, May 7, 1996.

38. Autobiographical Notes, LSE.

39. MS to LK, August 8, 1946, LSE, Box 7.

40. Steiner quotations about this score are from his original pencil sketch. MSS 1547, Vol. 31.

41. Sperling to MS, August 15, 1946, MSS 1547, Box 3, Folder 13.

42. For more on the film's production, see Rode, *Michael Curtiz*, 390–400.

43. "Mauve Music for Father," *Beverly Hills Register*, September 13, 1947.

44. Steiner quotations about this score are from his original pencil sketch. MSS 1547, Vol. 98.

45. Warner to MS, August 19, 1947, MSS 1547, Box 4, Folder 14.

46. Teller to Beatrice Steiner, December 5, 1946, MSS 1547, Box 1, Folder 8.

47. Scorsese provided an on-camera introduction for a home video release of the film.

48. Marilyn Ann Moss, *Raoul Walsh: The True Adventures of Hollywood's Legendary Director* (Lexington: University Press of Kentucky, 2011), 268–71.

49. Steiner, *The Real Tinsel*, 392.

50. Busch to MS, March 15, 1947, MSS 1547, Box 2, Folder 12.

51. Webb to MS, undated letter ca. April 1947, Box 4, Folder 1.

CHAPTER 22

1. Siodmak interview, *Weekend am Wannsee* (documentary, Perraudin Film Production, 2000).

2. Steiner quotations about this score are from his original pencil sketch. MSS 1547, Vol. 45.

3. Steiner, *Notes to You*, Chapter XIII.

4. MS to J. Huntington Hartford, July 6, 1960, MSS 1547, Box 3, Folder 2.

5. MS to LK, November 3, 1947, LSE, Box 7.

6. MS to LK, March 31, 1947, LSE, Oversized Boxes, 1.

7. "Singer Lee Blair and Steiner Back After Elopement," *Los Angeles Examiner*, April 3, 1947.

8. MS to LK, May 6, 1947, LSE, Box 7.

9. MS, *Notes to You*, Chapter XIII.

10. Summary of costs for 3961 Alcove Ave., 1951 document, MSS 1547, Box 2, Folder 7.

11. MS to William G. King, July 28, 1947, MSS 1547, Box 3, Folder 4.

12. Steiner, *The Real Tinsel*, 396.

13. Wieland Schulz-Keil, quoted by Tony Tracy, "Reflections of Huston," *John Huston: Essays on a Restless Director* (Jefferson, NC: McFarland, 2010), 205.

14. Scott McGee and Eleanor Quin, "The Treasure of the Sierra Madre," TCM website, http://www.tcm.com/tcmdb/title/2852/The-Treasure-of-the-Sierra-Madre/articles.html

15. Palmer, *The Composer in Hollywood*, 35.

16. JWM to author, August 30, 2016.

17. Palmer, *The Composer in Hollywood*, 37–38.

18. Steiner quotations about this score, unless otherwise noted, are from his original pencil sketch. MSS 1547, Vol. 161.

19. Behlmer, *Inside Warner Bros.*, 287.

20. MS to Huston, March 28, 1949, MSS 1547, Box 3, Folder 2.

21. Wald to Forbstein, December 11, 1947; Joe McLaughlin to Wald, December 17, 1947. See WBARC *Key Largo* Production Box.

22. MS to LK, December 1, 1947, MSS 1547, Box 2, Folder 1.

23. MS to Ronald Steiner, March 17, 1948, LSE, Oversized Boxes, 1.

24. MS sent numerous book proposals to publishers in 1947. See MSS 1547, Box 3, Folder 9.

25. Behlmer, "The Making of *Johnny Belinda* (Against All Odds)," *Johnny Belinda: Original Motion Picture Score* (Brigham Young Music Archive, 2005).

26. Negulesco, *Things I Did . . . and Things I Think I Did*, 126.

27. Steiner quotations about this score, unless otherwise noted, are from his original pencil sketch. MSS 1547, Vol. 89.

28. Steiner, *Notes to You*, Chapter XIII.

29. Ibid.

30. WBARC, *Johnny Belinda* Production Box.

31. MS to Wyman, January 22, 1948, MSS 1547, Box 4, Folder 2.

32. Steiner expressed bitterness over the loss in one of his final interviews, for the book *The Real Tinsel*, 396–97.

33. MS to Wyman, March 28, 1948, MSS 1547, Box 4, Folder 2.

34. Brendan Carroll, *The Last Prodigy*, 318–19.

35. JWM to author, August 30, 2016.

36. Ryan Brennan, "Bringing the Legendary Lover to Life: The Making of *Adventures of Don Juan*," *Adventures of Don Juan/Arsenic and Old Lace* (Tribute Classics, 2011), 8–19.

37. WBARC, *Adventures of Don Juan* Production Box.

38. Quoted by Behlmer, audio commentary for home video edition, *The Adventures of Don Juan*.

39. JVD, *It Didn't Stay in Las Vegas, Adventures of Don Juan/Arsenic and Old Lace*, 3–5.

40. Curt Hardaway, music notes, *Adventures of Don Juan/Arsenic and Old Lace*, 20.

41. MS to Antonio Rodriguez Moreno, October 26, 1954, MSS 1547, Box 3, Folder 8.

42. Steiner quotations about this score, unless otherwise noted, are from his original pencil sketch. MSS 1547, Vol. 1ab.
43. JWM, "Production Notes," *Adventures of Don Juan/Arsenic and Old Lace*, 42.
44. WBARC, *Adventures of Don Juan* Production Box.
45. Sherman audio commentary for home video edition, *The Adventures of Don Juan*.
46. Behlmer, *Inside Warner Bros.*, 308.
47. Wegele, *Max Steiner*, 78.
48. MS to Beatrice Steiner, May 6, 1948, MSS 1547, Box 1, Folder 8.

CHAPTER 23

1. Forbstein to Trilling, February 20, 1946. From the collection of JWM.
2. MS to Ronald Steiner, March 17, 1948, LSE, Box 1.
3. "Tribute Today to Forbstein," *Los Angeles Examiner*, April 25, 1948.
4. Janis Paige to author, August 19, 2016.
5. Autobiographical Notes, LSE.
6. MS to LK, January 6, 1949, LSE, Box 7.
7. Glenn Alexander Magee, "*The Fountainhead*: A Great, Flawed Film." *The Fountainhead: Original Motion Picture Score* (BYU Film Music Archives, 2004).
8. Ayn Rand, Appendix to *Atlas Shrugged* (New York: Signet, 1957).
9. Thomson, *Gary Cooper*, 96.
10. Palmer, *The Composer in Hollywood*, 38–40.
11. Steiner quotations about this score are from his original pencil sketch. MSS 1547, Vol. 63.
12. Magee, "*The Fountainhead*: A Great, Flawed Film."
13. "The Fountainhead," *Variety*, June 23, 1949.
14. MS to Ayn Rand, February 17, 1949, MSS 1547, Box 3, Folder 12.
15. MS to LK, January 6, 1949, LSE, Box 7.
16. Loan agreement signed by MS and Roy Obringer, March 7, 1949, MSS 1547, Box 4, Folder 1.
17. Sikov, *Dark Victory*, 272.
18. Hammond, "Max Steiner's Music for Bette Davis Films," 13.
19. MS to Victor Blau, September 30, 1949, MSS 1547, Box 5, Folder 10.
20. Steiner quotations about this score are from his original pencil sketch. MSS 1547, Vol. 21.
21. Davis, *The Glamour Factory*, 369.
22. MS to Charles Miller, February 22, 1950, MSS 1547, Box 3, Folder 8.
23. MS to LK, June 30, 1950, MSS 1547, Box 2, Folder 1.
24. Warner Bros. press release, undated (ca. 1951). Courtesy of Thomas Yotka.
25. Steiner quotations about this score are from his original pencil sketch. MSS 1547, Vol. 153.
26. MS to Steve Trilling, November 21, 1950, MSS 1547, Box 3, Folder 13.

27. Steiner, *Notes to You*, Chapter XIII.

28. MS to LK, January 13, 1950, MSS 1547, Box 2, Folder 1.

29. Quoted by Darr Smith, *Los Angeles Times*, 1950.

30. Steiner quotations about this score are from his original pencil sketch. MSS 1547, Vol. 68.

31. Williams to Warner, Jerry Wald, and Charles Feldman, May 6, 1950. Quoted by Ray Faiola, "The Score," *The Glass Menagerie: Complete Original Motion Picture Soundtrack* (BYU Music Archives, 2001).

32. Kate Buford, *Burt Lancaster: An American Life* (Boston: Da Capo Press, 2001), 102–104.

33. Steiner quotations about this score are from his original pencil sketch. MSS 1547, Vol. 59.

34. Contract between MS and Capitol Records, August 19, 1949, MSS 1547, Box 5, Folder 6.

35. MS to LK, May 17, 1951, Box 2, Folder 1.

36. MS to LK, June 11, 1951, Box 2, Folder 1.

37. Steiner quotations about this score are from his original pencil sketch. MSS 1547, Vol. 87.

38. "Song Recital," *(London) Times*, May 29, 1951. LSE, Box 1.

39. "American Soprano," *Stage*, May 31, 1951. LSE, Box 1.

40. The four letters quoted in italics are (in order): LK to MS, June 8, 1951 (MSS 1547, Box 2, Folder 1); MS to LK, June 11, 1951 (MSS 1547, Box 2, Folder 1); LK to MS, July 2, 1951 (MSS 1547, Box 2, Folder 1); MS to LK, May 17, 1951 (LSE, Box 7).

41. LK to MS, undated letter (late April or early May 1952), MSS 1547, Box 2, Folder 1.

42. LK to MS, September 2, 1952, MSS 1547, Box 2, Folder 1.

43. A deep dive into Cinerama history can be found at http://www.widescreenmuseum. com/widescreen/wingcr1.htm

44. Steiner, *Notes to You*, Chapter XIII.

45. Ibid.

46. MS to Lou Forbes, July 2, 1952, MSS 1547, Box 4, Folder 19.

47. Merian C. Cooper, "Adventure in Cinerama," *Weekly Variety*, September 29, 1954.

48. MS to Forbes, July 11, 1952, MSS 1547, Box 4, Folder 19.

49. MS to Forbes, August 5, 1952, MSS 1547, Box 4, Folder 19.

50. MS to LK, September 15, 1952, Box 2, Folder 1.

51. Steiner and Marie Teller handled invoices for the many orchestrators and co-composers on *This Is Cinerama*. There is no invoice among them for Max's work. In *Notes to You* (Chapter XIII), Steiner says that he worked "without any remuneration because of my admiration and affection for my friend Merian Cooper." He did, however, accept from the producer "a beautiful wrist watch which I still wear and treasure."

52. Steiner, *Notes to You*, Chapter XIII.
53. Steiner quotations about this score are from his original pencil sketch. MSS 1547, Vol. III.

CHAPTER 24

1. The Steiner-scored trailer can be found on most video releases of *House of Wax*. Its pencil sketch is at MSS 1547 (OS12, Folder 3).
2. JWM interview with JVD, February 7, 2011.
3. Robert Wise interview transcript, *The BBC Story* (1987).
4. Wise oral history, Academy of Motion Picture Arts and Sciences, February/April 2004, MHL.
5. "Steiner to Leave Post at Warners," *New York Times*, July 15, 1953.
6. "Steiner Leaves WB to be Music Pub," *Hollywood Reporter*, July 15, 1953.
7. MS to Michael Curtiz, July 20, 1953, MSS 1547, Box 2, Folder 13.
8. Curtiz to MS, July 21, 1953, MSS 1547, Box 2, Folder 13.
9. Steiner quotations about this score, unless otherwise noted, are from his original pencil sketch. MSS 1547, Vol. 17.
10. Steiner, *The Real Tinsel*, 397.
11. Newman to MS, April 12, 1953, MSS 1547, Box 3, Folder 9.
12. MS to Zissu, March 24, 1954, MSS 1547, Box 5, Folder 2.
13. Emanuel Sacks to MS, July 31, 1953, MSS 1547, Box 5, Folder 11.
14. MS to DOS, July 1, 1953, MSS 1547, Box 4, Folder 13.
15. MS to Dreyfus, September 17, 1953, MSS 1547, Box 5 Folder 7.
16. Ibid.
17. MS to Zissu, January 20, 1954, MSS 1547, Box 5, Folder 2.
18. JWM to author, 2016.
19. MS to Zissu, October 7, 1953, MSS 1547, Box 5, Folder 1.
20. "Caine Composer Asked to Write Hit to Order," *San Francisco Chronicle*, November 4, 1953.
21. MS to Joseph R. Carlton, June 21, 1954, MSS 1547, Box 5, Folder 11.
22. MS to Zissu, February 15, 1954, MSS 1547, Box 5, Folder 2.
23. MS to Zissu, June 1, 1954, MSS 1547, Box 5, Folder 2.
24. For *Sabrina* and *Magnificent Obsession*, see MS to Zissu, November 4, 1953, MSS 1547, Box 5, Folder 1. For *Strategic Air Command*, see MS to Zissu, July 19, 1954, MSS 1547, Box 5, Folder 2.
25. MS to LK, July 22, 1954, MSS 1547, Box 2, Folder 1.
26. MS to Zissu, February 15, 1954, MSS 1547, Box 5, Folder 2.
27. MS to Zissu, January 20, 1954, MSS 1547, Box 5, Folder 2.
28. JWM to author, August 30, 2016.
29. MS to LK, February 1, 1954, LSE, Box 7.
30. Ronald Steiner to LK, undated letter 1954, LSE, Box 1.

31. MS to Ronald Steiner, July 22, 1954, MSS 1547, Box 2, Folder 3.
32. LK to MS, December 6, 1954, Box 2, Folder 1.
33. MS to Zissu, January 20, 1954, MSS 1547, Box 2, Folder 2.
34. Ibid.
35. MS to Zissu, March 30, 1954, Box 5, Folder 2.
36. MS to Zissu, March 24, 1954, Box 5, Folder 2.
37. MS to Herman Starr, June 23, 1954, Box 5, Folder 10.
38. Ray Faiola, "The Marines, Warner Bros. and Max Steiner," *Battle Cry: Complete Original Motion Picture Score* (BYU Music Archives, 2004).
39. Ibid.
40. Syd Goldberg to MS, February 11, 1955, MSS 1547, Box 5, Folder 10.
41. R. J. Obringer to John Kotanan, December 22, 1954, MSS 1547, Leaney Collection.
42. MS to James Howard, April 5, 1955, MSS 1547, Box 2, Folder 4.
43. MS to Zissu, February 7, 1955, MSS 1547, Box 5, Folder 2.
44. Jacques Biroteau to MS, June 9, 1955, MSS 1547, Box 3, Folder 8.
45. Quoted by AFI notes on *Come Next Spring*, http://www.tcm.com/tcmdb/title/71281/Come-Next-Spring/notes.html
46. MS to LK, October 24, 1955, LSE, Oversized Boxes, 1.
47. For more about music in *The Searchers*, see Kalinak, Chapter 7, "What Makes a Man to Wander," *How the West Was Sung*.
48. Audio commentary, home video release of *The Searchers* (Warner Bros.). The score was not played by the London Philharmonic but by Los Angeles studio musicians.
49. C. V. Whitney to MS, December 9, 1955, MSS 1547, Box 4, Folder 1.

CHAPTER 25

1. MS to JWM; JWM to author, August 30, 2016.
2. MS to LK, April 17, 1956, LSE, Box 7.
3. Ibid.
4. Ronald Steiner to LK, April 21, 1956, LSE, Box 7.
5. Ronald Steiner to LK, October 26, 1956, LSE, Box 7.
6. MS to LK, February 15, 1957, LSE, Box 7.
7. Jewell, *Slow Fade to Black: The Decline of RKO Radio Pictures*, 188–93.
8. Jon Burlingame, "SCL's History: From SCA to CLGA to SCL," Society of Composers & Lyricists website, https://thescl.com/mission-and-history/
9. Raksin, Steiner eulogy, memorial service, December 30, 1971.
10. MS to LK, March 16, 1955, Box 2, Folder 2.
11. Steiner, *Notes to You*, Chapter XIII.
12. Ibid.
13. In his autobiography, Fuller wrote that during the 1950s he enjoyed the company of "nourishing people, like my musician friends Max Steiner, Victor Young . . ." Of

China Gate, Fuller wrote, "Max made sure all monies were paid to Victor's estate." Fuller, *A Third Face* (New York: Knopf, 2002), 330 and 341.

14. *China Gate* pencil sketch, MSS 1547, Vol. 29.

15. *Death of a Scoundrel* pencil sketch, MSS 1547, Vol. 43.

16. Quoted in album notes, *Band of Angels: Original Motion Picture Soundtracks and Scores* (Label X/LXCD 3, 1987).

17. Glenn Erickson, "Band of Angels," DVD Savant, https://www.dvdtalk.com/dvdsavant/s2212band.html

18. John Cocchi, album notes, *Marjorie Morningstar*. Screen Archives Entertainment, 2006.

19. Steiner was musical director of Wynn's Broadway revue *The Grab Bag* (Globe Theater, 1924–1925).

20. Wegele, *Max Steiner*, 86.

21. AFI Catalog of Feature Films, "John Paul Jones (1959)," https://catalog.afi.com/Catalog/moviedetails/53414

22. Autobiographical Notes, LSE.

23. Ibid.

24. Paige to author, August 19, 2016.

25. Hoover's involvement is detailed by Curt Gentry in *J. Edgar Hoover: The Man and the Secrets* (New York: Norton, 1991), 384, 446–47, and by the film's director, Mervyn LeRoy, in *Mervyn LeRoy: Take One* (New York: Hawthorn, 1974), 199–202.

26. Gentry, *J. Edgar Hoover*, 447.

27. Composer's Agreement, May 13, 1959, MSS 1547, Leaney Collection.

28. Paine Knickerbocker, "A Summer Place on the California Coast," *New York Times*, April 5, 1959.

29. MSS 1547, Leaney Collection.

30. See "A Farewell to Arms" pencil sketch, MSS 1547, Box OS11, Folder 25.

31. JWM, quoted in "*A Summer Place*: The Score," *A Summer Place: Complete Original Motion Picture Score* (BYU Film Music Archive, 2003).

32. Steiner, *Notes to You*, Chapter XIII.

33. JWM interview with JVD, February 7, 2011.

34. Blau to Mack Goldman, September 4, 1959, WBARC, *A Summer Place* Production Box.

35. David Simons, *Studio Stories* (San Francisco: Backbeat Books, 2004), 25.

36. Steve Sullivan, *Encyclopedia of Great Popular Song Recordings, Vol. 3* (New York: Rowman & Littlefield, 2017), 324.

37. Howard Thompson, "Summer Place Opens," *New York Times*, October 23, 1959.

38. Fred Bronson, *The Billboard Book of Number One Hits* (New York: Billboard Books, 2003), 75.

39. Ray Faiola, "*A Summer Place*: The Score," *A Summer Place: Complete Original Motion Picture Score*.

40. MS to J. Huntington Hartford, July 6, 1960, MSS 1547, Box 3, Folder 2.

41. The disco cover was recorded by none other than Percy Faith, shortly before his death on February 9, 1976. Bronson, *The Billboard Book of Number One Hits*, 75.

42. JWM interview with JVD, February 7, 2011.

43. Burlingame, "SCL's History: From SCA to CLGA to SCL."

44. JWM to author, August 30, 2016.

45. John G. Houser, "What's the Score?" *Variety*, April 26, 1961.

46. Undated letter ca. 1958 to 21 businesses and "all restaurants," MSS 1547, Box 2, Folder 3.

47. LK to JVD, May 7, 1996.

48. MS to Ronald Steiner, LSE, Box 7.

49. Ronald Steiner memorial obituary, LSE, Oversized Boxes, 1

50. "Max Steiner's Son Found Dead in Hotel," *Los Angeles Times*, May 1, 1962.

51. LSE, special collections.

52. Steiner, *Notes to You*, Chapter XIII.

53. LK to JVD, May 7, 1996.

54. *Los Angeles Times*, May 1, 1962.

55. JWM to author, August 30, 2016.

CHAPTER 26

1. Hazel Flynn, "Composer Loses, Regains Eyesight," *Citizen News*, June 11, 1963.

2. Henry Fonda, *Fonda: My Life* (New York: Dutton, 1981), 283.

3. Palmer, *The Composer in Hollywood*, 42.

4. Steiner, *Notes to You*, Chapter XIII.

5. Ibid, Chapter XIV.

6. JVD, "Max Steiner, Walt Disney, & Those Calloways," *Those Calloways: Original Motion Picture Score* (Screen Archives Entertainment/BYU Film Music Archive, 2013).

7. Ibid.

8. Ibid.

9. Silke, *Here's Looking at You, Kid*, 305.

10. Tony Thomas, "Max Steiner: Vienna, London, New York, and Finally Hollywood," 19.

11. Blau to Herman Clebanoff, December 16, 1964, WBARC, *Two on a Guillotine* Production Box.

12. JWM to author, August 30, 2016.

13. Silke, *Here's Looking at You, Kid*, 305.

14. JVD, "Max Steiner, Walt Disney, & Those Calloways."

15. MS to JWM, JWM to author, August 30, 2016.

16. Jack Smith, album notes, *The Searchers* (BYU Film Music Archives, 1996).

17. Steiner, *Notes to You*, Chapter XIV.

18. JVD, "Introductions and Acknowledgments," *The Max Steiner Collection*.

19. Max Steiner Music Society journal, Winter 1971.

20. Ibid., Spring 1972.

21. Ibid., November/December 1966.

22. JWM to author, August 30, 2016.

23. Ibid.

24. Max Steiner Music Society journal, 1967.

25. JWM interview with JVD, February 7, 2011.

26. JWM to author, August 30, 2016.

27. JWM interview with JVD, February 7, 2011.

28. Myrl Schreibman, "On *Gone with the Wind*, Selznick, and the Art of 'Mickey Mousing.'"

29. Ibid.

30. Steiner, *Notes to You*, Chapter XIII.

31. Behlmer, "The Recording," *Gone with the Wind: Max Steiner's Classic Film Score* (RCA Victor, 1974).

32. Elmer Bernstein, Steiner eulogy, memorial service, December 30, 1971.

33. Ibid.

34. Max Steiner Music Society journal, Summer 1968.

35. Ibid., Winter 1971.

36. Elmer Bernstein, memorial service, December 30, 1971.

37. JWM interview with JVD, February 7, 2011.

38. Albert K. Bender, "Max Steiner: The Humorist," Max Steiner Music Society journal, 1974.

39. Steiner, *Notes to You*, Chapter XIV.

40. Will of Max Steiner, signed June 3, 1969; LSE, Oversized Boxes, 1.

41. JWM interview with JVD, February 7, 2011.

42. Autobiographical notes, LSE.

Selected Bibliography

ARCHIVAL INSTITUTIONS AND ABBREVIATIONS

BRTD   Billy Rose Theatre Division, New York Library for the
        Performing Arts, New York, NY

HRC   David O. Selznick Collection, Harry Ransom Humanities
        Research Center, University of Texas at Austin, Austin, TX

LSE   Louise Steiner Elian Papers, L. Tom Perry Special Collections
        Library, Harold B. Lee Library, Brigham Young University,
        Provo, UT

MHL   Margaret Herrick Library, Academy of Motion Picture Arts and
        Sciences, Beverly Hills, CA

MSS   1547 Max Steiner Collection, L. Tom Perry Special Collections
        Library, Harold B. Lee Library, Brigham Young University,
        Provo, UT

RKOSR   RKO Radio Pictures Studio Records, Performing Arts Special
        Collections, University of California, Los Angeles, CA

THAUS   Theater Museum. Vienna, Austria

VATPC   Theatre & Performing Arts Collection, Victoria & Albert
        Museum, London

WBARC   Warner Bros. Archives, USC School of Cinematic Arts,
        University of Southern California, Los Angeles, CA

BOOKS AND ARTICLES

Allen, Jeanne T., ed. *Now, Voyager.* Wisconsin/Warner Bros. Screenplay Series. Madison: University of Wisconsin Press, 1984.

Banfield, Stephen. *Jerome Kern.* New Haven, CT: Yale University Press, 2006.

Barrios, Richard. *A Song in the Dark: The Birth of the Musical Film.* New York: Oxford University Press, 2010.

Behlmer, Rudy. *America's Favorite Movies: Behind the Scenes.* New York: F. Unger, 1982.

Behlmer, Rudy. *Inside Warner Bros.* (1935–1951). New York: Viking, 1985.

Behlmer, Rudy. "*King Kong*: The Eighth Wonder of the World." In *King Kong: Original Motion Picture Soundtrack.* Los Angeles: Rhino Records, 1999. Compact disc.

Behlmer, Rudy. "The Making of *Johnny Belinda* (Against All Odds)." *Johnny Belinda: Original Motion Picture Score.* Provo, UT: Brigham Young University (BYU) Film Music Archives, 2005. Compact disc.

Behlmer, Rudy. *Memo from David O. Selznick.* New York: Viking, 1972.

Behlmer, Rudy. "The Saga of *Gone with the Wind*." *Gone with the Wind: Original Motion Picture Soundtrack.* Los Angeles: Rhino Records, 1996. 2 compact discs.

Behlmer, Rudy. "Winning the West at Warners." *Dodge City/The Oklahoma Kid: Original Motion Picture Scores.* Provo, UT: BYU Film Music Archives, 2001. 2 compact discs.

Bennett, Robert Russell. *The Broadway Sound: The Autobiography and Selected Essays of Robert Russell Bennett.* Edited by George J. Ferencz. Rochester, NY: University of Rochester Press, 1999.

Berman, Pandro S. *A Louis B. Mayer American Film Institute Oral History of Pandro S. Berman.* Los Angeles: American Film Institute, 1972.

Bordman, Gerald. *American Musical Theatre: A Chronicle.* New York: Oxford University Press, 2001.

Bordman, Gerald. *Days to Be Happy, Years to Be Sad: The Life and Music of Vincent Youmans.* New York: Oxford University Press, 1982.

Brennan, Ryan. "Bringing the Legendary Lover to Life." *Adventures of Don Juan/Arsenic and Old Lace.* Los Angeles: Tribute Film Classics, 2011. 2 compact discs.

Burlingame, Jon. *Sound and Vision: Sixty Years of Motion Picture Soundtracks.* New York: Billboard Books, 2000.

Christlieb, Don. *Recollections of a First Chair Bassoonist: 52 Years in the Hollywood Studio Orchestras.* Sherman Oaks, CA: Christlieb Products, 1996.

Cooke, Mervyn. *A History of Film Music.* New York: Cambridge University Press, 2008.

Dagort, Aida Mulieri. *Harps Are Not for Angels.* Bloomington, IN: Xlibris, 1999.

Danly, Linda, ed. *Hugo Friedhofer: The Best Years of His Life: A Hollywood Master of Music for the Movies.* Lanham, MD: Scarecrow, 1999.

Darby, William, and Jack Du Bois. *American Film Music: Major Composers, Techniques, Trends, 1915–1990.* Jefferson, NC: McFarland, 1999.

D'Arc, James V., and John N. Gillespie, eds. *The Max Steiner Collection.* Provo, UT: Brigham Young University Press, 1996.

D'Arc, James V., and John N. Gillespie, eds. "Max Steiner, Walt Disney, & *Those Calloways.*" *Those Calloways: Original Motion Picture Score.* Provo, UT: BYU Film Music Archives, 2013. Compact disc.

Daubney, Kate. *Max Steiner's Now, Voyager: A Film Score Guide.* Westport, CT: Greenwood, 2000.

Decker, Todd. *Music Makes Me: Fred Astaire and Jazz.* Berkeley: University of California Press, 2011.

Dick, Bernard F. *Hal Wallis: Producer to the Stars.* Lexington: University Press of Kentucky, 2004.

Eyman, Scott. *The Speed of Sound: Hollywood and the Talkie Revolution 1926–1930.* New York: Simon & Schuster, 1997.

Faiola, Ray. "The Marines, Warner Bros. and Max Steiner." *Battle Cry: Original Motion Picture Score.* Provo, UT: BYU Film Music Archives, 2004. 2 compact discs.

Faiola, Ray. "*A Summer Place*: The Film, The Score, and The Story in Music." *A Summer Place: Original Motion Picture Score.* Provo, UT: BYU Film Music Archives, 2003. Compact disc.

Gartenberg, Egon. *Johann Strauss: The End of an Era.* State College: Pennsylvania State University Press, 1990.

Harmetz, Aljean. *The Making of* Casablanca: *Bogart, Bergman, and World War II.* New York: Hachette, 2002.

Haver, Ronald. *David O. Selznick's Hollywood.* New York: Alfred A. Knopf, 1980.

Jeongwon, Joe, and Sander L. Gilman, eds. *Wagner and Cinema.* Bloomington: Indiana University Press, 2010.

Jewell, Richard B. *RKO Radio Pictures: A Titan Is Born.* Berkeley: University of California Press, 2012.

Kalinak, Kathryn. *How the West Was Sung: Music in the Westerns of John Ford.* Berkeley: University of California Press, 2007.

Kalinak, Kathryn. *Settling the Score: Music and the Classical Hollywood Film.* Madison: University of Wisconsin Press, 1992.

Karlin, Fred. *Listening to Movies: The Film Lover's Guide to Film Music.* New York: Schirmer Books, 1994.

Kashner, Sam, and Nancy Schoenberger. *A Talent for Genius: The Life and Times of Oscar Levant.* New York: Villard, 1994.

Kaufman, J. B. "*The Three Musketeers*—The Film/The Music." *The Three Musketeers: Original Motion Picture Score.* Provo, UT: BYU Film Music Archives, 2007. Compact disc.

Kaufman, Louis, and Annette Kaufman. *A Fiddler's Tale: How Hollywood and Vivaldi Discovered Me.* Madison: University of Wisconsin Press, 2003.

Levant, Oscar. *A Smattering of Ignorance.* Garden City, NY: Doubleday, Doran, 1940.

Magee, Glenn Alexander. "*The Fountainhead*: A Great, Flawed Film." *The Fountainhead: Original Motion Picture Score*. Provo, UT: BYU Film Music Archives, 2004. Compact disc.

Maltin, Leonard. "As Songs Go By: All the Music of *Casablanca*" and "RKO Revisited." In *Hooked on Hollywood: Discoveries from a Lifetime of Film Fandom*. Pittsburgh: GoodKnight Books, 2018.

Mordden, Ethan. *Ziegfeld: The Man Who Invented Show Business*. New York: St. Martin's Press, 2008.

Morton, Frederic. *A Nervous Splendor: Vienna 1888–1889*. New York: Penguin, 1979.

Platte, Nathan. *Making Music in Selznick's Hollywood*. New York: Oxford University Press, 2017.

Pollack, Howard. *George Gershwin: His Life and Work*. Berkeley: University of California Press, 2007.

Rode, Alan K. *Michael Curtiz: A Life in Film*. Lexington: University Press of Kentucky, 2017.

Rosenberg, Deena. *Fascinating Rhythm: The Collaboration of George and Ira Gershwin*. New York: Penguin, 1991.

Rubey, Norbert, and Peter Schoenwald. *Venedig in Wien*. Vienna: Ueberreuter, 1996.

Schreibman, Myrl. "On *Gone with the Wind,* Selznick, and the Art of 'Mickey Mousing': An Interview with Max Steiner." *Journal of Film and Video* 56, no. 1 (2004).

Silke, James R. *Here's Looking at You, Kid: 50 Years of Fighting, Working and Dreaming at Warner Bros.* Boston: Little, Brown and Company, 1976.

Slowik, Michael. *After the Silents: Hollywood Film Music in the Early Sound Era, 1926–1934*. New York: Columbia University Press, 2014.

Smith, Jack. "*The Searchers.*" *The Searchers: Original Motion Picture Score*. Provo, UT: BYU Film Music Archives, 1996. Compact disc.

Spivack, Murray. *An Oral History with Murray Spivack*. Beverly Hills, CA: Academy of Motion Picture Arts and Sciences, Oral History Program, 1995.

Steiner, Gabor. "My Encounters with Emperor Franz Joseph." *Neues Wiener Journal*, Vienna (1/12/30).

Steiner, Gabor. "Sixty Years Working in Theater." *Neues Wiener Journal*, Vienna (11/17/29).

Steiner, Max. "The Music Director." In *The Real Tinsel*, edited by Bernard Rosenberg and Harry Silverstein. New York: Macmillan, 1970.

Steiner, Max. "Scoring the Film." In *We Make the Movies*, edited by Nancy Naumburg. New York: Norton, 1937.

Stephan, Renate. *Johann Strauss, the King of the Waltz 1825–1899*. Vienna: Greiner & Greiner, 1999.

Suskin, Steven. *The Sound of Broadway Music: A Book of Orchestrators and Orchestrations*. New York: Oxford University Press, 2009.

Thomas, Tony. *Film Score: The Art and Craft of Movie Music.* Burbank, CA: Riverwood Press, 1991.

Thomas, Tony. *Music for the Movies.* 2nd ed. Los Angeles: Silman-James, 1997.

Thomson, David. *Showman: The Life of David O. Selznick.* New York: Alfred A. Knopf, 1992.

Traubner, Richard. *Operetta: A Theatrical History.* New York: Doubleday, 1983.

Vaz, Mark Cotta. *Living Dangerously: The Adventures of Merian C. Cooper.* New York: Villard, 2005.

Wallis, Hal, and Charles Higham. *Starmaker: The Autobiography of Hal Wallis.* New York: Macmillan, 1980.

Wegele, Peter. *Max Steiner: Composing,* Casablanca, *and the Golden Age of Film Music.* Lanham, MD: Rowman & Littlefield, 2014.

Whitaker, Bill. "Lost Worlds and Forgotten Music: Max Steiner's Legendary RKO Scores." *The Son of Kong/The Most Dangerous Game.* Provo, UT: BYU Film Music Archives, 2000. Compact disc.

Yates, W. E. *Theatre in Vienna: A Critical History, 1776–1995.* New York: Cambridge University Press, 1996.

Index

For the benefit of digital users, indexed terms that span two pages (e.g., 52–53) may, on occasion, appear on only one of those pages.